KU-048-454

A HILLHEAD ALBUM

GLASGOW, W2

'Old Bridge on the Kelvin at the Great Western Road, 1888'

William Simpson, R.I.

from original water colour in the People's Palace, Glasgow Green

A
HILLHEAD
ALBUM

Compiled & Edited
by
HENRY BROUGHAM MORTON

GLASGOW
W 2

© HENRY BROUGHAM MORTON, 1973

Printed in Great Britain by
Robert MacLehose and Company Limited
The University Press, Glasgow
for
The Trustees of the Late
CHARLES A. HEPBURN, M.C., LL.D.
1973

ISBN 0 9502034 3 2

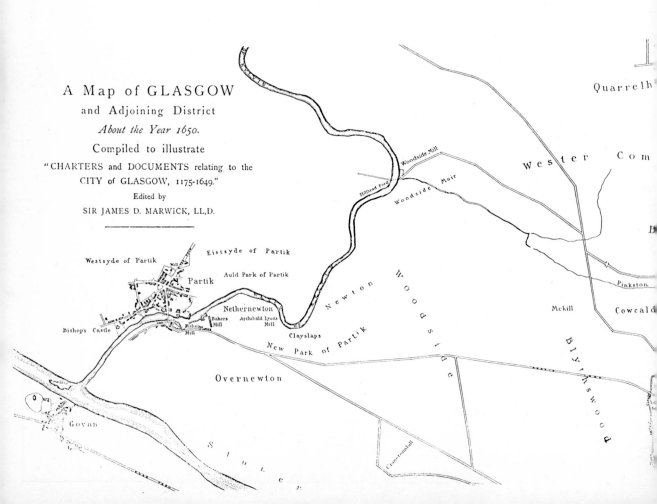

A Map of GLASGOW
and Adjoining District
About the Year 1650.
Compiled to illustrate
"CHARTERS and DOCUMENTS relating to the
CITY of GLASGOW, 1175-1649."
Edited by
SIR JAMES D. MARWICK, LL.D.

INTRODUCTION

HILLHEAD; a place-name quite often applied to the high part of a village or small town in Scotland. Add Glasgow and at once it acquires an identity of distinction that is not without considerable significance far beyond our island's shores.

Over the past hundred years, within its comparatively small area, the number of prominent people who were born or who have dwelt in Hillhead is such that it would require a substantial 'Who's Who' to list them briefly with due recognition. Even so, the number which has come within the scope of this work is by no means small.

A Hillhead Album is nothing more than the title implies. Its purpose is to preserve a mainly pictorial record of Hillhead, Glasgow, as it was and as it is still remembered.

It is the fulfilment of a mutual wish of Dr. Charles A. Hepburn and myself to make such a book available while there was still time to do so. His generation is now passing and mine is the rearguard. Both have experienced tremendous happenings in the history of this country. Consequently great changes have taken place in the life and character of Hillhead. Something of its early history is given to add depth of interest and this, with the appropriate maps and pictures, aids the visualizing of long-departed life and scenes of which very little record can now be traced.

The extent of the album and its fine quality are entirely due to Dr. Hepburn's enthusiastic encouragement and to his munificence in so willingly defraying production costs.

Unfortunately Dr. Hepburn died suddenly on 16th July 1971. By authorizing me to complete the book and by making arrangements for the final printing and the publishing, Dr. Hepburn's Trustees have fulfilled his wishes. *A Hillhead Album* is now his memorial in addition to being the testimony of his regard for the place of his birth and the centre of his life's interests.

5 Hillhead Street
Glasgow, W 2

H.B.M. 1972

HISTORICAL NOTE

THE MAKING OF THE Great Western Turnpike Road, authorised in 1836, undoubtedly led the way to developing the lands of Hillhead into a very desirable residential retreat with a direct route to Glasgow.

Until the first high-level bridge was constructed in 1840 to carry the new road across the River Kelvin, Hillhead enjoyed a pastoral isolation of considerable charm, lingering traces of which can be found here and there even today. Hitherto the only access from the lands of Blythswood was by the old route of the Bishops along the line of North Woodside Road from Dobbie's Loan and across Hillhead Ford and later by the low-set zig-zag bridge which remained under the new bridge until the reconstruction and final widening in 1891. Previously the main approach from Glasgow for horse carriages and waggons was through Sandyford by the Old Dumbarton Road, across the ancient Bridge of Partick and up the long-defined highway of the Byres Road.

It was part of a process which may be said to have begun in the late 18th century when to have one's residence in the new Miller Street, west of Glasgow Cross between Back Cow Loan and Argyle Street, was looked upon as being well out of town.

This western trend of residential desire continues today and now presses on beyond Bearsden and Milngavie, leaving in the various stages of its advancement surviving examples of sound planning and noble architecture.

It is the old story of change and decay and new birth with the offspring inheriting the merits or demerits of their progenitors according to the inspirations of their aims and beliefs and the quality of their smeddum.

In 1702 the lands of Hillhead were part of the great Blythswood Estates. They had been purchased about 1680 by Robert Campbell of Northwoodside, Dean of Guild in Glasgow, second son of Colin Campbell the first of Blythswood. Robert's daughter Janet inherited Hillhead at his death in 1694. On her marriage to Thomas Haliburton, advocate, of Dryburgh Abbey, in 1702 she sold Hillhead and Byres of Partick to Andrew Gibson the tenant and removed to her husband's estates in Berwickshire where, in the course of time, she became great-grandmother of Sir Walter Scott by her daughter Barbara marrying Robert Scott.

The Gibsons remained Superiors of Hillhead until about 1855 when the last James Gibson sold his Hillhead priority to his lawyer John Wilkie who resided in the original Hillhead House at the top of Great George Street.

In 1869, when the population had risen to 3,654, Hillhead became a Police Burgh with 9 Commissioners. Its police district came under the jurisdiction of the Chief Constable of Lanarkshire at Hamilton and included Kelvinside. The force comprised 1 inspector, 3 sergeants and 19 constables. Known as 'The Model Burgh' Hillhead at first resisted union with Glasgow but acquiesced when it obtained acceptable conditions. Provost Miller had been in favour of the annexation from the first proposal on the ground that they should not shrink their obligations to Glasgow.

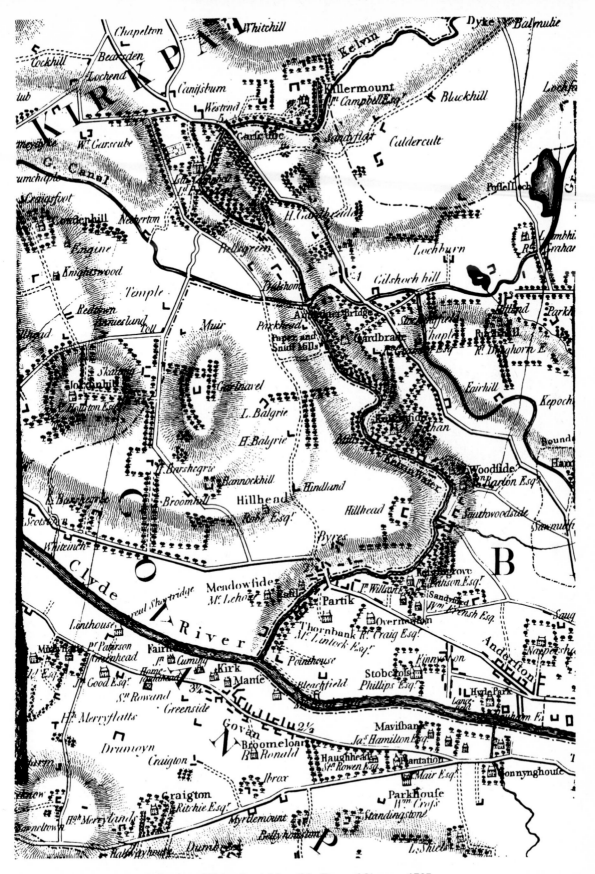

Section of Richardson's Map of the Town of Glasgow, 1795

Mrs. John Hamilton of
Northpark (Miss Helen Bogle)
by Sir Henry Raeburn. No. 519,
Oil on Canvas 762 × 634
(30 × 24$\frac{15}{16}$ ins.).   *University
of Glasgow. W. A. Cargill
Collection*

JOHN HAMILTON of Northpark was born in 1754. He was the
eldest son of the Rev. John Hamilton, D.D., minister of the
High Kirk of Glasgow and Moderator of the General
Assembly in 1766, who died in 1780 and whose tomb is in
Glasgow Cathedral.

In 1799 John Hamilton bought the small sequestered estate
of Northpark. In the following year he married Helen,
daughter of Archibald Bogle a younger son of Robert Bogle
of Shettleston, merchant in Glasgow. She died at Northpark
on 7th September 1825, aged 68 years.

John Hamilton was a merchant of extensive interests. He
was elected Provost of Glasgow three times and was regarded
by the citizens as a staunch upholder of Glasgow's good
name at home and abroad. The former Great Hamilton
Street, now part of London Road from Glasgow Cross, was
named after him. He is still commemorated in Hamilton
Drive, Hillhead.

Northpark House stood behind the line of Buckingham
Terrace, close to the short side street now known as Ruskin
Place, and looking north where the recently demolished
(1970) Queen Margaret Bridge spanned the River Kelvin.
Hence the name of Northpark given to the still existing
Northpark Terrace.

In Provost Hamilton's time there was no Great Western
Road and the route from the city to Northpark was by
Dumbarton Road and Byres Road. The once long avenue
to the house is now part of Hamilton Drive, Queen Margaret
Drive and top of Byres Road.

Provost Hamilton died at Northpark on 6th October 1829,
following a surgical operation, and was buried beside his
father in Glasgow Cathedral.

Robert Bogle, Junior, who purchased the estate of Gilmorehill in 1800, would appear to have been a nephew of Mrs.
John Hamilton of Northpark as he was a grandson of
Archibald Bogle of Shettleston. Both families had considerable landed interests east and west of Glasgow and were
related through inter-marriage in separate generations.

George Hamilton, brother of John Hamilton of Northpark, had a son, George John, who married Christina,
daughter of Henry Monteith, Provost of Glasgow. Their son
Christian Monteith Hamilton, Lieutenant-Colonel of the
92nd Regiment was the father of General Sir Ian Hamilton
who, in the 1850s, spent much of his early childhood amid
the gentle sylvan scenes at Hafton on the Cowal shore of the
remote Holy Loch.

From beside Kelvin Bridge

The Regality Club, Old Glasgow Museum

NORTH WOODSIDE
Sketch by A. Macgeorge, 23rd August, 1869

James Gibson of Hillhead, J.P. 1800–62, by William Wallace. (*With acknowledgment to unknown owner of original painting*)

JAMES GIBSON OF HILLHEAD

Born in Glasgow 1800, died at Dunoon 1862. Original projector of the Great Western Road. The last of the Gibsons of Hillhead, one of our old 'rentaller' families (i.e. families sprung from the 'rentallers' or tenants of the old archbishops) and long owners of Hillhead. The subject of this notice was descended from Andrew Gibson of Hillhead, maltman at Overnewton, who was younger son of John Gibson of Clayslap (which is now part of the West-End Park) and Overnewton (which marches with it) and was younger brother of the famous Walter Gibson of Balshagrie, a very notable 'promoter and propagator' of the trade of Glasgow, who was appointed Provost in 1688 and 1689 by the Archbishop of the Diocese, the last Provost so chosen.

From Catalogue of *OLD GLASGOW EXHIBITION*, 1894 (where painting was on loan).

James Gibson married, first, at Edinburgh, 1824, Jessie (Janet) 'only daughter of the late John Wilson, Lieutenant and Adjutant in the Canadian Regiment'. She died at Hillhead, 1826. He was married, secondly, 1835, at Westbank by the Rev. Mr. Leishman of Govan to Elizabeth, daughter of David Smith of Westbank, land surveyor, who is said to have laid out Great Western Road.

The Gibsons are buried in the churchyard of Govan Parish Church, Hillhead being within the Parish of Govan.

GREAT WESTERN ROAD BRIDGE OVER THE RIVER KELVIN NEAR GLASGOW

Erected 1839

James Thomson, F.R.S.E., M.R.I.A., Engineer

Old Glasgow Museum

GREAT WESTERN BRIDGE

Usually referred to as Kelvin Bridge, this is the present bridge carrying Great Western Road over the River Kelvin

Officially opened 29th September, 1891

From a drawing in 'The Bailie' when the foundation stone was laid on 9th April, 1890

Mitchell Library

Observatory

This photographic scene of about 1864 shows Lawrence Place, Crown Circus, Victoria Crescent and the Observatory. The ancient highway of Byres Road is indicated by the line of hedge.   *Glasgow Herald*

'The Old Mansion House of Hillhead.' Water-colour by Mrs. Hooker, exhibited in Old Glasgow Exhibition of 1894. This rural retreat stood between the south end of Granby Terrace (Hillhead Street) and Sardinia Terrace (Cecil Street) and disappeared when these streets were formed and built up in the sixties and seventies of the 19th century. *Glasgow Herald*

Granby Lane. Horse and cart on approximate site of Hillhead House. *May 1971**

*(Photographs with * were taken by H.B.M.)*

Great Western Road, Hillhead, c. 1890

Old Glasgow Museum

OLD HILLHEAD

These 'Notes on Hillhead' by Dr. Buchanan appeared in The Glasgow Herald *of Saturday, December 8, 1928. With the ensuing correspondence they form a most interesting description of Hillhead that is long gone but which could still be recalled personally by the writers. In addition they have the pleasing virtue of being self-correcting. Some slight curtailment has been made without loss of information.*

Hillhead is quite an old name, dating back several centuries. The land was a farm owned by Robert Campbell, son of Colin the first of Blythswood. It was sold in 1702 to Andrew Gibson, the rentaller, and his successors still hold the Superior rights.

Richardson's map of 1796 shows us what was the position of the farm buildings at a date when there were no other buildings on the hill. The farm steading was situated apparently just behind the southern part of Granby Terrace and subsequent maps show us that there was some building there until 1870 at least.

The approach to this farm was not an easy one as it was surrounded on three sides by the Kelvin. There was a ford at Woodside where the coal depot now is and North Woodside Road led to this ford down a slope in front of Rosebery Terrace; Dobbies Loan led into North Woodside Road across Garscube Road and so it came about that what is now University Avenue was, in the Ordnance Survey map of 1869, called Dobbies Loan. The ford at Woodside had a connection with the road over the valley between Hillhead and Gilmour Hill and was in 1820 called Woodside Road.

The building of the old bridge across the Kelvin and, still more, the bridge carrying the Great Western Road over the river must have made a great difference to Hillhead in 1837–38. Similarly the Gibson Street bridge must have helped greatly.

QUEEN MARGARET COLLEGE

The hill then was a steep grassy slope, with belts of trees and a group of trees round the farmhouse until about 1800. The first we can find of any house being built was that of Northpark, which was acquired by John Hamilton who was three times Provost of Glasgow and his son William was Provost twenty years later. Northpark is now Queen Margaret College. When Hamilton died in 1827 (*circa*) his son William succeeded him in the property. It was probably built early in the last century, for whilst Hamilton purchased the Grounds in 1799, it was some years later that he had to purchase ground in the line of Byres Road and Queen Margaret Crescent as a drive or entrance to his house. William did not occupy the house until about 1838. In 1832 Mr. A. M. Kirkland occupied it and in 1835 Mr. Wm. Shand of Craigellie was occupant. Mr. William Hamilton was in it for at least twelve years after 1838. These Hamiltons were the progenitors of General Sir Ian Hamilton.

In 1883 Northpark was purchased by Mrs. Elder and presented to Queen Margaret College and in 1893 was transferred to the University.

Soon after Northpark was built several villas were erected on the west bank of the Kelvin. These were Westbank, where Westbank Quadrant, etc., stand; Ashefield across Gibson Street at the corner of Smith Street; Janefield Cottage, Rose Cottage and one or two others. About 1840 it seems that building began to increase and we find names of several houses such as Thornville, Sauchfield, Lilybank, Laurelbank, Oakfield and Hillhead House. It is impossible to give names of all the inhabitants here but a few names may be connected with them.

Sauchfield, which is now Queen Margaret Hall, was, in 1840, owned by John Kerr, a well-known lawyer, who lived in it till 1859. His son-in-law John Napier of Robert Napier & Sons, lived in Sauchfield for many years. Lilybank which stood almost where the terrace of the same name now is was owned by a Dr. Fleming of Partick for many years. Thereafter it became the home of Provost John Blackie who died there in 1872. Later again it was occupied by Mr. J. B. MacBrayne. Hillhead House, now the property of the University, was owned successively by Mr. R. Dalgleish, by Mr. James Smith, by Mr. Hoggan and lastly by Provost Wilson of Hillhead. Thornville, which was standing until last year at the corner of Great George Street and Ann Street, was occupied for many years by Mr. McKeand; Oakfield, which stood until 1884 where Wellington Church now is, was occupied by Mr. Edward Railton, by Mr. Thomas Barclay, by Mr. James Ewing and by the Rev. James Taylor.

In 1842 William Govan senior built Laurelbank, a double villa standing beside Glasgow Street facing Oakfield Avenue. He lived in Laurelbank and his eldest son in the other half of the house until 1850 when he built Southpark. He and his family occupied the new house until quite recently. Laurelbank became well known as a school which still bears its name although, we believe, that the school overflowed into the house. Tyrefield which stood close to it was probably built about the same time. John King a former Provost of Hillhead lived in Tyrefield before going to Southpark Terrace. In 1850 there was a Mr. A. Hamilton living in Tyrefield, possibly a grandson of John Hamilton and in 1863 it was occupied by Mr. William Cree. Most of the houses mentioned so far had large gardens and were surrounded by beautiful trees whose foliage in spring and summer gave a semi-rural aspect to the entire district. Some other houses, as old perhaps as these, are Florentine Bank House, still standing at the top of

Gibson Street, Bloomfield, Oakvale and others.

It was about 1850 that terraces began to appear, first beside Great Western Road, then extending up on to the hill. Belgrave Terrace, St. James's Terrace, Hamilton Park, etc. were built about this time. Kelvin, Granby and Sardinia followed built in stages. Although the terraces advanced to a great extent until Bute Gardens and Mansions and University Gardens, etc. were built, the district remained quiet and residential. The western slopes were later of development than the eastern side.

Hillhead became a burgh in 1869 and the University came west a year later and gave a stimulus to growth. As late as 1870 there were no houses beside Byres Road from University Avenue to Ashton Terrace and there only a small group. From the site of the present picture house up to the Burgh Hall the only building was the low white-washed Curlers Tavern. The curling pond was on the west side of Byres Road opposite the tavern. The slopes of the hill were rough and a large brick factory had long existed here, leaving to the youth of the district a legacy of several deep water-filled clay holes. Kersland Terrace and Street with its large population was not built and the residents in Sardinia Terrace had an uninterrupted view over Horslethill Farm away to the Kilpatrick Hills. It was several years later that the Western Baths and Robart's Church were erected. Ashton Terrace at this time extended only to about No. 14 and there was only one small cottage between it and Dowanhill House.

Since the foregoing notes were written, it has been found that Northpark was occupied from 1873 to 1880 by Mr. John (of J. & M. P. Bell, pottery manufacturers.) The probability is that the old house was taken down in 1873 and the present house erected by Mr. Bell, but the site is different.

LESLIE BUCHANAN.

I have been informed by a correspondent that Sauchfield House and the house now Queen Margaret Hall was Lilybank.

L.B. 5 Royal Crescent, 12/12/28

24 Hamilton Park Terrace,
Hillhead, Glasgow.
Dec. 13, 1928.
My father, Mr. John Blackie, later Provost Blackie, entered on the occupancy of Lilybank in 1857, when I was five and a half years old. A few years after that he purchased the property which extended to about 10 acres. In 1864 a considerable addition was made to the house. My

father died there in February, 1873 and my mother resided there for several years after that. The house still stands the same externally as it was in the time of our occupancy, but I believe some internal alterations were made after the purchase by Mrs. Elder for use as a hostel for ladies attending Queen Margaret College.

Sauchfield House stood a little to the south of Lilybank and on a lower level and was entirely demolished to make way for other buildings.

Northpark stood behind Buckingham Terrace on the high ground in the middle of Hamilton Drive and its site is now occupied by Northpark Terrace. The demolition of Northpark and the building of the terrace took place previous to 1870.

I remember when the site of Queen Margaret College was occupied as a market garden by a man known amongst us boys as "Old Fraser". I don't think he lived there; the only erection in my memory is a sort of shed which he used partly as a shop and store and toolhouse. There was certainly no building of any importance on that site till Mr. Bell built the house that is now the college.

The original Hillhead House stood on the top of the hill between Hillhead Street and Sardinia Terrace and near the south end of Granby Terrace. I think the last occupant was a Mr. Colin Brown, a gentleman well-known in his day in Glasgow musical circles. The site is now built upon. I do not remember the name of the house now known as Hillhead House. When we went to Lilybank it was occupied and, I believe, owned by Mr. Dalglish: "Steenie Dalglish" as I often heard him called by my parents and others.

I well remember Mr. Stark's school

as I and my brothers were pupils in it, first in Kelvin Terrace, and later in Buckingham Terrace. It was quite a flourishing establishment for a number of years and I think most of the girls and boys in Hillhead at that time began their schooling there. The late distinguished chemist Sir William Ramsay was a pupil in my time and lived in Gibson Street below Oakfield Terrace.

JOHN J. BLACKIE.

———

Hillhead, December, 15. Hillhead did not at any time form part of "Old Glasgow". From its formation into a police burgh in 1869 with a Provost, Bailies and Commissioners of its own, until it was annexed to Glasgow, Hillhead had a separate identity and was part of the County of Lanark. Under self-government it was not long in becoming, as it continued during its independent existence to be, known as "The Model Burgh". It had several Provosts but never a Provost Wilson, as referred to by your contributor. The Wilson who occupied the house known in later years as Hillhead House was Mr. John Wilson, for several years M.P. for the Govan Division.

The original mansion-house on the estate was called Hillhead House and stood among stately trees within its own grounds opposite where Hillhead Gardens now stand. For some years before its demolition it was occupied as a boys' school known as Hillhead House School. There was no appearance of a farmhouse ever having been on the site. The old mansion house stood until about 50 years ago but never became the property of the University. Lilybank House still stands and is occupied as Queen Margaret Hall, a hostel for

female students attending Queen Margaret College and similar institutions. The late Lord Provost Blackie, while in occupation of Lilybank enlarged it and entertained there several distinguished visitors to the city, among whom were Mr. W. E. Gladstone when he addressed a great meeting in the City Hall, and H.R.H. the Duke of Edinburgh, second son of Queen Victoria, when he unveiled his father's (the late Prince Consort) statue in George Square.

Part of the garden wall of Sauchfield which was formerly occupied by Messrs. John Ker and John Napier, but never as Queen Margaret Hall, still stands opposite Bute Gardens.

The late Provost John King of Hillhead lived first in Laurelbank and thereafter in Tyrefield but never in Southpark Terrace.

Wellington U.F. Church stands on the site of a villa (not called Oakfield) formerly occupied by the late James Thomson, Professor of Engineering in the University from 1873 to 1889, brother of Lord Kelvin. My belief is that Oakfield now forms part of the east side of Oakfield Terrace.

Thornville was standing until a few months ago, but has since been demolished along with Laurelbank, Tyrefield and seven handsome modern self-contained dwelling houses known as Thornville Terrace to make room for the large public school which the Glasgow Education Authority propose erecting but which is not likely to add to the amenity of a locality formerly noted for its sylvan and picturesque character.

For many years the tollhouse stood on the south side of Great Western Road at the west end of the bridge then spanning the Kelvin. At this

Lilybank House c. 1850 (Alexander Thomson). The carriage drive entered at the corner of Bute Gardens where the road turned right to meet Great George Street. For a time Lilybank House was known as Queen Margaret Hall. *1957**

bridge dues were enacted for vehicles which were generally few in number and drawn by horses, entering or leaving Hillhead.

Laurelbank was built by Mr. Wm. Govan whose family were well known for many years in Glasgow, his eldest son, referred to in the notes, being a bailie in the city. It is many years since the Govans occupied Southpark House where they went to live after leaving Laurelbank. Southpark House was a few years ago presented by Lord Maclay for use as a female students' hostel.

The first public building, other than the old county police office in Byres Road, erected in Hillhead was Kelvinside Free (now U.F.) Church in 1860. The present burgh buildings in Byres Road were erected soon after the Burgh was formed. The Glasgow Academy was erected at Kelvin bridge about 1880. While Hillhead has passed, in the course of the last 70 or 80 years, from being a rural to an urban locality, it still retains many of its early characteristics. One of these is that there has been only one licensed house within its borders – the Curlers Tavern – in Byres Road, which probably derives its name from the curling pond referred to in the notes. Hillhead has been a quiet and attractive place of residence and can well do without some of the modern innovations which certain outsiders seem inclined to introduce into it but are not calculated to conduce to its peace and quietness.

F. P. R. FERGUSON.

NORTH PARK HOUSE, HILLHEAD

December, 16.
My father bought 6 Northpark Terrace then just built, in, I think, 1864. I was born there in 1865, the first of his family to be born in that house, North Park House must have been demolished, therefore, some time between 1862 and 1864. Mr. Bell's house, now Queen Margaret College, was not built then. I have a distinct recollection when a boy of seeing it built.

T.F.D.

HILLHEAD HOUSE

5 Royal Crescent, Glasgow, W.
Jan. 22, 1929.
Thanks to the kindness of various correspondents, I am enabled to supplement the notes regarding this interesting old house which you were good enough to publish on Dec. 8.

I may say that it is very difficult to obtain accurate information about houses which are now demolished and especially so when the house was not within Glasgow. Maps of Glasgow do not include Hillhead and are but rarely scrupulously accurate and also directories of Glasgow did not give much information as far back as 1850. I have been able to ascertain with a fair degree of accuracy that this old house stood until about 1876 or 77 just north of Great George Street and just west of Granby Terrace. From a correspondent who visited the house in its last days I have learnt that it was a long one-storey house facing almost south. It had lattice windows and had a stone-pillared doorway with a green painted wooden porch. It was even

then (1875) surrounded by fine old beech trees and there was still grass growing on what had been the garden. When he visited the house it was occupied as a school kept by a Mrs. J. L. Sutherland who did not reside there. This school was begun about 1872 and it last appeared in the directory of 1875. From 1866 to 1872 the house was occupied by Mrs. Colin Brown and from 1862 to 1865 Mr. James Smith of Smith, Beckitt & Co. occupied it. From 1859 to 1861 Mr. James Gibson was in the house and, it is of interest to note, that in 1862 Mr. James Gibson the last, I believe, of the family of the owners of Hillhead, died at Dunoon. From 1849 to 1858, Mr. John Wilkie, Writer, lived in Hillhead House, but before this I find no details in the Glasgow directories.

From J. O. Mitchell (*Essays*) it is learned that about 1845, possibly, Mr. William Connal of William Connal & Co. occupied the house as a summer residence and that, even further back, probably about 1825, Professor Jardine (possibly Professor of Midwifery) was in Hillhead House, probably as a summer residence also. I have been unable to ascertain if anyone possesses a photograph of the old house or a painting of any kind and would be very glad of information on this point.

LESLIE BUCHANAN

HILLHEAD HOUSE

Edinburgh, March, 1.
The correspondence about Hillhead and especially Hillhead House, has been brought under my notice and, having lived there as a child, I would like to make some reference to the subject, although references cannot be easily verified and memory is an uncertain aid.

As to the main access from Glasgow, I was given to understand that the ancient route for the "Bishop's Visitation" came out from his castle and down Dobbies Loan. It descended to a path beside the Kelvin, crossed the ford or the little bridge between Great Western Road and Gibson Street, then came up "Glasgow Street" passed the old house and continued down to Partick. This may explain the use of Dobbies Loan for University Avenue in 1869.

As to the situation of Hillhead House, it is rather a striking commentary on our city and its expansion to say that in 1866, my father, Mr. Colin Brown, took his family from Douglas Street, at Blythswood Square, to live in the country, as Hillhead then undoubtedly was, with its unpaved roads and very insufficient means of access. Some of your readers must recall the wooden steps down to Great Western Road at the end of Hillhead Street. The grounds of the house then extended for nearly the length of Hillhead Gardens and back to a lane beside "St. Bernard's Place". I understand three sketches of the house were afterwards shown in an "Old Glasgow" Exhibition in the eighties. I saw one of them by courtesy of a descendant of the late Mr. Gibson, but it was hardly sufficient to recall the house as we knew it in its last days. Since the sketch printed in the *Herald* was made it must have been considerably altered, probably by Mr. Gibson himself, as the "best bedrooms" were built above the old stone-flagged lattice-windowed service

rooms of a much earlier time. The date of 1706 was cut above the stable window, a detached building to the north, and this may show the alteration.

It was then an ideal house for children and I have delightful memories of the old garden, with an avenue of beeches and a row of elms which helped to hide it from the neighbours as well as from the newly made roads that manifestly encroached on our boundaries.

Your correspondent, Mr. Blackie, made a courteous reference to the musical interests which centred in the old house. Let me add that among many visitors the first John Curwen was a much-loved guest in it and that some of the successful beginnings of the tonic sol-fa movement were developed while he stayed there.

One personal reminiscence may be of general interest in the march of time. It is that of two other small boys who, with their nurse, joined our restricted circle on the grass in the days when conversational powers were limited. One of them now signs himself Cosmo Cantuar by the Grace of God and his brother is known and honoured in our East country.

I add an incident which came in the course of a great national upheaval and which shows how quickly history is made. My father had become responsible for the wellbeing of, I think, the first Japanese Samurai who came to this country to study shipbuilding, against great opposition by the then government. He afterwards became a viscount and guardian to the heir-apparent, but while he stayed with us I recall having opened the door of the dining-room and seeing a group of his friends sitting on the floor in eager discussion round a low stool which held tea. It was a council of the new Japan party, led by the famous Count Ito before their return to bring into being the great Empire of the East.

On another point, may I say that I think there is a little confusion between Mr. Hamilton's house of Northpark, which was surely built into Northpark Terrace, Hamilton Drive and Mr. John Bell's house on the opposite side of the road, beside "The Kibble" conservatory? The latter house was built by Mr. Bell with the thought of presentation to the city, and only the tragedy of an incomplete catalogue and unfinished will prevented it and its contents from becoming the property of the citizens. – Apologising for having fallen into "anecdotage" on a subject which may not be of general interest to your readers.

GEORGE GRAHAM BROWN,
Edinburgh 1/3/29.

HILLHEAD HOUSE

Royal Exchange, Glasgow, March, 4.
In the "Strangers' Book – Royal Exchange" I notice today an entry as under.

"1863, April 6:— Name: John W. Smith. From whence: Manchester. Address in Glasgow: Hillhead House. Introduced by whom: Jas. Smith. For how long: 1 week."

This should prove who was occupier at that date.

W.S.

Southpark Avenue (Ann Street) and Terrace before the Hillhead Burgh gas lamps were removed in 1959. *

HILLHEAD HOUSE AND GROUNDS

FOR SALE, by Public Roup, within the Faculty Hall, St. George's Place, Glasgow, on Wednesday, 7th. June, 1916, at Two p.m.

The ABOVE DESIRABLE SUBJECTS situate in UNIVERSITY AVENUE. The house is commodious. The grounds are well laid off, and extend per Title to 8944 square yards or thereby, and bound three streets.

Annual Ground Burden, One Penny Scots, if asked only.

UPSET PRICE £6000

For further particulars and orders to view, apply to Thomson McLintock & Company, C.A., 149 West George Street, Glasgow; or to Oatts & Rodger, Solicitors, 113 St. Vincent Street, Glasgow, the latter of whom have the Titles and Articles of Roup.

[Advertisement under PROPERTY FOR SALE, *Glasgow Herald*, May 1916, see correspondence on opposite page.]

Ivy Lodge, Gibson Street.
April 1970 *

Mitchell Library

Rus in urbe: in the heart of Hillhead.   *September 1962**

Southpark Avenue (Ann Street). An
almost century-old scene.   *1961**
(Old wall replaced 1970)

1869   1891

JE MAINTIENDRAI

BURGH OF HILLHEAD

Provost Bruce

Provost Miller

PROVOSTS

Robert Bruce - 1869–1875	John King - 1880–1886	Alex. S. Baird - 1887–1890
Henry Cowan - 1875–1880	J. B. Gilmour - 1886–1887	Robert Miller - 1890–1891

The first General Meeting of Commissioners after their election for executing the 'General Police and Improvement (Scotland) Act 1862' within the limits of the Burgh of Hillhead took place within the Session House of the Kelvinside Free Church on Monday the 21st day of June 1869.

Present:

Robert Bruce, 3 North Park Terrace; Andrew Paton, Oakvale; Frederick James Hallows, 2 North Park Terrace; Patrick Bruce Junor, 8 South Park Terrace; John Findlay, 1 Hillhead Gardens; Thomas Duff, 13 Hamilton Drive; George Russell Alexander, 11 Sardinia Terrace and Edward John Scott, 24 Sardinia Terrace. Letter was read from Henry Cowan, 13 St. James's Terrace apologising for his absence.

THE BURGH BOUNDARY

The burgh boundary was from the centre of the River Kelvin beside Westbank Quadrant at Smith Street (Otago Street) thence directly westwards and along University Avenue to Ashton Lane; along Ashton Lane to where it turns left and ends at Byres Road, thence along the centre of Byres Road and across Great Western Road to the eastern end of the Botanic Gardens from where the River Kelvin formed the remainder of the boundary to Kelvingrove Park (see extracts of Minutes).

THE BURGH CREST

The burgh crest, although of a simple style, was never officially authorised.

Old Glasgow Museum

1. JOHN F GILMOUR, Elected Commissioner 1887
2. WILLIAM FRAMER   1883
3. JOHN MAXTON   1884
4. G S ALEXANDER   1882
5. JOHN KING   1871
6. WM MACKIE   1873
7. ALEXA S BAIRD   1882

4. NEIL KENNEDY, Elected Commissioner   1885
7. JOHN MARSHALL   1881
10. JAMES MUIRHEAD, Burgh Clerk appointed 1851
11. JOHN C MACCALL, Burgh Treasurer   1884
12. THOS WRASKIE, Burgh Surveyor   1865
13. JAMES CHRISTIE, Medical Officer   1871
14. Inspector KIRKTON, Sanitary Inspector 18??

Jubilee Year of the Reign of Queen Victoria.

1887.
COMMISSIONERS OF THE BURGH OF HILLHEAD,
AND THE PRINCIPAL OFFICIALS.

1869	Plans for new streets and laying of sewers.
1870	Within Chambers of J. & W. Graham, C.A.
25th Feb.	Provost Robert A. Bruce in the Chair. (First mention as Provost who was also Chief Magistrate). Rendering accounts and arranging audit.
28th Feb.	Vote of thanks to Sir Edward Colebrooke and Major Hamilton (Members for County) for opposing Boundaries Bill. Enquiries to be made for suitable site for Burgh Buildings.
11th April	Clerk reported receiving from Mr. Robert Malcolm Kerr, the Proprietor of the ground at Victoria Road a confirmation of the Sale to the Commissioners of the piece of ground referred to last Monday.
13th May	The Clerk was instructed to write to Mr. R. D. Douglas as to the formation of a Police Court for the Burgh; and also to Mr. George Herbert, Eldon Street, as to the complaints that have been lodged as to the nuisance caused by his cows trespassing on or otherwise obstructing the pavement.
5th July	A letter was read from Messrs. Bannatynes Kirkwood and McJames on behalf of Mr. John Bell craving authority for erection of a self-contained Lodging in Hamilton Drive and the relative Plans were laid on the table. The Application and Plans having been considered it was found that Mr. Bell's Timber fence as shewn on the Plans encroached to the extent of six inches on the road and it was remitted to Mr. Wharrie to see that the Plans were rectified in this respect. On this being done it was agreed that the necessary authority would be given.
14th July	Petition against Tramways Bill.
8th Aug.	Mr. Thomas Wharrie, Surveyor, submitted Plans for new Burgh Buildings. Approved.
10th Oct.	It was agreed that a Plan should be prepared with the view of getting the Consent of the Proprietors to widen Victoria Street from Partick to Great Western Road and Mr. Wharrie was instructed to prepare said Plan accordingly.
1870	
25th Oct.	It was unanimously agreed to appoint Dr. Dobbie, 1 Kelvin Terrace, to be the Medical Officer for the Burgh under the Public Health Act, with a salary of Five Pounds, five Shillings per annum.
5th Nov.	Byars of Partick Road referred to as such by Mr. Wm. Burns, Writer in Glasgow, Agent for Inspector of Poor for the Parish of Govan.
1871	
9th Jan.	Building in east end of Belmont Crescent reported to be in dangerous condition.
26th Jan.	Under the estimates for the new Burgh Buildings, now reduced from the Sum of £6,811-14/- to the Sum of £5,740-10/-, it was resolved to recommend the Commissioners to proceed with the Front Building alone in the meantime.
2nd May	The Chairman reported the arrangements which the Committee had made in regard to the laying of the foundation stone of the new Burgh Buildings on the 13th curt. that day having been fixed in place of the 6th as formerly agreed upon. He also intimated that the stone was to be laid with Masonic honours and that the Band of the 25th Lanarkshire Rifle Volunteers was to be in attendance. It was agreed to have a special Meeting to complete arrangements on Friday evening first at Seven o'clock.
31st May	Commissioner's office, now 2 Oakvale, Gibson Street. To attend there 4th July.

The second Kelvin Bridge, built 1840, spanning the first bridge. Lansdowne Church, a fine achievement in the early work of John Honeyman was completed in 1863. St. Mary's Cathedral was still to be built and opened in 1871. *Annan*

19th June	Mr. John King of Laurelbank elected to the office of Commissioner.
27th July	It was remitted to the Magistrates to make arrangements to have the design for a suitable Coat of Arms for the Burgh prepared and submitted to the rest of the Commissioners. It was agreed that *The Glasgow Herald* should be got daily and filed in the Commissioners Office and, at the end of each year, be bound and the Provost was requested to order it from Mr. Stenhouse, Stationer, Hillhead.
9th Oct.	Agreed to form Hillhead Street at Granby Terrace and have proper outlet to Great Western Road.
14th Dec.	Commissioners agreed to co-operate with other burghs in opposing Glasgow Corporation extension schemes.
1872	
1st Jan.	To give up Oakvale office at Whitsunday.
25th Mar.	Approved offer from Sun Foundry to supply four lamps to be erected opposite Burgh Buildings at a cost of £13 each, said lamps to be the same in every respect as those erected opposite Provost Bruce's house in Hamilton Drive.
4th June	First recorded Meeting within the Burgh Hall.
14th Oct.	Application by Alex. Sloan, Secretary, for use of room in Burgh Hall for Curling Club Meeting. Granted for 5/-. University Avenue reported to be insufficiently formed levelled and paved from Gibson Street to Ashton Terrace.
1873	
3rd Jan.	Account from Messrs. Ratcliff & Tyler for gasaliers for the Burgh Hall amounting to £184-9/-.
14th April	After 15th May agreed gas supplies by Glasgow Corporation to cease and The Partick, Hillhead & Maryhill Gas Company to supply all public lamps. Flat flame burners to be used.
15th Sept.	Letter from Mr. James Drynan, Secretary, Hillhead Bowling Club, requesting use of Hall for Dinner of the Club on 17th October.
7th Dec.	First mention of City of Glasgow Bank as Proprietors in connection with the development of Belmont Street.
1874	
12th Jan.	A letter from Messrs. McGrigor, Donald & Co., Writers, on behalf of Professor John Nichol asking that the Commissioners should take over Ann Street and Glasgow Street as public Streets was read and remitted to the Streets Committee.
9th Feb.	Plan for Burgh extension produced.
13th June	Municipal Election notices posted on door of Parish Church of Govan as required.
12th Oct.	Gas brackets in common stairs to be lit from 15th August to 15th May. Proposed extension of Burgh.
10th Nov.	Approach by letter to Great Western Road Trustees to cause crossings to be made with square dressed stones at various points which included one across Great Western Road from Buckingham Street to the Post Office.
1875	
12th April	Proposal for amalgamation of Partick, Hillhead and Maryhill. Poor attendance at Meeting. Adjourned to further Meeting.
11th May	Application from Caledonian Cricket Club to erect Clubhouse opposite Belmont Crescent.
21st June	Following Municipal Election, Bailie Cowan elected Provost.
12th July	Agreement to combine with Partick and Maryhill in erecting a permanent hospital. Quarry behind Sandringham Terrace to be filled up and properly fenced by the Proprietors.
14th Dec.	First Class Manual fire engine ordered.

[continued

Courtyard behind Hillhead Burgh Buildings. Part of Fire Brigade stables and sheds can be seen on left. Site cleared and levelled when main buildings were demolished in June 1972. *1965**

Hillhead Burgh Buildings from Observatory Road, 1965. Built 1872. Total cost £13,000. Demolished June 1972. Hillhead district library to be built on site. Estimated cost £300,000. *1965**

Frieze in main meeting room of Hillhead Burgh Hall.   *1970**

Burgh Hall staircase. These two interior photographs were taken when the building had suffered much from being in a state of final disuse.   *October 1970**

BURGH OF HILLHEAD.

STAIR LIGHTING.

NOTICE IS HEREBY GIVEN, That the Commissioners of Police have, in terms of the General Police and Improvement (Scotland) Act, 1862, and particularly clause 131 thereof, resolved that the Lamps in all common stairs, passages, and private courts within the Burgh, shall in future be lighted all the year round from sunset to sunrise.

Under the clause above referred to, every occupier failing to have such Lamps lighted during the hours above fixed, will be liable to a penalty not exceeding 10s. for each offence.

By order of the Commissioners,

JAMES MUIRHEAD,
CLERK.

BURGH CHAMBERS, HILLHEAD,
9th June, 1890.

Kelvinside Free Church, Great Western Road, *c.* 1870, now
Kelvinside (Botanic Gardens) Parish Church

1876

7th March It was resolved to call upon Mr. Kay the Proprietor of the Curlers Tavern, Mrs. McCleary and Mr. G. C. Bruce all Proprietors of property on the east side of Victoria Street to lay pavement in front of their property. 8 feet wide of best Caithness Stone not less than 3 inches thick with ridged whin kerb stones in lengths of not less than thirty six inches by about twelve inches deep and six inches broad and the Clerk was instructed to issue the necessary Notices.

1879

8th Aug. The Clerk produced and read to the Meeting the Deliverance by the Home Secretary in the process raised before the Sheriff for the renewal and extension of the boundaries of the Burgh and it was ordered to be engrossed in the Minute Book.

AND WHEREAS appeals in terms of the said Act have been presented to me the Right Honourable Richard Assheton Cross one of Her Majesty's Principal Secretaries of State against the deliverance of the Sheriff by (1) Eleanor Montgomerie and Elizabeth Montgomerie and James Brown Fleming Proprietors of the Estate of Kelvinside in the County of Lanark and (2) James Bell and other Householders and Ratepayers in the Area annexed by the Sheriff to the Burgh of Hillhead.

And whereas enquiry having been directed by me into the circumstances of the case, parties have been heard in support of and against the said Appeals. Now therefore I do hereby in virtue of the Authority vested in me by the said Act sustain the said Appeals and order and adjudge that the Sheriff's deliverance be recalled and the prayer of the said Petition by the said Commissioners be refused and that the boundaries of the Burgh of Hillhead shall be the same as were fixed and determined by the deliverance of the Sheriff of the said County of date the sixth day of April one thousand eight hundred and sixty nine that is to say commencing at a point in the centre of the River Kelvin in line of the north march of the lands of Gilmorehill thence westward along said march of Gilmorehill till it reaches near to the stables or offices belonging to Gilmorehill and opposite to the western boundary of the Lands of Sauchfield, thence in a northwards direction across the parish road leading from Partick to Hillhead and along the march separating the lands of Donaldshill from the Lands of Sauchfield and Hillhead to the northern extremity of the said lands of Donaldshill till it joins the centre of the Road called the Byars Road or Victoria Street thence northwards along the centre of the said Byars Road till it joins the Great Western Road thence across the said Great Western Road to the eastern boundary of the Royal Botanic Gardens thence northeastwards and northwards along the said boundary of the Botanic Gardens at the junction with the River Kelvin and thence eastwards and southwards along the centre of the said River Kelvin till it reaches the foresaid point of commencement in line with the northern boundary of the Lands of Gilmorehill.

And I authorise this Order to be recorded in the Sheriff Court Books of the said County of Lanark.

Given under my hand and seal at Whitehall this Twenty first day of July 1876.
(Signed) Richard Assheton Cross.

12th Aug. Proposal that Burgh pay half for widening Kelvin Bridge.

9th Sept. Application from Mr. John Sheriff, Hon. Sec. Hillhead Musical Association, 13 Granby Terrace for use of Burgh Hall from October to April. Granted.

1880

8th Nov. Bailie John King elected Provost or Senior Magistrate.
Letter from Town Clerk of Partick offering use of their new Fire Engine.

1881

29th Aug. Application from Hillhead Parliamentary Debating Association for use of Hall.

1882

24th Feb. Notice received that levy of tolls on turnpike roads is to cease in May, 1883.

4th Apr. National Telephone Co. to supply direct telephone in Burgh Hall for £10 per annum.

1885

10th Aug. Covered dust cart ordered at cost of £26 following complaints of dust and ashes being thrown out of open carts.

1886

14th June The Clerk submitted an application from Mr. Peter Hepburn for permission to erect a retaining wall along the Kelvin in front of his property. The Commissioners agreed to make no objection.

2nd Dec. The Clerk submitted an application from the Secretary of Queen Margaret College requesting that a Crossing be made at the North End of Buckingham Street. Granted.
A Report by Mr. Brand on the Old Toll House and Weighing Apparatus at Kelvin Bridge was read and approved.

1887

9th May It was unanimously resolved that the salary of the Clerk, Mr. James Muirhead, should be increased to the sum of £150 per annum, commencing at the 15th curt. and that this salary should include the Clerk's charge for making up the Annual Voters' Roll.

13th June Photographs of Commissioners arranged to be done by Mr. Stuart.
Mr. Kennedy moved the square-headed Lamps with name-plates should be placed at the corner of every Street in the Burgh.

1888

7th June Bailies Farmer and Marshall and Mr. Mathie reported that they had been called to the Burgh Buildings this morning on account of a serious subsidence that had taken place in the South Gable Wall of the Building; that the four Tenants occupying the south side of the Building, viz: Inspector Simpson, Sergeant Simpson, Mr. Philip and Mr. Martin had been much alarmed, and that Inspector Simpson had removed his family and furniture to another house taken by him, and that he had also caused Sergeant Simpson's family and furniture to be removed. As the matter appeared to be urgent, they had authorised Mr. Philip to engage a house for himself in Roclea Terrace at the rent of £19-10/- per annum, and Mr. Martin to engage one in Great George Street at the rent of £23; that they had further instructed Mr. Brand to have the Gable shored up and to consult Mr. Bryden of Messrs. Clark & Bell, the Architects of the Building, in regard to this.

1891

5th Mar. Mr. Pirrie submitted a letter from Mr. Henderson, Windsor Terrace, Kelvinside, drawing attention to the danger attending cabs and other vehicles descending Hillhead Street to Great Western Road, when, after some conversation, it was agreed to erect iron posts 4 feet apart at the top of the hill, in Hillhead Street, with a red lamp in the centre, and Mr. Brand was instructed to see the work carried out.
It was also agreed, on the suggestion of the Convener, that Balfours & Co., Limited, should be allowed to erect in Great Western Road, between Cecil Street and Kersland Street, one Automatic Delivery Machine for the sale of postage stamps and cards.

18th Aug. The Provost on behalf of the Committee appointed to confer with the Town Council of Glasgow on the question of the proposed union, reported verbally the proceedings at the conference between them and the Committee of the Town Council.

(The last recorded entry was on 3rd September, 1891 and dealt only with problems arising from the construction of the Central Railway.)

(Glasgow City Archives)

LIST OF STREETS AND BUILDINGS, ETC.

When first shown on maps in

GLASGOW POST OFFICE DIRECTORIES

In general, with a few exceptions of earlier origin, completion of buildings took place from one to three years before appearing in these maps. The series began in 1847.

1847   First streets named in Hillhead are **Great King Street** and **Great George Street**. **Byres Road** and **Great Western Road** named. **Hillhead House** (first), **Saughfield House, Florentine House, Thornville, Gilmorehill House.**

1848   **Gibson Street** named.

1849   Three small unnamed buildings indicating position of **Curlers Tavern.** Nothing else on **Byres Road.**

1852   **Glasgow Street, Bank Street, Smith Street, Viewfield Terrace, Wilson Street, Ann Street. Lilybank, Tyrefield, Laurelbank. Hillhead House** (second) and **Parkview** indicated without name.

1853   **Buckingham Terrace** half completed from **Botanic Gardens.**

1854   **Buckingham Terrace** completed to **Buckingham Street.**

1857   **Hillhead Street** and **Cecil Street** named only. Tenements **Wilson Street** and fronting **Great Western Road** to **Great Kelvin Terrace** in **Bank Street.**

1858   **Sardinia Terrace, Granby Terrace, Belgrave Terrace.** All of **Buckingham Terrace** and **St. James's Terrace. Hamilton Park Terrace, Hamilton Drive, Northpark Terrace** (break – separate building indicated centre of Drive). **Oakfield Terrace** (both sides).

1859   **Southpark House. Victoria Terrace, Crown Circus, Lawrence Place.** Three self-contained houses indicated at foot of **University Avenue** below **Oakfield Terrace.**

1863   Half of **Ashton Terrace** from **Byres Road. Bothwell Place, Bothwell Terrace. Horslethill.**

1865   **Westbank Terrace. St. Silas Church.** Curling Pond in **Botanic Gardens** (Site of Lily Pond). Curling Pond on site of **Western Infirmary** next to **University Avenue. Southpark Terrace, Hillhead Gardens, Florentine Terrace, Florentine Place. County Police Station** behind unnamed **Curlers Tavern.**

1866   **Ashton Terrace** completed. **Lawrence Place** completed with **Elgin Terrace. Lawrence Street** named.

1868   **Hillhead Place** (**Bank Street**). **Nelson Terrace** at **Wilson Street.** A large rectangular 'Skating Pond' covered the area between **Albion Place** and **Ruthven Street.**

1869   Buildings in **Byres Road** from **Ashton Terrace** towards **Ashton Lane.** A few small buildings corner of **Albion Street** (Hunter's Corner).

1870   Buildings from middle of **Belmont Crescent** to **Hamilton Park Terrace.** Lower **Glasgow Street** and **Bank Street.** North side of **King Street** (**Gibson Street**) from **Smith Street** to Kelvin with short section in **Smith Street.** Half of north side of **Hamilton Drive** from **Hamilton Park Terrace.** Buildings on **Great Western Road** from **Belgrave Terrace** to Kelvin, **St. John's Terrace.**

1872   **Belmont Crescent** completed. **Victoria Crescent** and **Albion Place** (north side of **Albion Street**). **Alfred Terrace** and tenement **Great Western Road** west of **Sardinia Terrace** to position of **Kersland Street. Loudon Terrace,** north side of **Huntly Gardens.**

1873   Buildings completed on **Great Western Road** to **Kelvinside Church.** East side of **Kersland Street** to facing unbuilt **Vinicombe Street. Burgh Buildings.**

1875   **Caledonian Cricket Ground** on **Glasgow Academy** site.

1876   **Byres Road** built to **Ruthven Street,** also south side of **Ruthven Street. Hillhead Parish Church. Grosvenor Buildings, Byres Road** (halfway from **Elliot Street** to **Great George Street**).

1877   **Western Baths.** Half of **Gibson Street** from **Westbank Quadrant** to Kelvin.

1879   **Glasgow Academy.**

Byres Road in these maps, during the 1860s, is named up to
Lawrence Street and then becomes **Victoria Street.**

MAP
OF THE
PARISH OF GOVAN
1852.

ORIGIN OF STREET NAMES

Part of this information is taken from

The Origin & History of Glasgow Streets, by Hugh Macintosh (1902)

BUTE GARDENS In tribute to the Marquess of Bute, Sir John Patrick Crichton Stuart (1847–1900), benefactor to Glasgow University.

BYRES ROAD From the lands known as the Byres of Partick. At various times its spelling has been changed to Byars.

CECIL STREET Family name of 3rd Marquess of Salisbury, prominent Victorian statesman and Prime Minister.

COLEBROOKE STREET In honour of Sir Thomas Edward Colebrooke Bart., a popular Lord-Lieutenant of Lanarkshire.

COWAN STREET Henry Cowan, Provost of Hillhead, 1880.

CRANWORTH STREET Robert Thornhagh Gurdon, Baron Cranworth. Born 1829. Probably as proprietor.

ELDON STREET Earl of Eldon, Lord Chancellor, 1807–27.

ELLIOT STREET (CRESSWELL STREET) Named by the superior, Robert Malcolm Kerr, LL.D., in honour of his wife's grand-uncle General Elliot who successfully defended Gibraltar against the combined forces of France and Spain during the siege of 1779–83.

GIBSON STREET James Gibson of Hillhead. In 1822, to link Hillhead with Blythswood and encourage feuing, he built a small suspension bridge across the River Kelvin. He named it King's Bridge to commemorate the visit of King George 4th to Scotland. This probably explains why the lower part of Gibson Street was originally King Street.

GLASGOW STREET One of the first streets and named in Hillhead in the late 1840s. Probably given this name because of its long straight slope towards Glasgow.

GREAT GEORGE STREET Also one of the first streets planned to extend across Bank Street. Possibly named after George 4th.

GRANBY TERRACE Marquess of Granby. Born London 1852.

HAMILTON DRIVE John Hamilton of Northpark (1754–1829). Three times Lord Provost of Glasgow.

KERSLAND STREET From the superior, Robert Malcolm Kerr, Judge of the City of London Court.

OTAGO STREET Probably from Otago Province, South Island, New Zealand, to which many Glasgow people were emigrating when the street was named. Otago Street was originally the short section between Great Western Road and Glasgow Street, the remainder until the revision of street names was Smith Street to Westbank Quadrant and named after Smith of Westbank.

SARDINIA TERRACE Completed shortly before Victor Emmanuel Second, King of Sardinia became first King of a united Italy in 1861.

VINICOMBE STREET Said to be a Devonshire name. The wife of the superior, Robert Malcolm Kerr, was Maria Vinicombe.

Several streets got their names from local mansion houses. Others, in honour of Queen Victoria, were given the names of the Royal Palaces. Also chosen were names of famous families, or their estates, and fashionable districts of London. This applied more to Kelvinside.

Havelock Street and Lawrence Street were called after Generals who were prominent in quelling the Indian Mutiny of 1857.

BURGH OF HILLHEAD

NOTICE AS TO ASSESSSMENTS FOR THE YEAR 1890-91.

The Commissioners of Police for the Burgh of Hillhead hereby give notice :—

I. That in Terms of "The General Police and Improvement (Scotland) Act, 1862," "The Roads and Bridges (Scotland) Act, 1878, and as Local Authority under "The Public Health (Scotland) Acts, 1867, and 1871," they have assessed all Occupiers and Owners of Lands or Premises, within the Burgh, as from 15th May, 1890, to 15th May, 1891, as follows, viz. :—

Payable by Occupiers,—

"POLICE ASSESSMENT," - - - - at 1s. in the Pound.
"GENERAL IMPROVEMENT RATE," - - - - at ¾d in the Pound.
"SANITARY ASSESSMENT." - - - - at 1½d in the Pound.
"MAINTENANCE OF ROADS AND BRIDGES,"- - at 1½d in the Pound.

Payable by Owners,—

"SPECIAL SEWER RATE," - - - - at 1d in the Pound.
"GENERAL IMPROVEMENT RATE," - - - at ¾d in the Pound.
"MAINTENANCE OF ROADS AND BRIDGES,"- - at 1½d in the Pound.

II. That the said Assessments shall be payable within the Gas Office, Burgh Buildings, Hillhead, on the 7th day of November, 1890, and

III. That they have fixed the 30th day of October, 1890, as the date on or before which, Appeals in writing by any parties complaining that they have been improperly assessed, may be lodged with the Collector; and that the said appeals shall be heard in the Office of the Commissioners, Burgh Buildings, Hillhead, on the 1st day of November, with continuation of days until disposed of, commencing at half-past Nine a.m. of each day.

JAMES MUIRHEAD,
Clerk to the Commissioners.

Hillhead, 1st October, 1890.

GILMOUR & CARMICHAEL, Printers, 88 Maxwell Street.

Sundial in Garden of Florentine House. *1969**

I REMEMBER

✶

J. J. Bell

HILLHEAD

HILLHEAD was a suburb then, a burgh, with its own administration, police, fire-brigade, and so on. Though largely built up by my time, there were still, here and there, extensive vacant plots, which served very well as playgrounds for the numerous children. Here and there, too, were villas in their gardens, of a period previous to that of the rows of self-contained dwellings and tenements. The trees were not, however, confined to those gardens, and something of the rural survived in a dairy farm, or two, on the bank of the Kelvin. The side streets were paved with irregularly-shaped flat stones, between which, in some streets, the limited traffic allowed grass to grow. The pavements were mostly of asphalt.

On these pavements boys lashed their tops, spun their 'peeries', played at 'bools', dashed along with their little wheel-barrows, and 'ca'ed their girds'. Need I explain that a 'peery' was a top made to spin by a string wound on a spiral groove in the wood, an end of the string being held when the 'peery' was cast upon the pavement; that 'bools' were 'marbles' of baked clay; and that to 'ca' a gird' was simply to bowl a hoop? There was, indeed, a

saying, 'Ca' your ain gird!' meaning 'Attend to your own business.' On the pavement, too, girls disported themselves with skipping-ropes or 'peevers', known furth of Scotland as 'hop-scotch'. And what of the pedestrian? Well, the pedestrian – good-humouredly, as a rule – just took to the gutter. Such liberties were for the side streets, yet the main thoroughfare, Great Western Road, had its informalities. There, for instance, one often saw a constable in leisurely converse with a nursemaid, after he had greeted the occupant of the perambulator with, 'Well, Baby, how's Nurse?'

From which you may suspect that Hillhead was an easy-going sort of place – and so it was, in a way. Yet in another way, it was, though not unhomely, a superior sort of place, the inhabitants generally being both bein and douce – two words with delicacies of meaning not to be gained from the Dictionary. It would seem that they were not without a certain naive snobbery. Many of them did not wish to be identified with a common Street, and nearly every street was divided up into Terraces, Places, Buildings – you may yet discern the faded gold lettering on certain corners – and nearly everybody declared his or her address accordingly, to the confounding of stranger visitors and the miserable con-fusion of little boy and girl messengers, new to the district, especially on dark evenings. I was born in Bothwell Terrace – I have lost the number – where, with the best intentions, a ceiling fell on my cradle, and where, having forgotten his lancet, the doctor (not Dr. Bell) prepared my arm for vaccination with a darning needle, for which my mother never forgave him; but the first home of which I was conscious, was at 3 Great Kelvin Terrace, just across the way. Why 'Great', I have never been able to comprehend; for it is a short row, and the houses are not mansions. We continued to use the grander address, till, on a soaking Saturday night, at an hour that would shock us today, my father encountered a weary, weeping little boy, with a laden basket, seeking vainly for some bumptious Buildings or pompous Place. Thenceforth plain '8 Bank Street' was added to the note-paper, and all tradesmen instructed accordingly.

In my haste I once attributed to snobbery the nomen-clature of so many west-end streets, terraces, etc. – such as St. James's, Buckingham, Windsor, Marlborough, Grosvenor, Huntly, Athole; but now it seems just possible that the old builders may have been urged by a sub-conscious loyalty, since Queen Victoria was a very real and admirable personage to Glasgow, though it saw her seldom; and that having exhausted the Royal names, they descended gradually by way of some ducal ones. Let us, at all events, give them the benefit of the doubt. They builded well, as you may see by comparing one of their seventy years old erections with much of our modern domestic architecture. Indeed, I doubt whether the average modern dwelling, if set up on Great Western Road, would survive for five years the shudders caused by the traffic. I should certainly not want to live in it.

Great Western Road, which does deserve the 'Great', though progress has made the eastern section of it a bottle-neck, and two stretches of it (at the time of writing) the most perilous in Glasgow, if not Scotland, has other-wise changed but little, so far as Hillhead is concerned, since at the age of two, having escaped my guardian, I strolled across it, oblivious of the traffic, to demand from Mr. Hubbard, the baker, a cookie for my own use, gratis. I understand that the following duologue took place:

Myself (pointing): 'A cook!'

Mr. Hubbard (amiably): 'A cook! Certainly!'

Eventually, no doubt, the world will become sane, and all business be transacted on these simple, satisfactory lines. The Mr. Hubbard of the future, having gladly disposed of a cookie, may be seized with the desire for, say, a smoke. He will have only to step along to the tobacconist, and –

Mr. Hubbard (saluting): 'A corona!'

Tobacconist (pleasantly): 'A corona! By all means!' And so on.

Apart from the present crowding traffic and its clamour, composed of the harshest, ugliest noises that human genius can produce, the most notable change is to be seen at the corner of Bank Street, in the handsome building of Messrs. Cooper & Co. Its erection is now an old story, but before the warehouse arose, there stood on part of the site a pair of little villas, with small garden plots in front. On the railing of the western one a brass plate bore the legend, 'The Misses Rankin – Seminary for Young Ladies'.

Though not a young lady, it was to the Misses Rankin – or the Miss Rankins, as everybody called them – I was sent to receive my rudiments, which included Dancing, Deportment and Callisthenics, also Music. There is no

J. J. BELL (1871-1934)

The famous author of *Wee Macgreegor*, whose engaging adventures, first published in 1902, have never ceased to win new readers. This collection of vividly realistic short stories centred on the small son of a typical Glasgow working-class family at the beginning of the century first took shape when J.J. was stuck for a subject when his weekly article for the Glasgow *Evening Times* was pressingly due.

He tried to sell the copyright of the completed series but met with failure even after dropping his price from £10 to £5. Eventually by his brother giving him £50 to defray the cost, he had a small paperback printed with the now well-known cover design by John Hassall who then worked in Glasgow.

In his mature years his descriptive writings of a reminiscent nature also have a perennial appeal within their own reach of interest, the best selections being within the two volumes *I Remember* (1932) and *Do You Remember* (1934).

The first article and half of the second in *I Remember* re-printed here by courtesy of the publishers, Faber & Faber, constitute an important contribution to the contemporary life of his generation.

Horse tramcar of the 1880s at its Kelvinside terminus. At this time Crossloan Road (now Cleveden Road) was also known as Collins's Hill, the residence of Mr. Collins, the papermaker, being at the top. *Photo probably by Matt. A. Macdonald. Courtesy of Mr. Henry J. Crone*

accounting for the persistence of trivial memories. I still retain a clear vision of an upper room, on a very hot afternoon, the window open, a bee buzzing, myself at the piano, stumbling through the notes of 'We're a' Noddin'' – singularly appropriate music – and Miss Rankin sighing, rather than saying, 'Oh, dear, this is awful – one and two and one and two and. . . .' For a long time I have cordially agreed with her. A detestable tune, though none ever composed fitted its words better – an inspiration in dreariness.

Some of the old names still remain above the shops, but they grow fewer. The benevolent Mr. Hubbard's has lately gone, and that of Mr. Farmer, who sold 3 Great Kelvin Terrace to my father, also that of the draper, Mr. John Brown, at the Sign of the Crown, who was 'licensed to sell stamps', the nearest post office being at some little distance. Which reminds me that the postage stamps were far finer than those we have now; indeed, this country has had no dignified stamps since the 'Eighties. In the 'Seventies they bore the original and beautiful effigy of the young Queen's head, which filled the frame, no 'frills' being necessary. The penny stamps were red,

the halfpennies pink, and about half the present size, while the twopennies were a deep blue. Incidentally, there was no Parcel Post, and a telegram cost a shilling for twelve words – but the address went free.

Many of the shops have changed their trades. The china shop, where I bought my marbles, is a savings bank; the shop where, somewhat later, I bought sweets, in which the little lady's greeting was always 'It's pleasanter this evening' – whether it was a blizzard or a deluge – has become a bookseller's; the shop, a chandler's, where at the approach of the Queen's Birthday (24th of May) my brother and I purchased fireworks – squibs, zig-zag crackers, and whirligigs (Catherine wheels), one penny each; Roman candles, twopence; 'blue deevils', four a penny – that shop is now, I think, a shoemaker's. We always bought our fireworks too early, with the result that none were left for Her Majesty. The barber's – M. Leon Genin – at which, as a reward for having my hair cut, I was wont to receive a balloon, became, after some vicissitudes, a bank; the old Hillhead post-office is today a fishmonger's; another sweet-shop, famed for its 'jujube cuttings' – the trimmings of the slab from which the little squares, red, black or yellow, were cut – is a chemist's; and our old family chemist's is a baker's. I suppose the butcher's is the only food trade which has been unable to increase the variety of its wares, for even the fishmonger now sells farm produce, while the fruit merchant has long since added, at least, bananas. As for the baker, the confectioner and the chemist, when one regards their turnover in sheer luxuries, one can only opine that the Georgian has less respect for a shilling than the Victorian had for a penny. Yet the Victorian was mean neither to his friends nor to himself. What a Victorian of the older generation, returned to earth, would call the extravagance of these days might be partly explained to him by the fact that there are few large families to be provided for, while a multitude of middle-class women are earning money. Nevertheless, he would wonder helplessly at the expenditure outside the home – on motor cars, amusements, innumerable extras, and certain obvious feminine vanities; at the same time, he would be disgusted by the information that nearly all the jewellery displayed was worthless; and finally, about to return to his place, he would snap the question, 'Cannot you find any pleasures, without buying them?'

The street traffic was made up of carts, vans, an occasional carriage and pair, a stray cab or hansom, and tramcars, the service of which was adequate. The trams belonged to the Glasgow Tramway Company, who leased the road rights from the Glasgow Corporation. None of the routes exceeded three miles; all radiated from the centre of the City, that of the Hillhead cars, which were green, from St. Vincent Place. The penny tickets were white, the twopenny red, the threepenny blue. Boys 'collected' the tickets, the blue ones being rather rare. Boys also made friends with the guards – never 'conductors' then – and obtained rides for nothing. Inspectors were said to exist, though I never encountered one. There were fare stations, but no regulation stopping-places. You simply waved. If the driver did not see you, the guard pulled a leather thong, a bell tinkled above the driver's head, the horses heard and made ready to halt, while the driver applied the brake. Inside, a car held something like eighteen passengers, the double seat running the length of the unsheltered roof about the same. Ladies did not go up the narrow stair. When the car came over the bridge, a boy was waiting with a third horse to help it up the steep hill. As it ascended quite briskly, 'twas a sight to behold, in the early evenings, the gentlemen returning from business step nonchalantly off at the foot of their respective streets; but no lady would have dreamed of attempting the feat. At first the track ended at the Botanic Gardens; later on it was extended to Kirklee.

I have said that the horses understood the bell. The anonymous author of a humorous volume of the period called *Jeems Kaye* made use of the fact. 'Jeems' was a coal merchant, also a Colonel in the Volunteers. For the annual march out it was necessary that he should be mounted, and he hired a steed from the Tramway Company. With Col. Kaye at its head, the battalion marched bravely along till, when about to pass a car, the guard rang the bell. The intelligent charger came to a stop, holding up the entire battalion, and refused to proceed till the bell was rung again. It was not an incredible tale. Today the horse-tram seems an extraordinarily primitive means of transport, yet it served a generation in what were surely the most fortunate decades the middle-class of this country has known.

It seems unlikely that people will ever again ride in anything so fine and elegant as the carriage and pair, which with its dignity has all but disappeared from the rough and tumble of the street. Compared with the horseman, the cyclist must always be a grotesque. The rider of the early bicycle, on his graceful, spidery wheel, though elevated about five feet above his fellows, succeeded only in looking unusual – unless he was racing,

From *West Glasgow Record*   25th July 1893

BAND PERFORMANCE

Tomorrow night the 3rd L.R.V. under the leadership of Mr. James Wilson, give the following programme in the Botanic Gardens.

March	— Black Dyke	*Jubb*
Overture	— Le Caid	*Thomas*
Valse	— Eldorado	*Royle*
Selection	— Pinafore	*Sullivan*
Grand March	— Tannhauser	*Wagner*
Selection	— Life on the Ocean	*Binding*
Valse	— Schummerlied	*Coote*
Galop	— Madcap	*Reille*

V.   R.

QUEEN'S BIRTHDAY.

THE MAGISTRATES AND COMMISSIONERS
OF THE
BURGH OF HILLHEAD
RECOMMEND THAT
THURSDAY, 23RD CURT.,
BE OBSERVED AS A HOLIDAY IN HONOUR OF
HER MAJESTY'S BIRTHDAY.
ALEX. S. BAIRD,
CHIEF MAGISTRATE,

BURGH CHAMBERS,
HILLHEAD, 14th May, 1889.

Kelvingrove Park showing layout before Kelvin Way was constructed in 1914. Commonly known for many years as the West End Park, Kelvingrove Park was constituted in 1852 by the purchase of 66 acres at a cost of £77,945. With the addition of parts of the lands of Nether Newton, Clayslaps and Gilmorehill the area was increased to 87 acres. On the lower right corner of photograph can be seen the old red wooden bridge which led to the original entrance of the Art Galleries. *Annan 1905*

Official Opening of the Glasgow International Exhibition of 1888, by Edward, Prince of Wales. *Annan*

when he seemed miraculous. On Saturday afternoons bicycle clubs, led by a member with a bugle, wheeled rather solemnly along in single file, and in smart, tight uniforms – bound for a country run. Doubtless they created a stir among the farms and villages, whose folk would have something to talk about for a fortnight or so. Equestrians, of both sexes, on their way to or from the riding-track, a mile westward, were fairly frequent in Hillhead. It was unfortunate that the existence of a livery stable in the district should have given ribald message boys the inspiration to shout, 'Hey, come back! Yer hour's up!'

Excitements in Hillhead were not frequent. It was not, of course, impossible to get run over, and occasionally a man would be fined for 'furious driving'. Everybody, especially today, has his own idea of speed. To some of us Victorians a tramway car might appear to 'whizz along', or a hansom 'go like lightning'. The

supreme thrill was the Fire-Brigade; still, on dull days a chimney vomiting rich yellow smoke provided a welcome distraction, while in winter the fall of a poor horse on the frosty road quickly drew a gaping crowd. 'This has been a gran' day,' a message boy remarked to his chum, on their homeward way: 'A horse coupit, a lum a-low, and a man fell off a lorry!'

An event in spring was the Annual March Out of the 1st Lanarkshire Rifle Volunteers. Volunteering was an enthusiastic business, and it was a lengthy column of men in grey, helmets included, that marched out of Burnbank drill-ground, long since built over, across Kelvin Bridge, and gallantly breasted the western hill, led by a brass band. A pipe band was added later. 'A finer body of men I have never seen,' was the comment of the inspecting colonel, and that was the opinion of every boy in Hillhead, for the '1st Lanark' was *our* regiment, and most of us had friends or relations in it. 'There's my Uncle Bob!'

Bank Street showing Cooper's Tower and Great
Kelvin Terrace on left.   *April 1968**

Northwoodside House in early 19th century.
Original oil by A. D. Robertson in Glasgow
Corporation Collection

a youngster would proudly cry, but Uncle Bob, *aetat* 19,
would march on, with countenance as sternly set as ever
was countenance on the field of Waterloo. All the same,
a good many of us secretly wished that the uniform had
included scarlet tunics, like those of another Volunteer
battalion which sometimes took its outing through
Hillhead – a great, uplifting spectacle. There were cynics
in those days who spoke of 'playing at soldiers'. They
could not know that from the Volunteers were to come
the Territorials. The most deadly experience of the
Volunteers – as Volunteers – was the Grand Review of all
the Scottish regiments at Edinburgh, by Her Majesty
Queen Victoria, in 1881 – a day of pitiless rain, at the
close of which many a man returned as from a battle.
Some died.

Bank Street led to the University, and was therefore a
thoroughfare of some little importance, but in August
1888 it attained, for a few minutes, to honour and glory
by the progress of Her Majesty through it to Kelvingrove
Park, there to visit Glasgow's first International Exhibition. A little elderly lady in a bonnet, sitting erect in a big
landau, giving every now and then a nod – so she passed
by, looking serene and not bored. A year ago, the land
had acclaimed her Jubilee – fifty years on the throne, yet
with, as reigns go, many years still to come. The Exhibition had been opened in May by the Prince and Princess
of Wales, Her Royal Highness wearing a tight-fitting
costume with a very decided 'bustle', a floral bonnet, with
a veil to the tip of her nose, and carrying a prim little
muff.

Not long after Queen Victoria and her retinue had
passed, and the pavements and windows had become
vacant, an aged Italian, with barrel organ and monkey,
appeared. Possibly he knew nothing of the importance of
the hour, of Glasgow's first International Exhibition, of
the august Personage who had so lately preceded him.
It was his day for Bank Street, and calmly he began to
grind the 'Carnival of Venice', lifting peering rheumy
eyes to the windows. . . . To Bank Street also came
regularly a piano-organ, with a reel of somewhat lurid
pictures – battle-scenes – which slowly passed across a
glazed frame as the handle was turned. Its repertory,
year after year, included 'the *Marseillaise*'. Erratically
came a man with drum and cymbals on his back and
bagpipes in his hands, who looked as if he slept with them
all, and quite frequently two men with a Punch and
Judy show. But the itinerants most welcome to all but
juveniles arrived every Tuesday, and were the German
Band. The German Band had by then become a British
institution. There were superior persons who sneered, but
in quiet streets the Band was sure of its pennies.

Our band wore a sort of uniform and carried stands
for its music. Inferior bands existed, whose methods were
perfunctory, whose insignia were confined to their caps,
and who stuck their small sheets of manuscript on their
instruments, or did without. Our band carefully adjusted
its flimsy tripods, as if it were going to spend the afternoon
with us, secured its music to the frame with criss-crosses
of string, paused impressively, and then struck up, as one
man. There were five performers – a clarinet, cornet,
euphonium and trumpet – I cannot remember the fifth.
Invariably the first item was a rousing march. It was
followed by an operatic selection, say, from 'The

The First Lanark Rifles Gazette.

No. 1, Vol. I.] TUESDAY, 16TH NOV., 1886. [PRICE TWOPENCE.

CONTENTS.

Regimental Gathering and Presentation of Prizes,

THEATRE ROYAL, GLASGOW,

TUESDAY EVENING, 16th NOVEMBER, 1886.

PROGRAMME.

7-30 to 8 P.M.—2ND BATTALION BAND, BANDMASTER HOWELL, Conductor.

1.—OVERTURE,	"In Memoriam,"		Newton.
2.—SELECTION,	"The Bohemian Girl,"		Balfe.
3.—VALSE,..	"Mikado,"		Bucalossi.

8 P.M.—WALTZ, ... "Verena," Composed by Private MARSHALL F. REID. 1ST L.R.V.
1ST BATTALION BAND (ADAMS'), Conductor, H. J. O'NEIL.
DUMB-BELL EXERCISES, ... MEMBERS OF THE 1ST L.R.V.A.A.C.
INDIAN CLUB EXERCISES, ... Sergeant-Major CANSDALE.
8-10 P.M.—VOCAL MUSIC, ... MEMBERS OF GLEE CLUB.
8-20 P.M.—OVERTURE, ... "Merry Wives of Windsor," ... Nicolai.
1ST BATTALION BAND.

8-30. p.m.—PRESENTATION OF PRIZES.

*The names of Prize-winners entitled to appear will be found Marked * in Lists on Pages 7 and 8.*

9-0 P.M.—GRAND SELECTION, ... "Mefistofele," ... Boito.
1ST BATTALION BAND.
SWORD FEATS, by Sergeant-Major CANSDALE, Instructor, Gymnasium, Maryhill Barracks.
WALTZ, ... "Soiree d'Eté," ... Waldteufel.
1ST BATTALION BAND.
HORIZONTAL BAR EXERCISES, ... MEMBERS OF 1ST L.R.V.A.A.C.
9-20 P.M.—FANTASIA, ... "The Jacobite," ... Gassner.
1ST BATTALION BAND.
With Solos for Clarionet, Cornet, and Euphonium—Messrs. GREEN, HILL, and MERRET.
9-35 P.M.—FARCE, "A Waltz by Arditi," by JOHN OXENFORD, Characters by the MEMBERS OF THE
1ST L.R.V. DRAMATIC SOCIETY.
10-10 P.M.—VOCAL MUSIC, ... MEMBERS OF GLEE CLUB.

GOD SAVE THE QUEEN.

Bohemian Girl', which allowed of a cornet solo; then a waltz, probably by Strauss or Gung'l, or maybe Coote or Bucalossi. By way of compliment, no doubt, the fourth item was always Scottish. When it was ended, to the dismay of that section of Bank Street, the cornet player and another tucked their instruments under their arms and started off on a door to door collection. Each home was given every chance to contribute, the bandsman refusing to despair till he had rung at least three times. To cheer us during the collection the remaining trio performed a sparkling polka, the clarinet sustaining the melody. It always seemed to me that it would be a graceful act on the part of the reunited and rewarded band to play just one tune more. But no! Such a thing was simply not done by German Bands. The collectors returned, wearing inscrutable expressions; the music was unfastened, the stands folded up; and with the utmost nonchalance the band walked away.

A day was to come when it would walk away, never to return.

PAPA GOES INTO TOWN

ABOUT 8.30 began the pilgrimage of Hillhead's papas into town for the purpose of making pennies. Persons who were not papas set out on the same errand, but your attention is drawn to them merely in case you should care to spend some time in looking carefully for a woman or girl among them. This is going to be an attempt to picture, in the fewest possible strokes, the progress of an ordinary papa during an ordinary business day in the City of Glasgow, in the year 1880, or thereabouts.

But first a few words about the papas generally, who are coming down from the high terraces above the main road, or out of the side streets, some running after a tram-car and nimbly boarding it, without troubling the horses to stop, others making up their minds to walk into the city for the good of their health. A considerable number of them wear black coats and silk hats. Such a garb is almost certainly a sign that the wearer is a banker, or a lawyer, or a member of the Royal Exchange, or, of course, a cabby. But whether or not one wears a silk hat, it may be assumed that he donned, an hour or so ago, a stiff white shirt, a stiff white collar, and a pair of stiff white cuffs. As regards the shirt, it is known that such things as 'dickeys', or false fronts, do exist, though in Hillhead we do not mention them, except, on occasion, with a jocularly satirical air. It is most unlikely that any one of these papas, unless a slight chest weakness demands a shirt of flannel, carries such a sorry secret.

While the stiff collar is inevitable, the cuffs are *de rigueur*. They are really rather a nuisance, so quickly are they sullied by Glasgow's atmospheric grime. Man's inventive genius, however, has mitigated the worry, by providing a cuff which can be buttoned to the wrist-band – yet not only that, for the cuff is a double cuff which can be reversed. Care must be taken, nevertheless, to see that the cuff is securely attached to the wrist-band. Through neglect of this precaution distressingly awkward mishaps, have occurred. Lately, at a civic conversazione, a tall gentleman having shaken hands with a young lady

St. Vincent Place
looking east, *c.* 1894.
Terminus of Kelvinside
and Hillhead horse
tramcars
Old Glasgow Museum

JAMES HENDERSON & CO.,
COACHBUILDERS,

Beg to invite Carriage Connoisseurs to Inspect a Magnificent Stock of **Sporting Carriages**, also an interesting Collection of **High-Class Carriages**, comprising Landaus of all Styles, Broughams, Barouches, Double and **Single** Victorias, Park Phaetons, Stanhope Waggonettes, and Waggonettes of all sizes.
HIGHEST HONOURS at the GREAT INTERNATIONAL EXHIBITIONS at HOME and ABROAD.
GOLD MEDAL this Year at the International Exhibition, London.
BRANCH SHOW ROOMS—BOTHWELL CIRCUS.

The Bailie, 1896

seated on a low *fauteuil*, had the mortification of beholding his cuff remain on the fair one's wrist.

With collars, at present, are being worn four styles of neckwear: the bow, the knot, the fine scarf drawn through a ring, and the made-up sporting scarf, or 'poultice'. In the second and fourth a pin is usually carried, its head being often a jewel of price. Pearls, bloodstones, garnets, cameos, gold horseshoes, are favoured. Yet one may meet an elderly gentleman who wears none of these things. 'Why', demanded such a gentleman, 'should I fash about a tie when it canna be seen for my beard?'

Talking of beards, by the way, a friend, given to statistics, informed me once that having analysed the countenances of all the members of the Glasgow Royal Exchange, about the year to which I refer, he obtained the following percentages: beards, 83; whiskers, various, 10; moustaches only, 5; clean shaven, 2. He analysed also the hats: black 'tiles', 86 per cent.; grey ditto, 2 per cent.; hard felts, 9 per cent.; felts with flat tops, 3 per cent.

Our Papa, as I may call him for the present, is dressed in a dark grey lounge suit (though he would not know it by that name), under a dark light-weight overcoat, a 'pot' hat ('bowler' is still an 'English' word), a 'poultice', with a cameo of the head of Minerva; and, since he is not elderly, he carries a light stick of cherry-wood, with a narrow silver band. He is a little late this morning, so boards a tram. The inside is filled mainly with silk hats bending over morning papers – *The Glasgow Herald* or *North British Daily Mail*. An English journal is impossible in the morning, but you may obtain *The Times* and others, late in the day, from Mr. Porteous, Exchange Square. There is one lady in the tram, but she is merely going with her husband to catch a train. Our Papa goes upstairs, and lights a small cigar with a vesuvian.

The green car crosses Kelvin Bridge, which they are talking of widening. On the other side is a red-car terminus; and farther on, at St. George's Cross, you may take a blue car all the way to Crosshill, on the south side of the Clyde – rather an adventure, if you are not used to it. New City Road is just as drab as it will be fifty years hence; Cambridge Street, wardrobe of 'cast-off clothing', just about as dreary. Here are situated the tramway stables, where fresh horses are waiting, and where the conductor, running up to the office, hands in his money bag and receives another containing 3s. 6d. in small change. To coming generations these methods will seem clumsy and fussy; yet the Tramway Company does not slumber. In order to encourage tram travel it has recently introduced, in perforated sheets, little oblong green penny coupons, thirteen for a shilling.

Sauchiehall Street is too narrow ever to become a splendid thoroughfare, and at present the only buildings of note are Messrs. Copland & Lye's warehouse and the new Galleries of the Fine Arts Institute, with their classic frontage. The winter exhibition of pictures and statuary will be opened presently, with a grand Conversazione, and afterwards, on Saturday afternoons, an orchestra will perform, led (as I remember it, some years later) by Mr. W. H. Cole. Renfield Street is undistinguished; the banks and insurance companies have not yet become builders; and the same might be said of St. Vincent Street, but for its view of Buchanan Street, a vista of broad pavements under buildings not too high, ending in the spire of old St. Enoch's Church – curious instance of a woman's name, St. Thenew, being corrupted into a man's. And no 'new' woman has ever raised the question!

At St. Vincent Place the journey finishes, and driver and guard prepare to transfer the horses from the east end of the car to the west. Papa proceeds into George Square. It is not so tastefully laid out as it will be for the next generation, but the familiar statues are there. The new building on the south side is the General Post Office. Its foundation stone was laid by Albert Edward, Prince of Wales, accompanied by his Princess Alexandra. As a very small boy, I looked down on the procession from an office window on the west side. Eastward, the mountain of stone, the Municipal Buildings, has not yet arisen, though it has been imagined. The foundation stone will be laid in 1883. On the north side, plain and dignified, already elderly, stands the George Hotel (to become the North British). At its entrance are two soldiers in scarlet coats and busbies, holding rifles with bayonets fixed, on guard, for there is a High Court these days at Jail Square, and at this moment the Judges are breakfasting in the Hotel.

Reprinted by permission of Faber and Faber Ltd
from *I Remember* (1932)

WEE MACGREEGOR Taiblet

"Taiblet's awfu' guid"
(WEE MACGREEGOR)

1/- per tin.

Registered

Sole Proprietors

Wm FARMER AND SONS GLASGOW.

*Courtesy of
Mr. Wm. Roy Farmer*

St. Vincent Place
looking west, *c.* 1894
Old Glasgow Museum

University Gardens. *May 1965*

BACKWARD GLANCES

(in my eightieth year)

◎

CHARLES A. HEPBURN

IN the year 1891 I was born in Bothwell Place which faced Great Western Road on the site now occupied by Caledonian Mansions. My father was one of the first merchants to establish his business in Hillhead, when the City was moving west. He made furniture and had a large depository known as Kelvin House in Otago Street. The basement of the building and ground floor flat were used by the Corporation as stables for the tramway horses. Although the horse trams were replaced by electric trams in time for the great International Exhibition of 1901, the stalls can still be seen. These flats are now used as garages. The stables were approached from the back of the building by a cobbled track, known as the Bishops' Road that led to the stepping stones which the Bishops had used for centuries to cross the Kelvin on their way to and from the Cathedral when their summer residence was at Partick Castle. These stepping stones can still be seen in summer when the river is low, a little north of the present bridge.

Bothwell Place disappeared at the close of the 19th century when the Caledonian Railway Company extended the low level line from Central Station to Maryhill via Kelvinbridge, Botanic Gardens and Kirklee. At the building of Kelvinbridge Station they also built Caledonian Mansions to serve as an Annexe to the Central Hotel. It was never used for this purpose, hence the curious architectural feature of this fine block of flats. When Bothwell Place was demolished my family moved to Parkview House at 2 Great George Street. My sister, Kate, carried me in her arms along to our new house. Parkview, as the name implies, originally had an uninterrupted outlook on Kelvingrove Park. The house still had a fine big garden where we were able to build trenches and stage fights between the Boers and Britons. The War in South Africa was raging at this time and a most unpopular War it was.

Semple's dairy stood on the south side of Smith Street. The cows grazed on the banks of the Kelvin. As kids we got a great kick out of herding the cows at milking time. The milk was delivered in cans with wire handles. During the day the cans were boiled in a great boiler. The noise of the rattling cans could be heard around the district. Semple senior looked like John Bull, but his son was tall and lanky. He was good for a chase when called 'Lanky', but as he used a long carriage whip you had to give yourself a good start. I made a mistake one day. I called 'lanky' without giving myself a big enough start. 'Lanky' drew his whip and I got the lash twice round my face. Unfortunately for 'Lanky' my big brother Brodie arrived on the scene. Brodie was the amateur Boxing Champion of Scotland at the time. I still remember vividly how Brodie took two steps into the middle of the street and struck 'Lanky' a smashing blow in the face. Despite the smarting double weals in my face I felt sorry for 'Semple' as he lay spitting teeth in the street.

Next to Semple's dairy on the south side of Smith Street was Henderson's Stables where hundreds of tramway horses were stabled. Henderson also provided broughams for the General Practitioners in Hillhead and mounts for the men of The Queen's Own Royal Glasgow Yeomanry, the only Cavalry Regiment in Glasgow. This was an elite corps which only patricians could join. Officers provided their own Chargers while Henderson supplied mounts for the men. The Duke of Hamilton was the first Major Commandant, while the Officers included gentlemen like Captain James Merry of Monkland, an old High School boy, who ran many famous racehorses, such as Thormanby which won the Derby in 1860. In their blue uniform, with gold bandolier, and plumed steel head-dress the regiment made a brave show at all the Royal functions in the City. They gave a good account of themselves in the South African War and again in 1914 when they were dismounted and served as Infantry in the trenches. The Corps still exists today as the 64th (Q.O.R.G.Y.) Anti Tank Regiment R.A. (T.A.).

There was tremendous excitement the day students from the University dropped a pro-Boer Professor over Gibson Street Bridge on the end of a mountaineering rope. There was hardly enough water in the river to wet the Professor's pants, but it certainly scared him stiff.

I woke one morning to the sound of marching men and martial music. I jumped out of bed, pulled on my clothes, and dashed up to Bank Street in time to see the Reserve Battalion of the H.L.I. making its way to Stobcross Quay to embark for Cape Town. This was the old Militia, most of whom were Irish navvies. Tough, rough and absolutely heartless, useless for ceremonial purposes, but in action the finest fighting material in the world. The drunks, with their wives, had been bundled into G.S. waggons which followed behind. All were singing the song of the day, 'Goodbye Dolly Gray'. Little did I realise that 15 years later, while serving in Flanders, I should be 'lent' to this same battalion on a special mission, when it had orders to carry out a silent raid on the German trenches at Hooge, a notoriously nasty section of the infamous Ypres salient.

Before the fine red sandstone tenements were built on the north side of Great George Street, the hill was vacant space from the back of Sardinia Terrace to the back of the shops in Byres Road. In summer this space made a grand playground. In winter, when snow was on the ground, it made a wonderful run for sledging. Children came from all corners of the City, with all kinds of curious contraptions in the shape of sledges, from super toboggans from Kelvinside, to tin trays from Tobago Street. There was a hump in the middle of the run, known as Majuba Hill. By judiciously steering over this hump one could get the thrill of a dangerous jump. Only the 'big' boys ventured this escapade. One night on our way home on the other side of Great George Street we jumped on the sledge at Ann Street to run down the hill. It made a great run. We had gathered speed, when to our horror, a handsome cab appeared across our track at Wilson Street. We could do nothing about it. We shut our eyes and waited for the smash. Nothing happened. We had run below the belly of the horse. We must have touched one of its legs because it shied and upset the cabbie who shouted rude words after us.

Erected in Sardinia Terrace, now Cecil Street, Hillhead High School opened on Monday, 13th April 1885 with Edward Ellice Macdonald as Headmaster and Mr. Wm. Walker, as Janitor. This was a superlative combination. The Headmaster took care of the educational side of the School while the Janitor, who had been Colour Sergeant in the Northumberland Fusiliers, attended to discipline from a desk inside the main door where he could deal with latecomers. Pupils could refer to the Headmaster as Macdonald but none dared call the Janitor as other than Mister Walker. Together they made Hillhead one of the leading schools in the City.

Mr. Macdonald was a great Headmaster, aloof to the point of being difficult, respected by his Staff and feared by his pupils. He was a big powerful man, with a bald head. When his bald head went red it was the sign of danger. A great walker and a good swimmer. He lived at Bearsden and walked to and from the school every day. At examination times he would take a bundle of exercise books home with him to check. He would work on until 3 or 4 in the morning and then walk out the Stockiemuir Road to the Whangie, see the sun rise, return for a cold bath and breakfast, then start his day's work at the School.

As Headmaster he made a regular practice of visiting classrooms in the afternoon. When he stumped along the concrete corridors the whole school shook. He burst into the English classroom one day when I was on my feet reciting Burns' 'Address to a Haggis.' I had just reached the lines 'but mark the rustic, haggis-fed; the trembling earth resounds his tread,' when Mr. Macdonald made his entrance. The timing was dramatic; the class roared with laughter. The Headmaster demanded to know what the joke was. Nobody had the courage to tell him. I was ordered to his room where I got six of the best. Ten years later when I was walking through the Lairig Ghru from Aviemore to the Pools of Dee I met Mr. Macdonald about halfway, walking in the opposite direction. We sat down in the heather and had a chat while we ate our sandwiches. 'Do you remember,' he asked me, 'many years ago while you were at school, I visited the English class when there was an outburst of laughter. For years I've wondered what caused the hilarity.' I told him. 'Why did you not tell me at the time? It would have saved you six of the best.' I told him I was much too scared. He apologised and all was well. In 1912 he lost his life while bathing at Cullen.

When I got the length of the Chemistry Class I learned how to make gunpowder. Long before the Tennis Courts were made in the West End Park the 6th H.L.I. – Harry Lauder's Infantry – with Tommy Lipton as Honorary Colonel, used to do Battalion drill on the vacant space in front of Gray Street. I made up a tin of gunpowder and, with a short fuse, buried it in a hole in the parade ground where the battalion turned about in its marching drill. The fuse was timed to blow the powder as the battalion about turned. It worked like magic. The bomb exploded in a cloud of smoke just as the ranks reached the buried bomb. Never have I seen such a sight. Soldiers in panic running in all directions. Tommy Lipton fell off his horse. This was by far my most successful practical joke, and the one that gave me greatest satisfaction.

Little did I reckon that a few years later I would parade with the outfit as a member of the Cadet Corps at the great Review held by King Edward VII in the King's Park at Holyrood when Volunteers from every corner of Scotland marched past the King. The 6th H.L.I. entrained at Yorkhill on Sunday night and arrived at Leith in the early hours of Monday morning. We marched up Leith Walk into the Canongate, bands playing and flags flying. Folks hung out their windows in their nightgowns and nightcaps as they did

Arch at University entrance opposite Hillhead Street. *June 1963**

Caledonian
Mansions fro
Otago Street.
1963*

Otago Street. *1968**

Charles A. Hepburn M.C., LL.D. (1890–1971)
Stephens Orr

in Jacobite days. We were billeted in McEwans' Brewery where free beer was on tap for the men with an unlimited supply of tuppenny pies. There was little demand by the men for the pies but we boys made a meal of them. I personally consumed seventeen, since when I have never looked at another. By the time the bugles sounded 'Fall In' most of the men were drunk, but they still managed to make a brave show as the battalion marched into position below Salisbury Crags.

Tommy Lipton, the Honorary Colonel, led the Battalion, mounted on a white charger. At a walking pace he was able to sit tight in his saddle, but as soon as the battalion passed the saluting base and had to double, it was too much for Tommy Lipton. He fell off, without however doing himself any damage. The King called him up and that started a life long friendship.

The ploy that has plagued me all my life is the memory of the young man who broke his big toe kicking an old bowler hat under which I had placed a brick. In the days when four out of every five ocean going liners were built on the Clyde, many of the 'black squad' lived in Maryhill. Work started at 6 a.m. and finished at 5 p.m. The noise of the hand driven rivets was the background music in Hillhead. These shipbuilders were 'fitba' daft. Finding an old bowler hat I was tempted to lay it on Bank Street, with a brick below it, as the 'black squad' was hurrying home from the yards. The first man to get his eye on the hat had a run and kick at it. He lifted it almost as high as the first storey. With a yell he grasped his boot and while he waited for an ambulance to take him to the Western Infirmary his language was more lurid than anything I have ever listened to in my life.

In 1901 when the great International Exhibition was about to open in the West End Park the burning topic in Hillhead was the question of season tickets. Season tickets cost a

Carving on east side of Caledonian Mansions. *1968**

'Parkview', 2 Great George Street. Its name was for many years fully justified. *1965**

pound for seniors and ten shillings for juniors. In a large family this was a serious problem. Running home from school for lunch I tripped on some scaffolding lying in the street and landed in the gutter. When I picked myself up I found a half sovereign below my hand. My season ticket problem was solved. Forgotten was my bleeding nose and broken teeth. When I returned to school I retailed my good fortune to Arthur Ferrier, the boy who shared the desk with me. The incident gave Arthur the idea for a topical cartoon on the subject of season tickets which was given a double page spread in the School Magazine. He used me as the model of the harassed father surrounded by a large family clamouring for 'seasons'. The likeness was so good that it took me many a long day to live it down. Arthur Ferrier went on to become one of the leading cartoonists in the country. He moved to London where he became a prominent member of the Savage Club.

The Great War broke out on 4th August 1914. Next day hundreds of members of the O.T.C. turned up at the University Union when the Captain of the University O.T.C. advised us to apply in writing to the War Office for a commission. This we did and in due course received a postcard to say our applications would be dealt with at a later date. Week after week passed without further word. Meanwhile the army was retreating from Mons. The situation was desperate. Then came news of the battle of the Marne. The situation was saved. The tide had turned, the war would finish by Christmas. Our services would no longer be needed. We would miss the show. In desperation we formed up in fours outside the Union and marched down the hill and along Argyle Street to the Recruiting Office in the Gallowgate where we enlisted *en masse* into Kitchener's army, and so was lost officer material so badly needed by the army when Kitchener's army was squandered at Loos on 25th September 1915, by French's failure to bring forward his reserves in time to take advantage of the initial breakthrough. A fault which sacrificed the cream of the youth of the country and cost French his command. The fear of the war being finished by Christmas became a grim joke.

I may not have brought any academic honours to Hillhead High School but I am sure I spilled more blood in upholding the honour of the school than any other scholar before or since. It was a tradition at the time when message boys, known to be good fighters, waited outside the School at four o'clock on Friday to meet the champion from the school. There was no argument or discussion. We simply retired to the Lane behind Alfred Terrace with our respective supporters, and got stuck into it. Many a bloody nose and black eye I got in the process. Fortunately for me Mr. Walker, the Janitor, always appeared on the scene when I was being badly beaten. Many years later, when bored in the trenches, and recalling these fights, I wondered how the Janitor's interference was so fortuitous for me. I suddenly realised that the Janitor must have watched these fights from the cover of the boys' lavatory and let me carry on as long as I was winning, but stepped in and stopped the fight when I was being beaten. In gratitude I saluted that fine old soldier.

Hillhead produced many colourful characters. Sir William Smith, the founder of the Boys' Brigade lived in 4 Ann Street. On the day of the Annual Inspection of the Battalion at Yorkhill Sir William was mounted on a charger provided by the army stationed at Maryhill Barracks. On one occasion the groom who took the charger to 4 Ann Street left it standing in the street while he went upstairs to tell Sir William his charger was waiting without. The horse followed the groom up the close and attempted to climb the stairs, causing great consternation. An excited crowd collected, but the groom, aided by Sir William and his two sons, the maids, and the bobby on the beat, soon succeeded in persuading the well trained charger to back down into the street, amidst sparks from its shoes and screams from the crowd. All was well. Sir William, like a good soldier, was still on parade with five minutes to spare.

Not to be outdone Dr. Somerville, who lived further along the street, founded the Girls' Guildry at Gilmorehill Church. Dr. Somerville was a typical example of the general practitioner of his time. Dressed in a square cut frock coat, with shepherd tartan trousers, patent button boots with

The Prince of Wales Bridge, West End Park, 1903. This was the main carriageway before the construction of Kelvin Way. *S. Greaves*

lavender tops, an immaculate tile hat, and a flower in his buttonhole 'to bring an air of brightness into the sickroom'. Russell, the florist in Great Western Road, had standing orders to provide these flowers.

When Dr. Somerville retired he became President of the Society for the Conversion of the Jews. As President his chief task was to collect funds for this illustrious cause. With this purpose in mind he wrote to his friend Dr. Hawthorn in London: 'My dear Hawthorn, I am delighted to hear you have put up your plate in Harley Street where I'm sure you will be a great success. While I have no wish to remind you that, when you were a struggling medical student, I was able to be of some help to you, now that I am President of the Society for the Conversion of the Jews I should be pleased if you could see your way to help by sending me a couple of guineas.' Hawthorn wrote back to say: 'My dear Somerville, I'm sorry I cannot see my way to send you a couple of guineas but I shall be pleased to help, if you care to send along a couple of Jews I will do my best to convert them.'

James Laird, the cabinetmaker, with a furniture shop at the end of Kelvinbridge, lived in a most attractive villa on the north bank of the Kelvin on the side opposite Kelvinbridge Station. Laird in his leisure hours was a keen gardener. Amongst other things he grew tomatoes in his glass house, but he was never able to compete with the luscious tomatoes grown by Wells, the stationmaster at Kelvinbridge Station, who was also a keen gardener who cultivated the opposite bank of the river. The river was narrow enough to enable these keen rivals to carry on a conversation. Laird persuaded Wells to give him a cutting of his famous tomatoes. As the season advanced Wells asked Laird how his tomatoes were doing. In reply Laird said, 'Wait a minute and I will show you'. Going into his greenhouse he pulled off a little tomato about the size of a marble, and just about as hard. Laird threw the stunted specimen across the river. It caught Wells in the eye. That ended this gardening friendship.

Dr. Pollok, who lived in Belgrave Terrace, was a typical example of the general practitioner who served devotedly as family doctors in the Hillhead district in the days before the Health Scheme was developed, when large families were the rule rather than the exception. Dressed in a frock coat, tile hat, shepherd tartan trousers and button boots, the Doctor did his regular rounds in a brougham. In those days the family doctor was more than a mere medical man. He was also guide, philosopher and family friend. He brought the bairns into the world and watched over their welfare throughout their lives. He attended weddings and funerals as the first and most faithful friend. The National Health Service, whatever its benefits may be, can never equal that.

Dr. Pollok was a good amateur organist. Music was his recreation and solace in a hard working life. A dedicated elder of Wellington Church, he was proud to take his place at the plate at the entrance to the Church on the first Sunday of each month. With this purpose in mind the well-dressed Doctor was conscious that the foot of his trousers were rather the worse for wear. He had a new pair made in time for his turn at the plate. His tailor delivered the new trousers on Saturday morning. When the Doctor tried them on he was horrified to find they were too long in the leg. He asked his wife to cut a couple of inches off the bottom and turn them up another two inches. His wife asked him to get, Margaret, the daughter, to do the job as she was going to the theatre. The daughter said she was sorry she did not have time since she was going to a party. The daughter, in a fit of remorse, returned early and shortened the pants. Later his wife, on returning from the theatre, repeated the performance. On dressing for church the Doctor was shocked to find his new trousers much too short and he had to make do with the old frayed pair.

In my young days Great Western Road from Kelvinbridge

Dr. William Francis Somerville (1858–1926). Founder of the Girls' Guildry in 1900 (now embodied in The Girls' Brigade). Resided at 14 Southpark Terrace when Professor W. Macneile Dixon lived at No. 2.

to the Botanic Gardens was the shopping centre for the West-End of Glasgow. The ladies from the bigger houses did their shopping in broughams or carriages and pairs, and no Rolls Royce ever conveyed a more dignified air of opulence. Shopping was part of the social graces. The shopkeeper was considered a part of the family circle, business being conducted in the friendliest possible spirit. Some of the shopkeepers were colourful characters, such as Paddy McQueen, the grocer at the corner of Belmont Street. Butter in those days was sold from small barrels. Paddy cut the barrels in half. The price card on one half was 10d per lb. while the price on the other half was 8d per lb. When the half barrel with the 10d per lb. ticket was empty the 10d ticket was transferred to the 8d per lb. half barrel. In those days people bought the best. They judged quality by price. Assafrey, in Caledonian Mansions, was considered the most exclusive sweetshop in Glasgow. Assafrey chocolates were famous. They cost threepence a quarter pound. Hubbard, the bakers, were renowned throughout the Western Isles for their fine teabread and London buns. These London buns were no ordinary London buns. They were Hubbard's speciality. As boys we hung about the bakery in Belmont Lane until a batch came out the oven. These buns were as big as bread plates. They cost a penny. No other London bun has ever tasted as luscious. There were two brothers, both of whom did splendid mission work in Maryhill. In the early morning the women from the mission paraded with pillow cases which were filled, free of cost, with the previous day's teabread. The Hubbards were real people.

Cooper's corner was famous as the meeting place for assignations, and the starting point for cycle runs and distance walks. The most noted was the walk to the top of Ben Lomond, see the sun rise, and be back at Cooper's

'Great Western Road, Hillhead, looking east.' Original pencil drawing by Muirhead Bone, No. 38 in 'Glasgow : Fifty Drawings, 1911.' *Art Gallery & Museum, Kelvingrove*

corner within 24 hours, a distance of 65 miles. Many boys did this walk while they were still at school. Further west there was Robert Cappell, the chemist. Cappell was a great character who served his customers as guide, philosopher and friend, and medical adviser. Cappell never closed. In emergencies people called from every corner of the City. His sons did well. One is a Professor at the University and the other is a leading light in the church.

John Fyfe, the draper, had his single storey shop next to Hubbards. The reason for this was because these shops were built above the railway tunnel which could not carry any additional weight. Davie Fyfe, the son, unknown to his father, ran a Boxing Club in the evenings in the back of the store, with local boys as members. All went well until Davie was knocked out for the count one night. When he failed to come round the boys in panic ran for the father and so ended the Boxing Club.

Speirs & Frame, the plumbers, occupied the corner at Bank Street. Mrs. Speirs lived in the flat above the Shop. As a collector of antiques Mrs. Speirs attended auction sales. She went to a sale in Grosvenor Terrace where she bought a lot of silver at what she thought was a cheap price. Much to her horror she discovered at the end of the day when she came to pay the auctioneer that the price she had been paying was per ounce and not per article.

Peter Dickson, the shoemaker, had the shop next door. Peter made the finest handmade shoes in the country. They were expensive, costing £5 10/- per pair as against 16/6 for the best quality factory-made shoes sold in Buchanan Street, but Peter's shoes outlived by years the factory-made shoes. Customers came to Peter from all parts of the country.

Russell, the fruiterer and florist, was further west in Rokeby Terrace. All his fruit and flowers were home grown. Business men, living in Bearsden with gardens and glass-houses, would stop their carriages on their way into the City and drop off garden produce. During the strawberry season queues of jam-makers waited to buy rejects. The black grapes from the Kippen Vine were always in demand for the sick-room. The Kippen Vine was the largest vine in the world. It was cut down in recent years.

William Farmer & Son, grocers and wine merchants, occupied the corner of Ann Street. They did a particularly high-class trade, specialising in rice grown in different parts of the East. William Farmer was a prominent churchman and elder of Wellington Church.

Leishman, the butcher, occupied a shop nearby. He did a grand business with the hotels in Oban, but to catch the 6 a.m. train from Buchanan Street Station, Leishman had to start work at 4 a.m. He was a great worker. He would still be selling his famous sausages at 6 p.m. and then take his books home to write them up after tea. The 8-hour day was then unknown.

Mrs. Balharrie, the tobacconist in Great Western Road, was given her shop by way of compensation for the loss of her husband in the *Daphne* disaster. Her husband had been a shipwright. He was employed in the building of this ship. In those days it was the practice for the men who built a ship to stay aboard at the launching ceremony. When the *Daphne* was launched it turned over on its side. Most of the men on deck were saved, but the men with their heads sticking out the portholes were drowned. Mrs. Balharrie's husband was one of them. A relief fund was raised by the Lord Provost. Mrs. Balharrie invested her share in a tobacconist shop, and a most successful business she made of it.

No city in the country has an approach road to compare with Great Western Road. Its old-world charm, dignity and scenic quality is unique. Before the days of motor cars, when the horse-trams turned at the Botanic Gardens, the stretch of this gracious promenade from Byres Road to Bingham's Pond was used on the Sabbath by the fortunate folks who lived in the West-End as a church parade, between noon and lunch time. The 'best' people paraded in the middle of the road while the ordinary folks used the blaes-covered sidewalk. The young ladies delighted to display their elaborately trimmed and flowered hats, their long trailing skirts – which they held up as they walked – their bustles, feather boas, tippets and muffs. In those days a lady's voluminous attire started with a foundation garment called combinations. It was covered by a chemise, to which was added lacing stays, covered by a bodice; then came at least three ankle length underskirts, the first being of flannel, the second made of lawn and the third was a frilled silk underskirt which rustled loudly when the lady moved. Her outer dress was a trailing skirt and a tight fitting buttoned jacket. She wore hand knitted three ply woollen stockings, held up by long knitted garters, and black button boots of beautiful soft leather, sold by Saxone in Sauchiehall Street at ten shillings a pair! The elderly matrons dressed in black with dolmans and 'Queen Victoria' bonnets. The girls wore ankle length dresses and long hair down to their waist, until they were old enough to achieve their ambition to wear 'trailers' and put their hair up. The men marched in a military manner in square cut frock coats, shepherd tartan trousers, patent leather button boots with cloth uppers, silver topped sticks and shiny tile hats, and all

boasted of a well developed 'corporation' on which was suspended a gold Albert. Most boys wore the kilt but the few from English boarding schools paid the penalty for being there by wearing 'Eton suits', long trousers and tile hats.

I was married in 1920. I took my bride to Paris for our honeymoon. Walking down the Rue des Beaux Arts we saw an auction sale advertised. It was a sale of French Impressionist pictures. As we were furnishing and buying pictures we were interested. We had seen McChlery selling pictures in Sauchiehall Street so we went in to see how pictures were sold in Paris. The auctioneer had great difficulty in getting bids. A Renoir was put up. I got a kick from my wife which was a signal to bid. I did not like the picture so I did not bid. I was never allowed to forget that picture. It could have been bought for the equivalent of £40. This same picture was sold by Christie's in December 1968 for £750,000!

'Ah, gentle dames it gars me greet!
To think how monie counsels sweet,
How monie lengthen'd, sage advices
The husband frae the wife despises!'

7 University Gardens, 1970

Otago Lane. Scene for many years until the late 1920s of a busy blacksmith's shop where most of the local horses came to be re-shod.   *

The University and a Changing Hillhead

OF the five hundred and twenty years of its existence the University of Glasgow has spent one hundred years on the borders of Hillhead. But the decision to move from the ancient home in High Street had been taken some years before that. The earlier plan which came to nought would not have located the University in Hillhead and therefore needs no more than this mention. It was late in 1863 that an approach by the City of Glasgow Union Railway Company brought the scheme within sight and by the middle of the following year agreement had been concluded. Late in July 1864 the purchase was completed of the lands of Gilmorehill and about six months later the lands of Donaldshill and the property of Clayslaps had been acquired. Part of the ground was sold to the city and the Clayslaps land was exchanged for land for the Western Infirmary on Donaldshill.

The first sod was cut on 6th June 1866, by Professor Allen Thomson, the Convener of the Senate's Removal Committee. Nearby was Gilmorehill House, completed at the beginning of the century and said to have been one of the most attractive residences in the neighbourhood of Glasgow. It was not immediately demolished but became the offices of the architect and contractors until 1872. It stood where the West Quadrangle now is.

Building to the designs of George Gilbert Scott began towards the end of November 1866. It had been hoped for a time that Queen Victoria would consent to lay the foundation-stone. This proved impossible and the Prince of Wales agreed to do so. But the Princess decided that she too would come and a second foundation-stone was provided. According to the official record the ceremony on 8th October 1868, 'passed off without any untoward accident'. However, the account does exist that when the Prince stepped forward to lay the stone it rose in the air instead of gently descending. For a time it hovered and then slowly came down into its appointed place. The day was a notable one for Glasgow and for Hillhead. The Prince having received the freedom of the city then proceeded in procession with the Princess and his suite to Gilmorehill. The route was lavishly decorated. The gateway of the Old College which the procession passed bore the legend *Resurgat in Gloria*. At the Kelvingrove entrance to the West End Park there was a large floral arch with the word 'Welcome'. A wooden bridge specially constructed for the occasion spanned the river Kelvin and at the entrance to the University grounds (about where Pearce Lodge now is) there had been erected another arch bearing among other devices the Prince of Wales feathers. The Court and Senate received the royal party in Gilmorehill House and there the honorary degree of LL.D. was conferred on the Prince and Princess, and on Prince John of Glücksburg uncle of the Princess of Wales the first graduation ceremony in the new home.

The last meeting of the Senate in the Old College took place on 29th July, 1870, and classes met for the first time in the new buildings at the beginning of Session 1870-71. Work was, however, still proceeding, and it was not until 1872 that full possession of the quadrangles was obtained. Still much remained to be done to complete the original scheme. In 1884 the Bute and Randolph Halls were built and in 1888 the spire added to the tower.

Despite one or two incursions into the neighbourhood, for a long time the University kept within the confines of the Gilmorehill site. The increasing needs of teaching had been met by the erection of buildings for Botany, Natural Philosophy and some of the medical sciences at the west end and at the north east the Engineering building and temporary extensions for Chemistry and some provision for anatomy and surgery. Indeed fifty years ago the only 'pockets' in Hillhead were Queen Margaret College (now the B.B.C. Scottish Headquarters), the Women's Union at 67 Ann Street (Southpark Avenue) and Hillhead House where the Reading Room is today. The Queen Margaret College building began life as North Park House, which in 1883 was presented by Mrs. John Elder to Queen Margaret College for a women's college. The fascinating history of the movement for the higher education of women is not, however, part of this article. When in 1892 University degrees in Glasgow were thrown open to women the College buildings were handed

Lion and Unicorn staircase removed from the Old College and embodied in Gilmorehill buildings facing Professors' Court. *Scottish Field*

War Memorial Chapel, University of Glasgow, dedicated 1929. *Architects:* John Burnet, Son, & Dick. *Annan*

over to the University Court and there University classes for women were held until in 1935 the buildings were sold. In 1917 the family of Mr. Walter MacLellan gave Hillhead House to the University and here the department of psychology was housed and other smaller departments had rooms. Apart from one or two houses, particularly in Wilson Street (Oakfield Avenue), which were let for residence, the University's physical possessions on Hillhead fifty years back were not numerous.

In 1920 the University was still coping with the large increase in numbers occasioned by the return of the men from the war of 1914-1918. These men had lost, many of them, about five years and they were determined to make up for those years. They worked hard and played hard but they also had thought for the generations of students to come and seeing the deficiencies in the provision for social and physical recreation they set out to remedy them. Student Welfare was their deep concern. In 1921 there was launched a scheme to raise funds for students' hostels, for the Unions, and for Athletic Grounds. Here was an excellent and successful example of co-operation of senior and junior members of the University as well as of the generous response of the public and certain individuals. From this time it could be said the University began to look to the area to the north of University Avenue as the logical area in which to find room for development. In 1922 the house No. 1 University Gardens was purchased and converted to use as a Union for women to replace the inadequate premises in 67 Southpark Avenue, which reverted to residential use for many years thereafter. About the same time house No. 2 University Gardens was given by Mr. J. M. Robertson for use as a professor's house or hostel or other University purpose. A room of this was incorporated into No. 1 and the remainder became a professorial house: the house No. 1 Lilybank Terrace was acquired in its place and opened after the necessary conversion as Robertson Hall (a residence for women students) in 1926. It now forms part of the premises of Laurel Bank School.

In 1924 Queen Margaret Hall (which has since reverted to its original name of Lilybank House) was transferred to the University by the Queen Margaret College Association which in 1894 had opened it as a residence for women students.

If the needs of the women students for extended Union premises were great, those of the men were greater but could be provided only by a new building to replace that opened in 1885 and later extended. The site chosen was at the east end of University Avenue where Stenhouse's bookshop and two detached houses stood. In 1931 this new building was opened and the work of converting the old building for a

Union for the women was begun. House No. 1 University Gardens then became teaching accommodation for a number of the smaller departments. The University was now fully and logically committed to finding the extra space which was required in the part of Hillhead immediately to the north of Gilmorehill. From time to time houses which had come into the possession of the University either by purchase or by gift were used for teaching purposes and lent themselves easily to that use.

Meanwhile major building to meet the ever-growing needs of teaching and research had been going on in Gilmorehill and a Zoology Building, the west wing of the main building and the University chapel had been built and came into use by 1930.

It was inevitable that space for further large buildings would have to be found by the acquisition of property which might subsequently have to be demolished. But this must not be haphazard. The University Court commissioned Sir Frank Mears to prepare a development plan (subsequently re-appraised by Mr. J. L. Gleave and by Sir Hugh Wilson) and as a result of this application was made for the zoning of the area bounded by University Avenue, Ashton Road, Byres Road, Great George Street and Bank Street under the Town and Country Planning (Scotland) Act, 1947. This was duly granted. Already, however, by 1959 the first large teaching building – the Modern Languages building – had been planned and completed in University Gardens. The process has been a continuous one and University Gardens now has in addition the Queen Margaret Students Union (1968) and the Mathematics Building (1969). In Bute Gardens has risen the Adam Smith Building (1968) which now fronts Lilybank House, for many years known as Queen Margaret Hall, a hall of residence which was transferred to new quarters in Kirklee. The massive new Library (1968) – the first stage of that project dominates the hill – the Refectory (1966) forming a back-curtain to the Reading Room, and the Stevenson Physical Education Building (1960) provide much used – and appreciated – facilities. The most recent teaching building is the Rankine (Engineering) Building (1969). Southpark House, for long a residence run by the Church, is now the University's Television Centre. Teaching is carried out in a large number of the houses in the development zone and beyond it.

Nearing completion at the western boundary of the zone is the large Boyd Orr Building. Other buildings are planned for an early start. Much of this programme has necessitated the demolition of houses and further buildings cannot be erected without more demolition. Nevertheless it is hoped to retain as much as possible of some of the terraces.

The impression which an account of the influence of a large and growing urban university must give is one of change. It is true that the University has imposed many changes on Hillhead. But that is not its total contribution to the area. It has given a long succession of distinguished and colourful men who have served the University and who resided in Hillhead or whose daily paths led them through Hillhead. There is no area which could not be but enriched by the presence of distinguished Principals of the University such as John Caird, Robert Herbert Story, Donald Mac-Alister, Robert Rait, Hector Hetherington, and such professors as Lord Kelvin, Sir Richard Lodge, Richard Jebb, Gilbert Murray, F. O. Bower, James Cooper, J. S. Phillimore, William Macneile Dixon, George Milligan, D. Noel Paton, W. R. Scott, J. R. Currie, Charles Martin, T. S. Paterson and E. P. Cathcart – by no means an exhaustive list. But one must not forget the constant presence in the area of large numbers of young men and women, many of whom have carried to distant parts of the world fond memories of the time when Hillhead was so much part of their lives.

April 1971   R.T.H.

1, 2 & 3 Florentine Gardens. *1931**

WESTERN MEDICAL SCHOOL

THIS extramural school opened in 1880 under the Presidency of the Faculty of Physicians and Surgeons. It occupied the top floor of the Stenhouse building in University Avenue below Oakfield Terrace. It owed its origin to Dr. Knox of the Western Infirmary who saw the local advantages of such a school at that time. In the winter and summer sessions it had over 80 students. It closed shortly after the end of the Great War of 1914-18.

The first prospectus, produced by Mr. Stenhouse in 1881, gives the following information.

ANATOMY: A. Ernest Maylard, M.B., B.S., Lond.
Formerly Demonstrator of Anatomy and Senior House Surgeon, Guy's Hospital, London.

SURGERY: D. N. Knox, M.A., M.B., F.F.P.S.
Dispensary Surgeon, Western Infirmary.
also teaches
The Practice of Medicine; Midwifery and Diseases of Women and Children; Materia Medica and Therapeutics; Forensic Medicine and Public Health.

Class fees: First Session £2-2/-; Second £1-1/-; Anatomy £4-4/-; including practical anatomy.

THE GLASGOW SCHOOL OF MEDICINE

by JOHN PATRICK

There were other extramural schools in Glasgow in former days; the Portland Street Medical School and the Western Medical School – but they were on the whole short-lived though serving a useful purpose in their day. The extramural schools of Glasgow have not only possessed teachers of their own of great eminence, they have also provided an excellent ground for men who rose to higher spheres in the University. Many University professors first made their name as teachers in these extra-academic schools, and when the time came they carried with them scientific and teaching reputations, the lustre of which was, not as a rule, dimmed by the more serene and stable atmosphere of the University.

from article in book for B.M.A. Meeting, Glasgow, 1922

Spoons which belonged to Andrew Gibson of Hillhead. One has the date letter 'e' 1685–86 (James II): The other has the date letter 'K' 1690–91 (William and Mary) They bear the Glasgow Mark of Robert Brook who established his business in 1673. Property of Dr. J. Gibson Graham. *Photographed by Rupert Roddam 1971*

Old lamp-post at University Avenue between the back of Oakfield Terrace and the site of the Stenhouse building now occupied by the Union. *1965**

WELLINGTON CHURCH

MINISTERS

Rev. James Black, D.D.	1868–1913
Rev. David W. Forrest, D.D.	1894–1899
Rev. George H. Morrison, D.D.	1902–1928
Very Rev. Ernest D. Jarvis, D.D.	1928–1958
Rev. Stuart W. McWilliam, M.A., S.T.M.	1959–1972

Wellington Church, University Avenue. Designed after the style of the Madeleine by T. L. Watson, 1883.

THE BEGINNINGS of Wellington's history can be traced back to 1754 when a section of the Secession Church in Glasgow, then in Shuttle Street, decided to erect a new church in Havannah Street later known as 'The Havannah'.

Some of the members of the Havannah Street congregation lived in the village of Anderston, a pleasant place of about 1500 inhabitants, mostly engaged in handloom weaving, cotton-spinning and bleaching. Many of the houses were cottages, others two and three storey flats, while a number of fine residences in the west were owned by wealthy Glasgow merchants. For their own use these members had built a meeting-house in Cheapside Street. In 1792 they went a step further and presented a Petition of Disjunction to the Presbytery. This was agreed to and as a result a separate congregation was formed under the name of the Associate Congregation of Anderston, a session being constituted on 26th December.

The following summer, on 1st August 1793, the Rev. John Mitchell was inducted as the congregation's first minister, the call having been signed by 56 members and 35 'hearers'– no ladies being allowed to sign. The stipend offered was £80.

Dr. Mitchell's ministry lasted for almost half a century and during it much was accomplished both at home and in support of work overseas. A noteworthy date, however, was 1827, for it was in that year that the move was made to the new church in Wellington Street. The cost of this new building was £10,000 and it was situated where the Alhambra Theatre recently stood.

Four years before Dr. Mitchell's death in 1844 the Rev. John Robson became colleague and successor. During Mr. Robson's ministry the size of the congregation increased steadily and it is interesting to note that in 1867 the number of members on the roll was 1,149. In the previous autumn, at a meeting of session, Dr. Robson had asked for an assistant and as a result of his request the Rev. James Black, D.D., of St. Andrews, was elected to be his colleague and successor.

Dr. Robson died in the early morning of Sunday (Communion Sunday) 11th January 1872.

The completion of fifty years' occupancy of the church in Wellington Street was celebrated by a special service on 18th November 1877, but it was not long before a decision was reached to move further west. By 1882 the site of Oakfield House in University Avenue was bought, and on Saturday, 11th October 1884, the present church was opened, the service being conducted by Principal Cairns.

The architect responsible was Mr. T. L. Watson of Glasgow, and a particularly interesting innovation was that an organ was installed, the first organist elected being Mr. Fred Turner who, though blind, continued for over fifty years. Site and church together cost £26,468 and it can bear repetition that for the ordinary collections at the three services held on the first Sunday, 12th October 1884, the total contributions amounted to £11,171.

There were to be further notable dates before the century came to a close. In 1885 the present constitution was drawn up by the session and managers, and in 1890 Mr. Alexander Allan – whose name has been commemorated in the Allan Hall – provided Stobcross House as the centre for the congregation's home mission work. Yet another memorable event was the completion of the first century of the congregation's history, celebrated just before the Rev. David W. Forrest's brief five years as colleague to Dr. Black.

The first fifty years of this century are spanned almost

Dr. George H. Morrison (1866–1928). Minister of Wellington Church 1902–28. Born in Holyrood Crescent across the Kelvin from Glasgow Academy where he was educated and of which his uncle Dr. Donald Morrison was first Rector. *Annan*

completely by the ministries of Dr. Morrison and Dr. Jarvis.

The Rev. George H. Morrison was called in 1902 from St. John's Church, Dundee, becoming sole minister in 1913 on the death of Dr. Black. Dr. Morrison made Wellington famous by his great treatment of simple themes, especially in his evening services when the pews of Wellington were filled from far and wide. In the early days of the B.B.C. he was the first Scottish minister to address the growing number of wireless listeners. In 1926, as Moderator, he presided over the General Assembly at Edinburgh.

Dr. Morrison died on 14th October 1928. Eight months later he was succeeded by the Rev. Ernest D. Jarvis of Muswell Hill Church in London who, in due course, also became Moderator of the General Assembly of the Church of Scotland, being installed in 1954, four years prior to his retiral from Wellington.

Wellington will be for ever grateful to the late Sir D. Y. Cameron for the beautiful setting he created when he supervised personally the installation of the Communion Table during the church interior improvements of 1933.

MORRISON OF WELLINGTON

In the 1920s when Hannen Swaffer the well-known Fleet Street columnist and religious controversialist was visiting Glasgow, a local member of the craft undertook to show him the University and Art Galleries. When walking up University Avenue Hannen Swaffer looked across at the imposing pile of Wellington Church and enquired of his companion, 'What god do they worship in this temple?' to which he received the prompt reply, 'A god by the name of Dr. Morrison.'

September 1961*

WELLINGTON

August 1970*

August 1970*

WELLINGTON

August 1970*

Southpark House, Ann Street (Southpark Avenue). Built about 1850 for William Govan. *1961* *

Florentine House, formerly Florentine Bank House, Hillhead Street. Early 19th century. Kitchen quarters could be of a much older period. *1961* *

Southpark House. *1970**

Miss M. A. Hannan Watson. *1938 Weir*

Laurel Bank School

HEADMISTRESSES

Miss M. A. Hannan Watson, M.A.	1903–1938	
Miss Janet Spens, M.A.	1903–1908	
Miss Frances Chambers, M.A.	1938–1946	
Miss M. A. Hannan Watson, M.A.	1939–1944 (in Glasgow)	
Miss Janet R. Glover, M.A.	1946–1959	
Miss Alexandra Smith, M.A.	1959–1962	
Miss Elma R. Mennie, M.A.	1963–1967	
Miss A. Jean B. Sloan, M.A.	1968–	

LAUREL BANK the first school founded by Scottish women graduates, had its beginning in September 1903. The founders were Miss Margaret A. Hannan Watson, M.A. (St. Andrews) and Miss Janet Spens, M.A. (Glasgow). Three University Principals gave their names as referees: Principal Donaldson, Principal Story and Principal Marshall Lang. Other referees were Miss Janet Galloway of Queen Margaret College and Dame Louisa Lumsden, first Warden of University Hall, St. Andrews.

Both Miss Watson and Miss Spens came of well-known Glasgow families long associated with civic administration and social advancement. Miss Watson's grandfather, Mr. J. Hannan, was convener of the Committee under Lord Provost Stewart which brought Loch Katrine water to Glasgow when, in 1859, Queen Victoria opened the Glasgow Waterworks at Milngavie. Miss Spens family was prominently connected with the legal profession her father being Sheriff Spens.

Miss Watson's aim was to found a school which would give girls a sound academic education and train them to be good citizens.

Lilybank Terrace
all of which forms the
present Laurel Bank School.
March 1965*

The discovery of a pleasant semi-detached villa to let with a good garden on the hill beside Glasgow Street established the school and gave it its name. The house was one of the few remaining mid-Victorian family residences in the district and had been the home of Provost King of the Burgh of Hillhead who later moved into self-contained Tyrefield House on the lower slopes of its larger garden next to Laurelbank, a procedure eventually followed by the school when Tyrefield again became vacant and suited the growing needs of Laurel Bank which had adopted a two-word spelling. Miss Spens, who still had class commitments in literature with the University, in 1908 relinquished her connection with Laurel Bank to become assistant to Professor McNeile Dixon of the Department of English. Her inspiring teaching in the early days of Laurel Bank is long remembered.

In 1915, like a bolt from the blue, intimation was received by Miss Watson from the Govan Parish School Board that they had bought all the ground bordered by Ann Street, Glasgow Street, Wilson Street and Great George Street, which included the double residence of Laurelbank, the two self-contained houses of Tyrefield and Thornville and the short Thornville Terrace.

Very fortunately No. 4 Lilybank Terrace was for sale and was found to be suitable. Playground facilities and future possibilities being favourable, Miss Watson, acting

with decisive vision, bought the property forthwith. No. 2 was added in 1918, No. 3 in 1929. No. 1 which had been at one time the residence of Robert Miller the last Provost of the Burgh of Hillhead, was not acquired until 1964.

To secure the future welfare of Laurel Bank School under the provisions of the Education (Scotland) Act of 1918, the management of the school was transferred in 1920 to an incorporated company, limited by guarantee, with Directors and Governors, one Governor representing the Glasgow Education Authority. Laurel Bank was the first private school to come within this scheme. In 1959 Laurel Bank was added to the list of grant-aided schools and began to receive a grant from the Scottish Education Department. The school which opened in 1903 with thirty pupils has now, in the 1970s nearly six hundred.

The original Directors were Lady MacAlister, Miss Frances Melville, M.A., B.D., Hugh R. Buchanan Esq., John Hope Gordon Esq., Miss Catherine Howden, Professor Latta and Miss M. A. Hannan Watson, M.A.

When in the course of time the Jubilee of Laurel Bank School took place in 1953, the occasion was crowned by the fine red sandstone building of the former Belmont Church opposite Lilybank Terrace becoming the Hannan Watson Wing; a fitting memorial to the loving devotion Miss Watson gave to her life's work for Laurel Bank.

REMINISCENCES

1903–1911

SEPTEMBER 1903! It is a long time ago now, and all that one remembers of those days seems leisurely, happy and easy. On the morning of the day that Laurel Bank School opened, I was led up Great Western Road, where the trams trundled along with open tops, and horses' hooves sounded on the setts of the street, to the corner of Oakfield Avenue, then called Wilson Street. At the corner where Glasgow Street met Wilson Street stood the semi-

detached villa where Laurel Bank began. That morning we entered by the front gate, but the 'pupils' entrance' was a wooden door in the high wall of the garden, some yards up Glasgow Street. To the end the little house had a countrified air, standing back from the street, with pointed gables and surrounded by trees and shrubs.

I believe I was the first child to arrive, and I have a clear picture of the cloakroom in which my buttoned boots were removed, and a very new pair of patent leather slippers were put on. I then went

Laurel Bank
from Wilson Street
(Oakfield Avenue) at the corner
of Glasgow Street, 1915.
*Photo by George Eyre-Todd,
'Scottish Country Life'*

Hannan Watson wing (formerly Belmont Parish Church).
June 1970*

upstairs with someone and was taken to a room where Miss Rankin was waiting for me. She wore a closefitting black satin blouse, decorated with black beads, and we sat side by side and read the 23rd psalm in the metrical version out of a well-worn Bible. Nowadays I suppose it would be an Intelligence Test, to decide that mystery called the I.Q., but the 1903 way has something rather good about it!

There must have been a delightful freedom and intimacy about that first year, for the numbers were small. A glance at the photograph taken in March 1904, of the whole school, shows about thirty girls. Some of the staff are there, in the incredible hats and neckbands of the period, and Miss Watson and Miss Spens stand in the middle of their flock, and seem to one's elderly eyes very young to be embarking on such an enterprise. The Head Girl that year was Janet Greenlees. We, who were in the lowest forms of the school, looked upon her with great awe, for she had her hair in a 'bun' on top of her head. I suppose she was about seventeen. We admired her greatly and used to follow her about when we were out in the garden at 'Break', hoping for a word or even a look from her.

I remember very little about lessons that first year. Miss Spens took us for Reading, and our reading book was the Odyssey of Homer, Butcher and Lang's translation, rather a stern beginning for Form II. One by one my three or four companions were reduced to tears by the length of the names they had to read, and eventually Miss Spens and I were left alone.

The move to Tyrefield, which came before long, was very thrilling, and we all helped to carry chairs through a gate from the garden of the old house to the new. The new building was delightfully large, and the garden a great joy. We began to have our individual gardens then, an older girl and a younger together. They were not very ambitious, I think, these gardens. We bought bedding-out plants at local florists and put them in, and fought a losing battle with pests and stray cats. There was a little tool shed where we played at 'houses', tidying it up and making coloured paper curtains for the small grimy window. I seem to remember that a great deal of time was spent in holding the door against those whom we disliked for the moment.

After so long, what one remembers is only a few unrelated incidents. It may be that only the happy memories remain, but I feel sure that for this to be the case the prevailing atmosphere must have been a happy one, and certainly the friendships made in these first schooldays have greatly enriched the years.

ISABEL M. STEVENSON

Looking down Great George Street to Byres Road.   *May 1965**

Laurel Bank School, 1904

1904–1910

ON looking back across the years, what we remember best about Laurel Bank School is its freedom, not freedom from discipline, but freedom of outlook – a rare thing for a Girls' School in those days.

To one of us, coming from an old-established English High School, the discipline seemed almost too flexible and the absence of traditions a real lack, and only later did one realize the wisdom that allowed tradition to grow slowly and naturally, or the great gain of the homely welcoming atmosphere fostered in part by the private house in which we started.

The wise and gracious personalities of Miss Watson and Miss Spens made themselves felt through the whole school. The reading of Philippians iv. 8. seemed to give the keynote. It still echoes in our ears, and we think on these things.

The Spring term especially has impressed itself on one's mind. There were the little gardens, like graves, which they often turned out to be – graves of unfulfilled aspirations, for the flowers would *not* come up as expected!

Lessons were under the apple trees in blossom; in the 'breaks' Gathering Tig was played by all the girls, until that form of amusement palled, and it was 'go as you please.' Life was then made hazardous by the Diabolo experts, or rather, non-experts.

In winter a barrel organ used to come – until it was stopped – and play tunes of the day outside the Fourth Form windows. It was quite impossible not to speak or work in rhythm with 'Alexander's Rag-Time Band' or whatever it was. The mistress in charge was *not* amused! While at prayers the devotions of the back row were all too often disturbed by the jingling thrilling passage of a troop of Scots Greys returning from exercise.

Then there was the pride in the so uncomfortable straw hats with their green and white ribbon and badges, chosen and designed by the girls themselves. There was the dreadful occasion when a mother tried to alter the green badge to white – 'Change our badge? Never!' – and the resistance movement was born.

On thinking over these far-off times, we now realise what a well-balanced, well-chosen team our mistresses were. Outstanding among them were Miss Watson and Miss Spens, whose complementary characters and gifts provided the sure foundation on which today's great and well-established School has been built. Miss Watson was the leader and planner – wise, kind and far-seeing, whose well-loved personality has made the connecting link during all these fifty years. When troubles came one could always appeal to her in sure and certain hope that all would be well. Even the most tiresome pupil could never feel misunderstood. Every girl was treated with the same unfailing patience and loving-kindness, which cannot be forgotten. Miss Spens was a brilliant scholar with such burning enthusiasm for her subjects, above all for English Literature, and such charm in imparting them that few of us failed to catch her enthusiasm. We remember her beautiful voice reading Gilbert Murray's translation of the Greek Tragedies; she taught us Wordsworth's greatness – even Peter Bell's donkey became eerie and awe-inspiring, instead of a figure of fun, when interpreted by her.

So cherished are the memories of our two first Headmistresses, and so deep and lasting the influence of their teaching by speech, and still more by example, that after almost fifty years we are only the more grateful and more conscious of our debt.

Of our other mistresses we can only speak of some, and of them but briefly: Miss Chambers, who carried on, enlarged and strengthened the School and its now well-established traditions; Miss Rutherford, with her fine scholarship, her absolute integrity and uncompromisingly high standards; Miss Violet Young, who made music interesting, even to the unmusical; Mrs. Jackson, who opened our eyes to the beauties of the thrilling world of the Italian Renaissance. We have happy memories, too, of Miss Corner, Miss Lindsay, Miss Taylor, Miss Raeburn and Miss Elgin.

Then there were the girls, and of these we remember best our own contemporaries, many of them accompanied or closely followed by a younger sister or even brother – girls with a wide range of homes and backgrounds, destined for a variety of careers, but all, we believe, imbued with the same spirit: the desire, conscious or unconscious, to repay to their fellows some part of the great benefit they had received from their School.

E. SCOTT (Elspeth Campbell)
M. MACAUSLAN (Marjorie Mechan)

From *Laurel Bank School*, published in Jubilee Year.

3 Hillhead Gardens
(19 Hillhead Street).
*1971**

Doorway to private grounds between Bute Gardens and University
Gardens Lane. *May 1963**

Oakfield Avenue, shortly before demolition of remainder of Oakfield Terrace
on right. University Engineering building now occupies site. *1965**

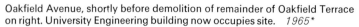

George Eyre-Todd (1862–1937)
Scottish historian, publisher and editor.
Secretary of the 1911 Exhibition.
Resided at 7 Oakfield Terrace.

JAMES MILLER (1860–1947)

An architect who introduced refreshing originality and distinction to much of his work. He was architect to the Caledonian Railway Company and gave pleasing character to its Coast Stations at Gourock and Wemyss Bay, and to the Princes Pier Station at Greenock of the Glasgow & South Western Railway Company.

He made notable contributions to local developments in the nineties when he designed the Railway Stations of Kelvinbridge and Botanic Gardens, Caledonian Mansions, Belmont Parish Church (now part of Laurel Bank School) and the buildings of the Glasgow International Exhibition of 1901. For many years he resided at 3 Hillhead Gardens (19 Hillhead Street).

Grand Entrance, Peristyle and Dome, from Exhibition Bridge. Glasgow International Exhibition 1901. Opened 2nd May in the name of King Edward VII by the Duke and Duchess of Fife. *Annan*

Glasgow International
Exhibition, Kelvingrove Park
1901. Royal Party arriving on
Opening Day attended by a
detachment of The Royal
Scots Greys
*Annan. Courtesy of
Mr. Henry J. Crone*

COLONEL HUGH MORTON

Colonel Hugh Morton of the Third Lanark Rifle Volunteers; a regiment noted for its marksmanship at Bisley and for its dexterity on the football field. Colonel Morton commanded the Third Lanark during the last years of Queen Victoria's reign. From 1895 to 1906 he resided at 25 Ashton Terrace which had been the first manse (1868–74) of the Rev. Walter Ross Taylor of the then Kelvinside Free Church.

For some years Colonel Morton's brother, T. Corsan Morton, later Keeper of the National Gallery of Scotland, assisted Fra. Newbery in the Life Classes at the Glasgow School of Art.

FRA. H. NEWBERY (1854–1946)

Headmaster of Glasgow School of Art from 1885 to 1917. His alert mind, practical vision and wise administration guided the School through a period of great change which he met in a most meritorious manner, being also an artist in his own right. He saw the 'Glasgow School of Painting' flourish and helped it to achieve the wide recognition that remains. He had a high regard for the work of Charles Rennie Mackintosh and, no doubt, was more than pleased when the winning design submitted by John Honeyman & Keppie in 1897 for the new building on the heights of Garnethill proved to be entirely the conception of their young draughtsman.

From 1886 to 1893 Fra. Newbery lived at 2 Queen Margaret Crescent. He then moved round the corner to 6 Buckingham Street which was his home for 20 years. His last residence in Glasgow was at adjacent 9 North Park Terrace (51 Hamilton Drive) which he occupied from 1913 to 1918.

Annan 1898

CHARLES RENNIE MACKINTOSH (1868–1928)

Charles Rennie Mackintosh, architect and artist in interior design, who gave British architecture a shot of near genius that is still felt and which brought him international fame.

From their flat at 120 Mains Street (Blythswood Street) at Bath Street Charles and Margaret Mackintosh in 1906 went to live in Hillhead at 6 Florentine Terrace which formed the gable end of this row of main-door dwellings. Here he transformed the interior with the same joyous artistry he had lavished on the Mains Street flat.

In 1914 his partnership in the firm of John Honeyman & Keppie was dissolved. Later in the same year the Mackintoshes closed their house in Hillhead and departed quietly from Scotland, going at first to Suffolk.

Annan. c. 1902, Courtesy of
Keppie, Henderson & Partners

1961

DEPARTURE

AND

NEW BIRTH

6 Florentine Terrace.   *April 1963**

6 Florentine Terrace (78
Southpark Avenue) and
Florentine Lane 1961
(demolished April 1963).   *

Ann Street (Southpark Avenue)   *Summer 1961**

70 University Avenue. Home of Sir J. J. Burnet in the early years of the century.   *1970**

Gas lamp at entrance to 6 Florentine Terrace.
January 1959*

c. 1900

JOHN KEPPIE (1862–1945)
Architect

From being chief draughtsman with Campbell Douglas & Sellars he entered into partnership with John Honeyman in 1889 and formed the firm of John Honeyman & Keppie. In the same year Charles Rennie Mackintosh joined as draughtsman and, in 1904, became a partner.

From 1880 to about 1904 John Keppie lived in the family home at 42 Hamilton Park Terrace. Latterly he lived with his two sisters at No. 16 which was their last home in Glasgow.

Gardeners' bothy in grounds formerly of Hillhead House.   *Summer 1961**

42 Hamilton Park Terrace.
*June 1970**

c. 1900

SIR JOHN JAMES BURNET (1857–1938)
Architect

An architect with a distinguished career in which he attained the highest professional honours. Son of John Burnet, a Glasgow architect, he became senior partner of Burnet, Son & Dick. His international reputation was made after he established his chief office in London.

His work in Glasgow included the original Fine Art Institute, Charing Cross Mansions, 1–11 University Gardens, Kelvinside Railway Station, Kirklee Railway Station, Alhambra Theatre and the Cenotaph, George Square.

Hepburn House, 7 University Gardens. *September 1970**

◄ Looking northwest across University Avenue from the University tower. University Gardens is in the foreground and Bute Gardens behind.
1905 Annan

Back of Florentine House,
top of Gibson Street.
1961*

Belgrave Terrace.
Built 1856. *1970**

Looking northeast ▶
from the University tower
across Hillhead towards
Kelvinbridge and
Woodlands Road.
1905 Annan

Balcony at 12 University
Gardens. *Architect:* J. Goff
Gillespie of Salmon & Gillespie,
c. 1900.   *August 1970**

Numbers 1 to 11
University Gardens.
Architect: Sir
J. J. Burnet, 1896.
August 1970*

Lamp at residence in Bute
Gardens of Sir Victor Warren,
Lord Provost of Glasgow,
1949–52. *1963**

Bute Gardens, from Hillhead Street. Demolished 1965. *1963**

Belmont & Hillhead Parish Church, from Huntly Gardens, *c.* 1937. *Salmon*

Sunday Parade, Great Western Road, 1900. *The Bailie*

BELMONT & HILLHEAD PARISH CHURCH

Dr. David Strong

IN 1871, when byres and cows and extensive grassland were still a general feature of Byres Road, an iron church stood alone in a field. The site is now bounded by Ruthven Street, Athole Gardens and Roxburgh Street. Here, in this simple structure, with pulpit supply arranged from week to week, a congregation grew which, only a few years later, moved into the splendid edifice that had arisen almost on the site of Horslethill Farm.

Church records refer to the ground acquired as being in Victoria Park, possibly a title of an ephemeral nature associated with the temporary re-naming of Byres Road as Victoria Street during the period of its early development.

A heartening total of subscriptions for the new church had enabled the managers to make prompt plans for the erection of a permanent building in keeping with the architectural care evinced in adjacent residential extensions where full rein was given to the classical inspirations of notable native architects.

During preliminary discussions a wish had been expressed by members who had worshipped in Sandyford and Park Churches to dispense, if possible, with interior pillars, as these, however beautiful, tended to obstruct both seeing and hearing the preacher. With this in mind, the architects, Messrs. Douglas & Sellars, in due course submitted their proposals. After various conferences and considerations plans were agreed upon which made this building unique of its kind in Glasgow as the approved design was clearly a copy of the 13th century Sainte Chapelle in Paris but modified to suit the site, the cost and the character of Presbyterian worship.

Due to horizontal coal-workings, fairly common to the district, substantial piers, following the outline of the future church, were sunk through the coal-workings to the solid rock beneath. The piers were united by arches and on this deep and firm foundation arose Hillhead Parish Church. The Opening was a most memorable one and took place on 8th October 1876 when Principal Caird officiated in the morning and Dr. John Macleod of Govan in the evening. In a short time all the sittings were fully occupied.

On 3rd December 1950, the congregations of Belmont Parish Church and Hillhead Parish Church became one within the Hillhead building.

Byres Road and Hillhead Parish Church. No. 37 in 'Glasgow: Fifty Drawings' by Muirhead Bone, 1911. *MacLehose*

MINISTERS

Ministers of Belmont Parish Church

Rev. J. Fraser Grahame, D.D.	1886–1919
Rev. Stuart Crawford Parker, B.D.	1919–1923
Rev. W. L. Levack, D.D.	1923–1935
Rev. A. R. R. Reid, D.D.	1936–1950

Ministers of Hillhead Parish Church

Rev. David Strong, D.D.	1872–1913
Rev. Walter R. Lacey, M.A.	1914–1922
Rev. A. E. Warr, B.D.	1923–1933
Rev. W. D. Maxwell, Ph.D., D.Litt., D.D.	1934–1950

Ministers of Belmont and Hillhead Parish Church

Rev. A. R. R. Reid, D.D.	1950–1958
Rev. G. M. Denny Grieve, B.D.	1959–

Portico of Belmont and Hillhead Parish Church.
Summer 1970*

Hillhead Parish Church from Observatory Road at Grosvenor Crescent.   *1908 Valentine*

Old coach-houses and hay lofts,
Grosvenor Crescent Lane.
April 1970*

Grosvenor Crescent Lane. *April 1970**

Population "Hillhead". Dec. 1889

Year	Residents			Servants			Total		
	Male	Fem	Total	Male	Fem	Total	Male	Fem	Total
1888.	2991	3746	6737	2	1359	1361	2993	5105	8098
1889.	3069	3861	6930	2	1406	1408	3071	5267	8338
Increase	78	115	193		47	47	78	162	240

	"Kelvinside"								
	M	F	T	M	F	T	M	F	T
1889	3013	2231	5244	18	1547	1565	3031	3778	6809

Police Census   *Glasgow City Archives*

*A bunch of the boys were whooping it up in
the Malamute saloon;
The kid that handles the music-box was
hitting a rag-time tune;
Back of the bar, in a solo game, sat
dangerous Dan McGrew,
And watching his luck was his light-o'-
love, the lady that's known as Lou.*

The Shooting of Dan McGrew
Songs of a Sourdough

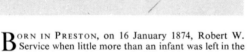

Robert W. Service

BORN IN PRESTON, on 16 January 1874, Robert W. Service when little more than an infant was left in the care of his three maiden aunts in Kilwinning until he was recalled to the family fold in Glasgow.

In the Glasgow Post Office Directories of 1881 to 1888 the name of the occupier of the main-door flat with basement at 8 Roxburgh Street (then known as Roclea Terrace) is Robert Service. In the issues of 1890 to 1901 the listing indicates the family occupying the slightly larger but similar flat at 18 Roclea Terrace. (His home, therefore, appears to have been in the friendly territory of Kelvinside across the 'Great Divide' of Byres Road.)

About 1875 Govan Parish School Board acquired the building in Church Street belonging to the Partick Academy which had moved to Peel Street. In 1878 it was re-opened as Church Street Public School, the Headmaster being Edward Ellice Macdonald. Thither, a year or two later, went Robert W. Service with his brothers until 1885 when it was entered in the log book on April 20th: 'About 130 Hillhead children left to go to new School in Sardinia Terrace'. Robert W. Service was one of these. (The present Church Street School of red sandstone, was built in 1903 along with the swimming baths.)

Apart from his near miss in correctly naming the north side of Roxburgh Street and his apparently purely fictional Ferndale Terrace, the foregoing factual information tallies with these extracts from his first 'adventure into memory' which he called *Ploughman of the Moon* and wrote in Hollywood during 1943–44 following his last moment escape from war-torn France.

In 1889, at the age of 15, Robert W. Service was apprenticed for six years to the Commercial Bank of Scotland at their Stobcross branch. Seven years later he resigned from the St. Vincent Street branch, to which he had been promoted, and emigrated to Canada as a steerage passenger, arriving in British Columbia with $5 in his pocket. After several years of rough living, which took him as far as California, he returned to Canada West.

In his 28th year he found himself in desperate straits. It was then that his handwritten reference (fortunately retained) from the Scottish bank came to his aid and got him accepted on the staff of the Canadian Bank of Commerce. Having proved satisfactory he was transferred to the far north branch at White Horse in the Yukon territory. There, while men converged from all parts of the world to wrest a fortune from the frozen earth, Robert W. Service found that he had discovered a gold mine of his own by the use of no other implement than his pen.

With the royalties from his books piling up he became attracted to Europe. Shortly before the Great War (in which he served as an ambulance driver) he had settled in France and married a Parisian lady. They had a house on the Riviera and one at Lancieux in Britanny. With his wife and daughter Iris he visited Kilwinning in the summer of 1948. He had intended making a return visit but, on 12th September 1958, at the age of 84 he died from a heart attack in his Lancieux home.

His poems appealed to millions and made him, at least, a dollar millionaire. He was also a novelist, his best success being *The Trail of '98*. His racy narrative verse made many books and editions. The zest for living his own way of life is well portrayed in his two autobiographies, *Ploughman of the Moon* and *Harper of Heaven*.

MY SCHOOL-DAYS

ROBERT W. SERVICE

remembered from across the world

(These extracts from *Ploughman of the Moon* (1946) are reproduced by permission of Ernest Benn Ltd., the publishers of his two volumes of autobiography and *Collected Verse*.)

DRAB SCHOOL

OUR HOME was in a four-storey block of flats called Roselea Terrace. Opposite it was a similar block called Ferndale Terrace. Their sole rustic suggestions were their names; for they were both grim and gloomy, and only in high summer did the sunshine gild our door-mat. But it was a highly respectable street, where we lived in genteel poverty. Our flat was number nineteen, the biggest and the last in the terrace. It was on the ground floor and had a basement.

We paid forty pounds a year for the flat, but generally had to borrow money to meet the rent. As time went on we had to turn the drawing-room into a bedroom, owing to the family increase. There was a downstairs sitting-room we called the nursery, where I sat till midnight reading yarns of adventure when the house lay asleep. Then I would stumble to bed and know nothing more till awakened in the morning by Papa pulling the clothes off me. That was his way of making me get up. . . . Roselea Terrace stopped at our house and gave on a vacant lot we called the Hollow. It was full of pot-holes and clothed with rank grass and nettles, but it was our beloved playground. Board fences surrounded it, the

crevices full of earwigs. It was priceless to us, as otherwise we would have been obliged to play in the streets. Although only a squalid wasteland, to our notion it was precious country where green things grew and the air was fresh. I have no doubt that sunken field did much to help our growth.

At eight in the morning we were routed out of bed, and after a cat's-paw wash we had breakfast of porridge (either under-cooked or burned), a roll and a straw-flavoured egg. Gulping it down, we were bundled off to school. As a rule we were late and had to run, leaving the smallest blubbering in the rear. There was no protective spirit among us. The youngest had to look out for himself. Fortunately the roads were safe, cabs and drays forming most of the traffic. Accidents were rare. The streets of my youth were fresh, calm and innocent.

The school was in a dubious region between slumland and respectability. It was dingy, grey and shabby, but we used to run most of the way to get there in time to play. When the whistle blew, the playground would be jammed with boys playing games. Every Friday, being washing-day at home, we were allowed to take a lunch to school. This consisted of an egg sandwich, with bread and jam. It took us five minutes to bolt it, after which we

Roxburgh Street. No. 18 is just beyond the lady in white.   *August 1970**

had the rest of the hour for play. The Masters wore shabby tail-coats and swung straps as they paced the floor. At my first school canes had been the instruments of discipline, but here thongs of leather were the symbols of authority. One can imagine the young Master going to the leather merchant and carefully selecting the tool of his trade. 'Let me have a nice supple one with tails that flick around the fingers.' . . . Or 'Maybe I'd better try one of those broad heavy fellows. Perhaps it would be more effective if I soaked it in brine. Let me swish it through the air to get the balance of it.' What would a Master be without his faithful strap?

There was a technique in swinging it. A turn of the wrist, and it would lacerate the hand. But most of the Masters played fair. Only when they were exasperated did they resort to that vicious twist. On the other hand, a flat delivery would raise a blister. Two strokes were the average and the maximum was four. After four it was a long time before the hands regained their feeling, and one was lucky if they were not cut open. But no one thought of complaining. We would grin ruefully and tell our chums we had been given a good licking. We would be proud of our bruises and boast how we could take it. The unwritten law prescribed that one must never be a cry-baby or a sneak. We dare not tell our parents, for they would have replied: 'Well, you must have deserved it. Spare the rod, spoil the child. Corporal punishment is a part of education.'

Maybe they were right, for was not the theory backed by ages of convention? Flogging was supposed to toughen the race. But in my case it had a contrary effect. I resented my strappings, and there was one in particular that even to-day makes me grit my teeth with rage. The German Master said something that set the class laughing, and he picked me out as a scapegoat. I was sent down to the Head to be flogged. He was a bearded man in a frock-coat and he took from his desk a black strap. 'The whole class was laughing, sir,' I protested. He answered: 'I cannot punish the whole class, so I will make an example of you.' And he did. That was the only time I got six. But though my hands were numb he did not

break my spirit. Towards the last I was feeling distinctly murderous. It was not so much what he did to me as the gusto with which he did it. I found myself eyeing a heavy ink-well on his desk and wondering what would happen if I hurled it at his head. It was red ink too. I believe another lash would have made me do it.

One does not forgive and forget punishment that is severe and unjust. Years after, when I heard he had been drowned while bathing, I laughed for joy. Yet I have no doubt he gave no further thought to the matter and would have been profoundly surprised at my lasting resentment.

In the lane behind the playground we frequently staged fights. I would say to another boy, 'I can lick you,' and he would reply: 'I don't think you can.'

'Well, meet me in the lane after school.' So all the class would know and assemble to cheer or jeer.

Sometimes the school janitor, an old soldier, would intervene. 'Fighting's a blackguardly thing,' he said to me, as he marched my opponent and myself to the class Master. 'You fought in the army,' I protested. But he would not argue the matter. I disagreed with him. It is good for boys to fight, I thought. But the Master had to disapprove, so he gave us both a light one. Then he looked at me quizzically. 'Who won?'

'He did,' I said, pointing to my companion. But the latter, not to be outdone in generosity, insisted I was the victor. So the Master said: 'Well, I suppose it was a draw; but don't make any return match, or I'll really warm your palms for you. Now shake hands.'

On account of the boxing lessons Pat had given me I acquired the reputation of a scrapper. Luckily no one knew how little I knew, and the bluff worked. I do not think I was yellow, but as I never got a real licking I cannot be sure. And before I could find out, I was beyond the blubber age. For there comes a point in a boy's life when he discovers he no longer cries when he is hurt. When I was ten I crushed my hand in a gate and the pain was agonizing. But it was forgotten in my amazement to find I did not howl any more. I was on my way to be a man.

Byres Road
at Lawrence Street.
1908 Valentine

Of my companions at this school I recall only one, and he was unforgettable. He sat next to me, a boy with a pale face and a big head. One day I noticed that he was making drawings, and he showed me one.

'It's the Fat Boy in Pickwick,' he told me gleefully. 'When he's not eating he sleeps.'

I admired the drawing, which was copied from Phiz. He had a lively sense of humour, and, though he did not shine at his lessons any more than I did, he was more avid and precocious. In fact, I was rather awe-struck to find that he had been able to absorb a *real novel*, as my reading was confined to penny dreadfuls and papers like *Ching Ching's Own*. My friend high-browed me, and sought to wean me away from Jack Harkaway and Deadwood Dick, but without success. *Eric, or Little by Little* gave me a pain in the neck, while *Tom Brown's School Days* repelled me by its moral platitudes. He tried to interest me in the *Boy's Own Paper*, known as the B.O.P., and endorsed by the public schools. No doubt it was *pukka*, but I was not. I liked stories by Manville Fenn and Talbot Baines Reed, but constructive articles such as *How to Rig a Model Yacht* or *How to Stuff Birds* left me cold. So my apostle of uplift failed in his effort.

I mention him because to-day he is known as Britain's Best Journalist. He is the London Editor of a famous daily paper and has published many books. Cabinet Ministers consult him, and mandarins of letters weigh his words. One of his brothers is a famous etcher who has been knighted; while another is skipper of a big Atlantic liner, and himself an author of note. I used to call him Jimmy, but now I call him James. He still high-brows me and I love it.

I left this school in a glow of triumph. We had been told to do an essay on COAL, and the subject pleased me. So I sat down and found myself writing with surprising ease. Ideas crowded on me, and words came to clothe them so willingly I wondered what had gotten into me. It was my first experience of Inspiration. I finished in a mood of exultation. I knew my work was good; indeed, I knew it was better than the combined class could do. When the essays were handed back to us the teacher did not return mine. Instead he said: 'Here is one I want to read aloud.'

He did so, while I hung my head in embarrassed shame. I blushed when he indicated that I was the author, and the other boys laughed derisively. To write well was to be considered a sissy. Afterwards he took me aside.

'Did no one help you?'

'No, sir.'

'Not even your father?'

'He's not capable,' I said, a little contemptuously.

'Well, it's a pity someone could not take you in hand. If you were well trained you might bud.'

I did not know what he meant, and he left it at that. But I was leaving next day for another school, so after I had packed my books I went to him and said: 'Good-bye and thank you, sir.' He was surprised and shook hands with me, saying: 'You're the only pupil who ever said good-bye to me.' I went away rather wistfully, wondering if I had not done it to show off.

IT WAS a gallant struggle to bring up a family of ten on two hundred pounds a year, and Papa and Mama should be given all credit. Especially as they kept up a front of *bourgeois* respectability. Behind the scenes our standards were proletarian. We boys slept in the flannelette shirts we wore during the day and would have considered serviettes at table a form of swank. I was fifteen before I bought my first tooth-brush. But we were clean and healthy, for we had a bath with soap every Saturday night. I believe we all used the same hot water.

At home it was a struggle to make frayed ends meet, yet each day we trooped off to what was then the Finest School in Scotland. There we were lucky, for it was brand-new and only five minutes from our house. It was a show school. The city fathers were proud of its beauty. It was equipped for science, art and domestic economy. Visitors were shown round *ad nauseam*. It made the swanking private academies look cheap. The Masters had University degrees and were hand-picked, while the Head wore a stove-pipe hat. It was a dream school dumped down almost at our door.

Here I remained until my final expulsion. I had the same teacher for three years and came to have a liking for him. He was a bantam of a man, with bandy legs and a big red moustache like a viking. To me he was a hero because he had been a famous football right-winger, and had won his international cap. That far outweighed any scholarship in my eyes. For a while I worshipped him. Then one Saturday afternoon in a side street I saw him stagger out of a pub. Once he pitched and fell, picking himself up with difficulty. I shrank into a door-way. How thankful I was he had not turned my way! I was as hurt as if I had received a clout on the face. I never told a soul about it. Most boys would have blabbed, but nothing would have made me sneak on him. No longer was he a hero in my eyes.

I was inclined to dramatize my difference from other boys. One time the chap next to me was called up for speaking in class. The Master was going to punish him when I stepped forward.

'Please, Sir, I was speaking too. I deserve to be punished as well as him.'

Said the Master: 'You should say "as well as he," so I'll punish you for bad grammar.' And he did too, quite enthusiastically. Thus I was snubbed for my quixotic priggishness.

My chief failing was a pertness that amounted to impertinence. One time I was punished for this, and I remember it because it was the last occasion I ever received the strap. I think I had been making sketches in class, and I did not question the justice of the chastisement. Unless one got a licking every few days one suffered from an obnoxious sense of virtue. It was up to us to qualify for another strapping, and to grin to the class on returning to our seats. In this case I may have felt that my quota of punishment was about due. However, the Master told me to wait until after school, which was a low-down trick, as it deprived me of the satisfaction of showing my classmates how pluckily I could take it. Always the exhibitionist, I was glad to hold the centre of the stage for a moment, even if it was a painful one.

Now our Master had a habit of saying: 'You know, this hurts me more than it hurts you.' We all thought this was rubbing it in, especially as he put on a sad expression as if he really meant it. That look of grief really enraged me; so after he had given me two with a gusto that made me squirm, he added his formula of regret. As I turned away I muttered something, and he called me back.

'It seems you have some criticism to make of my conduct. What did you say?'

'I said I wished it hurted me in the same way it hurts you.'

'Ha! And no doubt you wish too that it hurted *me* in the same way it hurts you. You are a Realist. Well, in future I won't punish you physically. You can now go home and write for me a hundred times: I am a Realist.'

So I went home and by lashing three pens together tried to reduce my task by a third. It probably took me more time than the actual job would have done, but I had the great glee of outwitting authority.

I was always thinking out ways to cheat the Powers That Be, and one of them was my patent palm-shield. I cut a sheet of transparent mica-like material to the shape of my hand and equipped it with an elastic band so that it lay flat on my palm. At a little distance it was invisible. The chaps were enthusiastic, so it was decided we must try it right away. We selected a Master who was short-sighted. We would have preferred him a little deaf, but one could not ask too much.

I had some difficulty provoking him into punishing me, for he was a mild man who taught mathematics; but at last I succeeded in rousing his wrath. He invited me to step on to the floor and produced a broad strap. All the chaps were agog with anticipation. Boldly I held out my right hand with its celluloid sheath. I saw his eyes glisten with satisfaction as he flung back the strap and swung it down with all his force. CLACK! It was a sound like a pistol-shot. The air between my palm and its shield was so violently expelled the crack made me jump. It also made the Master jump. I plunged my hand into my pocket, and there I left my protective device. Then taking out my hand I wrung it as if in pain. The boys

rocked with laughter. The Master was puzzled. He examined his strap, then my hand, then told me to go to my place. After which he turned on the grinning class, singled out six and gave each a proper one.

My invention was voted such a success some suggested I should patent it. Many wanted to borrow it, but I did not believe in overdoing a good thing. I was trying to figure out a way of eliminating noise, when the Bad Boy of the school insisted on demonstrating it. He was hard-boiled and consequently a hero in my eyes, so I gave it gladly. But alas! he was over-confident and was detected. Thus the only invention I ever mothered, my Pupil's Palm Protector, died stillborn.

When I was close to thirteen we had a wonderful summer and I spent three glorious months by the sea. In that time I changed almost beyond recognition. I came back a head taller, with a cracked voice and the hint of a moustache. Physically I felt the equal of any Master in school, so that I went round with a chip on my shoulder. When a teacher growled: 'You deserve a proper thrashing,' I gave him a contemptuous stare as much as to say: 'Try it.'

Oh, I know I should have been ashamed of myself, taking advantage of my strength to bully my Masters. They could not have a brawl with me that would end in a fight. I put them in an awkward position and they knew it. A year ago they would have beaten me, now they left me alone. I am afraid I was not a very nice boy, but all my life I have resented authority. It is by a man's vices you know him best. My record is one of shame and un-worthiness. But all my faults and follies are part of me; so in painting a self-portrait let truth prevail. In most of my classes I was lazy, unambitious, and a dreamer. If the subject did not interest me my mind wandered. I drudged through mathematics, was fair at French and good at German. Grammar and spelling bored me, and all my life they have never seemed to matter much. History kindled my imagination while geography brought me dreams of far lands. But in one class I was superlatively good – English Literature. Oh, how I adored it! There I shone a star and astonished even the Master by my knowledge.

The reason is that I had become a ravenous reader. I devoured books with febrile intensity. Night after night I would sit in the nursery under the whining gas-light until long after midnight. I read any book that interested me, but chiefly fiction. My appetite seemed insatiable. To begin with I exhausted the boys' books; Ballantyne, Mayne Reid, Jules Verne and others. Then I went on to more adolescent fare. My first novel was *Ivanhoe*. How-ever, it was the only one by Scott I could ever get through. The others I found boringly descriptive. Harrison Ainsworth was more to my taste, and I read nearly everything he wrote. My first Dickens novel was *Pickwick* which I enjoyed, while I read most of the others with delight. Captain Marryat was a prime favourite and Samuel Lover pleased me. I liked humour and character, but a lively story interest was my chief demand.

Every Saturday Mama would give me a penny for a book at Miss Bell's Circulating Library, on condition that

18 Roxburgh Street (Roclea Terrace).
Courtesy of Mrs. Sweeney.   August 1970*

I got one for her. Her favourites were Mrs. Braddon and Mrs. Henry Wood, but later in life she read detective stories with absorption. My own taste improved rapidly, so that I came to recognize quality in writing and to appreciate characterization and atmosphere. Between ten and twenty I did the bulk of my life-reading. What little knowledge I have of the classics I gained in those years. That was to follow later, however; in the meantime I pursued my adventures in the fiction of the day. It was exciting enough. Stevenson, Rider Haggard, James Reid, Besant and Rice – all held me spellbound, till I heard Papa shouting: 'Come to bed!'

One day the Master announced to the class: 'We have among us a budding Ben Jonson or maybe a suckling Shakespeare.' With that he produced a manuscript he had found in my desk. It was a five-act historical tragedy and consisted of a scenario and the first act. In the end all the characters perished in a bath of blood.

The class laughed, so again I felt that sense of shame. I was furious with the Master, and if one of the boys twitted me about it in the playground, I flared up and was ready to fight.

After literature, my favourite was the drawing class. I loved to draw and would spend hours with pen and ink copying from books. Thus engrossed, time seemed to pass with amazing rapidity. When I was not boring into a book I was poring over an illustration and trying to reproduce it. I would gloat over the work of Phil May, Will Owen or Raven Hill, enjoying its smallest detail.

It was this love of drawing that took me every Saturday to the Public Library where I would take out old volumes of *Punch*. The jokes were often less than funny, but the pictures were more than interesting. So boyish was I that one of the clerks objected to issuing me a book and called the head of the department. 'How old are you?' he asked.

'Eleven, sir,' I told him; whereat he looked at me benevolently through his spectacles.

'Well, you're the youngest reader we've ever had; but you seem to have a good head on your shoulders, so we won't discourage you.'

Ah, those Saturdays in the Public Library, and my joy as I trudged three miles of streets to my city of books! At noon I would go to an eating place and have cake and tea over a marble-topped table. It cost twopence, but it was a feast to me. What matter the poor fare! I was young and free, and my capacity for bright dreams was unlimited. Never was I more happy, and this because I felt so blissfully *alone*. When other boys of my age were playing games and idling away their leisure, I was living in an imaginative world of my own.

I was never popular at school. I was too much of a lone dog and I disliked games. Only on the football field was I in demand because I weighed ten stone. As centre forward I was valuable in the scrum, but I thought it very stupid spending half the game in a pushing mob. I really preferred Soccer to Rugger. However, we were little snobs and thought the former too plebeian.

There was much competition to get into the team, so that we who made it were inclined to be cocky. We wore tasselled caps in the school colours. My shorts were very short, and when I walked to the football field I kept my macintosh partly unbuttoned, so that my bare knees

Hillhead High School (now Primary School), Cecil Street. Opened 1885. *May 1961* *

might show. I imagined people saying: 'Fine specimen of a lad. No doubt Captain of his school.' Whereas no doubt they were thinking: 'Silly young ass. Thinks himself a puling International.' Maybe I did dramatize myself to some extent. Youth must have its dreams, its vanities. It needs a certain equipment of conceit to affront the realities of life. But the only time I distinguished myself in school football was when I split my shorts, and the opposing team was so convulsed with laughter at the sight of my bare buttocks that they allowed me to run in and score a try.

Partick Academy. Erected 1850. Building sold about 1875 to Govan Parish School Board and re-opened on 2nd September, 1878 as Church Street Public School.
William Greenhorne, 'History of Partick' (1928)

Façade of former Queen Margaret College. In 1938 this building became the nucleus of the Scottish Headquarters of the British Broadcasting Corporation whose Administration Offices now extend halfway along Hamilton Drive. *1970**

Old Copper Beech Tree in Queen Margaret College grounds. Died 1895. Photographed by Professor Mills about 1890.
University Archives

From written Address presented to Queen Victoria
on the occasion of her visit to Queen Margaret College
on 24th May 1888

Queen Margaret College, the first and as yet the only College for women which exists in Scotland is interested to place within the reach of women a course of higher instruction similar to that offered to the students in the Universities, and to give training such as is found at Girton, Newnham, Holloway, and other Women's Colleges in England. It originated in an Association for the Higher Education of Women formed in Glasgow in 1877 and was reincorporated in 1883 as a College which was named after Queen Margaret of Scotland, the earliest patroness of learning and culture in this kingdom.

Queen Margaret College from
the northwest, 1914.
Glasgow City Archives

Close-up of gate at entrance
to former Medical Buildings,
Queen Margaret College.
1970 Robert Cowper

QUEEN MARGARET COLLEGE

Queen Margaret College was originally Northpark
House. It was built in 1869 to the design of J. T.
Rochead for John and Matthew Bell, two eccentric
bachelor brothers who made a fortune from their
Glasgow Pottery in Stafford Street. The name was
adopted from the former mansion house of Northpark
on the site of which Northpark Terrace was built in
1866.

Top right opposite page

Looking across to the new Queen Margaret
Bridge (opened 1929) from the old bridge built in
1870 and demolished in 1970. Mr. John E. Walker,
Coachbuilder, who owned 100 acres of North
Kelvinside, built the bridge to connect his property
with the part of Hillhead he owned on the south side
of the Kelvin. The City of Glasgow Bank had built
Belmont Bridge to link their property north and south
of the river. The Bank's 28 acres extended to the
Great Western Road Bridge. A failure to agree when
the carriage drives were constructed up to the
boundaries of the two properties is said to account
for the barriers that still linger in Doune Gardens
and La Crosse Terrace.

7.30—10.0

**A Programme
for the opening of
BROADCASTING HOUSE,
GLASGOW**

7.30 The Rt. Hon. WALTER ELLIOT, M.P., will give the opening address

introduced by

Mr. R. C. Norman, Chairman of the BBC

and

Mr. F. W. Ogilvie, Director-General

Before the opening address Metrical Psalm xxiv (vv. 7-10) will be sung, and the Rev. Professor Archibald Main, D.D., D.Litt., Chairman of the Scottish Religious Advisory Committee of the BBC, will offer a prayer of dedication

A vote of thanks to Mr. Elliot will be proposed by Mr. Melville Dinwiddie, Scottish Regional Director of the BBC

7.55 app. Interlude of Scottish Dances played by the Strings of the BBC Scottish Orchestra (leader J. Mouland Begbie), conductor Guy Warrack

8.0 WILL FYFFE
supported by the BBC Scottish Orchestra (leader J. Mouland Begbie), conducted by Kemlo Stephen

8.25 THE GLASGOW ORPHEUS CHOIR
Conductor, Sir Hugh S. Roberton

8.55 THE THREE COLLEGE BOYS
Graduates in Rhythm and Harmony

9.0 A JAMES BRIDIE PLAY
specially written for this occasion—the first play to be written for broadcasting by the distinguished Scottish dramatist

Producer, Gordon Gildard

9.25 GAELIC SONGS
James Macphee (tenor)

9.35 TUNES FOR EVERYBODY
The BBC Scottish Orchestra (leader J. Mouland Begbie), conducted by Ian Whyte

10.0 *Time Signal, Greenwich*
THE FOURTH NEWS
(including Weather Forecast)
NEWS TALKS and SPORT

Facsimile Programme as published in the *Radio Times* for Friday, November 18, 1938. *Courtesy of B.B.C. Scotland*

1962*

Entrance of Medical Buildings, Queen Margaret College. The design is officially that of John Keppie, but the hand of Mackintosh obviously participated. Much of the building remains but is closely encompassed by the build-up of departments of the B.B.C.
1970 Robert Cowper

Medical Buildings, Queen Margaret College. Built 1895.   *University Archives*

Former coachman's house above stable and carriage quarters in Ashton Lane. About 1910 they became the chauffeur's house and the garage for Dr. Marion Gilchrist's prim dark green Wolseley laundaulette.   *1969**

Janet Galloway LL.D.

From 1877 Honorary Secretary of Glasgow Association for the Higher Education of Women which became Queen Margaret College. She devoted her life to its interests and died at her post on 24th January, 1909.

Marion Gilchrist
1864–1952
L.L.A., M.B.C.M. 1894
Glasgow Herald

5 Buckingham Terrace, residence of Dr. Marion Gilchrist. *1970**

First Women Doctors

WHEN I became a registered medical student, my home was in Burnside and the nearest railway station was Rutherglen. The low level service from there by the Caledonian Railway was a great boon as I could travel direct to Botanic Gardens Station almost at the door of Queen Margaret College. Its grounds were most spacious with two magnificent purple beeches on the right hand lawn where, on summer afternoons we had tea made on a portable gas ring linked to the house main. Twopence per individual per week bought us milk, biscuits, tea and sugar with enough over at the end of June to have a strawberry feast with cream. Some of our studies required our attendance at mixed classes at Gilmorehill which called for considerable physical effort to arrive in time as, of course, there was no transport. The period I knew was from 1905 to 1911 when I qualified. The class of operative surgery entailed our attendance at Queen Margaret College at 6 a.m. to 9 a.m. and 3 to 6 p.m. This work was arranged thus and crowded into a fortnight because our lecturer, Mr. J. Hogarth Pringle was chief of three wards at the Royal Infirmary. Among my fellow students was Doctor Katherine S. McPhail who, with the help of Doctor Leonard Findlay of Royal Hospital for Sick Children at Yorkhill, pioneered the establishment of a children's hospital in Serbia where it was pitifully required following the outbreak of war in 1914.

When, in 1895, Doctor Marion Gilchrist qualified in medicine, she acquired the additional distinction of being the first woman medical practitioner in Scotland, if not in Britain. Thus it was that Dr. Gilchrist sorely resented the setting up in Glasgow as general practitioners of Dr. Elizabeth Pace and Dr. Alice McLaren, graduates from the Royal Free Hospital, trained in London. They started in Newton Place while Dr. Marion Gilchrist assisted Dr. McGregor Robertson, a well-known general practitioner in Hillhead.

Women doctors were increasing in numbers all over the country and in order to uphold their interests local associations were formed, e.g. in Scotland – Scottish Western, Scottish Eastern and Aberdeen. Dr. Gilchrist elected to become a member of the Scottish Eastern Association in order to mark her disapproval of Dr. Alice McLaren and Dr. Pace, but by 1917 the great increase of women in Medicine brought about the formation of the Medical Women's Federation with headquarters in London, and a three-yearly president elected for the whole country. Dr. Gilchrist had then to submit to becoming a member of the Scottish Western Association, and as I was at that time president of the Scottish Western Association of the Medical Women's Federation I gave a Hallowe'en Party to the Scottish Western Members in my house at 2 Lynedoch Street and there it was my pleasure to have Dr. Alice McLaren and Dr. Marion Gilchrist drinking tea together.

Dr. Elizabeth Pace had retired from practice on her marriage to Dr. A. Maitland Ramsay. Dr. Marion Gilchrist was appointed Ophthalmologist to Redlands Hospital for Women in 1917.

ELLEN B. ORR, M.B., CH.B., F.R.C.S.G.

THE BOTANIC GARDENS

A FINE SUMMER SUNDAY AFTERNOON, almost a hundred years ago, would find many of the wealthier families of the City in the Botanic Gardens, enjoying the floral displays outside and the exotic plants in the glass-houses. The West-end was now a prosperous residential area and the University had recently moved to Gilmorehill near-by. Everything on the surface seemed to favour the future development of the Gardens. They were run by the Royal Botanic Institution of Glasgow and only members and their families and friends could use them freely. An attraction, recently negotiated with John Kibble, was the Kibble Art Palace, which had been brought from his home in Coulport and re-erected in the Gardens. It contained plants, ponds, fountains and statues to admire and musical soirées were held in it. Disraeli and Gladstone delivered their rectorial addresses there.

During the summer months public promenades were held in the Gardens with a military band playing. The plant collections were always being added to by donations from abroad from missionaries in Africa like David Livingstone, from the captains of trading vessels – and from the trenches before Sebastopol. Plants were also exchanged with other gardens in Britain. Many of the prominent citizens of Glasgow – the Lord Provost, city merchants, professors of the University – were connected at one time or another with the Institution. The Gardens were well known throughout Britain, due largely to the interest taken in them in their early days by Sir William Hooker, who was Regius Professor of Botany at the University of Glasgow from 1820-1841 and who described and illustrated many of the Glasgow plants in his scientific works.

The Gardens were founded in 1817 as a result of the enthusiasm and energy of Thomas

Great Western Road at Botanic Gardens Railway Station and entrance to the Gardens, 1905. *Annan*

Botanic Gardens Bandstand (demolished June 1965). *May 1963**

Botanic Gardens main entrance. *May 1970**

Hopkirk the Younger, a grandson of one of Glasgow's tobacco lords. Hopkirk and a few friends had enlisted the help of the University and prominent citizens to raise funds for a botanic garden. The Crown contributed and granted a royal Charter. An eight acre site was purchased at what is now Fitzroy Place, Sauchiehall Street, and Hopkirk donated his considerable plant collection to form the nucleus of the new Garden. The University was to receive plant material for its students and the use of a lecture room. The rapid westward expansion of the City in a short time made the site unsuitable for the growing of plants and a site was therefore purchased on the new estate at Kelvinside. The plants and glasshouse were transferred there and the new Gardens were officially opened on 30th April 1842.

The financing of the Gardens had always been difficult and the economic circumstances in Glasgow during the 19th Century laid greater strains upon them. They did not receive any regular official grants and by the 1880s, in spite of many efforts to raise money, it was becoming impossible to maintain the Gardens properly. A loan was received from Glasgow Corporation and, with it, the now dilapidated range of glasshouses was rebuilt and the lease of the Kibble Palace was bought out. But, in succeeding years, it was found impossible to repay even the interest. The Corporation took possession as creditors in 1887 and the Gardens were closed. When the City of Glasgow Act, incorporating Hillhead and Kelvinside, was passed in 1891, it was stipulated that the Gardens were to be maintained in perpetuity.

Since the take over the Gardens have carried on their earlier traditions. The link with the University has been continued and plant material is still supplied for the use of students. The plant collections have been built up over the years and are now particularly strong in orchids. The collection is rich in tropical species and conservation work is done to maintain and propagate species threatened in their native habitats. In addition to this botanical function, as public gardens they also provide information through lay-outs, exhibitions and informative labelling. In these ways the Gardens are carrying out the aims of the original founders of a hundred and fifty years ago.

E. W. CURTIS, 1971

Main Walk and Glass-houses.   *1905 Annan*

The Weeping Ash. Transplanted in 1840 from the old Gardens in Sandyford. *February 1971**

THE 'PEA-TREE WELL'

This rustic well first became a favourite place to stroll to early in the 19th century when the song 'Kelvingrove' had become popular. It was written by Mr. Thomas Lyle, a Glasgow surgeon, who set it to an old melody whose pleasant flowing movement is still to be heard. Here is the first verse:

Let us haste to Kelvingrove, bonnie lassie, O,
Thro' its mazes let us rove, bonnie lassie, O,
Where the rose, in all her pride, paints the hollow dingle side,
Where the midnight fairies glide, bonnie lassie, O

The famous well was overhung by an old laburnum tree, called in Scotland the 'Pea-Tree', from the pods of seeds like small peas which hung in clusters from the branches. The old Scotch word 'Pea-Tree' not being generally understood, it was often corrupted to 'Pear-Tree' but as no pear tree grew near the spot, this name was quite inapplicable, and gradually degenerated into 'Three-Tree' Well. This sylvan scene disappeared during the building of Kirklee Railway Station and the surrounding roadway.

Constable Wm. Hughes on point duty
at Botanic Gardens. *c. 1925*

The well-remembered sundial at the end of the broad walk. (In the 1960s the gnomon, which cast its shadow on the dial, was stolen.) *September 1959*

James Rourke, Horticulturalist (1905–1969). Born in Botanic Gardens Lodge when his father was foreman gardener before becoming curator. Always intensely interested in his work 'Jimmy' knew every inch of the Gardens. He had a sly wit that never failed to raise a smile when answering any query. For many years he had a dog which he had saved from drowning in the Kelvin. At the time of his promotion to Deputy Superintendent of the Queen's District of the Parks Department in June 1965, his abode was at Lansdowne Church where he had been church officer for 16 years.
1968 Campbell R. Steven

Near the entrance to the main 'Hothouses'; many Hillhead children of other days will remember this passage-way to the high pond where the goldfish darted below the big floating leaves. *1965**

'Donald' the last working horse kept in the Botanic Gardens. He came in December 1954 and was retired to the Linn Park in June 1970. His stable was behind the main glasshouses.
F. G. Rodway 1970

Lily and goldfish pond in the Kibble ▶
Palace (opened 20th June, 1873);
always an attraction for toddlers.
1914 Glasgow City Archives

At Lowther Terrace in the afternoon of Saturday, 4th June, 1960, a few hours before the departure of the last tramcar on Great Western Road.

The Kibble Palace and the steeple of Kelvinside (Botanic Gardens) Parish Church. *July 1964**

Hamilton Park Drive (formerly Hamilton Park Terrace). *April 1970**

Great Western Road, Hillhead, at Buckingham Terrace. *c. 1950 Valentine*

Queen Margaret Bridge (Walker's Bridge) from North Kelvinside, erected 1870, demolished 1970. *1914 Glasgow City Archives*

Evening Times   Hillhead Bowling Green and Clubhouse.   *October 1958. Courtesy of Mr. W. L. Little*

HILLHEAD BOWLING CLUB (from Centenary handbook)

THE first green of the Club was in Bank Street. The *Glasgow Courier* of 5th July 1849, in reporting the opening dinner held in Cook's Regent Hotel, Buchanan Street, on 3rd July, gives some interesting details. It says:

It may be stated that the club had its origin at Hillhead, in consequence of a few of the gentlemen residing on the hill suggesting to Mr. Gibson, the lord of the manor, that a small patch of ground, which last year was a potato garden, should be allotted as a bowling green. This he readily acceded to at a nominal rent. The club now boasts upwards of fifty members. The play ground is 110 feet long, by about 90 feet broad, and besides having about 20 feet of a fine shrubbery walk, commands a beautiful view of the Kelvin, and the surrounding scenery, being about 130 feet above the level of the Clyde.

In 1858 a committee was appointed to consider what could be done in view of the approaching expiry of the lease, and after negotiations, a suitable site was leased from Mr. William Govan of Southpark in what was known as Lilybank Street. The new green was opened in 1860, the following advertisement appearing in *The Glasgow Herald* of 30th April:

HILLHEAD BOWLING CLUB

THE NEW GREEN, at the South End of Sardinia Terrace, will be opened for the Season on Tuesday, 1st May, at Six o'clock p.m. Gentlemen desirous of joining the Club are invited to visit the Grounds, where they will obtain forms of application and every information.

The green was opened for play on Saturday 19th May, and a 'General Opening' was held on 29th May for which the following clubs were each invited to send a rink: Albany, Willowbank, Wellcroft, Partick, Govan, Bellahouston, and St. Vincent.

The cost of preparing the green was about £600. Towards covering the cost sums of £1 and upwards were borrowed from members at 5% interest. The Club held the ground on a twenty years' lease, and the debt was to be repaid to members within that period. In 1864 two additional rinks were laid out as a small subsidiary green.

The move to the third green at Hamilton Drive took place after long negotiations. In 1875 a large committee was formed to ascertain whether the neighbouring proprietors would give any support in the event of the Club deciding to purchase the green which it then occupied, but there is no record of what this committee did. At the Annual General Meeting in March, 1876, a committee was formed to enquire and report regarding the ground at Hamilton Drive. This committee met with difficulties. In May of the same year a letter was received on behalf of the Directors of the Botanic Gardens, proposing a meeting to consider the possibility of forming a bowling green in the Gardens for the Hillhead Club. Although the offer of the Botanic Gardens Directors seems to have presented a possible basis of negotiation, the Directors of the Club decided to make another approach to the Hamilton Drive proprietors, but once again they came up against difficulties. So they tried once more to arrange for the purchase of the green occupied by the Club, but found the price prohibitive. They next tried to get some ground from the University, but were unsuccessful. They also tried to get ground belonging to the Academy, but although the matter was discussed at length, the parties could not come to an agreement. Meanwhile it was necessary to do something, as the lease was about to expire, so the Annual General Meeting in March 1880 empowered the

Curling in Hillhead. The old gentleman is said to be the Rev. James Rennie. Date is possibly in the 1890s. This section ceased in 1919, the tennis ground having become unsatisfactory to flood in winter. *Mitchell Library*

Directors to lease the green then occupied for one or more years if they felt that advisable. Before the end of 1880 a satisfactory agreement was reached with the Hamilton Drive proprietors, and at a special General Meeting in December, the President was authorised to sign the memorandum for lease, and the Directors were given authority to form the new green.

Before the close of the negotiations the proprietors expressed a desire that the Club 'make a bank 12 feet wide between the green and the boundary of the ground next to Hamilton Drive, said bank to be planted with shrubs so as to screen the view of the green entirely from the road and thus prevent parties from gathering to look on at the game.' The Club was not prepared to guarantee to make so wide a bank, but 'they would endeavour either by shrubbery or a hedge or other authorised fence to effect the object aimed at by the proprietors.' Plans were prepared by March 1881 and estimates were called for. It was decided to lay out the ground to the north of the green to serve as a curling pond in winter and a tennis court in summer.

The green was opened on 27th May 1882. A game of seven rinks was played between the Past President (the President being ill) and the Vice-President, 'but after a few heads had to be discontinued owing to rain coming on. Notwithstanding the broken weather there was a large attendance of members and friends. Among the latter was Provost King of Hillhead who congratulated the club on the acquisition of so handsome a green which he declared was a great ornament to the neighbourhood.'

In 1905 the Directors arranged for a new lease of the ground for 25 years after the expiry of the existent lease in 1910. This early arrangement was made because certain expensive repairs were necessary and it was felt inadvisable to undertake them before being assured of security of tenure. In 1890 the Directors had bought 1/25 share of the ground for the Club, an action approved by a General Meeting of the Club with one dissentient. In 1914 Glasgow Corporation considered buying the ground, but did not pursue the project. The University eventually bought the ground all but the 1/25 share belonging to the Club. In 1924 the University court desired to purchase the Club's share, but the Club was unwilling to part with it for a long time. It was only in 1934 that it finally agreed to sell. In 1935 the ground was acquired by the B.B.C. from whom the Club held a lease but due to extensive building plans of the B.B.C. the inevitable closure of Hillhead Bowling Club took place in October 1958.

Queen Margaret Road from Hamilton Drive (built over in 1970 by the B.B.C.). *1961**

'The Kelvin from the North at Botanic Gardens, 1864' (Scottish School). Wm. Glover (1848–1916) (as given on title plate). Date on canvas is '84' and likely to be correct. *Oil Painting in People's Palace*

I RECALL . . . . *George Sheriff*

PLACID and respectable is the general tone of living in Hillhead which I recall in my young days.

I was born at 45 Lilybank Gardens in 1889 and lived there until 1906 when we moved to North Kelvinside.

The development of Hillhead at that time was orderly and, I should say, consisted almost entirely of the building of the red sandstone tenements on the sloping ground west of Kersland Street and between Great George Street and Vinicombe Street. This must have taken place about the beginning of the century. I associate their construction with the time of the 1901 International Exhibition. So I can't be far out. Before these buildings went up the area between Kersland Street and Cranworth Street was known as 'the waste ground'. With sufficient snow in wintertime it was a favourite place for sledging and, very often, the scene was quite a busy one. At the foot of the hill stood the Western Baths which go back quite a long time before my day. I had an uncle who had a propensity for diving into the pond from the gallery. There used to be a pillar box at the Great George Street end of Kersland Street and I remember before the buildings went up, my father taking me there and pointing out Ben Venue in the Trossachs.

In the last phase of Queen Victoria's reign I cannot recall any particular residents of note near us in Lilybank Gardens apart from Dr. Wallace, editor of *The Glasgow Herald* and Principal Story of the University. This latter household caused some amusement in the Gardens by an unconventional advertisement in *The Glasgow Herald* which simply stated 'Mrs. Story requires a cook'. The only local 'characters' which my memory retains from that far off period are 'the wee glass man' so called from his belief that he was made of glass and would break if anyone touched him; and old Miss Russell of the well-known business of Thomas Russell the florist and fruiterer in Great Western Road. Miss Russell was credited with knowing the intimate history of every Hillhead family on her order books. The source of this came from her excellence as a listener and sympathiser. Miss Russell's tears would flow copiously at the merest hint of a hard luck story with the result that she heard many of them. She was a good business woman, as was also one of my Sheriff aunts who went into the shop one day to buy a cucumber. The specimen offered was too big so my aunt said, 'Can you halve it for me, Miss Russell?' 'Certainly, Miss Sheriff,' replied Miss Russell, cutting off about one third and proceeding to wrap it up. 'Are both halves the same price?' queried my aunt. 'Oh yes, Miss Sheriff.' 'Then I'll take the other half' said Miss Sheriff.

About the turn of the century the Hillhead Post Office was on the other side of Byres Road – a little to the north, where Bayne & Duckett now are – and the 'Female Assistants' which was, I believe, their official status were at that time a by-word for general snappishness to customers. An uncle of mine went in one day to get a penny stamp but the ladies were engaged in a private conversation which they continued without paying any attention to him. As Uncle Arthur was not the man to put up with this sort of thing from public servants he raised his stick and rapped it soundly on the counter. At this one of the ladies turned and called out, 'Well? What do you want?' 'I want to send a telegram.' 'Can't you see the forms hanging up in front of your eyes?' retorted the lady. 'Take one and write out your message.' My uncle did so, but this time awaited the lady's pleasure without showing any further signs of impatience. When the lady eventually came over and took the form to count the words, she looked up with a startled expression and asked, 'Do you want to send this?' 'No, I don't,' he replied, 'but if I did, you would have to send it.'

The telegram read 'POSTMASTERGENERAL LONDON. LADY ASSISTANTS HILLHEAD POST OFFICE GLASGOW TOO BUSY GOSSIPING TO ATTEND TO CUSTOMERS'.

The Hillhead Burgh Hall was used on Sunday evenings during the winter by Mr. John W. Arthur, a very religious business man who lived in Athole Gardens, and who used to hold a service there for the boys and girls of Hillhead and Kelvinside who were strictly segregated – boys on the one side, girls on the other. Mr. Arthur liked to make the meetings as impressive as possible and I remember on one occasion his way of doing so was to have a large screen on the platform with sheets of brown paper pasted on to it. When he wanted to emphasise some special point in his address he would go to the screen and tear off one of the sheets of paper revealing an apposite religious picture underneath.

Mr. Arthur had four sons of whom the most remarkable was the youngest, Charles. Charlie Arthur, as he was known, was an extremely able and sociable man who went out to India where he did so well that he became Lord Mayor of Calcutta, commanded the Calcutta Light Horse, earned a Military Cross in Mesopotamia, and was knighted. But, alas, he also became the President of the Calcutta Turf Club with all its presumed implications which was a great shock to his father.

My maternal grandfather had a flat in Kelvinside Terrace West and on coming in to breakfast one morning he discovered a wooden scaffolding being erected opposite his flat and on making enquiries he found that they were about to build Queen Margaret

Place. As he was determined not to be overlooked he at once gave up the flat and took another one in the east side of Kersland Street which had an unobstructed outlook, but no sooner had he got his furniture moved in than they started to build on the west side, right in front of him. As my grandfather was rather a short-tempered man the effect of this double blow can be imagined.

The Glasgow Academy Cadet Corps was formed, I think, in 1901. I joined it in 1902 and it was commanded by Captain Peter Couper, one of the English masters. The Sergeant-Instructor was the Gym master, Sam Stewart, who was (according to the boys) a veteran of Lord Roberts' famous march from Kabul to Kandahar in 1880. This historic event provided the theme for the Corps marching song which, sung to the tune of the Soldiers' Chorus from Faust, ran:

Who led Lord Roberts to Kandahar?
Who led Lord Roberts to Kandahar?

Who led Lord Roberts to Kandahar?
Surely it must have been Major-General
Sergeant-Instructor Sam!

Jack Buchanan, the celebrated musical comedy star, was educated at the Glasgow Academy and used to tell this story against himself. One day, at the height of his renown when his company was playing at the Theatre Royal, he thought he would like to visit the school and see one or two of his old masters, so off he went and, going up the stairs in the school, he encountered Dr. Temple, the Rector, running down with his gown streaming out behind him, a spectacle which any recollection of Dr. Temple always evokes. Jack Buchanan stopped, stood aside, and bowing politely said: 'Good morning, Dr. Temple' to which the Rector made the characteristic reply: 'WAIT! DON'T TELL ME! YES! BUCHANAN! You always were a fool, Buchanan, but you seem to have been able to make it pay.'   1971

'The Sixty Steps' viewed from the foot of Queen Margaret Place opposite the old Queen Margaret Bridge. *1936 Daily Record*

Great Western Road at Buckingham Terrace.   *May 1960**

Great Western Road from
Hillhead Street. Ruskin
(formerly St. James's) Terrace
on left.   *April 1960**

Great Western Road looking
west from Kelvin Bridge.
October 1959*

Back Lane at University
Gardens. Recreation garden
of Bute Gardens on left.
June 1963*

Hillhead Street, looking down
to University Avenue. *May
1963**

Bank Street at Great George
Street. *August 1965**

Great Western Road looking across Kelvin Bridge. Caledonian Mansions on right at Otago Street.   *1905 Annan*

Donald Morrison
Rector, 1866–99

The Glasgow Academy. Main entrance, Colebrooke Street.
Architects: Hugh and David Barclay, 1878. *May 1970**

THE
GLASGOW
ACADEMY

THE GLASGOW ACADEMY was founded as the result of a meeting of 'leading citizens' on 8th May 1845. A company was formed to control the proposed school and to secure premises or land on which to build a school. This led to the buying of a site on the east side of Elmbank Street and on this site the Glasgow Academy was built. The first session of the school (1846/47) was conducted in two houses in Renfield Street, and the new school was occupied in August 1847.

The passing into law of the Education (Scotland) Act in 1870 led to the establishment of School Boards. The Glasgow School Board took over control of the High School and, considering its premises in John Street no longer suitable, approached the Glasgow Academy Company with a view to purchasing the latter's schoolbuildings in Elmbank Street. This was agreed to in 1877 and the School Board took possession on 30th June 1878. The first Glasgow Academy Company was wound up but a second immediately took its place. The shareholders of the first

company were able to show a very substantial profit on their shares but most transferred their holdings to the new company, and these, with the addition of very many new shareholders, enabled the new Glasgow Academy Company to secure a site at Kelvin Bridge and there build the new Glasgow Academy. While both companies were 'profit-making', dividends were neither large nor regular. This second company controlled the school from 1878 to 1921.

John King, writing for the Academy's Centenary Book in 1946, describes his journey to school in the 1860s: 'Hillhead, where I then lived, was a rural suburb of Glasgow and the site of the present school was a "free coup"! In my daily tramp to and from the old Academy in Elmbank Street I traversed what was largely open country, with hedges, trees, and green fields on either hand. Woodlands Road justified its name; sauch trees bloomed in Sauchiehall Street; but the elms in Elmbank were but a memory.' He continues: 'A small boy named J. M. Barrie, afterwards Sir James Barrie, novelist and dramatist, entered the school at the same time as I but he was posted to the 2nd English Class while I was deemed fit for the 3rd, so I had not the pleasure of being his class-mate.'

By 1878 the site was no longer a 'free coup'. It had been built up and developed into what was then a first-class cricket ground by the Caledonian Cricket Club who had spent more than £1000 in levelling, turfing, fencing and building a pavilion. To this ground they had brought not only famous cricket teams but even Canadian Lacrosse players. The Caledonian was the only club in Britain to give this party a guarantee and were rewarded by a substantial profit on the transaction. (Is there any connection between this event and the name, Lacrosse Terrace, of a road off Belmont Street?) The Caledonian had been neighbours of the Academy and Academicals at Burnbank playing fields near St. George's Cross, and Academy boys had played for the Caledonian Club both before and after the foundation of the Academical Club. Tom Chalmers and the Carrick brothers were perhaps the best known; the former a member of the first Scottish Rugby team and J. S. Carrick, also a Rugby internationalist, Secretary of the Academical Club, and President of S.R.U., but best remembered as highest individual scorer in cricket for a very long time with 419 not out for West of Scotland v Priory Park.

There must have been many sad hearts and divided loyalties when the Caledonian Club was ousted from its ground to make way for the new building because this led directly to the demise of the Club. Perhaps the most affected of all was Mr. H. E. Crum-Ewing, a former player of the Caledonian, who in 1878 was not only President of the Caledonian C.C. but first President of the Glasgow Academical Club (1866-79).

When the Academy Company planned its new beginning at Kelvin Bridge competition for the sons of Hillhead householders was not anticipated but shortly after the transfer Kelvinside Academy was opened at Kirklee and the Govan School Board (into whose district the Hillhead area fell) decided to open a secondary school in Cecil Street – Hillhead High School.

Glasgow School Board felt that they too must cater for their more westerly children and opened Woodside School in 1882.

From 1878 to the end of the 1914-18 War the control of the school rested with the G.A. Company and the only addition to the original four-square building was that of a Science and Art block to the north of the main building in 1902. Internally, and especially after the coming of Edwin Temple as Rector in 1899, there were many innovations. The *Glasgow Academy Chronicle* first appeared in 1899 and has continued to the present day to record the events of school and Academical importance. In October 1901 the *Chronicle* records, 'The directors have sanctioned the forming of a Cadet Corps to be attached to the 1st Volunteer Battalion, H.L.I. a regiment commanded by an old Academy boy, Col. R. C. Mackenzie.' So began the Cadet Corps, later the Officers Training Corps, and, later still, the Combined Cadet Force with not only an Army section but Naval and Air sections also. The importance of this training has been demonstrated by the records of boys from the school in the two great wars. In the First War (1914-18) 1,469 former pupils served in the forces and of these 327 were killed. Of the very many winners of decorations two must be singled out each having won the Victoria Cross – Lieut.-Colonel W. H. Anderson, H.L.I., and Lieut. Donald Macintosh, Seaforth Highlanders.

In 1910 was instituted the 'House System' and it is interesting to note that the geographically small house of 'Hill' with boundaries of the Clyde, the Kelvin, Great Western Road and Byres Road was greater numerically but also more successful in sporting contests than the other houses of North, South and West. The boarding house began about this same time in Lansdowne Crescent and later moved to a house in Belmont Crescent to which was added, at a later period, the house next door presented to the school by the brothers Smith, Stanley and Douglas, sons of Sir William Smith the founder of The Boys' Brigade. The presiding genius of the Boarding House for many years was the famous J. C. Scott, even better known as sports master at the Academy from about 1900 till his departure in 1919, to become Headmaster of Hutchesons' Grammar School. The debt owed to this man not only by school sides but also by Academical sides from 1905 to the great days of the 1920s is incalculable.

Before the end of the 1914-18 War many suggestions were made regarding a suitable war memorial. As a result, in 1921, the Glasgow Academy War Memorial Trust was established to guarantee the continuance of the school on an independent non-profit making basis. The shareholders of the Glasgow Academy Company either gifted or sold their shares to the new Trust which took over all the assets, and liabilities, of the old Company. The sum raised for the War Memorial was sufficient to take over the school, to establish the Trust, and to guarantee the ordinary running of the school. Since then extra-ordinary capital expenditure has been met from the proceeds of Appeals to former pupils and friends. The Academy is the only school in Glasgow completely independent, receiving no grants from either local or national Educational Authorities.

The fact that in 110 years the Academy has had only four rectors Donald Morrison (1861/99), Edwin Temple (1899/1932), F. Roydon Richards (1932/59), Basil M. Holden (1959-) speaks for itself regarding the outstanding ability of these men but surely some credit is also due to the men who chose them. All four were young on appointment and this shows that the Directors or Governors must have had rare insight into their possibilities. A brief glance at the Chairmen of the Governing body shows that all except one were leaders in the business life of Glasgow but with many other interests. John W. Arthur (President of Directors 1912/20) had been captain of the Academical XV for the first seven years of the club, as captain had signed the challenge to England which led to the first Inter-

13 Belmont Crescent. Last residence of Sir William Smith, Founder of The Boys' Brigade. Gifted by his sons to The Glasgow Academy. *May 1970*

national, had played a distinguished part in Scotland's victory on that occasion and two years later had played a part in the formation of the S.R.U. He conducted Sunday School classes in the Grove Institute, and Sunday evening meetings in the Hillhead Burgh Halls. Sir Robert C. Mackenzie (1920-44) was the first Chairman of Governors of the G.A.W.M.T. He had had a distinguished career in the Volunteers and Territorials and commanded a battalion in the first war. He too had played rugby for Scotland and was President of the Scottish Rugby Union in 1924-25. At an earlier period he had been the saviour of the Academical Club, of which he had been both Secretary and President, in a time of great financial stress in the 1890s.

Two later Chairmen follow much the same pattern. Sir Tennant Sloan (1948-57) was the exception to the line of Glasgow businessmen having served in the Indian Civil Service with great distinction. He played in Scottish Rugby teams between 1905 and 1909, was Captain of the Academical XV in 1906-07, and President of the Club 1946-49. The present Chairman, W. Maxwell Simmers, played for Scotland 28 times between 1926 and 1932, was Captain of the Club 1929-31, President 1953-55, and President S.R.U. in 1956-57.

The Academy has a fine record in sport especially Rugby Football and this has been reflected in the successes of the Academicals at different periods in the last hundred years. Six Academicals played in the first International match against England in 1871 and, through the years 80 Academicals have gained some 370 caps for Scotland. The peak period of the Club's success was in the mid-twenties which was the era of J. B. Nelson, J. C. Dykes, Herbert Waddell, and W. M. Simmers. These four gained 88 caps between them but in the same period, between 1922 and 1932, twelve other products of the Academy gained 27 caps. Fourteen Academicals have become President of the Scottish Rugby Union, the most recent being George G. Crerar. After the first International match of 1871 The Rugby Union was formed and three Scottish clubs joined, viz. Edinburgh University, Glasgow Academicals and West of Scotland. A meeting of representatives of Scottish clubs was held in the Academy (then in Elmbank Street) in March 1873 after the Third International against England at Partick when it was decided to form a Scottish Union (later S.R.U.).

In Cricket the record of school and club is not so distinguished. Before the formation of the Scottish Cricket Union in 1909 many Academicals achieved fame, but not usually when playing for the club. (J. S. Carrick and Tom Chalmers, both Rugby internationalists have already been mentioned.) Since 1909 nine players have gained 35 Scottish caps while I. A. R. Peebles played in thirteen Test Matches against Australia, New Zealand and South Africa between 1927 and 1931.

J. W. Dallachy is the third Academical to be appointed President of the Scottish Cricket Union. He was Treasurer of the S.C.U. for thirty years, was Secretary of the Academical Club from 1935 to 1960, has been Secretary to the G.A.W.M.T. since 1953, and was Captain of the Academical Cricket Club in 1932 when the Rowan Charity Cup was won for the second time.

At Golf eight players have represented Scotland on fifty-one occasions and R. C. MacGregor represented Great Britain against U.S.A. in the Walker Cup in 1953.

In Athletics the school has produced many distinguished performers. In earlier days R. S. Stronach (also a Rugby Internationalist) was Scottish Hurdles Champion from 1900 to 1907 and British in 1904-05-06. Later Ian Borland, Roy Hamilton, John MacIsaac, Hugh Barrow and Patrick Maclagan have represented Scotland at Commonwealth Games or other contests.

The highest honour members of the G.A.W.M.T. can confer on their fellow Academicals is to appoint them Honorary Governors and the present list of these (without honours, decorations or degrees) reads as follows: Lord Balerno of Currie, Professor-Emeritus C. A. Campbell, Thomas R. Craig, Dr. Hugh O. Douglas, James T. Dowling, Gilbert J. Innes, Lord Muirshiel of Kilmacolm, Dr. F. Roydon Richards, T. G. Robinson, Lord Sinclair of Cleeve, Sir Tennant Sloan, Stanley Smith, Lord Strathclyde of Barskimming.

Of past Honorary Governors perhaps the best known have been General Sir Archibald Hunter, Sir George Adam Smith (Principal of Aberdeen University), Professor Dr. James Moffat, Dr. Charles L. Warr (Dean of the Thistle and of the Chapel Royal, Scotland), Lord Lindsay of Birker (Master of Balliol), Professors J. H. Teacher, W. K. Hunter and J. M. Munro Kerr (appointed, at same time to medical chairs at the University of Glasgow), Sir D. Y. Cameron, Walter Elliot, Sir John T. Cargill, D. Norman Sloan, Colonel G. H. R. Laird, Lord Bilsland of Kinrara, Rear-Admiral W. S. Chalmers, Major-General D. A. H. Graham and Lord Reith of Stonehaven.

Going outside the lists of Honorary Governors there must be added the names of Sir James M. Barrie, O. H. Mavor (James Bridie) and Jack Buchanan for literature and the theatre, and of Jim Mollison the maker of so many pioneer record flights.

The teaming of Walter Elliot and O. H. Mavor at school caused some difficulties especially to that upholder of the establishment, A. M. Stevenson, later a Rugby Internationalist, and later still Moderator of the Presbyterian Church of Australia. Proceeding to the University to study medicine the two left their mark on the life and traditions of the University before, deserting medicine, they became politician – statesman and author – playwright respectively.

In the field of journalism Alastair Warren today occupies the editorial chair of *The Glasgow Herald*.

A. R. FORRESTER, 1971

Gardens of Belmont Crescent.
May 1970*

GLASGOW
ACADEMY
CADET
CORPS
1902

1 Nigel Watt
2 Hume Brodie
3 Arthur Mair
4 Robert Morton
5 — Watkins
6 — McKinnon
7 Norman Miller
8 James Armour
9 Richard Rose
10 Alex. Frew
11 — Fraser
12 — Dron
13 John Mavor
14 — Ralston
15 Peter Hally
16 — McBeth
17 — McGregor
18 — Russell
19 — Rose
20 — Haldane
21 Hector Gilchrist
22 — Dishington
23 — Rose
24 Alan Lawrie
25 — White
26 — Rose
27 — Lindsay
28 Osborne Mavor
29 — Paterson
30 — Schultze
31 Leonard Dutton
32 Fred Napier
33 — McConnell
34 — Pattison
35 — Thomson
36 —
37 John Reith
38 — Sandford

39 Frank Carruthers
40 — Miller
41 — Roemmele
42 Alex. Kay
43 — McConnell
44 — Watts
45 — Brown
46 Hugh Brown
47 Charles McLintock
48 — Benzie
49 Halliday Hannay

50 Ernest Collie
51 Stanley Smith
52 John Herbertson
53 —
54 — Davidson
55 William Fraser
56 Forrest McLellan
57 John McFarlane
58 —
59 David Clark
60 — McKissock

61 Alex. Scougal
62 — Rennie
63 David Strathie
64 Mark Aitken
65 — Doddrel
66 Sydney Smith
67 — Brodie
68 — Whitson
69 Jasper Howat
70 Matthew White
71 George Sheriff

72 —
73 James Wordie
74 — Dunlop
75 Gilbert Shanks
76 — Murdoch
77 Ralph Brown
78 Colin Black
79 Fred. Russell
80 — McWatters
81 Albert Tessier
82 Thomas Clark

83 — Parker
84 Ernest Perry
85 Walter Galbraith
86 James Allan
87 John Brown
88 — Tatlock
89 — Herbertson
90 Norval Lindsay
91 Roy Balloch
92 — Kellock
93 —

94 — Cree
95 — Rose
96 — Rose
97 Harry Rowan
98 —
99 — Roxburgh
100 — Martin
101 Charles Arthur
102 Peter Couper
103 Samuel Stewart
104 Alex. Stevenson

Edwin Temple, Rector, 1899–1932. *Annan*

The Glasgow Academy. Main Building. *May 1970**

Hillhead High School O.T.C. and Glasgow Academy O.T.C. on Church Parade at Barry Camp, July 1 1914. *Courtesy of Mr. A. C. Young*

Ralston

GLASGOW ACADEMICALS 1st XV, 1925–6

Standing — M. A. Allan ; T. R. Murray ; A. S. Dykes ; Archd. Watson, Esq. ; R. Findlay ; J. Findlay ; D. N. Walker.
Sitting   — J. Gilchrist ; J. C. Dykes ; H. Waddell ; J. B. White (*Captain*) ; J. B. Nelson ; A. K. Stevenson ; W. S. Dobson.
In front   — R. C. Warren ; W. M. Simmers ; W. Moore.   J. N. F. Blackater (*absent*).

SCOTTISH CHAMPIONS

All Matches :	Played 23	Won 22	Lost 1	Drawn 0	Points for, 609	Points against, 89
Championship Matches :	Played 19	Won 19	Lost 0	Drawn 0	Points for, 508	Points against, 50

Embossed burgh plaque set in Kelvin Bridge.
July 1970*

Position of plaque on S.W. side of Bridge.
July 1970*

Rear of Botanic Gardens
Railway Station, at daffodil
time.   *April 1969**

Recreation grounds of Bute
Gardens, looking towards
Hillhead Street. New Library
of University now occupies
site.   *May 1963**

Bandstand, Botanic Gardens
(demolished, January 1965).
May 1963*

Burgh gas lamp purchased
and re-erected in a Hillhead
back garden in 1959 when all
street gas lamps were removed.
May 1963*

King Edward VII Postbox
in wall of Lansdowne Crescent
private gardens facing Great
Western Road.   *June 1970**

eft: Broad Walk,
Botanic Gardens.
August 1963*

ght: Otago Street
at Glasgow Street.
August 1963*

eft: Kelvinbridge Railway
Station booking office.
Caledonian Mansions on
left and Lansdowne
Church in distance.
August 1963*

ght: Recreation garden
on hill at Gibson Street
above Oakfield Avenue.
June 1968*

★

Ever of thee I'm fondly dreaming,
   Thy gentle voice my spirit can cheer;
Thou wert the star that mildly beaming,
   Shone o'er my path when all was dark
    and drear
Still in my heart thy form I cherish,
   Ev'ry kind thought like a bird flies to
    thee!
Ah! never till life and mem'ry perish,
   Can I forget how dear thou art to me?
Morn, noon and night, wher'e'er I may be,
   Fondly I'm dreaming ever of thee,
   Fondly I'm dreaming ever of thee.

WITH TONIC SOL-FA.

EVER OF THEE

BALLAD
WORDS BY
George Linley
Music by
FOLEY HALL.

London,
W. PAXTON, 19, OXFORD STREET, W.

eft: Gibson Street
from Eldon Street,
Park Road on right.
June 1970*

ght: Ashton Lane.
September 1964*

★

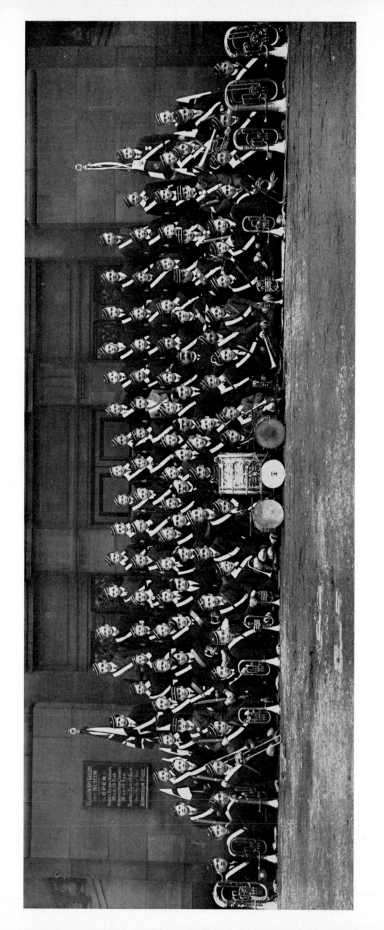

SIR WILLIAM SMITH WITH THE 1ST GLASGOW COMPANY OF THE BOYS' BRIGADE

Kelvingrove Park, 1913

Commemorative tablet on wall of Free College Church Mission, North Woodside Road, Glasgow. *July 1970**

Members of the 1st Glasgow Company at the North Woodside Hall in the 1920s

Sir William Smith as Colonel of the 1st L.R.V.

The Founder of The Boys' Brigade prior to a Battalion Inspection

Bower Street, formerly Bruce Street and originally Hillsborough Terrace where, from 1892 to 1906, Sir William Smith had his home at No. 12 in the flat on the right above the lamp. *August 1957**

4 Ann Street, now Southpark Avenue. Built 1874. *March 1969**

THE

BOYS' BRIGADE

& HILLHEAD

FOLLOWING its formation as conceived by William Smith, the first muster of The Boys' Brigade took place in the Woodside Mission Hall of the Free College Church on 4th October 1883. Twenty-eight boys paraded under their Captain and his two Lieutenants the brothers Hill.

Despite doubters, its success soared. Smith's courage and divine gleam proved to be on the right lines.

Early in 1885, with five Companies building up rapidly, the Founder realised the need for greater organisation and for a clearly defined Constitution to meet the possibilities of The Boys' Brigade becoming a national movement. And so, in his home at 4 Ann Street on 26th January 1885, the historic Meeting was called which constituted itself into the Council of The Boys' Brigade. Present with the Founder were J. R. Hill, J. B. Hill, J. S. Couper, J. B. Couper, F. P. R. Ferguson, E. W. Hamlen and W. Nicholl.

Sir William Smith (knighted in 1909) had a heritage of upright living firmly disciplined by exemplary military service. His father was an officer of the 7th Dragoon Guards.

His grandfather saw long service with the 78th Highlanders (2nd Seaforths) eventually becoming Adjutant while serving under the Duke of Wellington. Sir William maintained the family tradition by joining the 1st L.R.V. and, in due course, he became Colonel of the Regiment. It is noteworthy that several of the first Captains of The Boys' Brigade had also been officers of this crack volunteer battalion known as 'The Greys', their uniform, including helmet, having the same heather hue as the hodden-grey of The London Scottish.

Since coming as a boy from Thurso to stay with his Fraser uncle and aunts at 28 Hamilton Park Terrace, William Smith always had his Glasgow home in Hillhead. On 5th March 1884 he married Amelia Pearson Sutherland in her mother's house at 18 Ann Street. The adjacent building containing 4 Ann Street had been built only ten years previously when the Smiths made their first home in it. In 1891 they decided to move to the first floor flat at 12 Hillsborough Terrace round the corner in the same block. This was the family home until 1906 when he acquired the main-door house at 13 Belmont Crescent which was to be Sir William Smith's last residence and situated back to back with his first in Glasgow.

On 7th May 1914, while in his sixtieth year, he attended a great Display by the Brigade in the Albert Hall. The following day he collapsed in his London Office and died of a cerebral haemorrhage two days later.

On 30th April 1971 the official world membership of The Boys' Brigade amounted to 255,495.

Alfred Terrace at Hillhead Street. *May 1960**

In 1917 Rogerson succeeded William Farmer & Son at 1 Rokeby Terrace who, in 1878, had moved to these new and extensive premises from 1 Craiglaw Place at the corner of Wilson Street (Oakfield Avenue) where the business was established in 1853. In 1944, Cooper & Co. acquired the business from Mr. Rogerson. *Courtesy of Mr. John Barrie*

CHARLES WILSON'S PROPOSAL FOR WEST BANK OF THE RIVER KELVIN, NORTH OF GREAT WESTERN ROAD

J. Burbridge 1859

People's Palace

Where Belmont Crescent and Colebrooke Street were formed and, later, the raised ground on which the Glasgow Academy was built. Wilson had designed the Park Circus area and, with Joseph Paxton, laid out Kelvingrove Park in 1854.

Clock tower at Cooper's Corner, Bank Street and Great Western Road. Built 1875. *July 1970**

Stevenson Memorial Church, northeast end of Belmont Bridge. *Architect:* J. J. Stevenson, 1902. (Church of the 1st Glasgow Company, The Boys' Brigade, since 1927.) *February 1971**

osebery Terrace, Wood- e Road. *1970**

Kelvinbridge Station of the Caledonian Railway Company. Branch line from Central (Low Level) to Maryhill.
Opened 1896. *c. 1930. Courtesy of Professor C. J. Fordyce*

HILLHEAD RAILWAY STATIONS

HILLHEAD, like other of Glasgow's inner communities, received the benefits of local rail travel into the city centre and outwards to other Clydeside neighbourhoods much later than was the case in English cities of comparable size. The tenement system had created a compact town from which suburban sprawl did not become seriously noticeable until after the Second World War.

When the railway did come to Hillhead it came, in fact, too late but, because of other developments such as the electrification of the trams, on what turned out to be too optimistic a scale for its time to be profitable on the short distances involved. Plans had been discussed for years, but when the two railways to serve Hillhead were eventually opened it was within a few months of each other.

The Glasgow Central Railway, authorised in 1888 (and soon after taken over by the Caledonian Railway) performed miracles of tunnel engineering along Argyle Street and then turned north at Stobcross to provide a passenger service with stations at Kelvinbridge, Botanic Gardens and Kirklee, which began on 10th August 1896, with trains at 15-minute intervals.

A few months later (its official opening was on 21st January 1897, although it had started work for one abortive day on 14th December 1896) the Glasgow District Subway opened a station at Kelvinbridge and one in Byres Road named Hillhead which provided a 4-minute circular service under the Clyde and into the city centre.

The Central line, based on the Caledonian Railway's Central station, was connected with another Caledonian satellite, the Lanarkshire and Dunbartonshire Railway. It was of the standard gauge of 4 feet 8½ inches with Caledonian rolling stock, and was mainly worked for most of its life by the 0-4-4 tank engines designed by J. F. McIntosh, a development from a small engine designed by Dugald Drummond. From 1915 William Pickersgill who was to be the last locomotive superintendent of the Caledonian adopted McIntosh's design with only slight modifications, so these suburban tank engines were to run successfully right on into the era of railway nationalisation – and the closure of the Central Low Level Line.

Engineering work for the line had been of an exceptional nature, requiring underpinning of closely packed city buildings, and a method of tunnelling which interfered as little as possible with the traffic – including horse trams – on streets whose surface was only a few feet above the tunnels. Three years after completion of the line the resident engineer, Donald Matheson, was appointed engineer-in-chief of the Caledonian company.

The line from Stobcross went under the Park from a sharp curve beneath Kelvingrove Street. It emerged near the junction of Park Road and Eldon Street, skirted the River Kelvin and was then carried over the river to Kelvinbridge station. When from there it traversed Great Western Road there was a rising gradient of 1 in 80 to Botanic Gardens station. Here the station was actually under the Gardens, but the buildings, the booking office and waiting room were above ground beside the main entrance to the Gardens. The work of the architect James Miller, the buildings were described in 1896 as 'furnished with gilded domes – in the Old English style of architecture'.

For a long time after the closure of the line part of the Botanic Gardens station building was used as a cafe much visited by young people. It was destroyed by fire in 1970.

A tunnel of 220 yards – in which a royal train of King George V is said to have hidden overnight in the First World War – took the railway under the Botanic Gardens before emerging at the approach to Kirklee station, a station whose elegance and almost rural charm was still just discernible under the layer of decay, rubble and destruction which had afflicted it since closure. After Kirklee the line divided, one line swinging west to Dawsholm the other going forward to Maryhill.

The attractiveness of station buildings failed to compensate passengers for the discomforts of travel behind a steam locomotive through narrow tunnels. On the underground systems in Glasgow of both the Caledonian and North British Railways Mr. Hamilton Ellis once wrote, 'Of these fuming burrows, the less said the better. Unelectrified, they have grown old in sin.' Since then the N.B. line has been redeemed by electrification and become part of the successful 'Blue Train' system.

Lacking electrification, which would have been a boon to a city increasingly strangled by surface traffic, the Central line lingered and died. Its passengers were easily diverted, first to the trams, then the motor buses, and then the irresistible private motor car. Botanic Gardens and Kirklee stations closed in 1939,

John MacKay 1972

Caledonian Railway Locomotive No. 419

This 0–4–4 tank engine was built at St. Rollox in 1907 to the design of J. F. McIntosh. It is virtually the same type as the engines designed for work on the underground lines of the C.R. suburban system in Glasgow (the Central Low Level lines which ran through Hillhead, etc.), except that those for the underground services had condensing equipment, and were distinguishable by a waste steam pipe running from the smoke box back to the water tank. This engine is now in the possession of the Scottish Railway Preservation Society, and is frequently worked 'in steam' at their Falkirk depot.

Gibson Street Bridge. Horse covers place at gable-end of tenement where covered footway sloped to Kelvinbridge Station. *1963**

Back view of Kirklee Railway Station, opposite pathway to 'Halfpenny' Bridge in Botanic Gardens. *August 1967**

tunnel right under Hillhead on the line of Glasgow Street – reaching there the greatest depth of the system: 155 feet below street level – before curving south to the station in Byres Road. Kelvinbridge is one of the widest stations on the line; Hillhead with a platform length of only 82 feet, the shortest.

A hoist installed to take passengers from Kelvinbridge station up to Great Western Road was disused for many years, but has now been renewed, and again only one flight of steps, up to the level of South Woodside Road, has to be climbed to reach the main road.

The carriages on the Subway, which are worked as two-coach trains, are the same rolling stock as was used from the opening of the service. Twenty of them were supplied in 1896, 10 in 1897, 24 in 1898 and the remaining six between 1901 and 1913. Since they were adapted from cable operation to d.c. electric traction each train has a motor coach instead of a 'gripper' coach. The lighting and comfort have been improved, and the coaches are kept in smart condition, but they remain the oldest rolling stock in the world on a city underground electric railway – and among the most efficient.

From its opening the Subway prospered until, like the other suburban railways of Glasgow, it suffered the blasts of competition from the electrified tramways. It recovered, however, to reach a peak of popularity after the Second World War.

Nearly 20,000,000 passengers were carried by the line in 1969, and in the year ended November 1970 1,280,190 passengers bought tickets at Hillhead station and ordinary passengers bought 941,413 tickets at Kelvinbridge station.

The station at Kelvinbridge provides an additional facility intended to help reduce traffic congestion in the centre of the city. In November 1965 Glasgow Corporation started a 'Park and Ride' scheme based on Kelvinbridge station and the car park which had been established in the old goods yard. Motorists could leave their cars and for the price only of a parking fee make a return journey into town by Underground between Kelvinbridge and St. Enoch or intermediate stations.

In 1970 12,290 passengers paid 1s (5p) for two hours' parking at Kelvinbridge and a return journey to town, and 21,716 paid 2s (10p) for all-day parking and a similar return journey.

It now seems a great pity that Hillhead's two railways were not developed as hindsight shows was necessary for the city's wellbeing. The Subway might have been linked at Buchanan Street (and given an escalator there) and St. Enoch with an Eastern Circle as proposed in 1944. More important – and this still could and should happen – the Central Low Level line which served Kelvinbridge, Botanic Gardens and Kirklee should have been electrified as an urban 'metro', a rapid transit system running along Argyle Street, underground through the heart of the city, with interchange points. But that is a matter of importance and decision far beyond the boundaries of Hillhead.

L. V. BEHARRELL. 1971

on 6th February and 24th April respectively. Kelvinbridge survived until 4th August 1952, although goods traffic continued until the whole line closed on 5th October 1964, and Kelvinbridge goods yard later became a car park.

The Glasgow Subway started with the advantage of never having to run steam engines in its tunnels. This 4-feet gauge line, about six and a half miles long, with 15 stations on its circle, was worked by moving cables. This method of operation continued when the Subway was taken over by Glasgow Corporation on 12th June 1922, but the line was eventually electrified in 1935 when – in an attempt to improve the railway's "image" to match its new motive power – the name was changed to 'Underground'. Glasgow, of course, still calls it 'the Subway'.

Making the tunnels for the Subway also had its difficulties. Originally it was planned to take the line from Kelvinbridge station straight along to Botanic Gardens and then south under Byres Road, but that was not possible as the Central Railway had already obtained powers to tunnel under Great Western Road between Kelvinbridge and Botanic Gardens. The Subway, therefore, had to turn slightly south from Kelvinbridge and

Entrance of railway tunnel from Kelvinbridge to Kirklee. *1970**

Botanic Gardens Station of the Caledonian Railway Company, shortly after being opened.
'Architect', 20th June, 1904

CENTRAL LOW LEVEL RAILWAY

I have three personal recollections of this branch line of the Caledonian Railway Company.

The first is of the long covered footway that sloped down to Kelvinbridge Station when, in the sunshine of early childhood at the dreamily quiet corner of Park Road and Gibson Street, we used to run down this glazed wooden corridor with raised voices re-echoing from its spacious length until we saw a porter at the other end when we would scamper back. This convenient access beside the gable end of the tenement at the Eldon Street bridge, with Park entrance on the other side, must have been a busy place at the time of the 1901 and 1911 Exhibitions.

The second is seeing the stately chocolate-brown Daimler with the Royal Coat of Arms in front of its flat roof as King George Fifth and Queen Mary set out from Kirklee Station during their several days' visit to industrial Clydeside at the time of the Great War. At the end of each day the Royal train was backed into Botanic Gardens tunnel for the night. A military guard was provided by a detachment of the Glasgow Highlanders. Beautifully kept, with its cluster of uniquely designed red sandstone buildings, Kirklee Station was the pride of the Caledonian Railway Company. In 1971 the last vestige of it vanished after being cruelly vandalised since the closure of the line.

The third is of the early 1920s when I travelled regularly from Botanic Gardens Station to Central (Low Level). Occasionally beside the entrance at the loop siding used by the blue Oatlands tram whose terminus was then at Botanic Gardens a horse cab would draw up with passenger and luggage for a main line connection. While the outside of the station was rather pretty with its gilded domes the massive mahogany interior and black and white marble floor had little daylight. The soft royal blue upholstery of the first class carriages was pleasingly comfortable, once you got inside, but oh the coom you got on your hand from the big brass handle unless a porter was available to open the carriage door for you !

H.B.M.

Gate at luggage entrance to Kirklee Railway Station.
August 1967*

Vista between
No. 2 Hillhead Street and
Alfred Terrace Lane, looking
towards H.H.S. in Cecil Street.
January 1969*

> '*E'vn winter bleak has charms to me*
> *When winds rave thro' the naked tree.*'
>
> BURNS

Buckingham Terrace from Hillhead Street. Alfred Terrace on left.   *January 1969**

Great Western Road at Botanic Gardens and Byres Road. *February 1935. Daily Record*

THE
GLASGOW CONSERVATOIRE OF MUSIC,

10 HAMILTON PARK TERRACE, HILLHEAD.

Principals { Mr. GILBERT J. FERRIER.
{ Mr. W. LINDSAY LAMB.

LIST OF TEACHERS.

PIANOFORTE.
Mr. Gilbert J. Ferrier.
Mr. W. Lindsay Lamb.
Mr. David A. Harley, A.R.C.O.
Miss Catherine Young, L.R.A.M.

SOLO SINGING AND VOICE PRODUCTION.
Mr. Frank L. Bamford.
Mr. Walter Lewis, A.R.A.M.
Miss Elizabeth B. Mackay.
Miss Jessie L. Geddes.

VIOLIN.
Mr. Frederic Siegl (Vice-Leader of Scottish Orchestra).
Miss Emily Buchanan.
Miss Beatrice Taylor-Smith.

VIOLONCELLO.
Mr. Edwin Angless.

ORGAN.
Mr. David A. Harley, A.R.C.O. (Organist of Berkeley St. U.F. Church).
Mr. Geo. T. Pattman, F.R.C.O. (Organist of St. Mary's Cathedral).

HARMONIUM.
Mr. David A. Harley, A.R.C.O.

RUDIMENTS OF MUSIC.
Mr. Gilbert J. Ferrier.
Miss Annie A. Craig (Stillie Bursar).

HARMONY.
Mr. Gilbert J. Ferrier.
Miss Annie A. Craig (Stillie Bursar).

COUNTERPOINT, ETC., MUSICAL ANALYSIS and COMPOSITION.
Mr. Gilbert J. Ferrier.

ENSEMBLE AND CHAMBER MUSIC CLASSES.
The Principals, assisted by
Mr. Frederic Siegl.
Mr. Edwin Angless.

LADIES' CHOIR.
Mr. Frank L. Bamford.

SIGHT SINGING and EAR TRAINING CLASS.
Miss Jessie L. Geddes.

ELOCUTION.
Miss Millie R. Wilson.

MODERN LANGUAGES.
French—Mons. Hector Rey, B. es L., B. es Sc. (Licencie d'Anglais, Paris).
German—Herr Friedrich Broecker (Assistant in German at the Glasgow University).

JUNIOR DEPARTMENT.

PIANOFORTE.
Miss Annie A. Craig.
Miss Jessie H. Fraser, L.R.A.M.
Miss Margaret Hanson, L.R.A.M.
Miss Margaret Mackinlay, L.R.A.M.

PIANOFORTE.
Miss M. Leonora Mitchell, L.R.A.M.
Miss C. T. Paterson, L.R.A.M.

VIOLIN.
Miss Isobel Marshall, A.T.C.L.
Miss Bessie Templeton.

The NINTH SESSION Begins on MONDAY, SEPTEMBER 4th.

The PRINCIPALS will be in attendance from THURSDAY, 31st AUGUST, till SATURDAY, 2nd SEPTEMBER, both days inclusive, from 10 a.m. to 1 p.m., 2 p.m. to 6 p.m., and 8 p.m. to 9 p.m. for CONSULTATION and ENROLMENT.

Prospectuses may be had on application to the Principals; from Messrs. Paterson, Sons & Co., Buchanan Street; or from Mr. Bowman, Sauchiehall Street.

Advertisement in *The Bailie*
August 30th, 1911

A Little Memory . . .

42 Lilybank Gardens which later became the Hillhead Registrar's office was our family home when I was a boy in 1911. The houses were very quiet and orderly and had stone carriage steps. We had as neighbours the Rev. Dr. Morrison, Rev. Dr. Moffat, Rev. A. Boyd Scott, Professor Robert S. Rait, Professor Medley and Professor Rennie.

On the other side of the barrier wall at the end of the Gardens there was a steep brae between the wall and the unbuilt half of University Gardens, where the road round was roughly defined and enclosed by a light fence. From the grassy heights near Queen Margaret Hall to the sunken bare 'cricket pitch' was a considerable distance and ended at a very high wall flanking Ashton Lane. Here we sledged in winter and tore down in summer in our low four-wheeled daisy-carts which gave the ground its name of 'The Daisy.' At the foot for many years two huge tree trunks lay below the gable end of Lilybank Gardens. It is all transformed and built on now.

. . . and a Musical Note

I have a few undimmed recollections of the musical life of Hillhead much of which is associated with that greatly-loved man A. M. Henderson, Organist of Glasgow University. His own reminiscences are delightfully recorded in his book *Musical Memories*. His home was at 3 St. James's Place. He received his first lessons from the blind organist of Wellington Church, Mr. Fred Turner and had studied in Berlin under Eugen d'Albert. He had a special interest in the harpsichord and the spinet. My sister Joan Phyllis Dixon for whom he had a high regard as a pianist, quite often accompanied him in duets. On one occasion they gave a much appreciated concert in the Hillhead Burgh Hall of Elizabethan music using harpsichord, virginal, and spinet. Mr. Henderson amused me once in a curiously sudden manner in Great Western Road by exclaiming excitedly 'Oh John, I have had such a terrible experience; I have just had a tooth out.'

Gilbert J. Ferrier had the Glasgow Conservatoire of Music at 10 Hamilton Park Terrace. His wife was a poetess and a woman of great grace and friendliness. About 1920 I used to join a number of young people of my own age at the Ferriers' when we were given tea and then discussed many things. The company often included John Chappell Sprott, the Walkers and sometimes Mr. Pullein, organist of St. Mary's Cathedral.

J. L. DIXON, 1971

A. M. Henderson (1879–1957). Organist of the University of Glasgow, 1906–1954. His residence, latterly, was at 67 Southpark Avenue. *Stephens Orr*

Souvenir.
The Queen's Own Royal
Glasgow Yeomanry

Meeting of Burgh Boundaries;
Partick and Hillhead southwest
of University Gardens. (Building
demolished 1971.)
September 1968*

Edward Ellice Macdonald
Headmaster, 1885–1912

Hillhead High School, Cecil Street (now Primary School). Opened 1885. *Architects:* Hugh and David Barclay.

HILLHEAD HIGH SCHOOL

ERECTED for Govan Parish School Board, Hillhead Public School was opened on Monday, 13th April 1885, with Edward Ellice Macdonald as Headmaster.

An enrolment of two hundred pupils of all ages on the first forenoon, and three hundred more by the end of the term on 11th June, proved that the expanding burgh suburb had indeed required a School. As Hillhead's reputation grew, its numbers increased. By 1894, when it was recognised as a full Secondary School by Govan Parish School Board, who then began to refer to it as 'Hillhead High School,' the roll was 900. As a matter of interest we may note here that sixteen years later on it had risen to 1,260.

In 1904-05 came a major extension, when the northern wing on the Great Western Road side was added and the attics built up to complete a full top flat. It provided a good occasion for introducing electric lighting and this was done throughout the School.

In 1913, with the problems of accommodation still increasing, there came a threat from the Scotch Education Department that, unless their regulations about size of classes were observed, full grant would not be paid. The School Board had to act. Despite the outbreak of war in 1914, the Oakfield Avenue (it was then Wilson St.) site was secured by 1915 for a new Secondary School.

In April 1914, the Headmaster recommended to the Board that the proposed new School should be planned to provide twenty classrooms, six laboratories, three art rooms, assembly hall, gymnasia, swimming bath, library and study rooms, adequate staffrooms, and storage space for O.T.C. and Clubs. All work on the project was suspended during the war. In 1919 the Govan Parish School Board ceased to be; and its successor, Glasgow Education Authority, in turn gave place in 1929 to the Education Committee of Glasgow Corporation. Despite these changes, however, the task of providing the new School was never lost sight of. Messrs. Wylie, Shanks & Wylie won the competition for a suitable design, and were appointed architects in 1921. Building began in 1929, just before the Authority handed over to the Education Committee. The new School was officially opened on Tuesday, 15th September 1931. The building, estimated originally to cost £183,000, had in fact been put up for £75,000. The saving was mainly achieved by omitting the top storey and the swimming bath which had been part of the original plan.

At this point let us record, for our own and future generations, the names of the original Staff of our School. Here they are:

EDWARD E. MACDONALD, *Head Master*; MARGARET B. RUSSELL, *Head Mistress*; William Moffatt, *Second Master*;

Central elevation,
Hillhead High School,
Cecil Street.
*May 1961**

James Watson; Daniel Ferguson; David Stormont; Catherine Macnab; Catherine Leslie; Jane Blane; Alexander Galt, *Science*; James Allan, *Singing*; William Walker, *Janitor and Drill Instructor*.

Of those twelve, the last to leave was Miss Leslie, who retired in 1927. Others, though not members of the original Staff, deserve mention in the roll of our founders. Two of them – Miss Esther Wilson and Miss Anna Jackson – joined as senior pupils in 1885, and, after serving as pupil-teachers, went on to take, with honours, the only University degree open to women at the time – L.L.A. (Lady Literate in Arts) of St. Andrews. Thereafter, they spent their whole teaching lives in Hillhead.

Though the work done throughout the School was of fine quality, as results in open competitive examinations showed, it was the brilliant teaching given in the Modern Languages Department that first and most immediately brought Hillhead into the front rank of Scottish Schools. In the Department, Miss Sara H. MacPhail and Miss Esther Wilson (the legendary 'Hetty') were the execu-

tants; to direct and inspire, Macdonald brought to the School the two most eminent teachers of their race and time in Scotland, Dr. Louis Lubovius and M. Louis Janton. For many years, till they retired in the 1920's, they came among us, genial, cultured, skilful, making languages live; in the early days, as pioneers of such work, they set an unrivalled standard. As early as 1892 Hillhead pupils gained one-fifth of all the Honours Grade Leaving Certificates in Modern Languages awarded in Scotland.

One more person inevitably claims an honoured place among our founders. The janitor, Colour-Sergeant William Walker, late The Northumberland Fusiliers, was a pioneer in the teaching of physical education. Without a gymnasium, he taught drill to every class in the School.

Walker was drill instructor to the Cadet Corps and O.T.C.: no Inspecting Officer ever failed to report favourably on the standard of the unit's drill. He was sole janitor, too, during his thirty-five years' service in the

Great Western Road, Hillhead. Sunday in August, 1968. (Compare with similar view in 1890.)   *

Standard Three, Girls, Hillhead High School, with Class Teacher Miss Paterson. Session 1911–12.   *Wohlgemuth & Co.*

School – and such a janitor that in 1897 H.M.I. could report with approbation upon 'the quite remarkable state of preservation of the buildings and furnishings' after twelve years' use. He exercised a unique formative influence on every pupil, and took a major share in maintaining the tone and discipline of the School. All who knew him remember him well; nature seems to have broken the mould in which such men were fashioned. He died in 1919.

Macdonald chose as the School motto that of the Burgh of Hillhead, originally from the arms of the House of Orange – 'Je Maintiendrai.' In his own time and in the years since, the School has lived up to it. We have noted the early successes. In the oldest-dated prospectus of which the School retains a copy are listed 62 University distinctions gained by F.P.s in 1906, excluding degree passes; a Bellahouston Gold Medal, a Research Fellowship, an M.D. with honours, and seven medals or first prizes are among them. In 1912, just before his untimely death while bathing at Cullen, Macdonald had the satisfaction of seeing James Schoenfeld's name first on the Bursary list. Since then, four Snell Exhibitions, two Herkless Prizes, a Brunton Memorial Prize, and a Ferguson Scholarship have been won by students from the School. Only from a solid, ever-tended foundation can such peaks arise.

To succeed Macdonald came Mr. Duncan MacGillivray, translated from the Rector's chair in Bellahouston Academy. Vital, vigorous, downright, explosively intolerant of slackness or deceit, 'jovial and royal with his equals, but to the poorest student gentle and attentive' – one could write for long enough and achieve no more than a faint outline of this great man's personality. His eye missed nothing except what his innate kindness and sympathy made him decide not to see; but what lingers most in memory is his interest in people. He knew all his pupils and all about them; his prodigious memory of them in after life was a constant amazement and pleasure. His name and fame (he was an Islay man) attracted to the School many pupils from the Highlands and Islands – an infusion mutually beneficial.

For School and F.P.s alike, the struggle for success in Rugby was long and hard, but by 1914 (when on the outbreak of war Club Rugby was suspended) the F.P. side under Charles A. Hepburn were fit and ready for a full programme of first-class fixtures. The School, with Messrs. Buchanan and Jordan in charge, had longer to wait for real success, but when it came it was resounding.

Swimming in Church Street Baths was an integral part of the School curriculum, certificates being awarded for various degrees of proficiency. John Thomson and John Service have added lustre to the School records by swimming for Britain in the Olympic Games.

Hughenden, by the time it was opened in 1924 (under the Hillhead High School War Memorial Trust Ltd., which governs, and provides facilities for all School and Club athletic activity) cost £16,000; but its real price was the lives of the 179 Old Boys who died that we might be free to enjoy it. The ground was officially opened on Saturday, 24th May 1924, by Sir Charles Cleland, and dedicated by Dr. Smith.

Since Rugby began in the School in 1903-04, the Rugby Captain had been regarded by the boys as School

Duncan MacGillivray, Headmaster, 1912–28. *Annan*

Captain: there was no title of School Captain, nor were there any monitors. Boys exercised authority only in limited spheres – as team captains, as N.C.O.s in the Corps, or in the discharge of specific duties allocated by Mr. MacGillivray. In 1919, however, he introduced a system, not of Prefects – he didn't like that name – but of Ephors. Eight boys were drawn, some by election and some by appointment, from the three senior forms – this was to preserve continuity.

About this time a picture in the Magazine showed Hilda Rosser, Marjorie Langmuir and Margaret McEwan, who were all semi-finalists in the West of Scotland Girls' Singles Tennis Championships in 1920. In the final, Hilda beat Marjorie. Margaret became Scotland's first woman architect, and had a share in drawing up the plans of the new School. In the same class was Vera Findlay, later Scotland's first woman minister. Hilda went back to South Africa; Marjorie returned to teach in School, and to create a record that may never be equalled by representing Scotland a total of fifty times in three sports – hockey, tennis and badminton. She captained the only Scottish Hockey side ever to beat England in England.

The School Orchestra was founded by Mr. Douglas Berry, of the English Department, in 1923. Its members – pupils, Staff, and on occasion friends – came in, at various levels of proficiency, for the love of music and the

HILLHEAD HIGH SCHOOL OFFICERS' TRAINING CORPS, (1917–1918)

Centre group from left:

2nd Lieut. J. W. Jordan (*mufti*), Capt. S. R. Skilling, Dr. MacGillivray, 2nd Lieut. C. M. Macdonald (*mufti*),
Sergeant Instructor Wm. Walker.

Sandyford Studio

Photo by Mr. Steele

HILLHEAD HIGH SCHOOL F.P. RUGBY 1st XV, 1933–34
Joint-Champions with Royal High School F.P.

Played 28.   Won 24.   Lost 4.   Points for, 632.   Against 189.

Standing, left to right — W. A. Mackinnon (*Hon. Secy.*); J. L. Cotter*; W. A. Ross*; D. McGregor; J. H. Levack;
H. Mackinlay; R. A. Hamilton; W. S. Macleod.
Sitting, left to right — W. C. W. Murdoch*; B. O. Dias; J. D. Niven; J. S. Thomson; E. A. Young (*Captain*); A. Ross;
I. E. Wilkie; E. W. Walls; A. Grierson.
Insets — I. E. Dawson (*left*) and R. M. Murdoch.

*Internationalists.

joy of making it. From squeaky infancy through tuneful youth, and despite temporary extinction during and after the 1939-45 war, it has expanded, and developed, now under Mr. McKendrick, Head of the Music Department, into a very fine combination indeed.

Choral singing and dramatics by pupils of all ages have long formed a feature of Hillhead concerts; the eyes of the elderly still light up with joy at the recollection of Miss Dick's infants battling it out as Tweedledum and Tweedledee. Miss Margaret Lochhead's French and German choirs led the way in broadcasting. The Dramatic Club has organised the previously sporadic production of plays, and have some fine work to their credit. Apart from those – and they are many – who have achieved distinction on the amateur stage, some of our former players, like Gordon Jackson and James McKechnie, have gone on to fame.

Inexorably the day came when Dr. MacGillivray had to demit office. He retired in a blaze of glory. Honours and thanks were showered upon him. The School hall was never so small as on that day, 16th February 1928, when he took farewell of his pupils.

The retiral in 1960 of Mr. William A. McNeill, Depute Headmaster and Head of the History Department, was a milestone in the Hillhead story. He served us longer than any other man ever on the Staff. William Walker not excepted – thirty-five full years. Upright and downright too, he exercised a profound influence on the general life of the School and on the development of generations of pupils, the latter by his scholarly teaching and human interest in individuals, the former by the diversity and tirelessness of his extra-classroom work. We rejoiced to hear that he had been honoured in his own scholastic country; in 1956, the Royal Historical Society awarded him the David Berry Medal and Prize for the most meritorious essay on a Scottish historical subject. Later, his University of Glasgow appointed him to a Senior Research Scholarship in Scottish Studies.

ALASTAIR D. CAMPBELL
from his compact handbook, *Hillhead High School, 1885–1961*

Hillhead High School (secondary), Oakfield Avenue. Opened 15th September, 1931. *Architects:* Wylie, Shanks & Wylie. *June 1970**

HEADMASTERS

HILLHEAD HIGH SCHOOL

Edward Ellice Macdonald	1885–1912
Duncan MacGillivray	1912–1928
Frank Beaumont	1928–1937
William J. Merry	1937–1949
James Paterson	1949–1959
Robert Q. Ferguson	1959–1965
Walter E. Wyatt	1965–1971
J. McCormick	1971–

HILLHEAD PRIMARY SCHOOL

J. B. Stewart	1945–1953
Oliver Barr	1953–1961
J. A. N. Morrison	1962–1970
G. Macintyre	1970–1971
J. Hamilton	1971–

(minus degrees, honours and decorations to avoid incompletions)

NOTABLE FORMER PUPILS OF HILLHEAD HIGH SCHOOL

include

E. Rosslyn Mitchell, lawyer, M.P. and distinguished orator; Robert W. Service, poet and novelist, 'The Canadian Kipling'; Lord Fleck, Chairman of I.C.I. and President of the British Association; Charles A. Hepburn, Scotch whisky proprietor, sportsman and benefactor; Walter Owen, Buenos Aires businessman, poet and interpreter of Hispanic epic poetry; Gilbert Highet, Professor of Latin, Columbia University; Sir John Rennie, Governor of Mauritius; Donald Inskip, Vice-Principal, University of Capetown; Sir Charles H. Wilson, Principal, University of Glasgow; Ian Sadler, expert mimic (ITMA); Alistair MacLean, best-selling novelist; Stanley Baxter, comedian and versatile actor; Ian McColl, Editor of the *Daily Express*, London; Professor A. J. Haddow, Administrative Dean of the Faculty of Medicine, University of Glasgow; Alastair Dunnett, Editor of *The Scotsman*; Clive Sandground, Editor of the *Scottish Daily Express*; William S. Gray, Lord Provost of Glasgow (1972–).

Oakfield Avenue (Wilson Street) showing terrace designed by 'Greek' Thomson, 1865. *January 1959**

Vinicombe Street. (Hillhead Picture Salon on left at Cranworth Street.) *1968**

HILLHEAD PICTURE SALON

Hillhead Picture Salon was built in 1912 by a private company. The site had been occupied previously by the low wooden buildings and yard of James Nicol, joiner and jobbing builder. The Salon was very stylish and rather grand in the newness of its first few years. In the foyer heavy curtains in rich mauve velvet added to the opulence and enhanced the allure of the mystery beyond. It was the time when the cinematograph portrayed a world of romance and adventure entirely apart from harsh reality. The doorman in military tailored uniform of light brown with gold braid, was a commanding figure with a waxed moustache. Herr Wilhelm Iff, a tubby little man who lived in Cranworth Street was the maestro of the orchestra. In his earlier days he was orchestral leader in the old Gaiety before it became the Empire Music Hall.

A remembered feature of the Salon's first few years is the proffered free tea and biscuits on small round trays, during the afternoon performance. In the Great War years a special attraction was the first American Jazz Band to visit Glasgow. It had a negro singer and one of his songs was 'My Curly-Headed Baby'. In the 1920s the Salon's regular patrons were sure of a personal greeting from the ever cheery, ever smiling Donald the doorman of that era. During elections Sir Robert Horne, Hillhead's popular M.P. from 1918 to 1937, always arranged to speak for a few minutes in the evenings.

In the challenging times for cinemas after the Second World War, the survival of the Salon was due to the Booth family who held out bravely until 1969 when Fyfe & Fyfe came from Partick and like two fairies waving a magic wand transformed the Salon into the most comfortable and up-to-date cinema in Scotland. In April 1970 the Salon re-opened with 'The Sound of Music'.

' Nearly time for the big picture.'
Courtesy of Mrs. Wood (Miss Booth)

THE WESTERN BATHS

WESTERN BATHS *(Quiz)*

This was not an inauguration, only a re-opening (1886). A chill October evening outside; lots of people crowded on the banks of the pond and in the galleries above making it a warm evening within; plenty of fun in watching the expert swimmers, good music conducted by Mr. Cole, and a little dance to follow. *A. S. Boyd 'Twym'*

THE Western Baths, Hillhead, had a musical evening on this night week, at which between 600 and 700 members and friends were present. The large pond, which is about 100 ft. long, was emptied and nicely laid out at the bottom with rugs, chairs, couches and afternoon tea tables. Among the gentlemen who contributed to the entertainment were Messrs. Barker (harp), Anderson (conjuring), Baynham and Brown (elocutionists), Foulds, Newton, Master Hill and a number of other gentlemen, whose efforts were very successful.

The directors of the Baths had arranged with Mr. Assafrey, of St. Vincent Street, to attend to the wants of the members, and altogether a very pleasant evening was spent.

The Bailie for Wednesday, February 13th 1889

Cranworth House. *August 1968**

In the period of 1910–1920 Cranworth House was the residence of George Henry Martin, Musical Director, Odeon Operatic Society; Conductor, La Scala; composer of 'The Song of Glasgow', etc.

For some years it was used for Dances and Receptions. In 1965 it was acquired as offices for Radio Scotland, a popular 'Pirate' broadcasting service transmitted from a former lightship moored off Troon. It ceased in August 1967 when its legal loop-hole was closed. Radio Scotland was promoted and run by Mr. Thomas Shields an enterprising advertising agent and former journalist. He died at the age of 47 in March 1968.

The Western Baths. Promoted by several local gentlemen and built in 1876. The photograph was taken about 1895, a few years before the red sandstone tenements were erected. *Annan*

Western Baths. Side view of entrance. *1969**

THESE well-known Baths in Cranworth Street, Hillhead have long been a flourishing institution, and were thronged with school boys after school hours.

In those days before the First World War the bathmaster was a Mr. Murray, a fine man, but afflicted with a cleft palate which gave to his speech a certain weirdness.

Once a year the Glasgow Academy held their annual swimming competition in the Baths. One of the popular items was life-saving. Mr. Murray in a blue bathing costume dived majestically in at the deep end and seized the outlet grating at the bottom of the pond. He was duly rescued and towed to safety at the deep end steps, by each competitor. On one occasion a member of the well-known Galbraith family, who had just learned to swim, rashly entered for this event. Mr. Murray had dived and was seen waiting to be duly rescued at the bottom of the pond. Young Galbraith dived but found the depth too much for him. Amid cheers and laughter he gave up leaving the bathmaster slowly asphyxiating beneath the waters. He finally emerged in no very good mood, black in the face and gasping for breath.

J. GIBSON GRAHAM, 1970

As Alison F. Blood said in her *Kelvinside Days* written during the 1920s in Ceylon when her thoughts strayed back to when she was Miss Anderson of Kelvinside.

'There were, of course, other baths in Glasgow, but when we said "The Baths" we meant "The Western Baths", and never supposed that anyone could think otherwise.'

HILLHEAD BAPTIST CHURCH

Dr. J. T. Forbes

MINISTERS

Rev. F. H. Robarts, M.A.	1883–1901
Rev. J. T. Forbes, D.D.	1901–1929
Rev. John MacBeath, M.A., D.D.	1929–1944
Rev. Guy Ramsay, M.A., D.D.	1944–1961
Rev. W. R. Martin, M.A.	1961–1969
Rev. T. Kerr Spiers, B.D.	1969–

THE promotion of Hillhead Baptist Church was the group idea of five members of Adelaide Place Baptist Church, when ninety years ago, there was no systematic method of church extension. In the whole Western section of Glasgow there was no Baptist Church.

On 6th December 1882, the first meeting of the promoters was held in Marston, the home of Mr. Macdiarmid, to discuss the matter. The subject was even then so far mature that it was decided to establish a church in Hillhead, the step to be taken with the utmost goodwill towards the church which those named were leaving.

The initial negotiations were carried through with eager precision and promptitude. It was decided that a site should be procured in the neighbourhood of Byres Road, and that the Rev. Frederick Hall Robarts of Richmond Chapel, Liverpool, should be invited to undertake the charge of the new movement.

Various difficulties arose which caused considerable delay, and ultimately the Hillhead Burgh Hall was engaged for six months for the conduct of religious services on Sundays and on Wednesday evenings. A prayer meeting was held on the evening of Saturday, 1st September 1883. On the following day the first services of the new congregation were held. Mr. Robarts preached in the morning. The Rev. William Pulsford, D.D., preached in the afternoon, and in the evening the Rev. William Landels, D.D., of Edinburgh, preached.

On 19th September 1883, the church was formally constituted with twenty-one members representing eleven different families. Mr. Charles A. Rose was appointed Treasurer of the church, and Mr. William Tulloch was appointed Secretary.

Services continued in the Burgh Hall until September 1884, by which time the church hall in Elliot Street was ready for worship, and the congregation entered into occupancy of its own premises. Progress was also made with the building of the church on the adjoining ground, and on 3rd May 1885, the church itself, was opened for worship.

During the early years of the church the Sunday School was one of the most prosperous and influential in the west of Glasgow. Its most notable period was during the reign of Mr. J. W. Arthur as Superintendent. It is right to speak of his 'reign'; he was a king in the realm of childhood and youth.

Following the passing of Mr. Robarts in July 1901, the Rev. J. T. Forbes, minister of Dublin Street church, Edinburgh, accepted an invitation to be successor to Mr. Robarts and entered upon his ministry in Hillhead on 3rd November 1901. Within the twenty-seven years of his ministry Dr. Forbes received 1,017 into church membership, an average of almost thirty-eight per year. His ministry was strong and vigorous on the intellectual side, united to intense moral earnestness and spiritual power.

Hillhead
Baptist Church.
Architect:
T. L. Watson,
1885.
March 1970*

Florentine Terrace on left, forming block with Nos. 1 and 2 Florentine Place (87 and 89 Gibson Street)

MY HILLHEAD

HENRY BROUGHAM MORTON

Edwardian days

'Edwardian days' is a slightly revised article from Milden Miscellany, *a pocket magazine I produced during the post-war period of my service as a War Reserve Police constable in Milngavie.*

Two years after the ending of the South African War the dawn of my world took place. The tower of the University loomed, a few hundred yards away, across the crown of University Avenue. Between the strident strikings of the great bell at the hour, the lighter quarter and half-hour reminders emphasised the hush of the cathedral city setting which ensued around the rural end of Ann Street where the Grecian (or Romanesque) pile of Wellington Church agreed in principle with the massive Gothic spread on Gilmorehill.

From that fragrant early world at the top of Gibson Street, in the very heart of Hillhead, where the lush foliage of ancient trees clustered and drooped above the buttressed red brick garden wall enclosing, down Ann Street, the policies of Hillhead House backed by Florentine Lane; out of their timeless record that is mine, sights and sounds come clearly again as I summon up remembrance of things past.

Opposite are the trim trees that line the lawn of Wellington Church from its side entrance to the Avenue. Up past Florentine Terrace and across Gibson Street, Southpark House on its high elevation and spacious garden with its tall sentinel trees confronts, with dignified restraint, the modest elegance of St. John's Terrace. Further along the clean empty stretch of Ann Street, towards Great Western Road, between Southpark Terrace and Wilson Street and below the thorn hedge in Ann Street, the old villas nestle in their cosy gardens while still preserving an air of being country retreats afar from Glasgow.

Apart from the rustle of leaves under a quiet sky that knows only the delicate sweep of feathered wings, few are the sounds to be heard. Between long intervals perhaps the creak of cart wheels and the measured slap of a Clydesdale gelding straining in the shafts, or the whirr of a private brougham accompanied by the staccato dig of hoofs on gritty road metal. On occasion, surface renewal brings the crunch of a steam road roller with its bell-like ping from the rumbling front cylinder as it races its flywheel and sends cotton wool bursts of steam tut-tutting from its long brass-topped funnel.

Those Hillhead days of the mid-Edwardian era I remember as dusty days of slow time. Where the open top Pollokshields white tram waited at its terminus near the gates, a four-wheeler or a hansom cab would turn out of the West-End Park and another would follow at a lazy trot. When they were abreast the drivers would let the reins hang loosely and sit back and chat while the horses leant heads downward in their unhurried ascent of University Avenue.

The memory of those cabs appearing on the hill at intervals (returning to stables in Ashton Lane) is among the first memory snapshots I have of life. The first one that flashes back is when I was a toddler of two in 1906. It is always the same one. On the pavement beside the grass plot outside the small tenement where I was born is a pram. It is a brown wicker pram. A plain shallow thing on high wheels standing at the top of Gibson Street. It is empty, for it is mine, and I am looking at it from across the street which is not broad and almost unknown to large vehicles because of the steep ascent from any point in the district.

This steadily fixed recollection is like the not too clear

North British Railway Company's P.S. *Kenilworth* from Craigendoran leaving Innellan for Rothesay. *Summer 1913. Stromier Vogt Collection*

but exciting realism of seeing a momentary scene in an old news film that has been re-issued many years later as a curiosity or a kind of paradoxical novelty that can be repeated over and over again at will.

The windows of our dining-room are on the grass plot level, for we lived in 'the close', and I know if I were to look through I should see a glass dish of beetroot on a white cloth half covering the crimson baize on the dining-room table.

There were only two floors above us in this small building which, with the one adjoining still gloried in its original name of Florentine Place. In this it was supported by the adjoining Florentine Terrace and Lane around the corner. What a variety of small excitements it holds there for me. Little trivialities of the golden age of life. Even the childish nightmares have their fond place. I can still remember the fearful faces that haunted me in dark corners of the house, or when I was left alone at night after being taken to the Art Galleries where I had been nearly frightened out of my skin by the reaction of my sensitive imagination to the sight of the fiendish masks of ancient Japanese warriors on dummy figures, which were, of course, to me, the real thing and would get out of their cases as soon as I passed and follow me home. How harmless are the horrors of the simple honest! The happy ending is always theirs.

Exit the pram and enter the one-man band. The descendant of the wandering minstrel and the court jester, he belonged to the coloured plates of knights and princesses and dragons and dungeons, and perhaps he knew the Pied Piper, for he seemed to appear from nowhere and to depart as magically. I see him from the same standpoint across the street. He is standing in the gutter or the syver as we called it. His jacket and trousers are of a light blue material with red piping. His stiff cap is high and conical and very similar to the tall shako which the postmen wore then. It is surmounted by a bell on a band spring. When it is required he nods his head. On his back is a fairly large drum with cymbals atop. By some mysterious device a cord controls them from his heel. A jerk of the foot and the cymbals

clash and the drum bangs. Affixed in front of his mouth is a set of pipes slanting from short to long and, finally, between his hands is a concertina. I remember him clearly, for I never saw him again, and his like I have never seen since.

Following this vivid memory a series of miniatures come pell-mell. I see a wide flowing dress of light brown, a narrow waist and a small body above it in front of the piano which is being played. All I know is that she is Mrs. Wix, a friend of my mother, and that she visits us occasionally and plays the piano, and that I like her. I am always waiting for her to turn around for I can never remember her face, although I somehow think of it as a pleasant small wizened countenance that her name did not exactly suggest. High up above my head my father is lighting a raw gas jet in the lobby. My mother and sister stand by with me in the dark, for we have all just come in. The hour is probably about nine at night: a late hour for us to be out, even as a family. As the gas flickers up like a yellow jewel against black velvet the delicious smell of dinner and salt sea air is still in my nostrils and my mother is still holding me up among a lot of people near a funnel, the whole of which is steadily moving with water all round us towards a lot of other people bustling about on thick wood in front of some tenements which, somehow, in my childish mind, I cannot reconcile with the altogether strange scene. Actually we had been to Rothesay for the day and had sailed all the way in the *Edinburgh Castle* from the Broomielaw and back. More than sixty years have come and gone since then and much has been shattered and lost. But the full bouquet of that heavenly smell of dinner remains, for it epitomises the plain sincere kindliness my young life knew in that period.

Cowboys and Indians are walking beside a hansom-cab in a procession of high excitement that is turning into University Avenue from the foot of Gibson Street. Jingling money boxes pause and pass beside the crowd of eager sightseers lining the pavements. It is my first glimpse of the students' fancy dress parade for the hospitals. Old Mr. Crawford, the joiner with the grey beard, has got into our garden and is doing something to our window. His dirty white pouch formed by a swathe of cloth around his coatless middle fascinates me. I am aware of my mother standing uneasily beside the railings. It may have been in later years it was explained to me, but I know in the memory of it that she has left the house key indoors and locked herself out.

A square wooden house on wheels has arrived at the close. I feel rather proud of the big horse munching its chop, for it is there because of us. And that includes me. It has been released from the shafts and is turned round and is waiting in the contented way of its kind. Mother is walking smartly out to speak to the men. The long feathers of her pheasant hat nod jerkily. The smell of straw, canvas and a furniture shop has been boxed up with our furniture. I am toddling beside the fine horse that has pulled our things into the roadway between Bute Mansions and Strathmore Gardens. The creaking van is bound for over the hill. Alone with that horse I am walking into another world.

It is the end of chapter one for me.

At H.H.S.

We had moved over the hill to the top corner flat at 14 Kersland Street. It was another world but it was still Hillhead and my increasing perception soon encompassed the old with the new. We had an additional room occupied by a lodger, usually a medical student or doctor (probably connected with my father being Secretary of the Western Medical School).

This financial aid to our household needs coincided with my being taken one day, up Kersland Lane to a great cliff of a building called Hillhead High School where I was presented to the infants' headmistress who called me darling and took me in hand. I was installed beside a little girl in a white muslin dress with a pink sash. She fidgeted a bit but said nothing. The wooden framed slates on which we were learning to form hooks and eyes with slate pencils when not in use were kept in slots at the back of the desks. This necessarily large class-room with one door leading to the main hall and headmaster's room and the other at the far side giving access to the cloakroom and playground is viewed in memory sixty years later; yet I still see rotund little Miss Ritchie smiling, coaxing, mothering and guiding us to do what we were told, along with Miss Boyd of the golden hair and altogether lovely personality. During that session a bright, plump young woman of similar stature came as assistant to Miss Ritchie. The new arrival's name was Miss Dick. I received individual attention from her once by way of a jet of water she squirted at me from a handbasin she was using when I entered the cloakroom when the school was skailing.

The boy I remember in this class was never in it; at least, not within my ken. How many times it happened I do not know but I can recall two of the occasions when his father opened the door and thrust him in, when, as soon as he saw us, he got the wind up and, before the door could be closed, slipped from his parent's grasp and disappeared. Perhaps he is now a professor in a distant university. I remember his name but I am not telling. While still in the infants' I had the experience of being escorted to see the headmaster, Mr. Macdonald. The occasion arose from my chalking the blue serge back of a little girl when going home down Kersland Lane. At the headmaster's room some remarks passed high above my head and, gravely, he gazed down upon me. I was taken back to the classroom and isolated on a front seat where I was told to 'stay there for the present'. But, of course, the present never came. Soon high summer was with us and a pile of prizes appeared. I was given one and so was everyone else. The fib attached to mine was 'General Excellence'. It was called 'In the Gypsies Van' and had a pretty coloured frontispiece of a horse-drawn caravan beside an encampment.

From the drowsy hamlet of Row on the Gareloch where lay the old Trafalgar veteran, the *Empress* training ship, we had returned from our summer holidays of 1912 to find the news on everybody's lips of the tragic death of Mr. Macdonald while bathing on holiday at Cullen. The burial was at Cathcart and my mother took me. Along with a detachment of the kilted cadet corps in their scarlet tunics with yellow facings, we crowded on to a yellow tramcar at Botanic Gardens Station. On the sloping ground amid the verdure of summer, I glimpsed freshly piled reddish brown earth through a break in the crowd and polished wood and glinting brass descending. But what I particularly remember when the obsequies had been concluded, was the band breaking into a gay tune as it marched away in quick time.

Miss Jessie Wilson, bright and spry and very neat in her tailored navy blue skirt and white silk blouse, made suitable reference to the tragedy when we re-assembled in Standard One before going on to Standard Two and pert but thorough Miss Leslie with her hair in a bun on top. Next year when we got into Miss Macdonald's Standard Three class further along the passage she seemed slender and taller than Miss Leslie. Miss Macdonald could be quite nippy. One morning, during the first lesson, the head of the boy in front of me suddenly lolled back on to my desk and, from his wide

John Jones who, for over 30 years with his brother Henry appeared regularly in the residential streets of Hillhead with their Punch and Judy Show. In his last years he strolled alone, occasionally being greeted by a grown-up patron of the past. He died in 1960 aged about 68. *1957**

open mouth loud snores usurped our attention until Miss Macdonald asked him if he was catching flies when a spontaneous burst of laughter woke him up. But it was no joke to poor Robert. His family kept a dairy and, hours before any of us, he had been up and out in the dark with clattering cans to deliver milk to half of Hillhead.

Rumours of the inspector from the Govan Parish School Board visiting the school kept us on our toes. The next morning Miss Macdonald told us he might be looking in and, sure enough, he did. The door opened suddenly and in swept Mr. McGillivray followed by a patriarchal figure with wisps of white hair fringing a pink pate and a face like Moses. It was Mr. Wallace, Bible Inspector of the Govan Parish School Board. Stepping forward he thrust his long grave countenance at us while his eyes stared at the great beyond in the direction of Kersland Lane. 'And what did Samson say'? he breathed from a throat that had long lost its resonance and, before we could hazard a guess, turned, bade Miss Macdonald good morning and vanished quicker than he appeared.

Wartime schooldays

That summer I was kicking my feet through the grass verge of the shore road at Innellan when a woman came out from the opening to our house and told me to come back at once as my father had decided we should all return to Glasgow as soon as possible. It was Wednesday, 5th August 1914. When we left to follow our two tin boxes and gladstone bag being trundled to the nearby pier, the morning sunshine had gone and a leaden look had come over the Firth. The wind had whipped up the greying sea and, through the veil of mist and spume I had espied the darting sleek shapes of destroyers in mid channel. With the slapping and thumping of the paddles creaming the wake of the *Kenilworth* as the pier receded, and rumours of a spy being caught near the fort, and sugar going up from a penny-threefarthings to sixpence a pound, we headed for Craigendoran, Partick and a Henderson's cab home.

My first memory of the school in wartime is of Mr. McIlwaine clearing out his desk and tossing various odd items to anyone offering to catch. I got a nice-looking thin red box that had once contained a Swan fountain pen. Mr McIlwaine was Captain of the O.T.C. and we had a very brief acquaintance of him as class teacher of Standard Four for, with the call to arms, he and his senior, Major McLean, soon departed to aid the formation and training of the H.L.I.'s new battalions. Gone for ever was the sight of Mr. McIlwaine's straw hat (boater or strawbasher) topping his broad-shouldered beefy figure dressed in a blue pin-stripe suit as he stepped out along the top of Cecil Street at dinner-time. I knew nothing of him as a teacher as he had no time to get to know us when we began our new session in his class. A year or so later the school got word of the approximate time when his battalion would be passing along Great Western Road on its return from a route march and we were all allowed out to cheer him as he rode past between the leading companies headed by a silver band playing 'Colonel Bogey' and the soldiers shouting 'hip hip' to our 'hoorays'.

But in that class of 1914 a great metamorphosis took place in our lives. We entered a world of happy wonder and fascinating discovery remote from war. This magic opening of our eyes to things of timeless adoration and tranquillity came to pass with the coming of a young man by name of J. Harrison Maxwell. He wasn't our teacher; he was our leader. The innovations he introduced were revolutionary by prevailing standards. We had an aquarium, a private library, competitions for a book prize, visits to museums in winter and rambles beyond Killermont tramcar terminus in the summer. In the baths of Church Street School, to which we marched down University Avenue with our rolled towels under our oxters, he would join us in the water and give heart and instruction to the timid.

Returning one Saturday from an outing in the Bardowie region beyond Summerston, I had come round by the old Queen Margaret Bridge to find the crossroads at Botanic Gardens strangely quiet and empty. The scene has been for ever impressed in my mind. A silence in which time seemed to stand still pervaded the whole crossing. As I stood at the kerb on the edge of the great emptiness and glanced west I beheld, abreast of Botanic Gardens Station, in the glimmering dusk, at the halt and quiet as the grave, a great host of men in dark dress and in martial order stretching into the distant rise to Kirklee. When I got home I was told it was 'Uncle David's Regiment', that they had been in billets in Troon where they acquired the name of 'The Featherbeds' and had been fitted out temporarily in navy blue uniforms because of a shortage of khaki.

In 1915, moving across Cecil Street to the former house known to us as the Annexe we returned to rigorous discipline, tinged by the biting sarcasm peculiar to Mr. Boag, especially first thing every Wednesday morning when he usually managed to get most of us lined-up for the strap if we didn't answer quickly enough to snap questions in French. He was a little dark man with sallow well-chiselled features and a quick pouncing look in his eye. Perhaps he considered his extra-exacting manner very necessary for we were now in Standard 5B; the fateful 'qualifying'. Downstairs was Class 'A' with Mr. MacAlister in charge. Florid of countenance he had a lean rugged face and prominent nose which he had a tendency to finger in a nervous involuntary manner when seated at his desk. Refugees had appeared in Glasgow and we got one; a tall lanky youth from Belgium dressed in pantaloons, black stockings, a blowsy kind of light blue jacket and a big bulging cap. Later, when their numbers warranted it, horse butchers' shops were opened in Glasgow to cater for their accustomed diet. It was in this former drawing-room in the 'Annexe' that Mr. Harrower, our visiting elocution teacher treated us to an example of his own virtuosity by enacting the roles of the aged Waterloo veteran, his niece and her soldier sweetheart in 'A Straggler of' 15' by Conan Doyle. It must have been his *piece de résistance* at that time for he mastered it well. He was old himself but had a trim martial neatness. In fact he looked like Lord Roberts. I can still hear his declaiming of the last words thundered out by the dying veteran as he re-lived the action which gained him the Victoria Cross. 'The Guards need powder! The Guards need powder! The Guards need powder! and by God, they shall have it!'

The following session of 1915–16 was a particularly memorable one for me. We were now in Louis Hamilton's class of Form 1B. Small, neat and efficient, he had a prominent tuft of delicate brown hair above his thinning temples. It was our second year of French and, through the circumstances of war, it brought us an exciting new experience in the person of a most polite and vivacious young Frenchwoman. Her attempts to pout her pretty lips to emphasise correct pronunciation were received more with derisive laughter than the attention she expected; and when she turned to the blackboard and revealed a large safety pin securing the back of her hobble skirt the merriment that ensued was, quite obviously, beyond her understanding. But we had to beware of the silver-bearded tapering face of Mr. Fitzgerald having a look over the clear top of the partly

Hillhead from the University tower. The gable-end of 78 Southpark Avenue (6 Florentine Terrace) can be seen in centre. Hillhead House on left and Wellington Church on right. *1937 Annan*

Great George Street
from Byres Road.
*1966**

frosted glass door before entering to take over from Mademoiselle. Mr. Fitzgerald was a natural gentleman and the teaching of English was his natural forte. I delighted in it. English composition and drawing were the two subjects that absorbed my attention. One day he caught a boy out on the floor beside the blackboard and causing much laughter behind Mademoiselle's back. He told him to stay where he was and went to fetch a strap. Mustering his ingenuity, of which he had plenty, Marcus promptly placed a pencil on the floor where he was left standing and, on Mr. Fitzgerald's return, pointed to the pencil which he averred had rolled down from the desk and that he had come out to get it. Fitzgerald was not the type to question the veracity of the statement and so he accepted it. But Marcus's chief skill lay in his fisticuff prowess after school, when, in any of the nearby lanes he would fulfil any engagement arranged for him. Less than ten years later it was no surprise to learn of him as Seaman Dickson, Welter-Weight Boxing Champion of the Royal Navy, serving in H.M.S. *Hood*. Under Mr. Fitzgerald's orderly control we received from his conscientious teaching excellent tuition in English composition. I fairly warmed to it especially after he selected my attempt at essay writing and read it to the class.

The grimness of war touched us lightly. It was so far away and outside the scope of our interests and comprehension. Mr. Craik came round to read his latest letter from H.M.S. *Inconstant* which the school had adopted in providing comforts. Uniforms of the Army, Royal Navy and Royal Flying Corps appeared on the hill as former pupils ventured to call back, some even braving a confrontation with their former teacher before a classful of boys. Less than a year after leaving his class, the surprising appearance of strap-happy Mr. Boag as an officer of the Royal Scots Fusiliers was indeed a surprise. I was at a front desk when he ventured to visit us and I can still see him clearly, one foot on a drop seat, elbow on tartan-covered knee and chin cupped in hand as he addressed us with great earnestness and sincerity: but what he said I cannot recall. I never saw him again, but years later, I heard that he had forsaken scholastic teaching after the war and had become minister of a Dennistoun church.

Mr. Hamilton's class of those mid-war years undoubtedly stands clearest because of the memorable occasion exclusive to myself which took place then. It evolved from a very trivial incident. On my way home from school a boy had been cheeky to me at what he thought was a safe distance. I was fleet of foot then and suddenly made up on him, took his cap off, laid it on the pavement and departed. Apparently instead of picking it up he went home and told his mother that I had stolen it. When she called at our house and saw my father I was brought in and told of the accusation and explained what actually had happened which seemed to conclude the matter. A few days later when the classes were lined up after dinner, we were among those in the open playground. The senior boys were on our right flank in the outer shed (now walled up) and at their head Mr. Lapsley in charge of us all. We were about to march off when the small but mighty figure of Mr. McGillivray swept into sight from the nearby stair. Bristling with imperious power and making the most of his commanding look of leonine majesty he shattered the momentary silence he had created by calling for 'the boy Morton'. Nobody stirred but it suddenly dawned on me that he had called my name and, as no one else answered to it I stepped forth sheepishly to be stunned by the voice of Majuba (how did he get that name?) hounding me up to his room as he announced to all and sundry that he would deal with me for 'stealing boys' caps.' When he arrived busily recharging his anger to the desired pressure he ordered me into a small side room. It had a table with a centre drawer which he opened and withdrew a formidable-looking strap with thick black thongs, and forthwith proceeded to give me six of the best (three on each hand) which he did with great vigour and hustle while I was still stupefied. I cannot remember blubbering. Perhaps I was beyond it. The stinging pain was excruciating and my hands felt like great wads of burning hot thick rubber. When I got back to the class, Louis Hamilton was kind enough to look askance and leave me to myself as I slipped into the seat I shared with George Hempseed and discovered a writing lesson was taking place and that I couldn't hold my pen.

Fifteen years later I was seated in the Perth/Inverness Express out of Buchanan Street Station. As the train moved off the corridor door opened and in came Dr. McGillivray and sat on an empty seat next to me. But it was a Dr. McGillivray without the power or the glory or even the academic raiment with trimmings: just a courteous elderly gentleman, comfortably dressed, with a grey homburg hat where the glossy silk topper used to repose. Discovery of who we were was inevitable and we had a delightful conversation ranging over this and that interesting recollection but all too short as I was changing trains at Stirling. Three weeks later it was midsummer in Edinburgh and there we were again in joyous surprise laughingly greeting each other in Heriot Row. I never saw him again. In place of Mr. Hamilton one forenoon we had Mr. Jordan from Form 1A. He seemed to relish being blunt to the point of embarrassment for when a boy made a polite request to leave the room he immediately queried, 'Did you get medicine this morning'.

I remember one bright sunny morning during the war being with others on the parapet of the roof beside the glazed sloping enclosure of the science rooms. There was a safety railing, otherwise we would not have been allowed out. The occasion was a flying visit over Glasgow by the newly-formed Royal Air Force. One or two were piloted by former pupils who had notified the school of their intention to sweep low which they did, and included some pretty slick manoeuvring, to our great delight. How gay they looked, those bi-planes of over fifty years ago, flashing silver in the sun, their fuselages bearing bright-painted rings of red, white and blue. Had it been a dull day I don't suppose it would have been so memorable. But it wasn't: and roses were shining in Picardy.

Great bleak and smelly places were the science rooms where delicate balances, bunsen burners and queer apparatus surrounded the massive square tables at which we sat. Mr. Craik and Mr. Tulloch had a room each. We were with Mr. Craik but one day Mr. Tulloch took his place and was busily impressing us with a successful build-up of gurgling glassware and trembling rubber tubing when it blew up in his face but without noticeable injury. Towards the end of the war Miss MacDougall, a former pupil and hockey internationalist, came as a teacher of botany. (During the Clydebank blitz of March 1941 she was killed at her air raid warden's post when Queen Margaret Road received a direct hit at its junction with the new bridge.)

Mr. Boyle was in charge of the Art Department. He was a quiet man and was assisted by Miss Huggins. In 1917 a young man named James Miller began his Art teaching at H.H.S. His painting talents have since brought him international fame and membership of the Royal Scottish Academy. In the 1920s I used to visit him in the studio near Blythswood Square which he shared in the evenings with George Ternent the creator of Mr. Potter in the popular strip cartoon of *The Bulletin*.

School for me ended in the summer of 1918 in Daddy Schultz's class of Form 2B. Daddy Schultz had a squarish, flabby, fleshy face which beamed in expansive geniality. A ready facility in lambasting us according to requirements enabled him to hold and retain power over the uppish tendencies of our age group. He was very fond of raglan balls, the curious name given to the flattened equivalent of black-striped balls. Quite often he would send one of us down to R. S. McColl's sweetshop, next to Hubbard's at the foot of the hill, for a quarter of his favourites. On his daily perambulations on the hill and Great Western Road he delighted in radiating benevolence to all who caught his eye. He lodged at the top of Park Road when he was not in the 'Blythswood Cottage' at the foot. Varied are the tales of his wranglings within that hostelry in the social hours of evening. But he was always genial and sober whenever I saw his gay portly figure with bowler hat cocked slightly over one bushy eyebrow of his rather heavy countenance spanned by a bulging white moustache delicately tinted with nicotine. His clothes were usually of a light shepherd's tartan loosely enclosing a bow-front covered by a bright fancy waistcoat. He looked more like a retired army major than anything else. In the lower deck of a tramcar, where the two long seats polished by the sitters faced each other, he beamed on everybody and the car seemed to sing for joy in a brief timeless unison of bliss.

Curlers' Tavern, Byres Road.
The only public-house within Hillhead.
*April 1970**

Dumbarton Road at entrance to Western Infirmary near Partick Bridge. *May 1960**

HILLHEAD HIGH SCHOOL DINNER
17ᵀᴴ H.L.I.
HOTEL MODERNE, CONTAY.
PICARDIE. 20ᵀᴴ JUNE 1916.

"SOMME" MENU.

HORS ,D'OEUVRES:

Sardinia Assorties

CONSOMMÉ":

Napoo.

POISSONS:

Soles Frites au citroon à la Gailes

VIANDES:

Boeuf rôti de la Picardie.

LÉGUMES:

Pommes de Terre rotis de Totley et Prees.
Haricots verts à la Codford.

DESSERT:

Tartlette d'Amiens aux Abricots.
Tartlette de Rubempré aux Cerises.
Bonbons de "Chocolat Dugout."

Fromage de Wensleydale.

Biscuits du Havre.

Café Noir.

VINS:

Champagne de Warloy
Banyuls Anthérien de la Chaussée.
Le "Cratur" de La Boiselle.
Lime Juice de l'Entente Cordiale.
L'eau minerale Perri(s)scope.

James Russell

Steven D. Reith.

Arthur M. Cohen

Archibald Lang.

J. A. MacDougall

A. Mackinlay.

Kingston Elliott

A. Allan Cruickshank.

Ernest Harris

J. Cruickshank.

Jno. Munro.

T. G. Watson.

A. Houston.

C. C. Stewart.

D. M. Thomson.

John McC. Kerr

J. Robert Parker

H. W. Jordan

SHOPS, SHOPKEEPERS AND OTHER THINGS

This recollection of Great Western Road is mainly of the period shortly before the regular run of life was disrupted by the holocaust of 1914.

Starting at Kelvinbridge, Mr. Ballingall strides again in his double shop facing Colebrooke Street. He looked more like a policeman than a chemist especially beside his diminutive and precise partner. But it was its wonderful variety of battery flash lamps, when such things were still novelties, that made this shop memorable to boys of my generation. A single shop next door was a branch of the Glasgow Dairy Company whose shops were always scrupulously fresh and clean, each featuring a white marble counter, brown veined, upon which reposed, at the far end, a large tapered bowl of sweet milk.

Here I am describing only the shops that have impressed themselves in my memory. The other shops can be identified by referring to the extracts made available from the Post Office Directories of varying periods. The Kelvinbridge Post Office was then across the road beside Lawrence the booksellers and at that corner of Belmont Street was the larger grocer's shop of McQueen. Frazer & Green, the well-known city chemists, occupied the higher corner of Belmont Street. Continuing on that side at Belmont Lane I remember A. & W. Paterson's boot and shoe shop at the corner before coming to Hubbard's and, also, facing Bank Street, a single grocery personally managed by the proprietor, Mr. George McVey, a little man with a walrus moustache a bowler hat and a long white apron secured round his shoulders. He had a similar shop in Byres Road facing Elliot Street (Cresswell) and it is there I mainly remember him. At a later period, although it must now be close on fifty years ago an unusually interesting shop was established beyond Hubbard's and below what was a photographic studio.

This was 'Far Cathay Handwork', a black and heliotrope single shop with its window full of intricate ivory work and delicate lace. Mrs. Crosbie owned this shop and she had a son William, born in Hankow, who was a student of considerable promise at the Glasgow School of Art. D. Y. Cameron's Hillhead studio designed by Mackintosh is now his. The centre piece of this row was an emporium with several windows. In huge lettering it was proclaimed to be Fyfe's Hillhead Warehouse which specialised in hard-wearing underwear such as semmits, combinations, stays, etc. Next to the close before coming to Chalmers the baker at the corner of Hamilton Park Terrace there was a licensed grocer's double shop by the name of Bulloch. To cross back again to Caledonian Mansions and follow on from the bank at the corner of Otago Street which was then the Union Bank the next corner (now occupied by the Savings Bank which had been on the other side of Great Western Road at Colebrooke Street) was long the premises of plumbers with which I associate two names, Moses Spiers and Charles Hegney & Son. Then came Leishman, the butcher, and Balharrie's well-known tobacconist shop. Hepburn's ironmongery with glowing copperware and a fruiterer's was, I think, between Balharrie's and Annacker's cold meat shop with its colourful tiling at the corner of Bank Street. A few yards from Annacker's, in Bank Street, beside the railings of Bothwell Terrace was Gemmell's which has changed very little since it gave me my first memory of being inside a shop of its kind. To try to see over the counter meant gripping it by my finger tips and pulling myself up (not to be connected with the Old Highland Whisky dispensed into gill bottles from small silver taps on big polished barrels).

Mr. Gemmell gave personal attention to all his regular customers. Pleasant, elderly and aproned is all I can remember of him but I can still see facing me on the floor across the left-hand counter the row of large black-japanned tea bins,

'Murray's' Byres Road, in 1935. The young lady in the doorway is said to be Betty Price who later went to America. *Courtesy of Mrs. Murray*

Cooper's Corner, Bank Street. *1970**

lined and decorated in gold with large Chinese signs, and semi-circular deep trays of cereals fitted on top with scoops for measuring them into thick blue or brown paper bags on the brass see-saw scales. In Mr. Gemmell's time, in fact until iron-rimmed wheels were giving place to rubber, Bank Street was roughly laid in stone setts that obliged lightly spring vehicles and cyclists to traverse it gingerly. Consequently, it was about as bereft of traffic as the purely residential streets. There was no Kelvin Way then and the big gates of the Park were closed at night. Cooper's prominent building with its turreted tower was like a large family grocers with the addition of a household emporium reached upstairs by an ornate central staircase from the patterned terra cotta ground floor with its several long counters from which cash was swished in little round clip-on boxes along overhead wires in a direct line to the cashier's cubicle. The momentum came from a spring arrangement by pulling down a handle like that of a W.C. and then releasing it. But the most lingering memory of Cooper's in its heyday when its vans were prominent in Hillhead, is the aroma through the ventilator of the side window in Bank Street from the revolving coffee-roasting machine with its wide mouthed brass funnel. What an exotic subtle scent pervaded those shops usually designated as High Class Provision Merchants & Italian Warehousemen.

The row of houses along Bank Street from Cooper's Corner was, at one time, better known as Great Kelvin Terrace and its back lane still claims this name. Between the end of this lane under the tenement in Great Western Road and Wilson Street (Oakfield Avenue) were Cappell's well-known green-fronted chemist's shop, a branch of Birrell's the confectioner, and A. L. Scott & Sons footwear premises at the corner. At the other end of the sloping greenery at

Belgrave Terrace a famous name in Hillhead was to be found on the corner shop in the tenement known as Rokeby Terrace at the foot of Ann Street (Southpark Avenue). This was William Farmer & Sons, a business very similar to that of Cooper & Co. but purely local and more personal in administration.

Farmer's was established in 1853 at 1 Craiglaw Place at the corner of Wilson Street (Oakfield Avenue). When Rokeby Terrace was built in the 1870's the business was transferred to the spacious premises of No. 1 at the corner of Ann Street. At the time of Mr. Farmer's death in 1902 he was said to have been the oldest merchant in Hillhead and also its first Postmaster. During the administration of Hillhead as a Police Burgh he was a Commissioner and Magistrate. Next in Rokeby Terrace came Vernal who sold the best quality of boots and shoes and then Danks the butcher with Mr. Hutton, courtly and gentlemanly both in manner and appearance, preparing his customers' orders at the well-scrubbed long bench against the wall. In the traditional fashion the sawdust covered floor bore no counter and in hot weather cooling water streamed down both windows. I think More's came next. This well-known stationer famous for note-paper had four shops; two in Hillhead, one at the top of North Street, Charing Cross, and the other in Hyndland Road opposite Clarence Drive. Here, at the other side of the close entrance was Russell the fruiterer whose four-wheel lorry with its protective tarpaulin slung from a horizontal rod conveyed well-filled baskets to the big houses.

I am sure there was a chemist's, a barber's shop, and, at a later period a branch of the City Bakeries between Russell's and John Murray & Son at the end of Rokeby Terrace beside the steps in Hillhead Street. Murray's was very similar to Farmer's in its varied stock of high-class provisions. Their high two-wheeled square shallow cart with outboard rigging from which one of the large baskets of groceries could be manoeuvred on to the head of the delivery boy, who used a pad shaped like a black pudding, was probably the last to be seen in Hillhead. This well-remembered firm's reputation as first-class family grocers extended to Bearsden and Milngavie where they had branch shops. The row of shops which seem to be set into the foundations of Alfred Terrace were constructed in the Nineties by a new proprietor of the terrace which had until then a frontage similar to that of Belgrave Terrace. The butcher's business known as 'The Northern Farmers' was among the first to come here. It closed in 1969 when its near neighbour one of the oldest branches of the 'Scotch Wool & Hosiery Stores' also ceased. I always remember between the ends of the two counters in this wool shop the vertical heater radiating an orange glow from its single globe shaped like a straight sausage. No other shop I knew had one like it. In the middle of this group was a milkshop called (Hundred Acre Hill Dairy)? On one side of it was a milliner's and on the other a neatly-stocked draper's shop which supplied caps for Hillhead High School. Lacey, the confectioner and a single grocer called Clark came next and McDougall's extensive china shop occupied the corner at the foot of the school hill. Visualising McDougall's, it is easy to see again Walter Hubbard's cream and gold baker's shop at the other side of Cecil Street and sense its atmosphere redolent of shortening and rich fruit London buns. Some there were who dubbed his customers from H.H.S. as 'Hubbard's Hard Scones', a sobriquet quite highly esteemed by those who regularly indulged their fancy. One of the first shops of R. S. McColl, the former Queen's Park player, came next to Hubbard's. A single shop, it featured two special items for the local pennies; a thick light brown stick of School Rock and pale smaller sticks wrapped designated Scout Poles. Particularly good were R. S. McColl's long firm bars of chocolate nougat. The double shop beyond was Ritchie the grocer I remember for its bottled sweets piled in the centre and the enamelled dish of water marked DOG on the pavement at the doorway. These dishes were common to many shops doing a high-class family trade. But the one I always picture was Ritchie's, a grocery business that had been long-established by William Andrew, the previous proprietor. Brechin's blue and white tiled butcher's shop had already been established when they took over from Finlay Bell & Co. in the 1870s. Brechin claim to have been, in 1880, the first butcher's shop to have '*THE* ELECTRIC LIGHT' installed, the power being generated by a donkey engine.

Between Brechin's and the close was Mackichan's brown varnished two-windowed fruit and flower shop which enjoyed a trade similar to Russell's. (Its tiled floor is still evident in Mr. Lowe's stationer and bookshop.) Mrs. Mackichan (Susan) in a big feathered hat, was always dashing about and making a great fuss of her customers. Next, past the close, was a shop with an interior that was quite monumental with its terrazzo floor and massive bevel-edged slabs for displaying all kinds of wet fish, crabs and lobsters at the front of the shop while about half a dozen assistants were busy filleting at the rear upon what was not unlike a big stone billiard table. Game and poultry occupied the other window beside the counter along with Palethorpe's sausages. This was Sawers main Hillhead branch and, at the end of the day, tall Mr. Taylor could be seen in his great thigh-length waders meticulously hosing about two-thirds of the shop after which the two ornate iron gates would close and bring the curved fish centrepiece in each into full view.

Its name has changed but the old-established business of McMillan, the chemist, remains pretty much the same within, even to the brass plate at the end of the counter and the fine gas jet which was constantly in use when sealing wax gave the professional touch to the closing of neat white packages. No indication is to be seen now of Barrie Paterson's the well-known stationers of yore where we used to get our school jotters, pencils, rubbers, etc., and Blackie's Model Readers with their lovely coloured plates. It must be many years since the British Linen Bank extended into the site of this memorable two-windowed shop and wiped out No. 695 Great Western Road. Campbell, the grocers, is the shop I see in memory at the other corner of Kersland Street. Craig the bakers came next to it with their tearoom at the back with ornamental glass windows in Kersland Street. All James Craig's shops like so many others of forty to sixty years ago were most tastefully designed. The famous name of Waddell was to be seen above the bright little shop next to Craig's. A great treat at the week-end was one of their well-filled steak pies, family size, in a wally dish with the little three-pronged wally funnel in the centre to let the steam out from the gurgling depths. Two spacious shops with large windows came next. The first was Paterson's high-class drapers which specialised in ladies' blouses and other feminine flimsies. The second was Chrystal Bell & Co., Italian Warehousemen & Wine Merchants which later became Stalker & McLennan. Though well-stocked the interior of this shop was so wide and deep that it gave the impression of being half empty. Beside it More's other Hillhead branch with its window full of boxes of writing paper, specimens of visiting cards, doyleys and general stationery seemed tightly packed. Where this tenement abruptly ends with the Commercial Bank adjoining Kelvinside Church, concludes what I can recall of the shops I once knew on Great Western Road. Attempting it makes me feel they are still there and like a Rip Van Winkle, I can almost believe, were I to venture down the hill, I would still be in time to get one or two rich penny London buns or tuppence worth of mixed teabread in Hubbard's before they closed and my *Evening Citizen* for a halfpenny.

The Byres Road

To go round the corner past the church is to unfold a scene of fuller memories for they come mainly from my later boyhood and early adult life. To everyone who grew up in its vicinity it has always been The Byres Road whereas the tendency to apply the definite article to Great Western Road, is more likely to be used when referring to it as a great thoroughfare. Probably because it forms the boundary between Hillhead and Kelvinside is the reason for the distinction given to Byres Road. Fifty years ago it had very little traffic in comparison with Great Western Road, and in the evening, you could look down its whole empty length with nothing to impede your view of the distant minarets of Harland & Wolff's mighty cranes on the other side of the Govan ferry; a vista now gone. Apart from a quick trotting horse yoked to a light vehicle the general movement of street traffic was leisurely and safe. Even the tramcars droned for, on their single truck, they were liable to swing quite alarmingly if they speeded up on a clear stretch. To illustrate how quiet Byres Road was in the period before the Great War of 1914, I can recall viewing from the foot of Elliot Street (Cresswell) the funeral procession

Police Constable Wm. Joyner in traditional uniform

Hillhead's stalwart crime deterrent on the east beat from Hillhead Street to the Kelvin (1950–62). Present uniform was adopted in 1952. Two well-remembered constables of sixty years ago were 'Mr' Rodger on the west side and 'Bowser' of the Belmont Street area.

of a fireman proceeding towards Botanic Gardens at a slow walking pace. About fifty mourners on foot solemnly followed the horsedrawn fire waggon which bore the coffin upon which reposed a helmet of black leather and brass.

It may surprise many people to be told that the Hillhead shops in Byres Road are only those on the East side extending from Kelvinside Church to Ashton Lane. Yet both sides are looked upon generally as being in Hillhead as far down as Highburgh Road. But the feeling of this half of Byres Road belonging to both Kelvinside and Hillhead is amply confirmed in many ways. There is a family oneness about it all, happily exemplified by Hillhead and Belmont Parish Church being in Kelvinside and Kelvinside Parish Church being in Hillhead. So with equal regard for both sides of this ancient highway (which, in the early days of the Burgh was known as Victoria Street) let's see what the television of memory can enable me to depict of the shops I knew and which boys and girls of my generation will, no doubt, also remember with other memories of their own.

To state one's place of abode in Hillhead as Prince of Wales Terrace would surely suggest a palatial terrace similar to Grosvenor. Buckingham or St. James's. Probably the outstanding elegance of these splendid terraces when Hillhead was being feued out to tenement builders had much to do with the flamboyant fashion of providing a gilt-edged address to dwellers up closes in side streets or above shops in main thoroughfares. Anyway the fact is, once upon a time, Prince of Wales Terrace was to be seen in gold lettering above Alexander Kennedy's furniture shop, the first in the tenement on the left in Byres Road on the other side of the church. In addition to selling fine furniture this shop was also the local receiving office for Castlebank Dyeworks, the reason being that Mr. Kennedy was the proprietor of both. Harvey's family grocer's came next. Walker's fishmonger business must have been in the adjacent premises a very long time as I don't remember its not being there. The big double-faced clock which projected over the pavement beyond Walker's not only proclaimed the time clearly but indicated that here was Mr. Peden, watchmaker and jeweller.

The following shop like Peden's had two medium-size windows. This was Bell's the confectioners and tobacconists. It was run by two maiden ladies with round crinkly faces very much alike. Their aged father with a purplish nose sometimes appeared from the door in the centre of the partition that spanned the shop at the end of the counters. When I was about six this shop was the scene of an unforgettable experience. I had climbed up to the shelf above the kitchen dresser where my mother kept her house-keeping money and there I purloined a penny with which I slipped out of the house and down Vinicombe Street to Bell's. One of the sisters came to attend to my order which was a halfpenny worth of butter nuts and I placed the penny on the counter in front of my nose. As she turned to get the appropriate glass jar I stood gazing at the penny, possibly with thoughts of what to do with the change, when a hand appeared in front of my face and closed on the coin and I heard a voice saying 'That's not yours'. I turned and there was my sister quietly shutting the half door behind her. A more straightforward remembrance of this shop with its 'rosebuds' and French tablet (a long flat type of 'boiling' dark brown and white edged with pieces of almond in the centre) was its charmingly pleasant scent of cachoux, especially the tiny silvered ones like ball-bearings which you could buy in miniature cricket bats of coloured tin. The presence of the butcher's shop of Mr. Blackwood between Bell's and the office of the Glebe Coal Company I recall in an incidental manner to my main interest here which I used to eye with wishful thoughts. This was a very fine family governess car and sleek pony

beautifully harnessed which stood outside, mainly at weekends, when Mr. Blackwood would come down from his flat upstairs and drive out towards Anniesland. I loved the look of this equipage with its light brown varnished bodywork and gay yellow wheels. The extensive premises at the corner of Vinicombe Street were occupied by Fleming the ironmonger. Like Shaw Walker's in the city, Fleming's was a household name to several generations within its own domain. To the young it was the place to get your bicycle repaired. In Byres Road one window had an attractive display of cycle accessories surrounding, on a stand, a splendid specimen of a Humber bicycle, its glistening black frame gold-lined and a half inch similar effect round the centre of the wheel rims. In those comfortably distant days before the Great War the elite makes were the Humber and the all-black Sunbeam with its oil bath gearcase.

Burgh buildings and Elliot Street

Here at Vinicombe Street in 1911 I saw the Hillhead Picture Salon being built. I remember wandering in under the wooden scaffolding and making friends with the workmen. I especially recall the one-legged night watchman who, one evening, sent me to buy a tin of cocoa and gave me a halfpenny to myself with which I bought a big bar of nougat.

Was the electric power station on the other corner of Vinicombe Street in existence in my time? Memory fails me here. Perhaps there was a smaller one. But everyone knew the Burgh Hall for its social, religious and political meetings, or as the place where they learned to dance or attended the A.G. Meetings of their local Associations. The only thing that sticks in my mind about the Burgh Hall is when my sister and I were drawn there in the Spring of 1918 to hear a man prophesy that the world would end on a certain Monday that was approaching fast. Later going up reluctantly to school one beautiful morning I suddenly recollected in Kersland Lane that this was the day the world was to end and it bucked me up tremendously to note that they had a rare day for it.

The Police Station was at the left side of the Burgh Building. A grim-looking place it was with its entrance dark and foreboding and its heavily barred dungeons at the back where, on the far side of the courtyard, were the Fire Brigade quarters. The Cleansing Department was down the lane on the other side of the main building for there I can still recall the red panelled carts, each deep and low slung on two great wheels. Two things I particularly remember about these vehicles; the clicking sound of the steel pins jumping in the broad metal hubs as the wheels rumbled over the cobbles in the back lanes and the velvet pink and white square muzzles of the massive heads of the giant Clydesdale horses, the like of which I have seen nowhere else. A few bushes and a grassy stretch covered the remainder of the ground to Elliot Street. On this facing the Byres Road pavement were two or three huts one of which was used by Mr. McDougall, the local veterinary surgeon. Above his door was a model of a dog's head; a schipperke which, along with pomeranians, pugs, pekingese, fox and Irish terriers, was a popular breed fifty to sixty years ago.

In Elliot Street, halfway between Byres Road and the Burgh Court Lane a cabman's rest was supported clear of the gutter by little iron wheels obviously used originally to haul it into position for it had been a fixture long before my time. It stood out from the pavement and had a tin chimney. Cabs and horse-drawn delivery vehicles which had come a considerable distance such as the four-wheel yellow and green two-horse lorry of the Gleniffer Laundry, the two-wheeled high cart of the Victoria Park Laundry, Bailey & Clark's single horse lorry that traversed the residential streets supplying families direct with syphons of aerated waters and the two-horse Montgomerie's Ber-

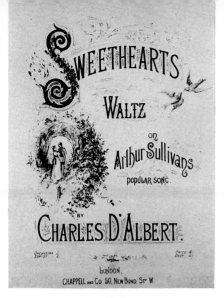

John Tobia of 'The Gardens Cafe',
known as 'John's'.
Weir

Courtyard lane of Burgh Buildings, Byres Road, showing entrance
to former Police Station. *1965**

adler's', a household name
in Hillhead and district for
se on a century. Corner of
bservatory Road and Byres
oad. The lamp denotes the
trict of Kelvinside. *c.* 1910.
*Courtesy of Mrs. Allison
(Miss Sadler)*

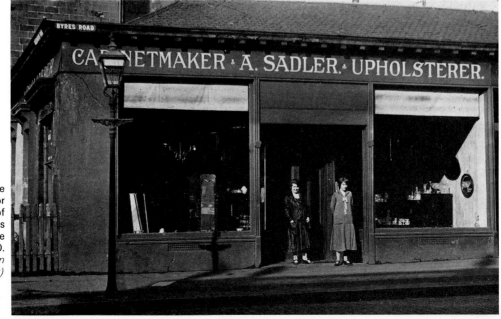

Byres Road from Great George Street. *Summer 1927**

maline bread van from Ibrox appeared regularly at noon. Although seen in the district I doubt if the superior laundry van of Baikie & Hogg (a light vehicle styled like a brougham) ever patronised this homely encampment. With the men seated on the wooden benches before the well-scrubbed long table at the open door and the buxom woman dishing up their dinner and the horses nuzzling their nosebags on the ground and scattering a share to the fluttering birds, the mid-day scene at the foot of Elliot Street was one of peaceful contentment.

'John's', 'Miss Bell's', etc.

The shops in what was once known as Victoria Buildings began with the Clydesdale Bank. Then came the cream and gold single shop of John Tobia the flavour of whose ice cream was an absolute joy never equalled then or since. The name that went up on the shop in 1903 was 'The Gardens Cafe' but to his young patrons of over three generations it was simply 'John's'. Round and tubby he had the quiet disposition engendered by the sunnier climes of Italy and I am glad to be able to include his photograph taken by Mr. Weir.

Next door to 'John's' was another long-remembered shop that was a veritable magic cave to children. It had two windows and a very roomy interior. It had to be for its stock included newspapers, periodicals, stationery, fancy goods, a circulating library and a large and fascinating range of colourful toys. The diminutive ones within our occasional purchasing power of a copper or two caused many an anxious moment of indecision as we gazed at them in the alcove isolated across from the counter where they filled the shelves on three sides. Considering how well-known it was for at least fifty years to the families of Kelvinside and Hillhead, it seems almost unnecessary to state that this was

'Miss Bell's'. Even Robert W. Service remembered it when writing his autobiography in Hollywood. Between the close and Hillhead Post Office was Roxburgh the confectioner whose pokes of broken mixtures sometimes contained Swiss tablet and expensive chocolates slightly bashed. Did the Buttercup Dairy come next? I am not sure but there was a very narrow sweet shop next to the red painted tunnel entrance to the Grosvenor Garage alongside the P.O. Sorting Office in the lane behind. On the other side of the garage entrance kindly though severe-looking Mrs. Morrison had the ironmonger's and A. & W. Paterson had a double boot and shoe shop next to Thomson the hairdresser. The remaining three shops in this row although, if anything, a more distant memory are undimmed in clarity especially Francis Spite & Co. at the corner with its chemist's counter on the right and grocer's on the left. The two before it were Miss McInnes' tobacconist shop with its old-fashioned long yellow wooden seat of flat bentwood patterned with small holes and Mr. Mitchell's the only umbrella and walking stick shop in Hillhead. For me, at the entrance, it had a very special attraction in the stand of beautifully made miniature walking sticks, the handles perfect models of dog's heads and retailing at sixpence each.

Most of my recollections of Byres Road, especially down from Vinicombe Street date from our removal from Kersland Street to Great George Street in 1911 just above the part of Ashton Lane known as Great George Lane. Officially our address was 49 Lilybank Gardens but it was more readily identified as 163 Great George Street. At the impressionable age of seven I got to know this vicinity particularly well. I wasn't too particular with whom I associated. I remember getting to know a Glasgow Academy boy who told me he would require to get his parent's permission to join me again at play. His father was a lawyer and so was mine; but he lived in a three floor main door house in Albion Street whereas ours was only a three room and kitchen top flat. He is now a partner in a well-known legal firm and we are still friends.

I have very grateful memories of red-nosed and gentle voiced Mr. Duncan who was in charge of the chemist's side of Francis Spite & Co. Bolting my breakfast in my hurry but not in eagerness to get to school, a codfish bone became stuck in my throat and my mother in desperation took me to Mr. Duncan who stood me on a chair and with the right degree of professional calmness told me to say 'ah' and, at the second attempt with a pair of forceps skilfully withdrew the three-pronged obstruction. When Templeton took over from Francis Spite, Mr. Duncan acquired the old-established chemist shop of his namesake Joseph Duncan in Gibson Street. A few yards up Great George Street from Francis Spite was the office of the Hillhead District Registrar of Births, Deaths and Marriages. The one shop here was Ross's Dairy from which a great clattering of milk cans with long wire handles emanated every morning. Mr. Tipaldi, black-haired and debonair, had newly established his hairdressing business at the opposite corner of Great George Street, while Hall's plumber shop stood, as it does to-day, indifferent to the passing of

time quietly back below the end of the corner tenement, where Mr. Crawford of the long grey beard had his joiner's yard down the side. An old tenement with grass plots and street level entrances occupied the space between the yard and Great George Lane. In Byres Road past the close next to Tipaldi a vacant single shop showed signs of becoming a fruiterer's. One sunny afternoon a day or two later, I was day-dreaming about the pavement there when a sturdy-looking man in a cap beckoned to me from the shop entrance and gave me an apple and a penny to deliver a bouquet of flowers to a main door in Hyndland Road opposite Queensborough Gardens. Without knowing it I had supplied the first delivery service of George Todd, Fruiterer & Florist whose business was to flower and flourish into many branches. Almost thirty years later; it would be about two months after the Clydebank Blitz, I was in police uniform with gas mask and steel helmet slung across my great coat and I was standing on the Milngavie Road just below Kilmardinny waiting for a bus to take me to Milngavie Police Station (the Lillie Gallery is now on the site) where I was due on duty at 2 p.m. Time was getting short and there was no sign of a bus when one of the good solid pre-war dark blue Austins drew up and I was offered a lift by a stoutish gentleman accompanied by a pleasantly plump lady. When

Ashton Lane Works of Barr & Stroud Ltd., 1901
Courtesy of Barr & Stroud Ltd.

The beginnings of Barr & Stroud Ltd. took shape in an attic above the shops at the entrance to Hillhead Subway Station. It was their first workshop and the year was 1895. Bigger premises soon became necessary and these were obtained in Ashton Lane. The move to Anniesland was made in 1904.

1 up in a two-storey tenement close in Hillhead flanked by main-door flats with gardens. Built 1874. *1971 **

I got inside I discovered I was talking to Mr. and Mrs. Todd who remembered me although I had been in London for nearly ten years before the war.

'The Wee Shop' and The Curlers' Tavern

To continue in the long ago the small low building next to Mr. Todd's first shop had one upper storey. This was the oldest building not only in the Byres Road but in Hillhead. Here an old woman (Mrs Gow) who lived at the back kept a 'Jenny a' Things' shop with two signs above the doorway; one in blue and white enamelled tin had the words 'Lyon's Tea sold here', the other of faded white painted wood announced 'Mangling Done Here'. In her blue cotton with apron Mrs. Gow looked like a country woman at the door of her cottage. Dividing the shop from the dark green and gold public house known as 'The Curlers' Tavern' was a pipe-clayed passage that went straight through to the back-yard and where the County Police Station stood a century ago. The public house occupied at least two thirds of the building. Even so, the interior was quite small and dark with a circular bar and a cubby private room. It had two windows. The smaller on the left of the entrance had white lettering and a red triangle stuck on it. The other had a big framed mirror advertising possibly Allsop's Beer and I think a coloured showcard or two for Barclay Perkins or Reid's Stout. It had then quite a different clientele to the Bohemian fraternity who encouraged its transformation

and development after the B.B.C. came to Queen Margaret Drive. But it had varied patrons then too, such as cab drivers, tradesmen, stablemen, itinerant musicians and the Jones brothers who left their Punch and Judy props and stand in a secluded corner of Elliot Lane. It still had much of the look and atmosphere of the wayside country inn that had stood through the centuries and could remember when, according to legend, William 3rd (or was it Charles 2nd?) came riding towards Glasgow on this lonely highway and spotting the inviting hostelry called a halt for refreshments. Finding it shuttered and barred, the landlord was quickly routed out and told to open up in the name of the King which he did with such satisfaction that William (or the Merry Monarch) bestowed upon the inn the right, by Royal Charter, to be open day and night, Sundays included, in perpetuity; but what happened to the vellum document is another matter. Incidentally the Curlers' Tavern has always been and still is the only public house within Hillhead.

Beside the Subway

It was after he was demobbed in 1919 that Henry Murray took over 'the wee shop' in the Curlers' building and made it a thriving newsagent's and packed miniature emporium for everyday small requirements. The tobacconist shop adjoining the tavern had the name of Mackenzie and featured its own special pipe tobaccos from 4½d an ounce. Before the age of the motor car many of their best customers using the Subway entered or left by the side door where, in addition to the main stream of passengers, we boys intercepted them for the much coveted cigarette cards then issued, such as 'Historic Events' and 'Overseas Dominions'. By providing additional shelter with its pillard canopy to the pavement edge the Subway entrance was a favourite trysting-place easily spotted at a distance. Its exclusively peculiar smell, said to be of Archangel tar, was stronger in those days of cable traction but, like most Glasgow people, I have always found it to be pleasantly agreeable. The employees of the Glasgow Subway Company wore a light brown uniform while the tall military figure of the chief inspector, also in brown, with his gold-braided cap and frock coat looked like a resplendent Bandmaster or General of a Foreign Power. The Company showed great enterprise in selling its advertising space and some of the richly-coloured large square cards that curved above the car seats were quite memorable. One I always remember advertised the Union Transit Co. and depicted a gaily-coloured globe of the world being carried on a red Sentinel steam waggon. Mrs. Dunlop of the Castlebank Bakery also had a large shop window within the Subway entrance but no side door. She served in the shop and always wore a hat to denote her proprietorship which was then a common custom. Beside the turnstile there appeared to be an entrance to upstairs premises.

Art matters

Two single shops followed Dunlop's. I think Gibson & Reid, the dry cleaners had the first; I know the second was occupied for many years by Mr. Stewart, a thin frail man with a conscientious interest in the services he rendered. He was our local picture frame maker and supplier of oil and water-colour paintings done on the premises. You could buy a competent work in a golden frame at his regular price of 3/6d, but for a masterly oil painting in a heavier moulding you would have had to go as high as 6/- (30 pence) or even more. One scene I can still visualize with ease as it was nearly always in the window, even after it was sold, for another soon appeared from the backshop perhaps larger to fit the next freshened-up frame. A pleasing composition and obvious good seller it was copied from a coloured book illustration which I came across many years later in the second-hand department of Thin's bookshop in Edinburgh.

It showed a yellow and green foreground surrounding a Highland sheiling in front of which an old woman with a white mutch was feeding hens. In the distance could be seen a ridge of blue mountains. We owned a genuine 'Stewart' which came within the scope of my father's art patronage. Being more of a scholar and tutor than a business-seeking lawyer, he was content with simple needs which sometimes made things pretty difficult especially for my mother. The only other two pictures I knew him to buy were a small coloured engraving after Meissonier which he got in Davidson's where Craig's Rhul Restaurant eventually arose next to Watt Brothers and opposite Sime's second-hand bookshop and an etching of a medieval French scene by 'Gaujean' which he acquired on a clearance occasion from Alexander Duthie in that once beautiful row of shops in Sauchiehall Street across from Holland Street. He was so pleased with this purchase that he told Alexander Reid, the Art dealer, whom he was wont to stop and speak to in the lunch hour when Reid often stood at his open door in West George Street. In the eighteen sixties they had been classmates in the High School, when it was in John Street, along with G. L. Watson who designed the Lipton yachts and Hugh Hopkins, Antiquarian Bookseller on an international par with Reid. With such a life-long association he didn't mind divulging to Reid that he had paid 2/6d for his prized signed proof from Duthie, to which Reid replied 'It wasn't dear'.

Memory connects with so much at this part of Byres Road that I am prone not only to linger but deviate. Perhaps it won't be amiss.

When 'The Grosvenor' came

After the double-windowed ice cream shop of the Mazaroli brothers there was a pend under this row of shops with small attics. An old retired coachman stood there regularly for years, his gnarled countenance set like chiselled granite. The pend led to a stable yard and smiddy partly open to Great George Lane where the ring of the anvil resounded at the back end of Lilybank Gardens. The left wall of a single shop that stood out from Ashton Lane formed the other side of the pend and, after the Grosvenor Picture House was built, became Henderson's Cab and Funeral Office.

Here, at what was the Hillhead Burgh Boundary, ruddy-faced Mr. Horn perched high on his two-wheeled milk cart must be acknowledged emerging once more from Ashton Lane. In the next row of shops, a break in alignment set them back several feet from the lane entrance. What the first was I forget but everybody knew Horn's Dairy with its yellow varnished front and blue and white tiled interior where Mr. Horn's three raven-haired fresh-complexioned sisters in purple overalls diligently dispensed their quick-selling lines of dairy produce. Apart from the small black cab office of Henderson with its deep blue opaque half window gold-lined at the top, I am unable to recall the one or two other shops that were there until 1921 when along with the cab office and Henderson's stables at the back they were cleared away to allow the Grosvenor Picture House to be built. To jump into the Twenties I can remember standing in the shell of the auditorium when the white new wood of the floor had been only half laid. And I can remember the two big pictures The Grosvenor opened with on the 3rd of May 1921. They were 'Helen of the Four Gates' featuring Alma Taylor and 'Eastward Ho' with William Russell. What a great swell Mr. Lomax, the Manager, was in his full evening dress. Richard Daeblitz conducted the orchestra and was the innovator of the famous Chorus Nights. Mr. James M. Hart was the first operator but soon became Manager, a position he held for close on forty years. Orr, the house decorators, were a little further along next to Sommerville the butcher. Then came Bryson's doing a first-class trade in stationery and the best periodicals such as the *Windsor* and *Strand* magazines, *Punch* and the *Illustrated London News*, and at Christmas the beautiful Annuals especially *Pears'* with two lovely colour plates issued separately and all for 6d. At the corner of Ashton Terrace was the green and gold grocer's and wine merchant's premises of Wm. Frame & Sons who apparently had some affinity with Sommerville the butcher as they had similar shops together in Kilcreggan.

South of the Border

To record one or two special memories beyond Ashton Terrace I have come within the precincts of that former Burgh of ancient roots at the foot of Byres Road.

It must be over thirty years since Miss Barclay came from the Gibson Street end of University Avenue to re-establish her restaurant at the corner of Ashton Road where she catered so excellently for her appreciative customers. I remember it as being previously an electrician's. Now, in June 1971, as I write, within weeks of her death, the building has also departed up to and including the shop which had particular personal interest for me in the year 1919. Latterly this was Lee's second-hand bookshop. Then it was a music shop, its red paint faded with age. At its entrance, dangling above the pavement, a red and white enamelled sign of The National Telephone Company announced YOU MAY

Entrance of
Hillhead Subway Station, 1937
Courtesy of Mr. David L. Thomson

TELEPHONE FROM HERE. Inside, behind a breast-work of loosely piled sheet music reigned Mrs. Rae crowned by a large feathered hat like ferns in a miniature conservatory and surrounded by a jumbled variety of musical instruments, while her husband, a teacher of the piano, kept to his own domain in the flat above. Fussy and excitable, Mrs. Rae had an eagerness to suit her customers which enabled my mother to arrange the purchase of my greatly desired gramophone which I remember seeing for the first time with its beautiful blue fluted horn perched upon one of the two pianos that stood opposite the counter. Of the three Zonophone records that went with it, along with a box of steel needles, I still possess 'Sweethearts Waltz' which has 'See-Saw' vocal waltz on the other side. 'Sweethearts' always recalled fond memories of other days to my parents. It has the tuneful swing that must have been irresistible in the stately days of the waltz. I once heard 'See-Saw' on the wireless but 'Sweethearts' seemed to survive only in this one recording by the Black Diamonds Band. My father could remember it in the 1880s as a great favourite at the splendid Balls of the 1st L.R.V. in the St. Andrews Halls, the composer, Charles d'Albert, formerly ballet master at Covent Garden, having resided at nearby 9 Newton Terrace when, in the 1870s, he held dancing classes in the Queen's Rooms at La Belle Place. Forty years after I got my first records, I came across a copy of J. J. Bell's *Do you Remember* and in the chapter on Melodies and Memories read that when in Neil Munro's house in Helensburgh one evening their conversation having veered on to the subject of old tunes Munro suddenly asked Bell if he had ever heard, or heard tell of, a waltz called 'Sweethearts'. He had known it long ago but had 'lost' it and ever since, had been seeking someone who knew the tune and from whom he might recover it. Fortunately, J. J. managed to get a copy for Neil Munro's piano and all was well. In such ways are we reminded that the present is simply an extension of the past.

Partick vignette

With the clanging rumble of a yellow tramcar for Langside turning from Highburgh Road towards Church Street, I find my feet again, but before recalling the Byres Road shops back from what is actually Dowanhill and Kelvinside to Botanic Gardens junction, a note is due on where the red Dalmuir and the blue Scotstoun West trams lumbered smoothly or, with metallic clash and bells sounding careered across the foot of Byres Road.

What would Hillhead have done without Partick? After all there were no pawnshops in Hillhead. Partick was a territory into which I always liked to venture. In addition to having a homeliness peculiarly its own, on a Saturday night its bustling portion of the Dumbarton Road was like a half-Eastern bazaar with the Soft Shoe Shuffler doing his turn opposite the dazzling Star Palace, Willie Ferrie with Kilmarnock bonnet and clappers giving his jingle and reciting his homilies at the foot of Hyndland Street, the silver band of the Salvation Army marching to its regular stance at Gardner Street and a ventriloquist, a hot chestnut man and a political spouter or two at Peel Street; lascars and turbanned figures, bent on finding bargains, led by their serangs from the City and Anchor Liners (Bombay and Calcutta) or 'Paddy' Henderson's (Rangoon) at Yorkhill or the Queen's Dock. And if you wanted a furtive feed of fish and chips, you nipped down to Partick until it became more convenient and almost respectable to be seen entering Osborne's which opened up about 1920 in Byres Road opposite Highburgh Road and almost on the verge of Hillhead.

Back to 'The Botanics'

To me as a boy in the era of Mrs. Rae, Tennent's, corner public house with its hidden interior looked a mysterious place especially when the military-looking man in the blue brocade uniform like a Lieutenant of Police or Superintendent of an Institution stood on guard. Between it and Miller's chemist shop at Albion Street, I can recall only Boyle's Irish butter and egg shop with its huge baskets of eggs at 11d a dozen. Crossing to Colquhoun's block I come again to the bright efficient grocer's shop of James & George Hunter at the corner of what I recently discovered was once Albion Place before the opposite side of that street was built.

Next to Hunter's was Stead and Simpson's boot and shoe shop (altered but still there). Then came Currie the chemist with the large red and blue bottles in the windows which most chemists displayed then with a large replica of a pestle and mortar protruding above the entrance. If you saw small compact and dignified Mr. Currie in the Byres Road you would be sure to meet the aroma of a Havana cigar, whereas Mr. Miller, tall, lanky, mentally engrossed and inclined to stoop was never without his curved 'Sherlock Holmes' pipe as he wended his way home up the other side of the road. Colquhoun's was at its best when the bakehouse abutted on the side lane. Well-groomed Mr. Colquhoun in his beautifully polished brown shoes saw to that. It was a time when Glasgow's leading family bakers such as James Craig, Walter Hubbard and William Skinner took a great pride in maintaining the highest quality of goods and service in their well-appointed shops and delightfully opulent restaurants.

Up the bent Ruthven lane, alongside Colquhoun's lane, leading to what was Price's Livery Stables, a self-contained villa dated 1870 is still to be seen at the bend. James King, a classmate of mine at H.H.S. lived here, the family-owned King's Dairy at the back being the last in Byres Road to have a byre with cows. Apart from Mr. Todd's large additional shop which I think came later than the time I am stravaiging in I can recall only three shops in the group between Ruthven Lane and Ruthven Street. The first, beside the lane, was Williamson the butcher, whose daughter Helen was in the infants' class with me. In the middle of this short row was a fruiterer's which must have been before Todd's time. Above the shop were the initials S.P.Q.R. which tended to make people remember it. There was nothing about the buxom proprietress weighing root vegetables in a hooked bucket on an iron stand to suggest a conscious connection with the Roman insignia; it was simply a modest way of expressing a hope that a small profit produced a quick return. Annacker's colourful cool-tiled cold meat and sausage shop, similar to that at Bank Street, was at the Ruthven Street corner, There was, of course, no official pedestrian crossing here; only a red-painted tram stop on each side of the Byres Road. At the other corner of Ruthven Street there was the grocer's called Hay: then came the Maypole Dairy where the flashing manipulation of the wooden butter pats was something to behold in wonder. The larger frontage of Boyd's fish shop I remember only too well. One Saturday morning while at breakfast we heard a great rumbling sound tearing down the hill accompanied by shouting and ending in a loud crash. I hurried out to see what it was and found that a coal horse had taken fright at the top of Great George Street and bolted with the lorry straight down the hill into Boyd's fish shop. Although released with difficulty from the broken shafts, it had not fallen and, despite several bad gashes, it was able to walk away.

In keeping with their other branches the James Craig baker's shop with its black and white marble floor was always brightly attractive with a hint of *art nouveau* in its appropriately functional design. On the other side of the dividing close Birrell's glowing display of shaded lights on its toothsome products nestling amid cascaded folds of silky pink was a constant lure for romantic generosity to respond to the bewitching spells of the deepening night by buying a 2 lb. box of Milady chocolates instead of what, perchance, might have been, only a few hours earlier, a quarter of a vanilla toffee. In the dark evenings these two shops beamed like beacons straight up Great George Street until about 6.30 when Birrell's continued alone in its rosy vigil until 11 o'clock at least. Among young people of more than one generation Birrell's was favoured especially for its molasses candies at 2d a quarter pound. The entrances of Birrell's and Hugh Miller's grocery were together as also were the next two single shops. These were Blair the bookseller and stationer (also known as the Grosvenor Library) and Pollock the jeweller. Small, elderly, grizzled and smartly attentive Mr. Blair I remember well because of the fascination of the array of neatly cased Collins' blue and Nelson red cloth-bound sevenpenny novels had for me. I would occasionally buy one simply to own it as I was too young to fully appreciate W. Clark Russell and Jack London, Captain Charles Gilson's 'In the Power of the Pygmies' and 'Submarine U93' in the *Boy's Own Paper* coming within my scope. Incidentally this beautifully printed large paged monthly with full-coloured glossy cover was priced at sixpence but sold at fourpence halfpenny. Pollock was also a watchmaker and like Mr. Peden's his premises were black and gold and had the same type of large black-framed clock protruding above its entrance. Fraser's no-counter butcher's shop took in two more windows and with possibly a single draper's, tall Mr. Kerr's licensed grocer's completed the corner into Roxburgh Street where the painters and decorators firm of George Sellers & Son had secluded business premises with a frontage of their own design. In trying to recall all these shops of fifty to sixty years ago, breaks are inevitable. In fact it is a wonder I can remember so many after all that has happened to me since, and to the shops. I say this for the shops beginning on the other corner of Roxburgh Street are just too vague for me to place or, possibly, they have remained much the same with a millinery shop at the corner and one or two single shops before Gentles' whose newsagent's single shop I can remember, especially the interior, as if it were still there.

Amid a varied stock, much of which had been undisturbed for years, in her 'widow's weeds' and crumply black hat sat meek Mrs. Gentles, seemingly resigned to life's tribulations, her sad eyes gazing wistfully across *Aunt Kate's Dream Book*, *Home*, *Chat*, *Chuckles* and *Lot o' Fun*, as she shifted an evening paper nearer to you and took your halfpenny because that was the price of the paper. In the back of the shop was a large cavernous recess which housed the remains of what had been, sometime in Britain's historic past, a circulating library of current appeal featuring such works as those of Wilkie Collins, Mrs. Oliphant, George Gissing and Emile Zola with the possible later addition of the new excitements daringly created by Elinor Glynn and Charles Garvice.

Bob, Mrs. Gentles' son, was quite a character. He assisted his mother in the shop and continued alone eventually with his two cats. A trifle wizened, and of slight stature, he had a chirpy manner and a quizzical look in his eye that let you know you couldn't get the better of him. This he exemplified occasionally in recounting his war experiences. A great sportsman, he was as regular as a clock in hurrying across to Hillhead Post Office in time for the two-thirty. In the early 1920s he took to playing the banjo. He had then cultivated a good connection up by Grosvenor Terrace and Huntly Gardens where he delivered the evening papers personally and was well-known below stairs.

Elder's shoe shop was there, as it is today, on the other side of Gentles' close. Then came the slightly recessed two-windowed fish shop of McCall. Facing Elliot Street, similar to the one opposite Bank Street, was the small grocer's business of George McVey who looked like Bairnsfather's 'Old Bill' in mufti. Bayne & Duckett's premises had, I have discovered, been the Hillhead Post Office until 1905 when it moved to its present position. I have an idea that A. & W. Paterson had a branch in this row, but I may be wrong. But I do remember the German barber with one leg and a crutch. He had a fiery nature and was liable to get drunk in the evenings. He had a single shop, prior to the Great War, just beyond the large frontage of the plumber's shop of George Miller & Son. About 1920, when Mr. McDougall had retired, Professor McColl succeeded him and had his veterinary surgery in the premises formerly occupied by the German barber. A. & E. Murray, drapers, were for many years at the corner where Loudon Terrace forms the south side of Observatory Road.

And now the shops of fifty to sixty years ago, which I have been reviewing in this television of memory, come to an end with the small row that stood alone and occupied half the ground facing the Burgh Halls from the north side of Observatory Road to Grosvenor Terrace Lane. The other half was a small field with a low wall broken by one or two tradesmen's huts. Eventually Wylie & Lochhead built their garage and showrooms on it. Apart from the Curlers' Tavern, these shop premises were surely the oldest in Byres Road until Grosvenor Mansions displaced them and incorporated the newest street premises. The most memorable

'Girlie', a Hillhead terrier and friend, 1968.
(Sundial partly re-erected in herb garden, Botanic Gardens.)

Gibson Street Bridge.
Built in 1894 by Caledonian Railway
Company when constructing line,
replacing Woodlands Road Bridge
built in 1853. *April 1970**

thing to me at this row is the container for household removals which rested on wooden props that allowed a horse lorry to be backed under it when required. It reposed beside Andrew Sadler's showroom and deeply recessed store and workshop. The setting had a grassy rural touch where the wooden container lay beside the stretch of red blaes footway that extended to the lane. There was a vintage quality about Sadler's shop for he dealt largely in best second-hand and sound antique furniture. It was a family business, well known to several generations in both Kelvinside and Hillhead.

In West of Scotland sanctums and drawing-rooms there are probably still many cherished photographs, some silver-framed, which bear the name of Ralston or Weir. Weir Bros. were well-established here, having continued the reputation of Ralston & Sons who began business in 1856 and who still exist in Glasgow as industrial photographers. I think the firm of Mackinlay the plumbers and electricians were also in this row although they had a large double shop opposite Havelock Street. I have a notion there was also a china shop, possibly another branch of McDougall's, and then nothing but the field. The few shops recently demolished at the side of what was then No. 1 Grosvenor Terrace are of a much later memory with the one at the corner of Grosvenor Terrace Lane becoming the last studio of Weir Bros. For many years a relic of the long past stood beside the railings on the low wall at the corner of Grosvenor Terrace and Great Western Road. This was a four-armed signpost the eastern arm of which gave the mileage to 'GLASGOW (Royal Exchange)'.   1971

The Palace of History and
Garden Club. Scottish Exhibition
of National History, Art and
Industry, Kelvingrove, Glasgow 1911.
Annan

RUGBY
RECOLLECTIONS

I WAS introduced to Rugby in 1906 when my big sister took me to Hampden Park to see Scotland beat the invincible side from South Africa. The score was 6 points to nil. It was in this match that Kenneth Macleod scored his famous try that is still regarded by surviving spectators as the most spectacular ever. Kenneth took a high dropping ball in flight and in a flash cut through the Springboks three-quarter line, beat the fullback, and touched down amidst tumultuous cheers from the biggest crowd of spectators ever to watch a rugby match.

Kenneth Macleod was the fantastic product of Fettes College and a triple Blue of Cambridge. He was picked to play for Scotland while still a schoolboy but his Headmaster would not grant permission. He won 10 Rugby Caps before he was 21. Kenneth was an astonishing athlete. At Fettes when 16 years of age he created a record for the High Jump which stood unbeaten for thirty years. He threw the cricket ball 122 yards. That record still stands. While still at school he would drop kick goals from halfway, with either foot. He was never beaten over the 100 yards and 220, either as a schoolboy or as a student at Cambridge. He was a scratch golfer. At 21, at his father's request, he switched from Rugger to Cricket. He was the first Scottish schoolboy to get a Cricket Blue at Cambridge. He captained Lancashire and on one occasion knocked up a Century against Yorkshire before lunch. His skill in Soccer was such that Manchester City were interested. A brilliant bridge player and a remarkable raconteur. A truly great ball player. He married four times. He died in Cape Province in 1964 aged 79.

The game against the South African side was the only International ever played in Glasgow. Although the game was played on a Wednesday afternoon such was the reputation of the Springboks that 50,000 spectators turned up. Never before had Rugby been seen by such a big crowd. It set the Scottish Rugby Union a serious problem. Edinburgh was the home of Rugby. Internationals were usually played at Inverleith, where only 11,000 spectators could be accommodated.

It was unthinkable that Internationals should in future be played in Glasgow. The solution of this awkward problem was to build Murrayfield.

Murrayfield was opened by England in 1925 when Scotland beat the Auld Enemy by 14 points to 12. The winning points being scored in the last minutes of the game when a magnificent dropped goal was manoeuvred by J. B. Nelson and Herbert Waddell. The crowd gave these Glasgow Accies a standing ovation.

The best Rugby side Scotland has ever seen was the famous Glasgow Academical team of 1925-26 when they won the Championship with a unique record. This remarkable side produced 9 full Internationalists and 3 reserves for Scotland. Their standard of play was so attractive that Rangers became concerned about losing so many spectators. Their shipyard supporters from Clydebank were turning up at New Anniesland in their 'bunnets' instead of crossing the river to Ibrox.

Hillhead High School F.P. – who shared the Championship with Royal High School F.P. in 1933-34 – were a fine side which played particularly attractive Rugby. It was not a heavy side but it was fit and won most of its games in the last 20 minutes. Jimmy Cotter and Ian Dawson reduced the Scissor pass to a fine art and were responsible for making this pass a popular feature of the game. Copey Murdoch was fast and effective in attack and a great kicker of drop goals. On one occasion at Hughenden, when playing against West of Scotland, 'Copey' dropped three consecutive drop goals from practically the same spot about 40 yards out, in the space of 5 minutes. This side produced 3 Internationalists.

The most historic try in the annals of Scottish Rugby was the one scored by Wilson Shaw, the current President of the S.R.U. when in 1938 he again defeated the Twickenham bogey, when he dodged through the English backs to score a thrilling try between the posts. The Scottish spectators went wild with joy and Her Majesty Queen Elizabeth stood waving in the Royal Box; forgetting, in the excitement of the moment, that she was also Queen of England.

CHARLES A. HEPBURN, 1970

Burgh of Hillhead Fire Brigade
Report For The Year Ending 11th November 1884
To The Honourable Commissioners
The members of the Brigade have attended at the Engine House
13 times for Drill & Cleaning Appliances
5 Alarms of Fire have been Reported to which the
    Brigade turned Out

Estimated Damages

1st at Mr Buchans 12 Westbourne Terrace on 11th Nov 1883 £ 20 – 0 – 0
2nd " Mr Fairleys 13 Great George Street on 15th " " £ 3 – 0 – 0
3rd " Mr Gladstones 4 Ann Street on 26th Jany 1884 £ 10 – 0 – 0
4th " Mr Hepburns Otago Street (Joiners Shop) on 9th Feb " £ Trifling
5th " Mrs Bells 19 Montgomerie Drive on 3rd April " False Alarm.

John P. Scott
Superintendent

Glasgow City Archives

WALKING home on winter evenings the long ribbon of Great Western Road unrolls itself before me in a glittering chain of light, a very torrent of earth-treading stars marking the straight running course to the opening river and all the glamour of the West. The friendly eyes of the traffic signals have for me a knowing little wink as they bid me stop, wait, go: the Neon lights blaze a lovely trail of blue, red, green, and amber, and the shop windows gleam for me like Aladdin's cavern.

Every tram and bus that streams past in a brilliant flash may be full, no doubt, of ordinary people like myself, but, for the moment, in the shining speed of their passing they assume the personality of riders in triumphal chariots, adventurers saluting the road to unknown hearths.

Placid Days

As I walk I fall to dreaming, picturing how this familiar road appeared on winter evenings when as a child I hurried or sauntered home from school. There were not so many lights in the streets of the Hillhead of that earlier and more placid day, only the tall standards tracing the tram lines as far as Botanic Gardens, and some years later extending to Hyndland Road, while up and down the long side-streets and through the quiet crescents and terraces the lamplighter dotted a little glowing trail. Shop windows were shuttered and dark at closing time, with no afterhour flaunting of their wares as we see to-day, and Venetian blinds screened the discreet illumination of incandescent gas or table and standard oil lamps in the comfortable flats and tall houses.

Cabs and Skates

Going out in the evenings, especially if you rode in a four-wheeled cab, was a small adventure for little girls in Red Riding Hood capes with fleecy 'clouds' covering their curls, straight fringes or long plaits, and for little boys in reefer coats, mufflers, and woolly gloves. The cab had a curious and, for us, entrancing smell of musty leather, mildew, and the stables. Thus we journeyed

gleefully through streets that had shed their everyday homeliness and become darkened tunnels of echoing emptiness to eagerly anticipated parties, and at Christmas time to the pantomime and the circus.

But better even than circus or pantomime for boys and girls in the Hillhead of long ago was Loch Burnie. First came frost, days and days of it – and anyone will tell you that in these good old days we very often had real hard winters – till on some bright morning under a sky like blue steel, the air still and brittle with frost, mysterious as any bush telegraph would flash round the school the magic message 'Loch Burnie's bearing!'. Then the lovely words 'Skating Half-holiday!', and soon there were eager feet crunching over the churned-up snow round the little loch.

Sabbath Calm

Winter Sundays in old Hillhead were quiet indeed. Church in the morning, followed by a walk out Great Western Road, perhaps as far as the boating pond, where we could joyfully and surreptitiously kick up with our Sunday shoes the thick tan laid down for riders. Then in the afternoon came Sunday School or Mr. Arthur's Meetings for boys and girls in Hillhead Burgh Halls.

Fantastic Future

Quiet, decorous, well-ordered old Hillhead, where, during the morning shopping hours, opulent carriages and pairs, or elegant one-horse broughams stood outside the shop doors and nearly everybody knew everybody else. The cinema was a nebulous dream of the future, the motor-car only vaguely spoken of, and the even more fantastic idea of flying in the air on a par with the wild prophecies of the tales of Jules Verne.

Those of us who knew it may recall its passing with regret, while admitting that as children we would have rejoiced in the flashing, sparkling lights and all the rushing turmoil of this present-day Great Western Road.

MABEL PENMAN
(*The Glasgow Herald*, 7th January 1939)

The Hillhead Duel

WHEN a Bearsden lady was visiting her Uncle Fraser in Somerset in 1962 he said to her, 'Do you know that I witnessed what may well have been the last duel in Scotland? It took place when I was a boy at Hillhead High School.' He then recounted the facts and she jotted them down as follows.

A quarrel arose in school between two boys. It became so bitter that they decided it could only be settled by a duel. A formal challenge was made and Seconds appointed. The weapons chosen were pistols which somehow were obtained for a few shillings. The site selected was vacant ground upon which Belmont Church was built a few years later. Below Queen Margaret Hall (Lilybank House) a solid wooden fence

extended across the field and a light paling at the Great George Street end.

The hour was fixed for late afternoon and, on the appointed day, the duellists arrived with their Seconds. The distance was paced out. The signal was given and the combatants fired. Happily their aim was not accurate. One bullet embedded itself in the Queen Margaret Hall fence and the other came to ground in Great George Street. The proceedings ended abruptly when a cry of 'police coming' caused the duellists and spectators to take to their heels along Lilybank Gardens Lane. There was great relief that no one was coming down Great George Street at the time.

One of the duellists was known as 'Putty', his father having a joiner's business in Hillhead. 'Putty' was eventually expelled from H.H.S. for putting beetles in the teacher's desk. Undaunted he joined the army as a drummer-boy and went off to the Boer War.

KELVINSIDE (BOTANIC GARDENS) PARISH CHURCH

THE practical vision that created this congregation grew from a meeting which took place on 13th February 1857, within 20 Kew Terrace, the residence of Mr. John Blackie, Senior. Foreseeing a major residential development about to be planned for the area west of Kelvinbridge, Mr. Blackie and several other leading members of the Free Church timely recognised the need for establishing a central place of worship among the new community likely to be formed within the next decade. Decisive action in this respect was encouraged also by the fact that the most westerly Free Churches were then the College Church in Lynedoch Street and St. Stephen's in New City Road. Through the initiative of Mr. Thomas Corbett, father of the first Lord Rowallan, the very desirable site at the junction of Byres Road and Great Western Road was secured at the price of 8/- per square yard. After various setbacks, including a change of architect, the foundation stone was laid by Mr. John Blackie, Senior on 4th September 1862. In the meantime a temporary church was in use at the corner of Byres Road and Observatory Road. This had been constructed at a cost of £800 and opened for public worship on Sunday, 6th November 1858. The Rev. William Traill of the Free Tron Church accepted the first charge in 1862 but, after four years, in the new church which was opened in 1863 he relinquished his incumbency for health reasons and moved to Elgin. Then from East Kilbride came a son of the manse from Thurso in the person of the Rev. Walter Ross

Taylor whose inspiring vigour, extending over nearly forty years, lighted a flame of faith in Kelvinside Church that remains.

The Boys' Brigade Company of Kelvinside Church, while retaining its original title The 4th Glasgow Company holds the honourable distinction of being the second oldest Company in existence, ranking next in order to the 1st Glasgow Company, that of Sir William A. Smith, the Founder of the Brigade. Its first Captain was William Nicholl who, with others whose names are on the Roll of Officers, had the honour of taking part in the historical meeting with the Founder in framing the Constitution that created the world-wide establishment of The Boys' Brigade.

Kelvinside Church is also memorably associated with the 5th Scottish Rifles, the Territorial battalion formed from the famous 1st Lanark Rifle Volunteers which was recruited mainly from professional and business men residing west of Charing Cross. In 1914, after war was declared, the 5th Scottish Rifles attended Church Parade the following Sunday morning in Kelvinside Church prior to leaving the city for their war-training station. The service on this momentously appropriate occasion was conducted by Dr. Thomson.

The well-known peal of eight bells was gifted by Mr. Nicol Paton Brown as a memorial to former pupils of Glasgow Academy and Kelvinside Academy and also to members of the congregation who made the supreme sacrifice in the Great War of 1914-18. The bells were rung for the first time on Christmas Day, 1917.

The Boys' Brigade (4th Glasgow) Company of Kelvinside Church, with their Officers and Chaplain, Rev. P. D. Thomson, D.D. Date unknown (possibly period of Great War). In 1928 Church extensions were built on this ground.

Dr. Walter Ross Taylor

MINISTERS

Rev. William Traill, M.A.	1862–1867
Rev. Walter Ross Taylor, D.D.	1868–1907
Rev. P. D. Thomson, M.A., D.D.	1907–1938
Rev. Alan Boyd Robson, M.A.	1938–

Kelvinside (Botanic Gardens) Parish Church from front of Botanic Gardens Railway Station. *May 1937. Salmon*

View from north front of church looking across to Botanic Gardens Railway Station. *May 1937. Salmon*

William Nicholl

One of the seven who attended the historic Meeting at Ann Street and first Captain of the Boys' Brigade Company of Kelvinside Church.

Portico, Byres Road entrance, Kelvinside (Botanic Gardens) Parish Church. *April 1970**

CAPTAIN ROBERT E. 'BOSS' YOUNG WITH THE 1ST GLASGOW SCOUT GROUP

Kelvingrove, 1914

1ST GLASGOW SCOUT GROUP

Some information about their Scout Headquarters situated at 7 & 8 Alfred Terrace, Hillhead, Glasgow W 2

Captain Robert E. Young was Adjutant of the four Glasgow Cadet Corps then in existence in 1907 in the four West-end schools. It was customary to hold an Annual Cadet Camp and in 1907 such a camp was held at Barry in the 'sunny month of June'. Many of the Cadets thought it was a great pity to suspend their comradeship of the summer until the next year's Camp. They discussed with Captain Young the possibility of starting some form of weekly meetings for at least some of their numbers. He agreed that it was a splendid idea and selected four squads of eight from each of the schools – Glasgow Academy, Glasgow High School, Hillhead High School and Kelvinside Academy – to start the scheme. Was this a prophetic glimpse of B.P.'s Patrols of eight or just a strange coincidence?

Towards the end of August 1907 arrangements were made to inaugurate the meetings of the four Patrols after the summer holidays were over and on the re-start of the schools in early September. At first the four Patrols met in Captain Young's home at 8 Athole Gardens. At a very early date it was obvious that some other meeting place was essential and a flat was rented at 6 Strathallan Terrace (now Caledon Street). Again what with increasing numbers and objections by neighbours to such unusual tenants another move had to be made. In May 1909, Captain Young spotted a house at 8 Alfred Terrace but it was too expensive for a young troop. One day, however, he met a Mr. Biggs, Scoutmaster of the then 5th Glasgow Troop on the same hunt. After a talk they decided to join forces, the original First Glasgow being divided into A and B Companies and the 5th Glasgow forming C Company. At a later date (I think around 1919) the house at No. 7 was also taken over and eventually the two houses were connected by a passage through the wall at first floor level. Considerable alterations were carried out in the early '20s after £2,000 had been raised at a bazaar. Electric light was installed in place of gas and a portable stage was constructed for concerts, etc. It was around 1941 that the First moved to temporary Headquarters in Great Western Road near Kelvin Bridge, in a large shop. From there they moved after the war to the mansion-house at 4 Victoria Circus which they purchased and a few years ago extended by a hall in the grounds costing around £13,000 (House purchased in 1944).

The First Glasgow claim to be the first Troop in the world and have been continually in operation since 1907.

Robert E. Young or Boss YOUNG as he was known to thousands of boys, died in 1940. He was the first County Commissioner of Glasgow and held that position from 1908 until his death in 1940. He was born on 9th August

Captain Robert E. 'Boss' Young

1877 and died on 7th February 1940. He was Group Scoutmaster of the First from its start in 1907 until his death. When he started the four Patrols in 1907 he very soon ran them on the lines of the new Scout Movement based on the pamphlet issued by B.P. and later on the lines of the fortnightly parts of *Scouting for Boys* which came out in January 1908.

Boss Young lived all his life in the West-end of Glasgow. His father lived at 8 Athole Gardens and was in business in Queen Street as Yarn and Rope Merchants. Boss went into the business and during the First World War spent a considerable amount of time in the Clyde area examining ropes for the Admiralty and shipping.

He had always called in at the County Scout Head-quarters around lunch-time before making his way home for lunch. The Headquarters were originally in Blyths-wood Square and after the war were moved to a Memorial House at 21 Elmbank Street, which had been purchased and equipped from a huge Bazaar held in St. Andrew's Halls. So his routine included a call around 12.30 at Elmbank Street then a walk along Woodlands Road to Park Road, up Park Road and then out Great Western Road to his home. On this daily route he met the boys from Woodside and Willowbank Schools coming out for lunch, mainly in Woodlands Road. Many were scouts but many were not. He seemed to know all of them by their name and also knew much of the home background. The boys would link on to his arms or shout 'Hullo Boss' as they passed. Then as he turned into Great Western Road, he began to meet the boys from Glasgow Academy (his old school) and then Hillhead High School – the same performance was continued – boys leaving off from his arms and company as they reached their home streets and more boys taking their places. And so he reached his own home, had his lunch and began his return along the same route meeting boys coming back from their lunch, etc. Later when his father died and the home at Athole Gardens was sold, he went to stay in the then Grosvenor Hotel at the corner of Byres Road and later he stayed in the Westbourne Private Hotel. His memory was remarkable – not only remembering names but details of brothers and sisters and home life. It must also be remembered that the First Glasgow Scout Group gradually became one of the largest units in the United Kingdom and had numbers between 200 and 350 at a time. It can be imagined over the years from 1907 until his death in 1940, there must have been hundreds if not several thousands through the First. And, of course, he also knew many other boys and leaders from other Troops in the City in the growing Scout Movement. At some week-ends he would go to Queen Victoria School for Soldiers' and Sailors' Sons, at Dunblane. He was a governor of the school. He would take four or five boys out for a run in his car and for a tip-top tea. Again he became well-known to generations of QV boys. (It was one of his tales that one day when passing Buckingham Palace, the sentry on duty whispered 'Hullo Boss' as he passed. An old QV boy!) The Scout Headquarters at Alfred Terrace were usually opened by Boss around 7 p.m. every night, including Saturday, and sometimes on Sunday afternoons. The HQ closed for the boys at 9.15 each night but Leaders were usually around until 10 or later. Then very often there was a Parade of the whole four Troops from Alfred Terrace at 2.45 on a Saturday, led by Boss through Dawsholm area to Acre Woods (now mainly Maryhill Park) where Scouting activities were carried out before marching home (with bugle band) to Alfred Terrace. Boss always led the Parade. Eventually the pattern changed and we lost Acre Wood.

Many of his former Leaders and Boys will readily admit to-day that their training in the First and especially in the art of leadership, paved the way for much of the success they have had in later life.

He was, of course, on many of the early Committees that were the pioneer spearhead of the new Movement and he was known to B.P. and to many of the pioneers of the early days of Scouting.

J. D. STEWART, 1971

THE WILLOW BANK
BOWLING CLUB

Upper Green,
Willow Bank Bowli[ng]
Club. *1970**

A well-remembered family business at corner of Albion Street and Byres Road. This branch was established in 1875 and closed down in 1960. It was managed by Mr. George Hunter whose nephew, Mr. James Mellish, is in centre of group. *c.* 1925. *Courtesy of Mr. J. Wilson Hunter*

THOUGH the early records of this Club have long been lost, its origin may be traced to the Bowling Green formed in 1695, when the Town Council disposed of ground in Candleriggs to Mungo Cochrane, with the restriction that it should be kept as such, in all time coming.

Cleland, in his *Annals of Glasgow*, states that 'in 1816 this old Bowling Green was acquired by the Magistrates and Council, on which to erect a Bazaar, and extended from the old *Herald* buildings at the corner of Bell Street and Candleriggs to the house which forms the entrance to the City Hall, and extended back to the Police Office Lane.'

Thus after 121 years' occupancy, the Club had to remove from Candleriggs, and a site on the west side of Renfield Street, between St. Vincent Street and Gordon Street, was secured.

In 1832 another removal was made westwards, a new green being laid down on the property called Willow Bank. The grounds were situated at the north-west corner of Bath Street and Douglas Street, and were famous for a well, much patronised by the families in the neighbourhood. The western boundary was a large orchard, which extended to Sauchiehall Street. In 1835 the present name was chosen and Rules were drawn up and printed for the first time. Some of the members, also about the same year, desirous of continuing good fellowship in winter, formed the Willow Bank Curling Club.

Later, in 1846, the Club leased ground in Elmbank Street, on part of what is now the site of the High School.

Being again compelled to find new quarters, and in order to prevent the necessity of such frequent removals from leased ground in consequence of the extension of the city, the Club purchased ground at Burnbank, and opened the green in what is now Willowbank Street, Woodlands Road, on 12th May 1859. In 1896 the ground was acquired by the Glasgow School Board, and the site is now occupied by Willowbank School.

At the instigation of several members of the Club a Company with limited liability, was then formed to purchase the plot of ground, now occupied by the Club, fronting Victoria Crescent, Dowanhill – the whole scheme having involved an expenditure of about £4,000. Two greens were laid, the dimensions of the lower one being curtailed owing to the crescent formation of the ground at that point.

The new Greens were opened on Saturday, 15th May 1897, under the presidency of the late Mr. John Pirrie, Buckingham Terrace. The turf for the upper green, removed from Willowbank Street and successfully relaid, was procured from Ayrshire in 1859 by the late Mr. William Anderson, C.A., and is acknowledged to be equal to any in the country.

(Centenary Year Booklet 1935)

Willow Bank Clubhouse. *1971**

Northpark Terrace
(35–51 Hamilton Drive) 1866.
Architect: Alexander 'Greek'
Thomson.
*May 1970**

Bank Street (Bothwell Terrace)
at Great Western Road.
*April 1971**

Bank Street from corner
of Great Kelvin Terrace
and Glasgow Street.
*May 1970**

Ashton Road. Cleared along with Sutherland Street to make new road opposite Highburgh Road. Lower half of Ashton Terrace remains on right. *1968**

Byres Road from south of Highburgh Road. *September 1970**

Byres Road from corner of Ashton Road. *April 1971**

Lookout at a North West Frontier fort. Not quite, but has some slight association of fact as this is where a narrow defile called the Khyber Pass ended above the Kelvin about a century ago. It is a rear view of Kirklee Railway Station from below the steep bank at this point. *1965**

South African War Memorial of the Highland Light Infantry, Kelvingrove Park. Erected 1906. *1965**

FIELD MARSHAL EARL ROBERTS OF KANDAHAR

Reining in his horse as he gazes towards the Khyber Pass in the North West Frontier (of the Botanic Gardens) where, at the time when he was advancing on the Khyber Pass in India, a tortuous pathway of this name led from Great Western Road over the hill behind High Windsor Terrace (Kirklee Terrace) to Kirklee.

This splendid memorial is at the top of Kelvingrove Park in front of where the two Crimea cannon used to be. The memorial is the work of Henry Bates, A.R.A. and is an exact replica of that erected in the Maidan, Calcutta. It was dedicated by Lady Roberts on 21st August, 1916. (In the photograph the rather charming inclusion of the amorous young couple was quite unexpected.)

September 1965*

James Barrack, Headmaster, 1878–81

KELVINSIDE ACADEMY

IN 1877 there was issued a 'Proposal for the Foundation of a Proprietary Educational Institution' to be called 'The Kelvinside Academy' – the undertaking to be named 'The Kelvinside Academy Company, Limited.' The document contained the following:

'While shareholders may confidently anticipate a satisfactory return on the Capital invested, the promoters have mainly in view to provide an Academy so conducted as to afford a guarantee that sound education in its highest branches shall be within the reach of all residing within the district.'

This might be called the first 'Prospectus', and £13,850 was subscribed. Ground at Kirklee extending to about three acres was fenced. A school building was erected estimated to cost about £12,000 but in fact, when completed, found to have cost £21,698 11s. A recent newspaper article referred to the Academy as one of a small number of schools in Glasgow which deserved to be preserved for the beauty of its architecture.

The school opened on Monday, 2nd September 1878, with 155 pupils, and by 1882-3 this had increased to 267. This remained roughly the size of the school into the new century, but by 1907-8 it had dropped to 194 and by 1912-13 to 137. During this period there was little change in buildings, but efforts had been made to secure playing fields. Waste ground near Dowanhill, then Hyndland, seems to have been used before the first official field in front of the school across Bellshaugh Road. Later came the use of ground at Balgray.

During the 1914-1918 war, 540 Academicals joined the Services and of this number 131 did not return. As a Memorial to those who died it was decided to set up a Trust to take over the ownership and control of the school from the Kelvinside Academy Company and to run the school on a non-profit-making basis. It was felt that this would ensure not only the continuation of the school but the continuation of the spirit of all those who had served, the survivors and their successors maintaining the memory of the fallen.

There was one very great difficulty. The Kelvinside Academy Company had accumulated the 'staggering' burden of a debt of about £46,000, and this had to be cleared before steps could be taken to raise a War Memorial Fund. How this was done makes a fascinating story which is told by William Brodie in his book *Kelvinside Academy, 1878-1923*. Dr. Brodie himself played a very large part in the negotiations which led to the affairs of the School being put on a sound basis.

The Kelvinside Academy War Memorial Trust was duly incorporated on 25th May 1921. The following year the field at Balgray was purchased from the Kelvinside Estate Trustees, from whom it had been leased for some years by the Academical Club. Later another piece of ground was secured on the north side and made into a first class pitch by which was erected a stand with changing rooms underneath. In the school there were only minor changes, the introduction of electricity and the turning of 'play sheds' into a Dining Room.

For the first fifty years of its existence the great majority of the boys leaving school went into 'business,' but there has always been a relatively small but extremely successful minority entering the Universities. An old number of the school magazine, about 1906, contains University notes from Oxford, Cambridge, Edinburgh and Glasgow, and the writers were not lone representatives of the school. Law seemed to secure many of the brightest, who later practised in London and Edinburgh, notably Fergus Morton, who, having spent all his schooldays at Kelvinside, went on to Cambridge and the English Bar, and as Lord Morton of Henryton to the House of Lords. Medicine and divinity also had their quotas. Just before the 1914 War and increasingly during the '20s and '30s, boys went into accountancy and many of the leading figures of Glasgow's commercial life to-day are of these generations.

Many well-known Kelvinside families have been associated with the school as Directors of the Company, as pupils, Academicals and Governors. Dr. William Brodie's name will always be associated with the foundation of the Trust, that of Mr. T. H. H. Warren with the Science Block, and that of Mr. James Bell, with the new Hall and Dining Room. To one generation the name of the Chairman of that day, Colonel Gourlay, will always be associated with a day spent in the grounds of Erskine Hospital, of which he was Medical Superintendent, on the occasion of the passing down-river of the *Queen Mary*. Another Academical and Director, Dr. J. R. C. Greenlees, holder of many Scottish Rugby caps, was called from a Kelvinside practice to become Headmaster of Loretto, an unusual but most successful appointment. At nearly the same time the Rector of the period, Douglas (Schulze) Miller, a Glasgow Academical often capped by Scotland between 1905 and 1911, moved to Aberdeen

Grammar School and some years later became High Master of Manchester Grammar School.

In early days men of widely different characteristics served the school, including the poet John Davidson, and George MacDonald, who later became head of the Scottish Education Department. From early in the century to the late '30s the solid core of the staff was supplied by these well loved and long lived stalwarts, Jimmy Loudon and William Fogo. Of this period, too, was D. H. Low who taught English and then French. At one time he had been an English Lecturer in Belgrade and tutor to the Serbian Royal Princes and could always be lured into the highways and byways of European interests.

The Cadet Corps has played a very important part in the life of the school. Founded in 1893 under the command of S. W. Gemmell as the 4th Volunteer Battalion Scottish Rifles Cadet Corps (Kelvinside Academy), it was the first Cadet Corps to be established in Glasgow and junior only to Glenalmond, Merchiston and Blairlodge in Scotland. Its association with the Scottish Rifles was a most happy one from which the Corps benefited greatly and which it remembers with gratitude to the present day. In 1908 it became the O.T.C. with more direct control from the War Office. In 1948 another change of name took place and it became the Combined Cadet Force with, in the case of Kelvinside, Army and Navy Sections.

From the earliest days Rugby Football has been the chief sporting activity and the school has provided its quota of international players. A decline in numbers just before the First World War led to the loss of many of the best fixtures, but with the expansion of the school since 1945 the situation has righted itself.

A. R. FORRESTER
From an article in *The Scottish Field* December, 1964

Douglas G. Miller, Rector, 1913–21

RECTORS

James Barrack (*Headmaster*)	1878–1881
James Macdonald	1883–1895
Bingham Dixon Turner	1895–1901
W. Cecil Laming	1901–1913
Douglas G. Miller	1913–1921
D. Morrice Low	1921–1928
Ian McPherson Bain	1928–1932
W. S. Clark	1932–1939
At Tarbet Hotel war years 1940–1945	
R. Murie	1945–1956
C. J. R. Mair	1958–

(minus degrees, honours and decorations to avoid incompletions)

The Cadet Corps in 1899

School Buildings. *Architect:* James Sellars, 1879

Kelvinside Railway Station, Great Western Road. Caledonian Railway via Partick Central and Crow Road Stations, *c.* 1930. Built originally for Lanarkshire & Dunbartonshire Railway in 1896.
Architect: Sir J. J. Burnet. *Courtesy of Professor C. J. Fordyce*

Semple's Balgray Farm, corner of Beaconsfield Road and Great Western Road, *c.* 1925. *Daily Record*

Lilybank Gardens, sloping down from No. 34. This side began with lofty three-storey flats, their two close entrances being Nos. 23 and 25 with the main-door of No. 24 in between. Here, at the rounded roadway from No. 1 on the high corner of Great George Street, a barrier wall divided it from the unbuilt half of University Gardens. The paved approach to the Boyd Orr Building now covers the site of No. 24.   *August 1971 **

The Hillhead Murder

COMMITTED in the dark shadow of night near the glimmer of a bracket gas lamp projecting from a high wall in Ashton Lane, it has remained unsolved these sixty years.

About 9.40 p.m. on Monday, 21st January 1912, Miss Aikman of 24 Lilybank Gardens (a main-door house) had arrived home and gone into the back bedroom when she saw, through the railings at the raised backgreen in Ashton Lane, two men engaged in a desperate struggle. Hearing a cry of 'murder' she opened her window and shouted that she would phone for the police. She then heard a thud and saw a man hurrying off in the direction of University Avenue. The police arrived promptly and found a man lying in blood coming from the back of his head. Some distance away a constable found an iron bar about two feet long. The man was removed to the Western Infirmary but died shortly afterwards.

From a bank book and papers found on the victim it was revealed that he was George Riddoch, silver engraver of 64 Buchanan Street. Also in his pockets were a sovereign, a half-sovereign, a sixpence and sevenpence halfpenny in coppers. It was learnt later that he was a bachelor aged 45 and lived at the Y.M.C.A. Residential Club in Bothwell Street. He was Chairman of the model section of the Scottish Aeronautical Society which had been using an upstairs workshop in Ashton Lane. But the workshop, after being closed for some months had been sold. This building, at the turn of the century, had been part of the first premises of Barr & Stroud Ltd. Since then it has been occupied by J. B. Stevenson Ltd. the motor body specialists.

There was nothing to explain the motive of the crime and the movements of the victim on the night of the murder remain shrouded in mystery from the time he left the Y.M.C.A. after having tea. One brief detention was made and two or three suspects checked and cleared. Later on it was rumoured that the police knew who the murderer was but lacked convicting evidence. Partick being in its last year as an independent Burgh, the former Hillhead Burgh police station was then a sub-station of the Maryhill Division. Superintendent Matthewson was in charge of the investigations. Among the officers assisting him was Detective Inspector Trench.

This excellent model of a traditional milk cart is to be seen in Tollcross Museum.
Rupert Roddam 1970
Courtesy of People's Palace

Hubbard's main Hillhead shop and restaurant on original site. Latterly part of City Bakeries Ltd. Closed down in December 1970. *April 1970**

Great Western Road from opposite Otago Street. *Early morning April 1970**

Great Western Road shops below Alfred Terrace. *May 1969**

In Kelvingrove Park.
Listening to Clydebank Burgh Band
on Sunday afternoon, 23rd August, 1970.   *

Pillar at the University Avenue entrance to Kelvingrove Park.
Originally with other three formed part of gateway to Woodlands
House in Woodlands Road.   *April 1966**

Drinking well in Park at
Park Road entrance.
*1962**

Yorkhill House, built 1805. The site is now occupied by The Royal Hospital for Sick Children opened by King George V and Queen Mary, July 7th, 1914.

Original entrance to Glasgow Art Gallery & Museum Kelvingrove. Opened in 1901 as part of the International Exhibition of that year. On the marble floor at the entrance was an iron turnstile in the charge of an elderly uniformed policeman. This entrance ceased to be used in December 1914 when Kelvin Way was completed and the approach road from Sauchiehall Street to the Argyle Street entrance was being constructed to suit the intended use of the building as a military hospital, a proposal which the military authorities rejected some months later. *May 1970**

Architects: Simpson & Milner Allen, London

A Man in Armour
signed and dated 1655?
canvas 54⅛ × 41⅛ ins.

Rembrandt (1606–69)
Graham-Gilbert Bequest 1877
Glasgow Art Gallery, Kelvingrove

After belonging to Sir Joshua Reynolds in 1764, *A Man in Armour,* almost a century later, was acquired for the Graham-Gilbert Collection at Yorkhill House.

John Graham-Gilbert, R.S.A. was born in 1794 in the Stockwell, Glasgow. His father was a West Indian merchant. In 1834 he married Jane, niece of Andrew Gilbert of Yorkhill. In 1838 his wife succeeded as heir to the estate and, in conformity with the terms of the settlement, he took the surname of Gilbert and removed to Yorkhill from St. Vincent Place. He died at Yorkhill in 1868. When his widow died in 1877 she left the whole of her husband's collection (having no issue) to the City.

King Edward VII and Queen Alexandra leaving Glasgow University during their State Visit to the city in May 1903. Windows on the right are of the Western Medical School in the Stenhouse building. *Scottish Field*

Memoir

I WAS born in Bute Mansions in 1890 and, during the course of my life in Hillhead I have dwelt in three other houses. In May 1968, I gave up my last residence at 73 Southpark Avenue (Viewfield Terrace) opposite No. 78 at one time occupied by Charles Rennie Mackintosh and which was demolished in 1963.

The acquisition by the University of the houses on both sides of Southpark Avenue had taken place and I was the last to leave.

Robert Knox (1790–1848) of Kelvingrove House had a son Robert who lived for a time in Royal Crescent. He was born in 1821. His daughter Helen (1857–1935) was my mother-in-law, having married William Cowan Finlay (1851–1925) who was born at High Windsor Terrace, Great Western Road, Queenstown, which is now Kirklee. Knox was a powerloom manufacturer and the Finlays manufacturers of gingham and pullicats. William

and his brother Hunter played rugby at Burnbank in one of the first teams of Glasgow Academy. Latterly their home was at 11 Granby Terrace. My mother-in-law, as a young woman, sometimes visited at Saughfield House from Royal Crescent.

The recreational building housing the swimming baths of the University cover the site of 3 Oakfield Terrace (75 Oakfield Avenue) where I lived from 1922 to 1939. Below us, on Gibson Street, there were three small villas with couchant plaster lions in place of pillars. They were between the lane and the small row of shops in University Avenue. Before the Union was built we could see the white tramcar at its terminus and hear its characteristic 'whine' as it came round the sharp rise from Gibson Street. Occasionally a tramcar overran the line when the night was dark or foggy and gave us a display of pyrotechnics when being towed back.

KENNETH STEVENSON
Kilmacolm 1970

MINISTERS OF
HILLHEAD CONGREGATIONAL CHURCH

Rev. Henry Herbert Snell, B.A.	1898–99
Rev. Thomas Templeton, M.A.	1900–07
Rev. John Safely, M.A.	1908–19
Rev. Herbert Henry Summers, M.A. B.Sc.	1921–27
Rev. Percy G. S. Hopwood, B.D., Ph.D.	1929–35
Rev. Vera M. M. Kenmure, M.A., B.D.	1936–45
Rev. Edward James Baker, B.A.	1946–50
Rev. Harry Escott, M.A., Ph.D.	1951–67
Rev. Bernard Lodge, B.D.	1968–

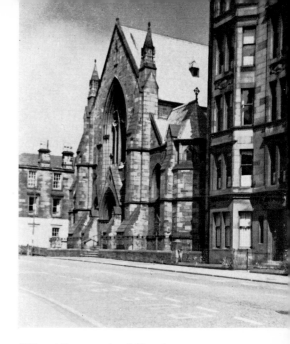

Hillhead Congregational Church,
University Avenue. *1970**

Miss Barclay's restaurant and Miss Davidson's tobacconist shop in University Avenue opposite Hillhead Congregational Church, 1928. *Courtesy of Miss Davidson*. Vacated in 1937 when Union extensions were planned for the site by the University. Miss Barclay moved to the corner of Ashton Road and Byres Road and Miss Davidson to the other end of Bank Street from which she retired in 1971 after being over 60 years in business.

Rev. Vera M. Kenmure

HILLHEAD CONGREGATIONAL CHURCH

HILLHEAD has always had a good quota of churches and amongst those is Hillhead Congregational Church situated in University Avenue adjoining Bank Street and opened on 26th September, 1890.

This is the oldest Congregational Church in Glasgow, the original building being near the Broomielaw in Ann Street (now Midland Street) going back to 1799. Rev. Greville Ewing became the first minister in 1800.

Many Hillhead people must recall with pleasure the preaching of such ministers as John Safely, H. H. Summers, and Dr. Percy Hopwood. More recently, the church was most fortunate to have the services of the very talented Rev. Vera M. M. Kenmure, M.A., B.D. who was the first ordained woman minister in Scotland. In recognition of her great powers as a preacher, she was appointed in 1951–52 the President of the Congregational Union of Scotland— the first woman to occupy such a post.

From 1946–50 the church had as its pastor the Rev. Edward Baker, whose tenure of office was most successful. Latterly Rev. Harry Escott M.A., Ph.D. author of *A History of Scottish Congregationalism*, was minister from 1951–67.

At present the church has a linked ministry with Partick Congregational Church, the pastor being the Rev. Bernard Lodge, B.D.

Amongst famous visiting preachers to the church in times past, were Rev. Silvester Horne (father of the late Kenneth Horne) and Dr. Maude Royden. Many well-known names come to mind as one recalls such members as Professor T. MacRobert, Professor A. A. Bowman, etc.

Hillhead Congregational Church prides itself on having had as its organist Alexander Gibson who later became the very famous Conductor of the Scottish National Orchestra. During his two years of office he gave two Organ Recitals in the church which were a sheer delight.

JEANIE McLEAN HILL, 1970

Lamp of Thomas A. Kerr, Lord Provost of Glasgow, (1952–55). The Lighting Department still maintain it for street illumination in front of his residence at 108 Otago Street. *May 1970**

White cars of Glasgow
Corporation Tramways
Department at their
University terminus.
1938. W. A. Camwell

Occasionally a tramcar overran
the ends of the rails and
ploughed into the tarmacadam.
The following car usually
managed to tow it back by use
of a coupling bar.

This recent extension of the Men's
Union viewed at night from a position
near the side of the church gives the
illusion of a white tramcar about to
turn from University Avenue down
Gibson Street as of yore.   *1971**

Gibson Street from the bridge across
the Kelvin. *May 1970**

WOODSIDE SCHOOL

◉

HEADMASTERS
1882–1932

left to right

George Murray (*inset*)
J. A. Petrie, Alex. Flint, (*standing*),
John Robertson (*inset*),
W. W. Russell, James Gibson,
William Law

*(minus degrees, honours and decorations
to avoid incompletions)*

Jubilee Magazine 1932

LET us look back to Woodside's beginnings as seen through the eyes of one of its famous Heads of the English Department, Mr. John Hutchison.

The real story of a school can best be told by its old pupils. But other details may be given. The site was bought by the old Glasgow School Board from the Streets Improvement Trust in 1880, and towards the close of that year was cleared of the tradesmen's workshops on it. The building rose during 1881, but it was not until 7th August 1882, that the school was opened and the first pupils were enrolled. The architectural style is a good example of Italian Renaissance (one refers, of course, to the older building) applied to an Educational Establishment, the Architect (Mr. Robert Dalglish) having designed it after a school he had seen in Florence. Such an island site, splendid for some purposes should, of course, never have been chosen for a school. But who then dreamt of the enormous increase of road traffic to come? It can be recorded to the credit of the old Board that it resisted for a time the extension of the tram cars to Park Road. (Shades of the No. 11 bus to-day!)

In 1886 the Park Church Hall was hired, although the new school in Hillhead, in Cecil Street, had attracted some families who came from beyond the then municipal boundary (the number of such children in 1883 was 351). With the growth of dwelling houses in the great vacant space between Rupert Street and Park Road (alas for the lost opportunities of school playing fields!) even this extra accommodation proved insufficient and the German Church that once stood in Woodlands Road was also used for some classes. Finally, more ground was accordingly bought, and the old whitewashed Blythswood Cottage and several other wooden and brick erections on it being demolished, the new building, also designed by Mr. Dalglish, was begun in June 1884, and occupied by higher grade classes and infants in April 1896. This building, grandiloquently characterised at the formal opening as of Italian Architecture, was of the central hall style favoured by School Boards of the '90s of last century, now considered quite out of date. The total cost of the two buildings may be of interest. The sum of £12,964 was paid for the whole site. The old building and equipment cost about £11,000, the new building a little over £19,000. Together, they provided accommodation for 1,600 pupils.

THE ALBANY

The continually increasing importance of Secondary education led to a noteworthy addition to the accommodation. There was a fine little building in West Cumberland Street (now Ashley Street), once the residence of a Lord Provost, and afterwards a private school, famous in its day. It had been taken over by the School Board, who, enlarging it, used it first as the Pupil Teachers' Institute. With the abolition of the P.T. system in 1910, Woodside School was at once chosen as a Junior Student Centre, and this Albany Academy became an annexe of Woodside. It was eminently suitable for secondary education, having the finest Art Room in Glasgow at the time (over which R. Lewis Sutherland, a former President of the Glasgow Art Club, reigned), a spacious laboratory and excellent classrooms. There was something particularly distinctive about this building away from the main stream of traffic, something academic and classic in its atmosphere that had itself an influence. For fifteen years it remained the

Woodside School from Woodlands
Road; Eldon Street on left and
University tower beyond.
May 1971*

Woodside Annexe: it was with reluctance that staff and pupils left in 1925 when the Albany became of all things, a clinic. But the wheel of time turned and the Albany was restored to Woodside some years after World War Two and, in the dying years of the school still remains its Annexe.

The school colours (maroon and silver) remain unchanged but under the wise guidance of one of Woodside's finest headmasters, Mr. John Petrie, the initials of the old badge being no longer applicable, an assistant Art master of the time, Mr. John McVean, had a new design approved in which the laurel wreath encloses the initial 'W' with the motto 'FORTITUDINE' beneath. The School was fortunate too, in having a brilliant young teacher in the Classics Department in the late '20s, James Erwin Dunlop, who besides being learned in Latin and Greek, had also the gift of Music and Poetry. He it was who gave Woodside its School Song – 'Fortitudine Vincemus' – which is bawled out lustily as occasion demands.

And what of Woodside's Former Pupils? Well, they are legion and have achieved fame in many spheres. One of the best known was William Power who became a West of Scotland journalist and writer. I quote from the article he gave to Woodside's Jubilee Magazine: 'I remember though not exactly as if it were yesterday, the morning of August 1882, was it not? when Woodside School opened. I had watched it being built, not long after as a very small child. I had seen the demolition of a cow-feeder's edifice on the site now occupied by the Swedenborgian Church in Woodlands Road.

About that time too, was also removed a print work that stood where Kelvinbridge Railway Station now stands. The whole space between South Woodside Road and Great Western Road, west of the Three Tun Tavern, was open grass, the Burnbank drill-ground of the 1st L.R.V. Even the horse car had not yet invaded those Arcadian heights and retreats!

I remember that morning of 1882 because I was among the first pupils to be enrolled. As we went in an ominous sound was heard and our hearts sank. Word ran back that one of our "push" had hanselled the headmaster's strap and got "six" for giving cheek.

But our forebodings were not justified. Mr. George Murray, the first headmaster – who came from Henderson Street – was a strict disciplinarian but a just and kindly man and an excellent teacher with a strong vein of pungent Scots humour.

There were two "kent faces" among the teachers. One was Mr. Potts, an able mathematician, who had been in the "Established Normal" where I had been a pupil for a few months at a very tender age – that being my only previous schooling – the other was Mr. John Ferguson, a distinguished looking young man with a pointed beard. His career, which would have been a brilliant one was cut short by consumption. The only lady teacher I distinctly remember was Miss Laird, the Infant Mistress, who was succeeded by the famous Miss Oliver Scott.

Apart from the annual inspection – in those days rather a nightmare to teachers and pupils – we were a boisterously happy crowd. Our chief school recreations were marbles and "slides" in the playground and on the neighbouring pavements, varied by arranged "fights", in which I did not shine. Once in a while the class was photographed by a gentleman called Wohlgemuth, a name which we shockingly mispronounced.

I left Woodside at thirteen to enter a bank. My whole schooling had amounted to four-and-a-half years: yet in the subsequent scrappy progress of self-education I discovered that in English, Latin, French, History and Geography, the foundation had been well and truly laid at Woodside.'

Thus saith Mr. Power. But what of Woodside's other famous pupils? Well, perhaps the best known is William Primrose (born 1904), who started out as a violinist but became world renowned as a specialist in the viola. He studied with Ysaye and played the viola eventually in the London String Quartet, touring with that group for five years in Europe and North and South America. He made his solo debut as a viola player in Rio De Janeiro and appeared in Italy, Spain, Canada and the United States where he eventually settled after becoming first viola with the N.B.C. Symphony

William Power (1873–1951) Author and journalist. Friend and neighbour of J. J. Bell in Hillhead. *1935 Annan*

Orchestra. He is still resident in New York at the time of writing.

Other F.P.s worth mentioning are Professor W. L. Renwick who reached his peak as Professor of English at Armstrong College, Newcastle-on-Tyne: Professor D. M. Blair, Dean of the Faculty of Medicine, King's College, University of London, and the popular B.B.C. documentary producer, Archie P. Lee, who edited the Woodside Magazine from 1926 to 1928. Woodside, of course, has given more than its quota of scholars to the Church and Teaching Professions. I mention just a few, viz., Rev. Archie Campbell and Rev. Andrew McLellan for the Church: Alexander Stewart (now a Glasgow Headmaster) and your contributor who is now the Sage of Garnetbank, a school which has supplied many pupils for Woodside, Garnetbank being one of its 'feeders'. Noted recently with pleasure was the appointment of former pupil David McNee as Chief Constable of the City of Glasgow Police.

But progress must not stand in the way of sentiment and so the Fates have decreed that Woodside School is to depart from its now unsatisfactory island site. A fine new Comprehensive Establishment (can one call it a school?) is being constructed alongside of and on the site of Kent Road School and by 1972 Woodside and some of its kindred, notably St. George's Road and Kent Road, will have amalgamated to form the new *Woodside Secondary*. We hope at least the old name will be preserved to carry on some of that tradition started up in 1882.

SAMUEL C. GREAVES, 1972

Interior of St. Silas English Episcopal Church. Erected 1863. *Architect:* John Honeyman. *Mitchell Library*

BURNBANK BOWLING CLUB

In the year 1865 a group of bowling enthusiasts in the west and north-west of Glasgow held a series of social gatherings to raise funds for the establishment of a bowling club in the Burnbank area of Glasgow. This effort was carried out under the guidance of Mr. George Sellars, who later was to become Burnbank's first President in 1866. Local support resulted in an immediate promise of credit up to £150 from the Union Bank of Scotland.

Colonel Campbell of Blythswood was then approached for a feu of some ground lying between the 1st L.R.V. Drill Hall in West Princes Street and Woodlands Road, exactly where Willowbank School now stands. The ground was procured at a rent of £20 per annum, and as there was enough space to lay out two greens, it was decided to do so, one of the greens being smaller than the other. Estimates for laying down the greens and erecting a bowlhouse were accepted, the work was commenced in January 1866, and the greens were opened for play in May. As the Club was situated in the district of Burnbank there was no problem about the choice of a name.

Two entrance gates were made, one a wicket-gate off Great Western Road, opening on to a path which led through ground then used as a showground by the Glasgow Agricultural Society, the other at South Woodside Road, now Woodlands Road. The cost of laying the greens and building the bowlhouse was approximately £300, an interesting figure in comparison with present-day costs.

It is a matter of regret that the official minute book of the Club from its inception in 1866 to 1874 was lost, so making it impossible to give much information about this vital period.

The Club was progressing very favourably

Clubhouse, Burnbank Bowling Club.
September 1970*

Where, it is said, a certain schoolboy, one John Reith, on his way to the Glasgow Academy from his father's manse in Lynedoch Street, first beheld the initials BBC.

German Church, Burnbank Bowling Green and Woodlands Road in 1908.
Valentine

until 1889 when the Directors received a notice to quit from the factor of the Blythswood Estate, because part of the ground, including the whole of the small green had been feued for building purposes. Protests being of no avail, meetings were hurriedly convened to look out for a new site, and after protracted negotiations with the Corporation of Glasgow the present site of our greens was secured.

This site was not, as some members think, a part of the West End Park; it had been used by the Corporation as a coup and a stone-breaking magazine. The frontage in Woodlands Road was used in some parts by tradesmen and shopkeepers. At the north-east corner there were a joiner's shop, a boot repair shop and a plumber's shop. It was some time before the huts were removed. The entrance was some forty yards east of the present one. The old turf was laid on the bottom green and new turf was bought for the top green. The Directors, aided by the members, held a bazaar towards defraying some of the expenses, and the magnificent sum of £900 was realised which went almost half-way towards the total cost of £1,960. The present greens were declared open on 27th May 1890 by Councillor Bilsland (afterwards Sir William Bilsland and Lord Provost of the city). But even in those days property was not always respected. For example, in the severe winter of 1892 the boys and girls of the neighbourhood noticed that the greens were frozen over, so they climbed over the railings and began to skate, a performance which was not looked on with a kindly eye by the members.

In 1903 consternation arose when the Corporation issued a notice to quit, as the ground was required for feuing. The members rallied to the call of the President, Mr. Wm. Mailer and the district was thoroughly canvassed. Three thousand one hundred and twenty-five householders in the area signed a petition which was presented to the Town Council, and after protracted negotiations the greens were handed over to the Parks Department. So the Club and its premises were saved.

When the German Church which stood in the north-west corner of the grounds was demolished in 1919 by the Corporation the ground was added to the site of the Club and laid out as a level lawn with flower beds.

from *Centenary Brochure*

Herbert's Farm of Woodlands in the late 1870s. Almost same site as Burnbank Bowling Club. *Old Glasgow Museum*

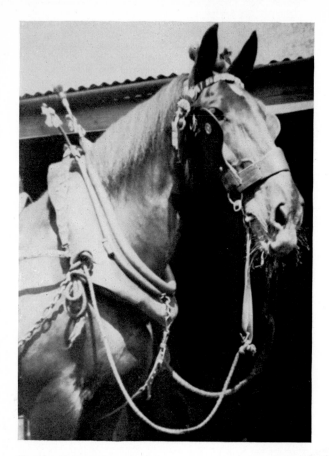

'Darkie', Helensburgh, 1955.
Courtesy of Miss Grace McHardy

Tribute

to

The Brave Days

of the

Horse

Horse tramcar leading final
parade of electric cars in Glasgow,
4th September 1962.   *Ian F. Hicks-Mudd*

Field (Howitzer Battery) Artillery, Kitchener's Army, 1915

Typical horse-drawn lorry amid
traffic on Bridge Street at
Glasgow Bridge, 1913.
Glasgow City Archives

William Beattie's splendid four-in-hand, in Bothwell Street, Glasgow, July 1939. (The horses survived the war.)
Daily Record

Bread van in wartime
February 1942.
Glasgow Herald

Hillhead Fire Brigade in 1913, the last in the city to have horses. The change to motor vehicles took place in November of same year when the horses were sold. *Courtesy of Glasgow Fire Service*

Hearse drawn by Belgian black horses. From being an ornate and cumbersome vehicle at the beginning of the century, the hearse had gradually evolved into this neat yet dignified carriage in the 1920s. *Courtesy of Wylie & Lochhead Ltd.*

First floor, Grand Hotel, Charing Cross, Glasgow. Shortly after noon, Monday, 21st October, 1968. Closed five days later after nearly a century of its memorable existence. Vanished early 1969.   *

Funeral carriages returning to stables. Passing Grand Hotel and Cameron Fountain at foot of Woodside Crescent. *1914 Annan*

Tea lounge of THE Picture House, Sauchiehall Street, opened in 1910. In 1925 the lounge vanished along with the palm court. The foyer was extensively re-constructed and, although it had been re-named the Gaumont, the cinema interior remained substantially the same to the last. It was demolished in 1972 at the same time as the former New Savoy building which adjoined it in Renfrew Street.

Courtesy of W. Ralston Ltd.

THE Picture House

To those who knew it during that first glorious phase which spanned the Great War period, THE Picture House was unforgettable.

'If you were intent on seeing "the pictures," you walked through a richly carpeted and pillared foyer with palm trees and divans snugly and invitingly placed. You then circumvented an embroidery of delicate greenery and flowers surrounding a beautifully-veined marble pond where large goldfish lazed or cruised majestically and fairy fountains danced their sprays from an island grotto. The spacious lounge, which now spread itself on either side, was dotted with groups of comfortable cane chairs, in front of which, on similar style tables, silver tea things glinted beside enticing French cakes. The whole effect made you feel you were in some splendid Palm Court of a Grand Hotel, and the inclination was to dally there instead of passing through the swing doors, beyond which, as you entered the translucent darkness, you were suddenly aware of a slight whirring noise above your head, and you followed the rays that came from its source until you slipped into a crimson plush seat and, in no time, found yourself "In Old California" where life moved silently in sepia tones, and sweet orchestral music stole up from below and wedded itself to the changing scene.'
Glasgow's Vanished Cinemas, Milden Miscellany 1948.

Institute of the Fine Arts 1901, 171 Sauchiehall Street. Built 1879. *Architect,* Sir J. J. Burnet. (Latterly occupied by Pettigrew & Stephens Ltd.)
Mitchell Library

BY SPECIAL APPOINTMENT PHOTOGRAPHERS
TO
HER MAJESTY

RALSTON & SONS
141, SAUCHIEHALL STREET
and
311 VICTORIA ST (BYAR'S ROAD)
Opposite the Borough Hall
HILLHEAD

GLASGOW

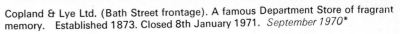

Copland & Lye Ltd. (Bath Street frontage). A famous Department Store of fragrant memory.   Established 1873. Closed 8th January 1971.   *September 1970*

1930

Copland & Lye
delivery van, *c.* 1920.
Courtesy of Mr. Kelly Ogg

Great Western Road at Buckingham Terrace. *June 1960**

Great Western Road at Hillhead Street. *Late June 1960**

Park Road. *June 1960**

Byres Road from Dowanside Road crossing. Grosvenor Picture House in centre. *April 1970**

Geological Note

The elevated part of Hillhead rises to 157 feet and is one of three local hills known to geologists as drumlins created by the Great Ice Age and composed of boulder clay and stratified sands and gravels. The other two are Partick Hill 179 feet, and Woodlands Hill 153 feet.

An Comunn Gaidhealach

For fifty years or more up to about 1930 the junctions of Byres Road and Queen Margaret Drive with Great Western Road formed the meeting-place on Sunday evenings of a great gathering of tall powerfully-built men and neat sturdy women.

For two to three hours they possessed the crossings, especially in the long summer evenings. A native of Hillhead attempting to make his way through this closely knit throng could feel like an alien. The only sounds to be heard were those of the Gaelic tongue holding communion with their individual inheritances from above the Highland Line to the farthest Hebrides.

Mostly they were off-duty police officers and female members of the domestic staffs of the well-appointed self-contained and terraced houses in Hillhead and Kelvinside.

Flying Machine Pioneer

Percy Pilcher a lecturer in Naval Architecture at Glasgow University lived with his sister in lodgings in Kersland Street. There between 1892 and 1897 they made models of gliders which, when built to full scale, he tried out on the slopes of Dunbartonshire near Cardross. In 1895 he achieved successful flight as an airborne pilot thus inaugurating the era of heavier-than-air flying machines. At a more developed experiment in Market Harborough in 1899 he was killed when his glider crashed in very bad weather. He was then 33 years of age

Hillhead Academy for Young Ladies, 12 Vinicombe Street

This establishment flourished in the Eighties and claimed to give a very complete education. The Principal, Mr. James Leitch accommodated resident pupils at his house, 21 Oakfield Terrace.

From 'The Glasgow Herald' Wednesday, 2nd October, 1878

The City of Glasgow Bank has stopped payment.

Great Western Road. Belmont Street on left. *October 1959**

The end of an era. 'Tweed' and 'Kelvin', the last of the Glasgow Fire Brigade horses, depart from Hillhead in 1913.
Courtesy of Glasgow Fire Service

TWO SPECIALTIES!

1.

"Royal and Ancient" Parchment.

A Delightful Notepaper of First-class Quality, and has
a Most Agreeable Surface.

PRICE.

5 Quires, in Box, - - - 1/- | 100 Envelopes, in Box, - 1/-

In Three Fashionable Sizes.   Specially adapted for Die Stamping.

2.

"Chad Valley" Marking Ink.

This fluid is guaranteed INDELIBLE, and after a prolonged trial
we have much pleasure in recommending it.

NO HEATING REQUIRED.   IN BOTTLES, **6d.** and **1/-**

J. BARRIE PATERSON,

Stationer and Printer,

695 GREAT WESTERN ROAD,

GLASGOW.

WALTER HUBBARD,

Family Baker and Confectioner,

508 GREAT WESTERN ROAD,
HILLHEAD

(FIVE MINUTES' WALK FROM BOTANIC GARDENS).

Famed Wedding Cakes.   Dainty Tea Cakes.
Scotch Shortbread.

LUNCHEON AND TEA ROOMS.

HIGH-CLASS PURVEYING.

Branches at
679 GREAT WESTERN ROAD;
486 DUMBARTON ROAD, PARTICK;
701 POLLOKSHAWS ROAD.

(Advertisements from Botanic Gardens handbook 1902)

Estd. 1873

JOHN McMILLAN, LIMITED, CHEMISTS.

17 GREAT WESTERN Rᴰ Sᵀ GEORGE'S CROSS

Compound Liquorice, or Prussian Powder
(FINEST QUALITY)
Dose.—A tea-spoonful at bed-time.

and 8, BUCKINGHAM BUILDINGS, HILLHEAD,
GLASGOW.

Now John Summers (Chemists) Ltd.

1869–70 (*selected list from approximately 900 insertions*)

Wilson Street, Hillhead

King, John, Laurel Bank

Viewfield Terrace, Ann Street, Hillhead.

Taylor, James D. D., Oakfield house

Ewing, Jas. Oakfield house

Smith Street, Hillhead Portman Place

1 Cochran, W. B.
2 Bishop, Robert
Burt, John
Fisher, Mrs. Archd. teacher of music
Edmiston, John, auctioneer
Wilson, James, Janefield cottage
Orr, James, dairyman, Kelvinside cottage
McArthur, John, wright, Rose cottage

———

Allan, James, Sr. 1 Grosvenor ter.
Alston, J. Carfrae, 18 Oakfield ter.
Anderson, Harvie, 14 Eaton Place
Blackie, John jun. (of Blackie & Son), Lilybank
Brown, Colin, Hillhead ho.
Brown, J. Berlin wool repository, 16 Bothwell Place
Brown, John, haberdasher, 13, 15 Hamilton Place, house, 11 Belgrave Terrace
Brown, Thomas, 6 Florentine Ter.
Bruce, Robert (of Woodside Paper Mills), 3 North Bank ter.
Burrell, A. M. 3 Hamilton Park quadrant
Chalmers, John, family baker, 12 Hamilton pl
Colquhoun, Alex. baker and confectioner, Ashton pl Dowanhill; house, Saughfield cottage
Cowan, Henry, 13 St. James's ter
Craik, Misses, teachers, boarding and day school, 16 Buckingham terrace
Cree, Wm. James, Tyrefield house, Wilson st
Cricket Club, Western Gilmorehill Park, Saughfield rd
Danks, Wm. butcher, 3 Craiglaw pl; ho. 17 Bloomfield pl
Dingwall, John, Post-Office
Dobbie, James, M. D. 1 Kelvin ter Great Western rd
Dobbie, Robt. livery stable keeper, Byars' rd

Dutoit, J. F. Frederic, professor of French, 10 Belgrave ter
Eadie, Rev. John, D.D., L.L.D. 6 Thornville ter
Ewing, George Edwin, sculptor, 13 Nelson ter
Farmer, Wm. family grocer and provision merchant, 1, 2 Craiglaw place: house, 3 Great Kelvin terrace
Faill, P. Salmon, teller, Bank of Scotland, 6 Hamilton pl
Gardiner, Joseph, Thornville ho.
Gemmell, John, procurator-fiscal, 5 Sardinia ter
Gemmell, John, family grocer, 18 Bothwell pl: ho. 15 do
Gibson, T. B. 3 Florentine pl
Gossip, Robt. (of N.B. Mail) 1½ Kelvin ter
Govan, Wm. Snr. South Park ho
Govan, Wm. Jnr. South Park ho
Hamilton, John, 1 North Park ter
Hegney, Charles, plumber and gasfitter, 1 Bothwell pl house 2 Otago st
Henderson, William (National Bank of Scotland), 1 Gt. Kelvin terrace
Hoggan, Andrew, Hillhead house, Saughfield rd
Jaap, John, pharmaceutical chemist, 10 Hamilton pl; ho. 23 Oakfield ter
James, Edward Dickson, head post-master of Glasgow, 9 St. James' ter. Gt. Western rd
Jones, Robert, slater and plasterer, 3 Wilson street; house, 2 Belgrave place
Junor, Patk. Bruce, agent, Clydesdale Bank, 8 South Park ter
King, John, Laurelbank
King, Robert, Parkview house, Gt. George st
Knox, Robt. jun (of Rainey, Knox, & Co.) resid. Saughfield house
Laird, John, upholsterer, cabinet, and venetian blind maker, 6 Bothwell pl
Lockhart, Oakvale, Hillh.
McAslan, William, teller, City of Glasgow Bank, 18 Bloomfield pl
Macbrayne, Miss, St. Bernard's pl
McKay, Rev. James, M.A. 1 Granby terrace
Mackenzie, J. F. C. (Capt. Royal Navy), 12 Hillhead Gardens
McLean, John, post-office
MacNair, J. S. Parkview house
Miller, Rev. Thomas, 1 Florentine pl

Morren, H. K. Post-Office, 6 West Bank ter
Morrison, Donald, A. M. rector of Glasgow Academy, 4 Victoria ter Dowanhill
Morrison, Rev. Jas., D.D. Florentine Bank House
Murray, John, tea and wine merchant, 4 West Bank ter: house 5 Bloomfield pl
Naismith, John (of McClure, Naismith, and Brodie) 2 Belg. ter
Nichol, John, professor of English literature, College: house 1 Southpark ter
O'Halloran, Michael, 6 Gibson st
Police Office, Byars' road
Post Office, 5 Kelvin ter
Russell, Wm. manager, Saughfield cottage, Dowanhill
Sawers, W. S. 14 Bothwell ter
Sheriff, Geo. (of Pollok, Gilmour & Co.) 13 Granby ter
Skene, William, physician, 2 Kelvin ter
Small, Francis, nursery and seedsman, Westbank house
Spiers, Moses, plumber, 2 Westbank ter
Spens, Wm. actuary, 3 Granby ter
Stark, J. M. Training Academy 25 Buckingham ter
Stenhouse, Alex. bookseller, stationer and librarian, 5 Kelvin ter; ho. 6 do.
Stewart, Robert Buchanan, 14 Sardinia ter
Stronach, Alex. (of City of Glasgow Bank) 3 Grosvenor ter
Sword, Robert, Marleybank
Taylor, Rev. Dr. Oakfield house
Taylor, Rev. Walter Ross, 25 Ashton ter
Tod, William, cashier, Clydesdale Bank, 22 Oakfield ter
Walker, John E. Cab office. 1 Hamilton pl
Wallace, Dr. Wm. analytical chemist, F.R.S.E., F.C.S. 8 Granby ter
Whyte, John C. Oakfield cottage
Zinkeisen, Victor, merchant, 7 Hillhead gardens

Victoria Street, Great, Byar's Road.

Landles, James, church officer
Orr, John, joiner
Police Office, County
Sinclair, Mrs. J. Curlers' tavern
Moore, John, grocer
Gallie, William
Dobbie, Robert, livery stables

Byres Road

Prince of Wales Terrace.

3 Kennedy, Alexander
5 Landles, James
Christian, J. C.
Templeman, Miss
McDonald, W. H.
Roebuck, W.
7 Harvey, J. & R.
9 Billing, R. R.
11 Watt, John, butcher
13 Beaton, Mrs.
Mellish, Andrew
Coulter, E.
15 White, Jas.
17 Alex. W. Peden
19 Fulton, D. & R. plumbers
23 Butters, Joseph

Ailsa Terrace, Hillhead (Vinicombe Street).

2 Drysdale, Robert
Ross, G. W.
4 Kennedy, Alex.
White, James
Watt, John
Baxter, John
6 Black, Mrs. D.
Wallace, Walter
Scouler, F.
6 Balfour, Andrew
McLaurin, G. A.
12 Hillhead Academy
14 Gemmell, Mathew

Victoria Street, Hillhead

Partick, Hillhead & Maryhill Gas Office
Burgh Buildings
Simpson, Thos. inspector
Connelly, Edward
Philip, James

Byres Road

Victoria Buildings, Hillhead.

4 Clydesdale Bank
Millar, William, agent
5 Delmore, John
6 Bell, C. stationers
7 Hutcheson, James
Gibb, William
Bell, Miss
8 Roxburgh, Robert
9 Munro, Wm.
11 Bushell, Miss
Coglan, M. P.
Maitland, J.
Brown, Thomas
13 McMorran, W. L. & Co.
McMorran, W. L. & Co.
14a Morrison, George
15 Billing, Rodger
16 Robertson, Miss C.
18 Taylor, Geo.
19 Ross, Oliver
20 Paterson A. & W.
21 City of Glasgow Steam Dyeing & Laundry Co.
22 Algie, Wm.

1909–10

Great Western Road

Kelvin Bridge Station (C.R.)

Caledonian mansions.

447 Roxburgh, Robt.
449 Ballingall & Co.
451 Dickson, Peter
453 Glasgow Dairy Co.
455 Templeton, J. R.
455A Hutchison, Miss A.
457 Arbuckle, J.
459 Union Bank of Scotland
——Otago street here
471 Hegney, Charles, & Son
473 Leishman, A., & Son
477 Bowie, W. & J.
479 Balharrie, Mrs.
481 Cochrane, W. P.
483 Hawthorne, M.
487 Hepburn, Peter
491 Speirs & Frame
493 Kennedy, Alex.
495 Speirs, John
       Logan, Mrs.
497 Annacker, Wm.
——Bank street here.
507 Cooper & Co.
517 Paterson, John
519 M'Dowall, R.
       M'Vey, Geo.
       M'Kinnon, Thos.
       Wilson, H.
521 Miller, F. & A.
525 M'Raith, John
527 Crawford, R.
       Mitchell, A.
529 Birrell, J. S.
531 Ferguson, James, & Sons
535 National Bank of Scotland
——Wilson street here

Rokeby Terrace.

595 Farmer, William, & Son
597 Assafrey, A. F.
599 Danks, William
       Hutton, Alex.
601 Campbell, Misses
603 More, Robert
605 Hyslop, Geo. R.
       Dunlop, D.
607 Russell, Thomas
609 Maclean, John
611 Thomson, William
613 Hutton, Alexander
617 Murray, John & Son
625, 627 Northern Farmers Ltd.
629 Vernal, W., & Son
633 Munn, W.
635 Jaegar, Dr., Sanitary Woollen
       System Co.
639 The Western Stores.
641 Greenock wool and hos. stores
645 M'Queen, Miss
647 The Hundred Acre Hill
       Dairy Co.
649 Logan & Beatson
653 Craig, James
655 Harley, W., & Sons
657 Campbell, T. S.
359 Young, A.
665 M'Dougall & Sons

Buckingham buildings.

679 Hubbard, Walter, baker
681 Roxburgh, Robert

683 Andrew, Wm., grocer
685 Brechin Bros.
687 Mackichan, S.
689 Beattie, G. N.
       Taylor, Miss
       Watson, W. R.
       Grant, Peter
       Macintosh, John W.
691 Sawers, Ltd.
693 M'Millan, John
695 Paterson, J. Barrie
697 Johnstone, Miss J.
701 British Linen Bank ;
       Henry Fairlie, agent

Sandringham terrace.

711 Campbell, John
713 Bank of Scotland;
       J. L. White, agent
715 Waddell, R. D.
717 Paterson, John
719 Arnott, Mrs.
       Gray, Archibald S.
       Paterson, James B.
       Black, Miss
       Provan, D.
721 Chrystal, Bell & Co.
723 Wallace & Connell, plumbers
725 More, Robert
727 Stewart, M., fruiterer
729 Armstrong, J. W.
       Barclay, A. J. Gunion
       Chalmers, A. G.

Hamilton Place.

536 Chalmers, J., & Co.
534 Cappell, Robert
532 Bulloch, John
530 Cappell, Robert
       M'Fadyen, Miss
526 Brechin Brothers
524 Fyfe, James
518 Ramsay, C. C.
514 Sawers, Ltd.
508 Hubbard, Walter, baker
——Belmont lane here

Belmont Place.

498 Paterson, A. & W.
496 M'Vey, George
494 Arroll, R. H., jun.
       Buchanan, Mrs.
492 Brown, William
490 Sauter, Chas.
488 Frazer & Green, chemists
——Belmont street here

Salisbury Place

478 M'Queen, Peter
474 Leitch, Miss Mary
472 Barber, F. W.
470 Campbell, P. & P.
468 Dallas, David
       Duncan, Thomas
       Neilson, Thomas
       Sawers, R. K.
       Thomson, Mrs. Janet
466 Lawrence, John
464 Paterson, James
462 Oswald, Frederick
458 Calder, Mrs.
——Colebrooke street here
——Kelvin bridge here

1910–11

Otago Lane.

Clark, D.
2 Erskine, J. R.

Otago Street, Hillhead. 24

19 Blakely, E. M.
27 Hepburn, P.
       M'Gowan, Bros.
29 Farmer, W. & Sons
35 Pullar & Co.
39 M'Donald, A., & Co.
42 Lindsay, D.
       Smith, Wm.
28 Horn, Jas.
       Melville, Mrs.
20 M'Callum, D.
18 Macindoe, Thos. & Lauder
12 Kelvinbridge Post Office
10 Hegney, C.
8 Findlay, James
6 Hegney, Charles, & Son

Byres Road

——Albion street here
215 Hunter, James & Geo.
217 Stead & Simpson, Ltd.
219 Colquhoun, Mrs. A.
       M'Culloch, Mrs. A. P.
       Hunter, George
       Young, George
221 Reid, J., & J. fruiterers
223 Currie, W. L., chemist
225 Colquhoun, Alex., baker
229 Graham, Mary
231 Stafford, Miss, hosier
233 Young, Alex.
235 Geddes, John
       M'Luckie, R.

Ruthven Place.

239 Hill, Miss
241 Lockhart, William
243 Williamson, Matthew
245 Walker, John
249 Gooding, H. D.
       Ronald, Robt.
253 Smith, J. G.
257 Annacker, Ltd.
——Ruthven street here

Grosvenor Place.

259 M'Intyre, John
261 M'Clure, Miss
263 Boyd, J. W. & Co.
267 Craig, James
269 Gossip, Wm. M.
       M'Kinley, Robt.
271 Birrell, J. D.
273 Johnstone, John
277 Russell, Robert
279 Pollock, M.
       Wright, D. B.
       Taylor, Thomas
281 Greenlees & Son
283 Hay, Alexander, grocer
285 Smith, Crawford
287 Pollock, M.
291 Fraser, James
295 Johnstone, Hugh
297 M'Dougall, Mrs.
299 Kerr, William
——Roxburgh street here

Windsor Place.

303 Rowand, Miss
305 Cameron, M.
309 Park Dairy Co.
311 Gentles, A.
313 Philip, James
       Wilson, John
315 White, James
319 Macmillan, Alex.
321 Bayne & Duckett
325 M'Callum, James
       Sherry, C.
327 Todd, James
329 Bowie, W. & J.
331 Bingley, & Co.
333 M'Vey, George
337 Murray, A. & E.
——Observatory road here
347 Saddler, A.
349 M'Donald, M. & J.
351 Weir, John
355 Sellars, G. W.
357 Brand & Mollison
359 Rattray, John, & Son
363 Henderson, James, Ltd.
367 Miller, G., & Son
379 Dixon, Wm. Ltd.
381 Bell, John
389 Ross, A. M'Kenzie

ESTABLISHED 1853.   Telephone No. 2142.

WM. FARMER & SONS,
WINE MERCHANTS,
HILLHEAD.

WHISKIES. To Connoisseurs and those whose health requires the most perfect quality of this article, WM. FARMER & SONS have every confidence in recommending their blends of Old Vatted Whiskies.

	Per Bottle.	Per Gallon.	Per Doz. Bottles.
Farmer & Sons "Own Blend,"	3/-	18/-	36/-
GUARANTEED 6 YEARS OLD.			
Highland Liqueur Whisky,	3/6	21/-	42/-
GUARANTEED 10 YEARS OLD.			

DETAILED PRICE LISTS of WINES, SPIRITS, and MALT LIQUORS on application.

(Advertisement from Botanic Gardens handbook 1902)

Prince of Wales Terrace.

404 Kennedy, Alex.
402 Landless, James
    Robertson, Miss
    Templeman, Miss
398 Harvey, J. & R., grocers
396 Billing, R. R., florist
388 Peden, Alex. W., jeweller
386 Kuttner, F. C.
    Drew, Wm.
384 Bell, Miss
382 Blackwood, William
380 Glebe Coal Co.
378 Butters, Joseph
376 Fleming, J. S.

——Vinicombe street here.

356 Hillhead Police Station
    Hillhead Fire Station
    Drummond, D.
348 Burgh Hall; W. Freer, curator
338 Sanitary office
    Dobson, James L.
336 Johnston, A. M.

——Elliot street here

Victoria Buildings

326 Clydesdale Bank
    Alex. Fyfe, agent
320 Bell, C., stationer
318 Kuttner, Adolph
    Clugston, R.
316 Roxburgh, Robert
310 & 314 Post Office
308 Bryce, George
306 Fraser, Lachlan
304 Hillhead Garage
300 Morrison George
296 Barker, Miss F.
294 M'Innes, A.
290 Hardie, R. & Co.
286 Johnstone, Andrew
284 Paterson, A. & W.
276 Spite, Francis, & Co. Ltd.

——Great George street here

Lilybank Buildings

266 Gibson, William
    M'Kenzie, Wm.
262 Kirkwood, James A.
256 Curlers' Tavern
252 M'Kenzie & Co.
250 Subway Station
248 Dunlop, Peter, baker
242 Campbell, Mrs.
236 Stewart, R. L.
230 Rossi, A.
226 Granger, John, Forrest & Co.
    Ltd.
224 M'Donald, D.

——Ashton lane here

Ashton Place.

202 Ferguson, R., & Son
200 Horn, William, dairyman
196 Cochrane, Miss
194 M'Culloch & Elrick
192 Henderson, Jas., Ltd.
190 Kirkpatrick, Thos.
188 Sommerville, J. & Son
186 Sommerville, J.
184 Andrew, William
182 Orr, John, & Sons, painters
180 M'Gibbon, D.
178 Bryson, James
174 Frame, Wm. & Sons, grocers

University Avenue, Hillhead

1 Hillhead Congregational
    Church
3 Milligan, Kenneth
5 Wilson, Mrs. W. A.
    Fisher, J.
    Petrie, J.
    Plotzker, B.
9 Hillhead U.F. Church
    University Lodge
    University Union

——University gardens here
——Hillhead street here
    Wilson, Mrs. J., Hillhead
    house

——Ann street here
    Wellington U.F. Church
70 Burnett, J. J.

——Wilson street here

48 Anderson, G. P.
44 Western Medical School
42 Stenhouse, A.
26 Watson, Miss
    Stenhouse, A.
12 McKenzie, M. K.
10 Simpson, J. C.
8 Hall, John W.

Gibson Street, Hillhead

3–5 Sanderson, Jas.
11 Brucciani, A.
15 Campbell, James
17 Newlands, John M.,
    painter
19 Orr, Wm.
21 Baxter, Duncan
    Hill & Co.
    Smith, W. T.
23,25 Sinclair, Miss
29 Docherty, Wm.
    Brockett, McFarlane
    Stewart, William
    Frater, Henry
31 McDonald, D.
33 Docherty, W.
35 Rose, Mrs. C.
37 Bannatyne, John

Westbank Terrace.

39 Ross, Charles
    Simpson, L. W.
    Gilmore-Cox, Jane, M.B.,
    C.M.
    Gilmore, D. G.
41 Robertson, John, grocer
43 Donaldson, R. W.
47 Temple, Mrs.

Gibson Street, Hillhead

Ashfield Terrace.

36 Speed, David & Co.
34 Duncan, Joseph
32 Duncan, Joseph
28 Gillies & Co.
26 Murray, John, & Son
24 Gillespie, Mrs. Jas.
    Smith, A.
    Brown, John, grocer
22 Blair, Miss
20 Roy, John & Son
18 Gardiner, John
16 McAskill, D.
    McPherson, Mrs.

12 Robertson, M.
8 Brown, C.
6 White, Jas.
    Smith, Wm. J.
    Thomson, D.
    Black, John M.
2 Grant, Miss

1929–30

Great Western Road

Caledonian mansions.

445 Roxburgh, M. C.
447 Perry, F. J.
449 Ballingall & Co.
451 Dickson, Peter
453 Glasgow Dairy Co.
455A Hutchison, Miss A.
459 Union Bank of Scotland

——Otago street here

471 Davidson, M.
473 Leishman, A., & Son
477 Bowie, W. & J.
479 Balharrie, Mrs.
481 Ogilvie, Robert
483 Halliday, J.
487 Hepburn, Peter
491 Speirs & Frame
493 Kennedy, Alex.
495 Logan, Mrs.
    Reeve, H.
    Mackay, A. S.
    Walton, Misses
497 Morton, Marie

——Bank street here.

507 Cooper & Co.
517 Bayne & Duckett
519 M'Vey, Geo.
    Cappel, D. F.
    Haddow, W. M.
521 Cochrane, A.
525 Cappell, Ltd.
527 Fraser, Alexander
529 Caldwell's Dairy, Ltd.
529A Birrell, J. S.
531 Buttercup Dairy Co.
533 Scott, A L., & Son
535 National Bank of Scotland

——Oakfield avenue here

595 Rogerson, R. & Son
597 Vernal, William, & Son
599 Danks, William
    Hutton, Alex.
601 Campbell, Misses
603 More, Robert
605 Henderson, A. M.
    Macfarlane, Colin
    French, W. T.
    Irving, Mrs. Margaret
607 Russell, Thomas
609 Thomson, Edith
611 Taylor, J.
613 Hutton, Alexander
    Fraser, Wm.
617 Murray, John & Son
625,627 Northern Farmers Ltd.
629 Sadler, A.
633 Pullar, J., & Son, Ltd.
635 Primrose & Primrose
639 Bell, A, & Son, Ltd.
641 Scotch Wool & Hosiery Store
645 Regan, Isabel
647 Buttercup Dairy Co.
649 Logan & Beatson
653 Currie, A., & Sons, Ltd.

655 Daintywear
657 Lacey, Ltd.
659 Gillespie, R. B.

Buckingham buildings.

679 Hubbard, Walter, baker
683 Chalmers Stores Ltd.
685 Brechin Bros.
687 Mackichan, S.
689 Beattie, G. N.
    Rennie, Andrew
    Stewart, Miss Ethelwyn
    Shields, Wm.
691 Sawers, Ltd.
693 M'Millan, John
695 Henderson, R.
701 British Linen Bank ;
    Henry Fairlie, agent

Sandringham terrace.

711 Bank of Scotland ;
    Matthew Pettigrew, agent
713 Craig, James
715 Waddell, R. D.
717 Paterson, John
    Wilson, M. & N.
719 Arnott, Miss
    Provan, D.
    Dallas, David
721 Stalker, Duncan
723 Rennie, Andrew, plumber
725 More, Robert
727 Commercial Bank; W. White,
    agent
729 Roberton, S.
    Bruce, David
    Cruden, Misses
536 Chalmers, J., & Co.
532 Rossleigh, Ltd.
530 M'Fadyen, Miss
    Jockel, Miss
    M'Lellan, J.
526 Brechin Brothers
524 Bamber, J. H.
520 M'Alpine, Mary J.
518 Crosbie, Mrs.
516 Smith, George
514 Sawers, Ltd.
508 Hubbard, Walter, baker

——Belmont lane here

Belmont Place

498 Paterson, A. & W.
496 Munn, Wm.
494 M'Kenzie, A. W.
    Hunter, J.
    Dobbie, Mrs.
    Lowe, Geo.
492 Brown, William
490 Ferguson, James, & Sons
488 Frazer & Green, chemists

——Belmont street here

478 Marshall, J, & Son
472 Barber, F. W.
470 Pullar, J. & Son, Ltd.
468 Williamson, A.
    Taylor, Mrs. Jas.
    Sutherland, Misses
    Bailey, E. W. E.
466 Lawrence, John
464 Kelvinbridge Post Office
462-458 Savings Bank of Glasgow
    (Hillhead Branch)

——Colebrooke street here
——Kelvin bridge here

Smith Street, Hillhead. W. 2

Janefield terrace

1 Laird, Mrs.
3 Taylor, W.
  M'Beth, W.
  Purves, T.
  Silver, Elizabeth
5 Wyllie, J.
7 College Laundry
  Rossleigh Cycle Co.
  Hillhead Window Cleaning Co.
9 Orr, David T.
  Geddes, A S.
  Graham, W.
  Leitch, D.
  Millar, Lewis
  Abernethy, J.
11, 13 Semple, R.
15 Hubbard, Walter, Ltd.
17 Rennie & Prosser
  Hamilton, Claud, Ltd.
23 Stokes, D.
25 Greyson, R. W.
27 Fraser, Wm.
29 Aitchison, Robert
  Tannock, J.
  Gray, J.
31 Graham, D. R.
  Stobie
  Dunshie

—— Gibson street here

Otago St., Hillhead. W 2

7 Wyllie, Mrs.
19 Blakely, J. H.
27 Hepburn, P.
  Montgomery, T., & Co.
29 Hepburn & Ross
39 M'Donald, A., & Co.
42 Lindsay, D.
  Gardner, A. M.
  Trocche, V.
  Bristo, C. H.
20 M'Callum, D.
12 Findlay, Jas.
10 Hillhead Motor Transport, Ltd.
6 Hegney, C. J.

1930—31

Byres Road

—— Albion street here

215 Hunter, James & Geo.
217 Stead & Simpson, Ltd.
219 Dixon, Misses
221 Reid, J. & J., fruiterers
223 Currie, W. L., chemist
225 Colquhoun, Alex., baker
229 Brown, J.
  Wilson, John
231 M'Kean, Wm.
235 Geddes, John
  Wilson, Hugh
  M'Callum, J. G.
  M'Grellis, Wm.
239 Connell, C.
241 Loudon, Thos.
  Rippon, T.
  M'Clure, T.
243 Williamson, Matthew
245 Walker, Thomas
249 Ronald, Robt.
  Bell, Wm.
  Stewart, F.

251 Ure & Young, bakers
253 Todd, Geo.
259 National Bank of Scotland, Ltd.

—— Ruthven street here

261 Maypole Dairy Co.
263 Boyd, J. W., & Co.
267 Craig, James
269 Gossip, Wm. M.
  Stewart, A C.
  Sproul, J.
  Harley, G.
  Cooper, J.
271 Birrell, Ltd.
273 Miller, Hugh
277 Boots, Cash Chemists
279 Pollock, M.
  Taylor, Thomas
  Thomson, W. D.
279 Gillespie, J.
  Thomson, J.
  Haddow, A.
281 Greenlees & Son
283 Caldwell's Dairy
285 Chisholm, F. H.
287 Pollock, M.
289 Birrel, Wm.
  Shaw, J. L.
  Curley, Jas.
291 Fraser, James
295 Akerman, A. E.
  Henderson, J. D.
  Tonner, R.
297 Scott, A. L. & Sons
299 Kerr, William

—— Roxburgh street here

303 "Anthonette"
305 Adam, J.
311 Gentles, Mrs.
313 Campbell, Miss
  Davidson, Mrs.
  Bain, Miss
  Law, John
  Gentles, Mrs.
315 Elder, W. S.
319 M'Call, James
321 Bayne & Duckett
325 Nicol, Mrs Jas.
  Bertram, Mrs. Helen R.
  Bertram, Miss A. M. M.
  Mason, Miss
  Calder, James
327 Todd, James
329 Bowie, W. & J.
331 M'Call, Prof.
  M'Call, J. R.
333, 335 Murray, A. E.
337 Spite, Francis, & Co., Ltd.

—— Observatory road here

347 Saddler, A.
349 Repairs Co.
355 Reid, Geo.
359 M'Kinlay Co.
377 Wylie & Lochhead, Ltd.

—— Grosvenor ter. lane here

383 Weir, John
385 Ferrier Bros.
387 Chalmers, J. & Co.
389 Grainger & Co.
391 Castlebank laundry receiving
  office

404 Kennedy, Alex.
402 Landles, Miss
  Sutherland, Mrs. Geo.
  Gray, A. A.
  Templeman, Miss
398 Fulton, R.
396 Walker, Thos., fishmonger
388 Peden, Alex. W., jeweller
386 Kidd, H. A.
  Flint, Mrs. D. Frame
  M'Laren, P.
384 Bell, Miss
382 Blackwood, William
380 Brand & Mollison
378 Ramsay, John
376 Fleming, J. S.

—— Vinicombe street here

360 Corporation Electricity Department
356 Hillhead Police Station
  Hamilton, James
348 Burgh Hall; J. Hercus, curator
344 Eagle Express Co.
340 Dixon, Wm., Ltd.
338 M'Dougall, Allan H.
336 Shaw, R.
334 Rex, Arnot & Co.

—— Elliot street here

326 Clydesdale Bank
320 Bell, D.
318 Gauld, J.
  Napier, J.
  Horn, Mrs.
316 M'Coll, R. S., Ltd.
314 & 310 Post Office (Hillhead)
308 Duncan, D.
  Smith, E.
  Barrie, J.
  Middleton, H.
306 Buttercup Dairy Co.
304 Hillhead Garage Co.
302 Duncan, D.
300 Morrison, George
298 Doherty, J. G.
  Wilson, E. C.
  M'Cauley, W.

  Fyfe, A.
  Russel, H.
  Taylor, J.
296 M'Dougall, Mrs.
294 Tobia, G.
290 Thomson, R. A.
286 Allan, Mrs.
  Martin, D.
  M'Culloch, M.
  Haviland, G. W.
  Allison, Miss
284 Paterson, A. & W.
280 Orr, Charles
276 Templeton, R. & J., Ltd.

—— Great George street here

272 Massey, A., & Son
266 M'Lean, N.
  M'Kenzie, Wm.
262 Todd, Geo.
260 Murray & Grant
256 Curlers' Tavern
  Green, John
252 Milligan, Wm.
250 Subway Station
  Watson, Wilson, & Co.
248 Dunlop, Peter, baker
242 Gibson & Reid
236 M'Meekin, H.
230 Marzaroli, L.
226 Henderson, James, Ltd.

—— Ashton lane here

202 Baird, R. S.
200 Horn, William, dairyman
198 Methvens Ltd.
196 Cochrane, Miss
194 Grosvenor Picture House.
190 Rosefield, M.
188 Blair, M. B.
186 Turner, James
  Stevenson, C.
184 Hailstones, Wm. W.
182 Orr, John, & Sons, painters
180 Wilkie, J.
178 Bryson, James
176 Selkirk, M.
174 Union Bank of Scotland

ACKNOWLEDGMENTS

MY MAIN SOURCES of research are fourfold. Therefore, in the first place, I would thank Mr. Charles W. Black, City Librarian of Glasgow, Mr. Roy Gillespie, Librarian of the Mitchell Library and especially the staff of the Glasgow Room over the last three years; Mr. Richard F. Dell, City Archivist of Glasgow, who has many official records of the Burgh of Hillhead neatly docketed in the comfortable seclusion of his invaluable department; Mr. Robert Blair Wilkie, Curator of the People's Palace and Old Glasgow Museum, for his courtly attention in making available important pictorial contributions that enhance the historic background; Mr. H. K. MacKay, Librarian of Baillie's Library and his assistants Mrs. Mary Manchester and Miss Isabel H. Paterson. Here I must express my most grateful thanks to Mrs. Manchester for her unerring ability in tracing elusive facts and dates. With these main sources I would include appreciation of the assistance I got from Mr. David Reid of Robertland, Archivist of the University of Glasgow.

For giving life to the general panorama by their special contributions I am much indebted to the late Dr. Charles A. Hepburn, Dr. R. T. Hutcheson, Mr. A. R. Forrester, Mr. E. W. Curtis, Mr. George Sheriff, Mr. L. V. Beharrell, Mr. Samuel C. Greaves, Mrs. Sheila Pinkerton, Mr. John L. Dixon, Mr. Kenneth Stevenson, Mr. J. D. Stewart, the late Dr. Ellen B. Orr who died at the age of 86 on 21st January, 1972, and who was the first woman to practise general surgery in Glasgow, and to Dr. J. Gibson Graham, great grandson of James Gibson of Hillhead.

While publishers' permission to include extracts from Robert W. Service's 'Ploughman of the Moon' is acknowledged within, I would add my special thanks to Madame Germaine Service for so kindly approving the notes on the local background of her late husband which I have included in the brief biography along with the famous first verse of 'The Shooting of Dan McGrew'.

My thanks are due to the Trustees of the National Library of Scotland for supplying photographs for reproduction of the local sections of the Ordnance Survey maps of 1861 and 1913 and of Richardson's map of 1795; to T. & R. Annan & Sons Ltd. for their help in finding suitable photographs from their famous collection and, similarly, to Mr. Andrew Hannah and Mr. Alasdair Auld of the Glasgow Art Gallery & Museum. I am indebted to the Glasgow Headquarters of The Boys' Brigade for making available the 1913 photograph of the 1st Glasgow Company and of North Woodside Hall and to the Glasgow Headquarters of the Scout Association for the photographs of the 1st Glasgow Scout Group of 1914 and Captain Young.

For their assistance in relative matters I thank the Chief Constable of Glasgow, the Firemaster of Glasgow, the Head Postmaster of Glasgow and the Controller, BBC Scotland.

For granting inclusion of the correspondence on 'Old Hillhead', also various photographic reproductions and the article by Mabel Penman, I am indebted to Mr. Alastair Warren, Editor of the *Glasgow Herald*. I thank Mr. Comyn Webster, Editor of *The Scottish Field* for two photographs and Mr. A. R. Forrester's selections from his article on Kelvinside Academy. For permission to reproduce photographs indicated, I thank the *Daily Record*.

For their co-operation generally and for lending photographs or supplying information or both, many thanks are due to the following; the late Miss Jeanie McLean Hill and the Rev. Bernard Lodge, Hillhead Congregational Church; the Rev. Stuart W. McWilliam and Mr. K. K. Weatherhead, Wellington Church; the Rev. Alan Boyd Robson, Kelvinside (Botanic Gardens) Church; the Rev. G. M. Denny Grieve, Belmont & Hillhead Parish Church; the Rev. T. Kerr Spiers and Miss Walker, Hillhead Baptist Church.
Miss A. Jean B. Sloan, Headmistress, Laurel Bank School; Mr. Basil M. Holden, Rector, The Glasgow Academy, in association with Mr. A. R. Forrester's article based on the Centenary book by permission of the Governors; Mr. Walter E. Wyatt, Headmaster, Miss Mary B. Rodger, Secretary, Mr. William Thomson of the History Department, all of Hillhead High School, also Mrs. Alastair D. Campbell, Islay, for granting extracts from her late husband's handbook on H.H.S.; the late Mr. George Macintyre, Headmaster, Hillhead Primary School; Mr. C. J. R. Mair, Rector, Kelvinside Academy; Mr. James R. Cuthbertson, Headmaster, Woodside School.

For their special help in various ways I am most grateful to Miss L. M. Cheetham, Miss E. Davidson, Mrs. William Fulton, Mrs. John M. Halliday, Miss Irmgard Lemkes, Mrs. Charles H. Morris, Mrs. Henry Murray, Miss Sheila Reid, Miss M. Allison Sadler, Mr. J. H. Clegg, Mr. Wm. Roy Farmer, Mr. Ross Higgins, the late Mr. Alfred G. Lochhead, Mr. Tom McLeod, Mr. W. L. Little of the former Hillhead Bowling Club, Mr. R. J. McKellar, Secretary, Willow Bank Bowling Club and Mr. Henry Gibb, Secretary, Burnbank Bowling Club. To the many who have assisted otherwise and for all expressions of encouraging interest when they were most welcome I tender my sincere thanks.

Finally I wish to thank Miss Elizabeth F. Aitken, private secretary to Dr. Hepburn, and my wife for much of the typewriting; Dr. Hepburn's Trustees for enabling me to complete the book and Mr. William Bryson of Robert MacLehose & Co. Ltd. for his assistance in the general work of production.

December 1972   H.B.M.

SUNDAY TELEGRAPH
PATIO
GARDENING

Line drawings by Charles Stitt

Colour photography by Michael Warren and the author

Garden sketches designed and drawn by
Kenneth Midgley

ROBERT PEARSON

Mahonia 'Charity'.

ROBERT PEARSON

Robert Pearson has been the Gardening Correspondent of the *Sunday Telegraph* since 1971. He was also, until 1985, the Publisher of Collingridge gardening books, and for many years before that the Gardening Editor of the Hamlyn Publishing Group, of which Collingridge forms part.

Trained at some of the finest gardening establishments in Britain, including the Royal Horticultural Society's school of horticulture at Wisley in Surrey, his entire career has been devoted to horticulture, journalism and publishing, apart from war service as a pilot in the Royal Air Force.

He is a Fellow of the Institute of Horticulture and a council member of the Royal National Rose Society.

His much-loved home with large garden is in Hertfordshire.

First published in 1974 by
The SUNDAY TELEGRAPH
Hamlyn Paperback revised edition 1979
Second revised edition 1983
This edition Telegraph Publications 1988
Copyright © SUNDAY TELEGRAPH and
Robert Pearson 1974, 1979, 1983, 1988

ISBN 0 86367 290 6

Telegraph Publications,
Peterborough Court,
At South Quay,
181 Marsh Wall,
London, E14 9SR

This book is sold subject to the condition that it shall not, by way of trade or otherwise, be lent, re-sold, hired out or otherwise circulated without the publisher's prior consent in any form of binding or cover other than that in which it is published.

All rights reserved. No part of this work may be reproduced or transmitted by any means without permission.

Front cover A patio garden in Ipswich, 1984, showing how imaginatively a wall of broken paving stones can be used to enhance a small space. *(Photograph supplied by Photos Horticultural)*

Typeset by KMWS Graphics Ltd, London, WC1

Printed and bound in Spain Graficas Estella, S.A.

Pearson, Robert
Patio gardening. – 4th ed.
1. Paved gardens. Ornamental flowering plants
I. Title
635.9'671

ISBN 0-86367-290-6

Contents

To Diana

Introduction

I have written this book because I feel deeply that a garden –
even the tiniest of gardens – can give infinite pleasure and
solace if used to the best advantage.

As land becomes more expensive – an irreversible trend –
and gardens consequently become smaller, it is inevitable that

*Pelargoniums (geraniums) and
fuchsias have the perfect foil in a
backdrop of tender mimosa and
bay.*

patio-type gardens will become more and more popular, for not only are these extremely attractive, but they are easy to look after.

Astonishing results can be achieved, even in those of pocket-handkerchief size. This book, however, is by no means solely concerned with the most constricted of patio areas, although these are kept very much in mind. For the patio garden is, in effect, an outdoor room, and rooms can vary in size. Also, it may not take up all your garden area but lead on to features of more traditional design. The possibilities, if not endless, certainly give plenty of scope for the enterprising garden owner.

The wonderful thing about gardening is the scope it gives us to be enterprising – especially in this country. Maybe it is something we give little conscious thought to, but the quite remarkable range of ornamental plants, from trees and shrubs to herbaceous perennials, annuals and bulbs available to the home gardener in Britain gives us all the opportunity to do exciting, even original things with whatever size plot we happen to own. Fortunately, too, the more go-ahead nurseries and seedsmen are always whetting our appetites with new offerings, and trying out some of these always adds zest to one's gardening, even within the confines of a small area such as we are concerned with here.

I would like to thank landscape architect Kenneth Midgley for providing the beautifully executed sketches of patio gardens which you will find on the pages which follow. These show what can be achieved when a sensitive eye is combined with a keen appreciation of plants and their use in settings of the kind we are concerned with. My thanks also to Charles Stitt for the outstanding line drawings of plants and, in some cases, garden features, which so splendidly set the scene and to Michael Warren for providing the majority of the colour photographs. Like Mr Midgley they are masters of their diverse arts. The photographs on the following pages were taken by myself: 39, 50-1, 55 (insert), 74, 83, 86, 90-1, 98-9, 122, 127, 130-1, 134-5, 139, 146, 154, 158 and 159.

Having said that, it only remains for me to express the hope that this book will prove helpful to you in your patio gardening – both in the planning and the execution.

Robert Pearson

1. Why a patio garden?

Why a patio garden? I can best answer this question by contrasting two gardens which, although of quite different character, both basically presented their owners with the same problems and opportunities.

The first lay behind a terraced house in the suburb of a large city and consisted of a plot perhaps 60ft (18m) long by 20ft (6m) wide. It had possibilities, for the light was by no means bad, there were walls to grow things on and the site was sheltered – but little had been done. A patchy lawn was surrounded on three sides by a rather sad-looking border filled in desultory fashion with a motley collection of plants. Opportunities had been missed, though I suppose even this garden gave its owner satisfaction of a kind.

The other garden was attached to a semi-detached home in an urban area, and the small corner site had been turned into a charming patio-type garden by the skilful use of plants and paving. Everything was perfectly in scale.

A small cherry tree in one corner led the eye round to a trellis-topped fence over which the tangled growth of *Clematis montana* spread to hide effectively other houses from view. Climbing roses enveloped the garage wall, flowering and foliage shrubs and perennials were growing in plant beds, and less permanent plants in a few containers stood on the paving slabs which linked with other features to give the garden balance and an air of studied calm. It was, to my mind, the kind of garden a family could live with and enjoy for many a year.

This garden had no eating-out area, but that is something which many patio gardens can incorporate if you have a taste for such delights. Can I use this as an example, though, of the necessity for foresight in garden planning? What you must have with an eating-out area is easy access to the house and kitchen, otherwise the continual to-ing and fro-ing will soon become an irritant and a bore. On-the-spot barbecue facilities are fun for parties but are not the kind of thing you want for everyday living.

The first site I mentioned could with little trouble have been

9

turned into quite a pleasant garden of conventional design. But with a good boundary wall, not high enough to cut out light, what an opportunity had been lost to turn it into a patio garden of real character and charm.

No plot is too small for this. After all, just think what countless plant lovers manage to achieve with a balcony garden or even a few window boxes. Imagination and enthusiasm are more important in gardening than space.

Why not go out into your garden now and cast an eye over the assets you already have? Perhaps you have good walls or close-board fencing on a couple of sides of your property, providing shelter and privacy and all kinds of opportunities to grow interesting plants. Perhaps there is a tree of suitable proportions which could form the focal point of a completely new design, or, say, you have a paved area already which could form the basis for a patio garden.

With any of these advantages the battle is already on its way to being won. But don't be deterred if you have to start from scratch.

Above all, be practical, and decide very early on just how much money you are prepared to spend. That is really the crux of the matter – the key to everything in the end.

Making a patio garden can also be a time-consuming business but, once made and planted, it is far more labour-saving than a conventional garden.

Opposite: *The natural elegance of wrought-iron furniture is enhanced by this intimate setting of flowers and foliage.*

2. Elements of Design

Gardening is something one should never be dogmatic about – it is often so much a matter of taste and opinion – but that will not deter me from saying that the key to success in patio garden making is simplicity of design. That is true of any garden making, but the limited scale of a patio garden makes it even more important.

So often too many features are included, too many plants are crammed into a small area with unsatisfactory or even disastrous results (which is not to say that you cannot 'mass' plants success-fully if they have a basic affinity).

Unobtrusive paving, a small flowering tree of delicate outline, a few choice climbing plants and some plant containers filled with gay geraniums, long-flowering fuchsias or hydrangeas may be all that is needed to create a garden of delight. But then, other features might be far better – it depends on the circumstances. I hope that in the pages which follow you will be able to pick and choose, from the features and plants described, those which will suit you best.

Planning your patio

If garden planning does not come easily to you I would suggest that you seek early advice from a professional garden designer or landscape architect, if only to get him or her to draw up a plan to which you can afterwards work. A trained eye would quickly pick out the good things about the site which could be exploited, and, just as important, advise on how less favourable aspects of it could be played down. But if you seek advice, do get an estimate in advance so that you know what your financial commitment will be.

One of the first things you must secure in your garden is shelter and a modicum of privacy, for there is no pleasure in being chilled to the bone, even on a sunny day, or in trying to relax in the public eye.

Although in a patio garden, with its space limitations, hedges are not always a practical proposition, they should not be ruled out altogether. A yew hedge which can be kept trimmed to a foot thick, for example, can be a delightful feature, but in general hedges take up far too much lateral room and draw too much goodness from the soil.

This plot, 30ft (9m) wide by 50ft (15m) long, is backed by a neighbouring building and enclosed on two sides by walls. (In other circumstances these last could easily be high fences.) Basically, the design takes the form of a pattern of rectangles outlined in a hard-fired brick and these interlocking shapes, together with the plantings and the garden furniture, give the whole garden a real feeling of being an outdoor room. Again, the trees - these could be something like Acer ginnala, Malus robusta *'Yellow Siberian', or one of the smaller-growing flowering cherries - balance the design and give the garden a different level of interest. The grass "carpet" makes a useful sitting-out area and contrasts pleasingly with the paving around it. However, if more colour is needed, this minute lawn could be a bed with flowering plants or such plants could replace the pool.*

This design illustrates how the simplest of shapes, allied to restrained planting, can please the eye and result in a garden which many home owners would find sympathetic and - very important - continue to enjoy over many years.

Opposite: *Paving and patterned brickwork lead the eye to the Mexican orange blossom,* Choisya ternata, *and the poker-flowered* Polygonum bistorta *'Superbum'.*

Brick walls can be delightful to look at and very sympathetic to plants, but they may, regretfully, have to be ruled out on account of cost, so one comes back to fencing of one kind or another. Wood is by far the nicest choice: best of all, close-board fencing or the overlap type which makes a good surface to grow plants on or against. But whatever your choice, don't make the screen so high that you cut out the light. Remember, too, that although you have to guard against chill winds both for the sake of the plants and yourself, a garden which is too much enclosed becomes almost too hot on very sunny summer days.

If you have a patio which leads into a main garden area, then open-work screen walling in precast concrete can, in short sections, provide just the right kind of division between the two – not too heavy, not too insubstantial.

House and garden walls in towns, exposed to years of industrial pollution, can take on depressingly dark shades, and when this happens it is well worth while colour-washing parts at least in white or perhaps a pastel shade. This will give the whole garden a quite different appearance and provide a congenial backdrop for plants.

Paving of one kind or another which will take the wear of continual traffic is, of course, a vital feature of any patio garden. Its quality sets the tone of the whole plot. Real stone paving or patterned bricks – of the special hard-fired quality necessary to withstand exposure to moisture and low temperatures – make surfaces of great aesthetic appeal, but it can be costly these days to cover even a small area.

Usually, it will be a case of opting for one of the proprietary brands of precast concrete paving slabs which are so freely available – and very attractive some of these can be. They come in various shapes and sizes, textures and finishes, and in a range of colours to meet most requirements and tastes. You will find them on display at builders' merchants, garden centres and major flower shows like Chelsea. It is worth taking the trouble to find just what you want.

Sometimes local councils sell off old paving slabs which are surplus to their requirements, and bargain lots can occasionally be obtained in this way. If it is of interest to you it is certainly worth inquiring at your local council offices, even if the answer is likely to be No.

It is often a good idea to break up the uniformity of paved areas by incorporating patterned areas of granite setts or cobbles, although it is best to keep the latter away from areas where you will walk frequently as they can be slippery in wet weather. Lovely effects can be achieved by making up simple designs in this way, especially around specimen trees.

Stepping-stones – circular, square or rectangular and made of artificial stone – can look delightful in association with appropriate

plantings. Indeed, they can be strong enough to be a design feature of some importance in a garden of the dimensions we are thinking of.

It might be helpful to know that if you intend using concrete in your garden, whether in the form of paving, steps, open-work screen walling, raised plant beds or the like, that the British Cement Association publish an excellent well-illustrated 28-page booklet 'Concrete Round Your House and Garden', which gives detailed advice on concrete as a material and how to make maximum use of it in the garden. It is available from garden centres, builders merchants and specialist retail stores or direct from Publications Sales, British Cement Association, Wexham Springs, Slough SL3 6PL, price £1.00, postage included.

One thing I would not use concrete for myself, unless I were getting a professional job done, is making a small pool, of the kind of size suitable for most patio settings. It is much easier nowadays to buy a glass-fibre pool ''off the shelf'', or a plastic pool liner for which – apart from the precautions I detail on p. 108 – there is little more preparation than the digging of a hole of the required size, shape and depth. Concrete pools are vulnerable to frost damage, especially if home-made mixtures are not of quite the right consistency or if they are too thinly applied to withstand the worst that the weather can throw up in its most arctic-like moods.

A small water feature complete with water-lilies and other aquatic plants – not too many – can add great charm to a patio garden, especially if edged with stonework effectively to hide from view the material of which the pool itself is made. It will be an even greater source of pleasure if you install a small fountain. Under-water lighting sets are also becoming very popular, and these can provide quite impressive effects. A two-lamp set, complete with low-voltage transformer, can be bought for quite a modest sum.

An interesting variation on this theme is to have the pool only partially sunk in the ground, and surround it with a low wall which can be used as a seat. For this again you could use precast concrete blocks and slabs.

A path of concrete paving with cobbles used to provide a variation in form and texture, can be pleasing to the eye.

Plants and planting

Plants in paving are always attractive, and I have suggested some suitable subjects for such a feature on pp. 144 to 146. Beds and borders for plants should not be overdone in a garden of this kind, for you must keep that essential quality I mentioned earlier, balance, constantly in mind; but within those limits a great deal can be achieved. I would always myself use a good leavening of plants with attractive foliage or form as well as those notable for the beauty of their flowers, so that there is the best possible spread of interest throughout the year. The flowering periods of most plants are relatively short while foliage and form can be enjoyed for at least half the year, and all the year round in the case of evergreens.

Of course, there are plants which possess two, and some even all three of these attributes -shrubs like *Paeonia lutea ludlowii* and *Mahonia* 'Charity' and perennials like *Alchemilla mollis*, the lady's mantle, the hostas and *Euphorbia characias* to name but a few.

Herbaceous perennial plants with special qualities certainly find a place in beds or borders, and perhaps some annuals to use as colourful 'fillers' in summer. Some climbing plants, too, these perhaps being grown on pillars to complement those grown on the house walls, fences and so on.

A fairly recent innovation is the raised bed, designed to help the elderly and the infirm to continue to garden effectively without bending down. A joy to many people certainly, but what I want to stress now is the value of the raised bed as a design feature in its own right. A raised bed in a paved area makes a splendid home for rock plants and dwarf bulbous plants, not to mention a dwarf conifer or two, miniature roses and small-growing shrubs like *Hebe pinguifolia* 'Pagei'; *Spiraea japonica* 'Alpina'; the dwarf willow, *Salix apoda*; and heathers like the lime tolerant, ruby-red, winter-flowering *Erica carnea* 'Myretoun Ruby' and, for summer flowering (and lime-free soil), the magenta *E. cinerea* 'Stephen Davis'. Such a feature can be a source of pleasure during every season of the year. A bed raised just a few inches above the level of the garden can also be valuable, strengthening the overall design.

Small-growing rock and bulbous plants can also be grown most attractively in trough gardens. Real stone troughs, though, of the kind one used to see in every farmyard, and the lovely old stone sinks which used to catch the overflow from village pumps, are becoming extremely difficult, indeed almost impossible, to obtain.

In the final analysis it is usually a case of making do with a trough made from reconstituted stone or perhaps a glazed domestic sink, although even these are not so readily available nowadays. Sinks can be effectively treated to hide the shiny surface, or one can mask the glazing with trailing plants. What

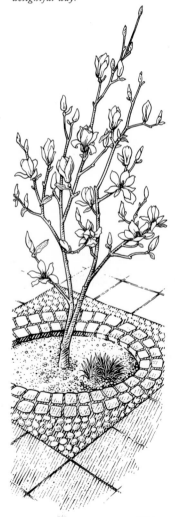

Paving, brickwork and cobbles frame a shrub or small tree in a delightful way.

Opposite: *It is particularly important in small gardens to provide interest for the eye at different levels, an objective which has certainly been achieved in this instance.*

you should *not* do is to attempt to grow alpines in plastic containers, which dry out far too quickly in hot weather for the good of the occupants.

Plant containers, whether they are large tubs, bowls and the like or window-boxes, have an important part to play in the patio garden, primarily, of course, as receptacles for housing short-term, seasonal plants; but not exclusively so, by any means. Numerous shrubs can be grown on a permanent basis in this way as well as fruit trees (see Chapter Thirteen) and perennials like the phormiums, if you take the trouble to top-dress the soil annually and generally look after them as I describe on p. 107.

What possibilities flowering bulbs, corms and tubers offer the patio gardener! Apart from the daffodils and tulips in their almost bewildering array, there are the hyacinths and small treasures like snowdrops, dwarf irises, grape hyacinths, eranthises and scillas, the crocuses, and easy lilies like the beautiful *Lilium regale*, all of which can delight the eye in the kind of intimate garden setting we are considering. In Chapter Nine I take a close look at the possibilities open to the patio gardener with a liking for this group of plants.

It may sound a little bizarre to suggest growing vegetables and fruit in the patio garden, and naturally I am not suggesting that this is going to fill your larder or deep freeze unit to over-flowing. But it is surprising, nevertheless, what produce can, on occasions, be raised on a small piece of ground or in plant containers. Even a small number of outdoor tomatoes, for instance, can be very prolific in a good summer, or you could grow runner beans or those delicious little Courgette marrows as well as lettuces, radishes and spring onions. Raspberries, too, can be grown in plant containers, strawberries in pots and if you have a bed at the foot of a north-facing wall there is a chance to make use of it by training a Morello cherry against it.

Trained fruit trees can look very attractive, and you could even find room for an espalier-trained apple or pear or a few of the same fruits cordon-trained. Even, perhaps, a so-called "family tree" in which three varieties of desert apples or three of pears are grafted on one bush-trained specimen (see p. 161).

Grass has a minor part to play in the patio garden, if indeed it has any part to play at all, but even a small ribbon of close-textured turf can be extremely effective if it is integrated into the overall design with care (see the designs on pp. 13, 64, 124 and 141). The fresh green colouring is soothing to the eye throughout the year and there is no better foil, in my opinion, for a multi-coloured border of flowers. Even a strip, say, of 4ft (1.3m) wide can have relevance in a small patio garden, but it must have a well-coiffured look if it is not to appear incongruous. Apart from regular trimming in the growing season, it must be fed and watered as circumstances demand.

Phormium tenax *cultivar*

A suggestion for the treatment of an area measuring only 20ft (6m) across and 25ft (7.5m) deep facing a bare wall and with flanking walls on both sides. Evergreen shrubs give the garden form and the two trees atmosphere, and this winter scene illustrates the point that the tracery of bare branches, as provided by the birch on the left, or even a winter-flowering cherry (Prunus subhirtella 'Autumnalis') as shown on the right, is a pleasure not to be under-rated. Low-growing ground-cover plants come into their own in such a setting, and need little attention. The stepping stones are discs of artificial stone, and the curve these describe, echoing the curve of the plant bed, give this patio garden a certain dramatic quality.

A small piece of statuary can add much to the beauty of a patio garden if it is well executed and used as a focal point of the design. I have seen beautiful effects created by framing such features with the foliage of shrubs and so on. Good statuary is not easy to come by – it may take time and patience to find what you want.

Choosing furniture and containers

If you intend to make a lot of use of the patio as an outdoor room, then it is worth taking considerable trouble over choosing garden furniture. Whether wood, metal or plastic is a matter of preference, and dependent to some extent on the kind of garden you have planned. High-quality wooden furniture – made of some really durable wood like teak or iroko – has an air of solidity which metal sometimes lacks, but if the whole atmosphere of the garden radiates lightness and grace then metal furniture may be just what is needed to set it off. Aluminium alloy furniture, in particular, can be very pleasing, likewise nylon-coated steel furniture with polyethylene seats. I find cane furniture very pleasing too in this kind of setting, but you have to have somewhere to store it when it is not in use.

Don't underestimate the aesthetic importance of containers. Like paving and garden furniture, these can help set the general tone of the whole garden. The severely clean lines of, say, a moulded asbestos-cement container or a concrete bowl may be just right in one setting, whereas in another setting something with more ornamentation, like the lovely glass fibre reproductions of period urns, vases, etc., one can buy, might be more pleasing and appropriate. These last can be extraordinarily reminiscent of the originals. Again, in a rather homely setting, hardwood containers, either with their natural finish or painted, the better to show off the flowers they will contain, might be a more suitable choice. Have a good look round and consider all the options before making up your mind.

A plan of campaign

Indeed, get your ideas thoroughly sorted out before you commit yourself to anything, whether plants, materials or furniture.

Then get the basic construction work completed as quickly as possible and take your time, if need be, over completing the planting and furnishing. Spreading the financial outlay in this way makes it possible to do rather more ambitious things than might otherwise be possible. It is a great convenience nowadays to be able to obtain from garden centres many good garden plants as container-grown specimens for immediate planting at any time of the year, so long as the weather is suitable. It means that you can take things calmly and gradually build up the kind of garden you want.

Lilium regale *(see p. 18).*

I mentioned earlier the importance of foliage and form – shapes in other words. Now a word about colour which it is always a joy to see used in gardens with sensitivity. What you need to keep firmly in mind is that green, in its infinite gradations, is always restful to the eye; the red end of the spectrum has just the opposite effect; blue is a lovely cool colour to enjoy on a warm summer day, while yellow is the colour which lifts the spirits, even when the sky is cloud-wracked. Go out into the garden on a dull day at any time of year and you will find that it is the yellow of flower, leaf or berry which introduces a joyous note. Grey foliage and white flowers will both give the garden a touch of sophistication if deployed with artistry. This is something, I am glad to say, which is being increasingly recognised by the gardening fraternity.

So, as I said at the start, keep the basic design simple. Use strong colours with discretion, especially those extrovert reds and oranges. Try to make different features relate to one another so that you have a unified garden rather than a jumble of disparate parts. In that way you will capture the peace and serenity which is the greatest gift that a garden – any garden, patio or otherwise – can give to its owner. Achieve that, and the patio will be a part of the home to which you will gravitate on every possible occasion.

Statuary and foliage combined can form the focal point of the design (see p. 21).

3. Climbing, Wall and Other Shrubs

Cistus skanbergii

Ornamental shrubs of one kind or another are the backbone of the modern garden, whatever its size. They are available in almost bewildering array, and provided one takes account of their special needs – if they have any – they are the easiest of plants to look after. An annual spring mulch, perhaps a little pruning, although this is not always necessary, and watering in the driest periods are just about all the attention many of them need. And look what they give us in return!

They are a natural choice for the patio garden, for a few, selected with care, and with perhaps a small tree to provide a different level of interest, form the framework for the whole design. Climbing shrubs, too, and non-climbing shrubs which are particularly well suited for growing against walls or fences, have a special importance.

There is something else to consider as well, if you are the adventurous type of gardener I hope you are, and that is the opportunity your patio garden gives you to grow shrubs and other plants which are on the borderline of hardiness. By definition a patio garden is an enclosed garden and that must mean that it provides plants with a greater degree of warmth and shelter than it is possible to find in a more open situation. Use it to the full. There are so many plants of excellence which fall in this category from cistuses (or rock roses) like *Cistus skanbergii*, a lovely 3ft (1m) tall and wide shrub which bears its papery-textured pink flowers in early summer, to sun-loving hebes like 'Great Orme' and 'Autumn Glory' – low-growing, evergreen shrubs which bear pink and violet-blue flower spikes respectively, the first from early summer, the second from July to autumn. Warm south- or west-facing walls provide an ideal background for things like *Abutilon megapotamicum* and *A. vitifolium* 'Veronica Tennant', the very showy *Fremontodendron* California Glory' (which you may know under its former, and less clumsy, name *Fremontia* 'Californian Glory'), the passion flower, *Passiflora caerulea*, and much else besides. More about these in a moment, and others which could give you great pleasure over the years.

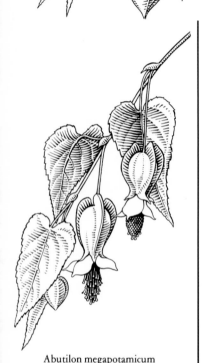

Abutilon megapotamicum
(see p. 23).

So, don't always play safe and go for absolute reliability whatever the weather, for you miss so much enjoyment that way. Accept the challenge. One thing nobody can do is to define exactly the degree of hardiness of any plant. It depends on so many different factors, from the microclimate to which the plant is subjected (aspect, light availability and the degree of warmth and shelter provided) to the soil conditions you are able to offer and, yes, imponderables. We all know of occasions when a plant has failed miserably in one place yet romped away in another not, on the face of it, very much different. It is that kind of thing which makes gardening so exciting.

Planting and cultivation
Before discussing specific plants, a word or two about more general considerations, including planting and basic cultivation. It is fatally easy to be so mesmerised by the charms of some particular plant as to disregard completely the conditions it needs to succeed. It is a trap to avoid. If a plant needs lots of sunshine or, conversely, light shade, or if it needs an acid soil rather than one which is alkaline, do not expect it to put up with quite the wrong conditions without complaint. It won't.

Container-grown plants, as I have said, are a great convenience, making the whole year a planting season. The reason is, of course, that when you remove a plant from a container you cause very little disturbance to the root system and it rapidly settles down again.

But nursery stock lifted from the open ground is a different proposition. It is lifted for dispatch only at the traditional planting seasons, the time, of course, when re-establishment in the garden is easiest and the least strain is put on the plant's resources. So with deciduous trees and shrubs it is from late October or early November, after leaf fall, until March, except when excessive wet or frost and snow make this impossible. With evergreens the best times of all for planting are from late September until late October and from the beginning of April to May; but, of course, you can plant in mild spells in winter if you take all the normal precautions.

The two optimum times I have mentioned are so good because the soil is reasonably warm at those times; yet the sun is not so hot that it will cause excessive transpiration through the leaves. Nor with a bit of luck will strong winds cause heavy transpiration either at those times of the year. It is not always realised that wind is as much an enemy as hot sunshine to evergreen shrubs whose roots have not yet started to function again efficiently in their new home, for unlike deciduous shrubs they have no resting period. For that reason they are much more tricky to re-establish.

If your plants arrive when the weather is unsuitable for planting because of frost, snow or heavy rain, leave the root wrapping on but take away the top-growth covering and place in some cool, frost-proof place until conditions improve; or heel them in in a specially opened up trench out of doors, just covering the roots with soil and firming with the heel. The latter treatment is to be preferred, if the bad weather lasts for more than a week.

A few other pre-planting needs. Cut off cleanly any damaged roots, just above the break. Make the planting hole just a little larger than the roots at their full spread, assuming that they are not in a soil 'ball'. Fork over the bottom of the hole and cover it with a thin layer of garden compost (if you have it available) before adding a little top soil. The hole should be of such a depth that the shrub will be at the same level when planted as it was when growing in the nursery – something you should be able to check easily as the soil mark on the stem is usually clearly visible.

Place the shrub in position – after you have put in a stout stake, if support is needed early on – and work good quality top soil in among the roots with the fingers, or, if there is a root ''ball'', around this. Firm with the foot, add more top soil, firm and repeat this procedure until the soil is slightly above the surrounding soil level. This is to allow for the small amount of sinking there will inevitably be as the soil settles down.

If the wind is a problem, and it should not be in a sheltered patio garden, it is always a good thing to shield newly planted evergreens for a time, on the windward side, with a temporary screen of hessian or polythene sheeting, supported by stakes. This will cut down considerably the loss of moisture through the leaves caused by transpiration. Help the evergreens all you can, too, in the post-planting period by watering as necessary and spraying over the leaves in the late afternoon.

Mulching around shrubs with peat, composted bark or garden compost, after the soil has had a chance to warm up in spring, will greatly help to conserve soil moisture during dry periods – but make sure, by periodically drawing back the mulch, that the soil is not dry underneath. Water, if necessary.

Clematis
Consider wall plants in the context of the typical patio garden and one's thoughts immediately fly to roses and clematis, both of which are available in wide variety. Both, of course, put on an impressive display, and they often make the loveliest of com-

panions. Ceanothus and pyracantha are other shrubs which make ideal companions for clematis.

Roses are dealt with in a separate chapter (see p. 79), so I shall say no more about them now, but turn your attention to the clematis, which have so much to offer the gardener between spring and autumn. From the earliest flowering species like the rather tender creamy-white *C. armandii* (an evergreen species and also needing a warm home), through the large-flowered hybrids to those yellow-flowered species *C. orientalis* and *C. tangutica*, which bring an end to the season, they provide so much of interest.

A special joy, I always find, is the May-June-flowering *C. montana*, the vigorous species so much grown in its rose-pink variety *rubens*. And indeed it is a lovely sight for a few weeks with its mass of blooms set off by bronzy-purple foliage and in the vigorous way so typical of the montanas reaching up to a height of 30ft (9m) or more on wall or roof. But I myself prefer the magnificent white-flowered *C. montana grandiflora*, dazzling in the full flush of it flowering with its myriad blooms set among fresh green foliage. Another beautiful variety is the soft pink 'Elizabeth', and many gardeners have an affection for the large-flowered 'Tetrarose', which has mauvish-pink flowers and bronzy-green leaves. These *montana* varieties will succeed on a wall of any aspect and they are delightful shrubs for the patio garden.

Like the large-flowered hybrids, *C. montana* and its cultivars, as well as other clematis species, like to have their roots in cool shade and their tops in sun. This is not difficult to arrange. You either grow leafy perennials around their base or just lay flat stones on the soil around the stems. Acid and alkaline soils suit them equally well. (You can obtain simple soil-testing kits from garden stores incidentally to determine the lime content of your soil, for when plants do have specific needs.)

Clematis are versatile, too. A vigorous species like *montana* is excellent for growing on trees as well as walls, and the less strong growing hybrids with their large distinctive flowers are ideal for pillars and fences as well as walls.

Let's start with early flowerers. It goes without saying that any climber which flowers in late winter (between January and March) must be a valuable acquisition, and that *Clematis cirrhosa* certainly is, especially in its form *balearica*, the fern-leaved clematis as it is called. The dark-green leaves turn bronze in winter and provide a telling foil for the pendant, pale greenish-yellow blooms which are marked reddish-purple on the inside of the sepals. In ideal conditions it will grow 15ft (4.5m) tall, but usually it is considerably less than that.

The very handsome *C. armandii* also grows up to 15ft (4.5m) tall, even 20ft (6m) on occasions, and what an asset it is at all times

Clematis tangutica
(see p. 29)

Opposite: *Apart from the fuchsias, this planting scene relies entirely on foliage effect through the wall-scaling* Hedera helix 'Goldheart', *spotted aucuba and* Elaeagnus pungens maculata.

27

Clematis macropetala

with its showy, glossy green leaves, each consisting of three leaflets up to 6in (15cm) long. It is a sight to see in March and April when the large clusters of creamy-white flowers are present. Much valued, too is its cultivar 'Apple Blossom', in which the flowers are pink-tinged. There is also a pure white cultivar named 'Snowdrift'. I would emphasise, however, that really warm, sun-drenched and sheltered conditions are needed by *C. armandii* and its cultivars. Likewise, *C. cirrhosa* and its cultivar *balearica*.

Growing 6ft (2m) or rather more tall is *C. alpina* with beautiful, smallish blue to purple, lantern-shaped flowers in April. It is an excellent choice for clothing a fence and, a not unimportant consideration, proved in recent arctic winter spells, the hardiest of all the clematis. Two excellent cultivars are the blue 'Frances Rivis' and 'White Moth' with double, white blooms. Another is 'Ruby' with purplish-pink blooms.

Another very beautiful clematis which always intrigues me with its pendant bell-shaped, semi-double flowers is *C. macropetala*, a species from Northern China and Siberia. These flowers are violet-blue in colour and are borne in May and June. A height of 10ft (3m) may be achieved but it is often rather less and it makes a splendid adornment for a fence or, as I once saw it grown, festooning a large garden ornament. 'Markham's Pink' is a colour variant of equal attraction.

The early, large-flowered hybrids make marvellous plants for growing in large containers or tubs, and I have more to say about these and other clematis suitable for such a role on p. 116. That splendid old cultivar 'Nelly Moser' belongs here; how attractive it is with its flowers of mauvish-pink, each sepal of that colour overlaid with a carmine bar. So does the lovely lavender-blue, cream-stamened 'Lasurstern', 'Bee's Jubilee', deep pink with a rose-pink bar on the sepals, and purple 'The President'. All of these flower in May and June with a second flush later in summer. Indeed, 'The President' is usually carrying blooms from May until September. There are many more cultivars to choose from.

Following these in flower, from June or July to August or September, are the mid-season cultivars like 'Marie Boisselot', pure gleaming white in colour and with cream stamens, 'W. E. Gladstone', lavender coloured and with purplish-red stamens, and 'Henryi', a hybrid with creamy-white pointed sepals and brown stamens.

The Jackmanii and Viticella hybrids are the rearguard, so to speak, of the large-flowered clematis, flowering from July to late August or September although a few of the first-mentioned type like the striking carmine-red 'Ville de Lyon' (which has bright yellow stamens) and the fine magenta-red 'Ernest Markham' are in flower by June to give a very long period of colour. It would be unthinkable not to mention also the violet-purple 'Jackmanii

Superba', for that is probably the most widely grown of all clematis.

With heights of up to 15ft (4.5m) in the case of the Jackmanii hybrids and 10ft (3m) or less in respect of the Viticella kinds – white-flowered, dark stamened 'Alba Luxurians' is one of note, the extraordinary velvety, deep purple 'Royal Velours' another – there is a lot of scope for enterprise in their display. The Viticella hybrids have a good colour range, do not suffer from that so far intractable trouble, clematis wilt (for which there is no cure at present although one may be on the way) and have small to medium-sized flowers which stand up well to exposure to bad weather.

The strong-growing mid-season flowering hybrids, the Jackmanii and Viticella hybrids and later-flowering species like *C. orientalis* and *C. tangutica* with heights of around 20ft (6m) are ideal for climbing through trees and shrubs in patio settings.

Clematis orientalis and *C. tangutica* flower in late summer and early autumn. In addition to the yellow flowers – bell-shaped and with very thick sepals in the case of *C. orientalis*, lantern-shaped in the case of *C. tangutica* – there is the attraction of the handsome, silky, silvery seed heads which both species carry in early autumn. You can expect both to make a delightful show against a wall.

With so many types of clematis – and there are plenty I have not even mentioned, all splendid garden plants in their own right – some logical system of classification is imperative and, following talks with clematis specialist Raymond Evison, whose knowledge of these flowers is unrivalled, I am following, with his permission, the eminently sensible scheme which he has adopted.

His classification is as follows:

Group 1 – Evergreen clematis, including *C. cirrhosa* and *C. armandii*; *C. alpina*, *C. macropetala* and *C. montana*.
Group 2 – Early, large-flowered hybrids and mid-season large-flowered hybrids.
Group 3 – Jackmanii, later-flowering, large-flowered hybrids, late-flowering species and their small-flowered cultivars, including *C. orientalis* and *C. tangutica*, which I discuss above.

Group 1 clematis need light pruning just after flowering; Group 2 should have dead and weak growth cut out and be cut back to a strong pair of leaf axil buds in February or March; Group 3 should be hard pruned down to just above the base of the previous season's stems in late February or March.

I have written at length about clematis because these climbers have such relevance to patio-gardening conditions. They can be hugely enjoyable.

Wisteria and honeysuckle
One of the best wall plants for a patio garden is the wisteria,
always attractive when in leaf and magnificent in early summer
when it is bearing its glorious racemes of fragrant, lilac-blue
flowers. But you must be able to give it a warm position, facing
south or south-west. It will, of course, climb to 30ft (9m) or
more.

What you can do, though, if you haven't the room to let one
climb is to have a standard specimen and grow it in a special
planting area in the paving. I have several trained this way in a

Cultivars of Clematis alpina, *like 'Ruby' shown here, are a glorious sight in April (see p. 28).*

grass setting and they are a delight with their branches twisting themselves into the most appealing oriental-looking shapes. They can, however, be quite expensive to buy, because of the training involved and few nurseries have them on offer.

There are two types of wisteria – the Chinese, mauve or lilac-coloured *Wisteria sinensis*, of which there are white and purple forms, and the Japanese *W. floribunda*, usually offered in its cultivar 'Macrobotrys', which is notable for the length of the bluish-lilac racemes of flowers. These can be as much as 3ft (1m) long. This also has a white-flowered form, *alba*, which can look

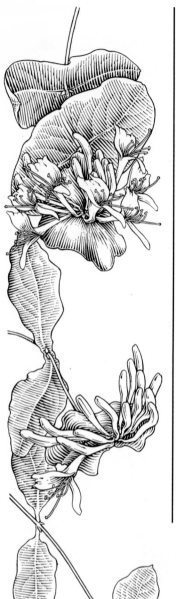

stunning in flower against a mellow stone wall. With these wisterias there is sometimes a modest second flowering in late summer.

Wisterias like a rich loamy soil best, but they are not really fussy about the soil they are given. Shelter and warmth are more pressing needs.

Those honeysuckles which are highly fragrant would be worth growing for that attribute alone, even if the flowers were less attractive than they are. They need a good loamy soil and conditions similar to those suggested earlier for clematis, i.e. a cool root run (which you provide by growing leafy plants of small stature around them) but exposure to sunshine for their top growth. Mulching in spring (after the soil has had a chance to warm up) wth garden compost, composted bark or peat is also something they greatly enjoy.

For scrambling up a post or over a fence I would suggest the early or late Dutch honeysuckles – both if you have the room, for between them they provide fragrance and attractive flower colouring right through the summer. The first, *Lonicera periclymenum* 'Belgica', bears purplish-red and yellow flowers in June and July; the second, *L. periclymenum* 'Serotina', bears purplish-red and creamy-yellow flowers from July to September.

Another honeysuckle of which I am especially fond is *L. japonica* 'Aureoreticulata', completely different to the last-mentioned cultivars with its mass of small oval leaves heavily netted with yellow veins to provide a very pleasing combination of yellow and bright green. It is these leaves which are the plant's decorative feature, not the small, wishy-washy-looking white to pale cream flowers which have little decorative value although they have good fragrance. An evergreen, it can loose its leaves in very severe winter weather but it soon puts forth fresh ones in spring after such an occurrence. In my garden it survived (if only just) winter conditions some years ago when, on several nights, the temperature fell to a low of 7°F (–14°C) and its com-

Lonicera tellmanniana

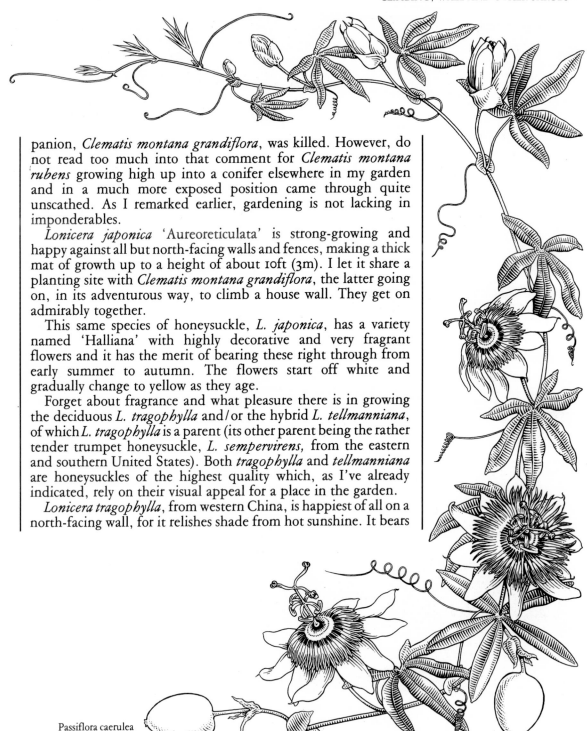

panion, *Clematis montana grandiflora*, was killed. However, do not read too much into that comment for *Clematis montana rubens* growing high up into a conifer elsewhere in my garden and in a much more exposed position came through quite unscathed. As I remarked earlier, gardening is not lacking in imponderables.

Lonicera japonica 'Aureoreticulata' is strong-growing and happy against all but north-facing walls and fences, making a thick mat of growth up to a height of about 10ft (3m). I let it share a planting site with *Clematis montana grandiflora*, the latter going on, in its adventurous way, to climb a house wall. They get on admirably together.

This same species of honeysuckle, *L. japonica*, has a variety named 'Halliana' with highly decorative and very fragrant flowers and it has the merit of bearing these right through from early summer to autumn. The flowers start off white and gradually change to yellow as they age.

Forget about fragrance and what pleasure there is in growing the deciduous *L. tragophylla* and/or the hybrid *L. tellmanniana*, of which *L. tragophylla* is a parent (its other parent being the rather tender trumpet honeysuckle, *L. sempervirens*, from the eastern and southern United States). Both *tragophylla* and *tellmanniana* are honeysuckles of the highest quality which, as I've already indicated, rely on their visual appeal for a place in the garden.

Lonicera tragophylla, from western China, is happiest of all on a north-facing wall, for it relishes shade from hot sunshine. It bears

Passiflora caerulea
(see p. 35).

33

the most beautiful narrowly-cylindrical, bright yellow flowers in clusters of 10 to 20 in June and July on a plant which climbs to a height of 15ft (4.5m) or so. *L. tellmanniana* – deciduous like *tragophylla* – grows to a similar height and has a similar flowering period, bearing bright yellow flowers which are tipped with bronze, a colour which suffuses the flowers at the bud stage.

More choice climbers

The climber everybody wants to grow, though, if they have the right conditions, is the passion flower, *Passiflora caerulea* – and no wonder when one thinks of the extraordinary beauty of those complex flowers whose various parts are supposed to represent Christ's Passion: a glorious amalgam of white petals, purplish-blue corona, and other shades as well. These flowers can be enjoyed for most of the summer and into autumn on a climber at least 15ft (4.5m) tall. For this, a warm, sunny wall is a necessity, and in good years rich yellow fruit will also be produced. If it gets cut back in winter there is every chance, too, in favoured gardens, that it will break again in the following spring.

A superbly decorative ivy for the patio is the Persian ivy, *Hedera colchica,* in its variegated form 'Dentata Variegata'. Large, heart-shaped leaves which are a mixture of green, grey and creamy-white – yellow, too, when young – give this climber real value as a patio plant, and it loves to trail along the ground as well as climb. Another colourful variant is *H. colchica* 'Sulphur Heart', (or 'Paddy's Pride' as it is also called) which has the centre part of its leaves boldly marked with yellow. Of the cultivars of the common ivy, *Hedera helix*, make a special note of 'Buttercup', which is really striking with its golden foliage (this gradually takes on a greenish tinge as the leaves age). Extremely popular, and rightly so, is 'Goldheart' (often misnamed 'Jubilee') with leaves heavily splashed with rich yellow. These and other ivies are remarkably easily pleased, for any ordinary soil suits them and they are not over-fussy about the amount of light they get.

Another delightful wall, fence or trellis plant for a sunny position is the self-supporting *Actinidia kolomikta*, around 10ft (3m) tall and with heart-shaped leaves of a darkish green marked at their lower ends with blotches of white and pink. It introduces a rather exotic flavour into the garden and will grow well given good drainage and a better than average soil. If you have a warm, sunny corner, too, you could also try that tender Chilean climber *Eccremocarpus scaber*, which can be highly decorative during summer with is racemes of red and organge tubular flowers, each about 1in (2.5cm) long. It is best in a lightish soil, for it needs to have good drainage, and you plant it straight from pots in May, after the soil has had a chance to warm up. A climber only for climatically favoured parts of the country, though.

Another climber which can be a wonderful sight on a house

Opposite: *The large-flowered clematis cultivar 'Bee's Jubilee' – May-June flowering with more blooms in August.*

Hydrangea petiolaris

wall is the true Virginia creeper, *Parthenocissus quinquefolia*, its pretty, deeply cut leaves turning to glorious shades of scarlet in autumn. It grows well given any aspect. The lovely *P. henryana*, with dark green, silvery-veined foliage, is best on north or west-facing walls. I almost hesitate to mention that rampageous climber the Russian vine, or the mile-a-minute plant. *Polygonum baldschuanicum* certainly deserves that last sobriquet (as it does the first, for it comes from southern Russia) because it is extraordinarily fast growing and will shin up a large wall in next to no time – and smother trees, too, given half a chance. Still, if you want an out-building covered quickly and effectively this is your plant, and the panicles of pinkish-white flowers borne in fluffy clouds in summer and autumn are attractive seen *en masse*. Any well-drained soil will do for this climber. A fine town plant, too, with no sensitivity to traffic-polluted air. I find I appreciate it more and more as time goes by.

The extraordinary adaptability and vigour of the Russian vine is well illustrated by a specimen I know of in a Yorkshire country garden which, although having its roots confined in a quite small container made from the same stone as the wall against which it was built, still covered this wall with the greatest of enthusiasm and very effectively. It was, however, fed lavishly each spring with well-rotted manure from the owner's stable.

A lot of gardeners seem to have no knowledge of the climbing hydrangea, *H. petiolaris*, a self-clinging species (it clings by means of aerial roots), which has its uses in the patio garden if you have an uninviting north-facing wall which you would like to cover to a considerable height. It makes a spreading leafy cover – the leathery leaves are heart-shaped – up to 20ft (6m) tall and as much across, and in June and July bears flat, white flower heads in some profusion.

Shrubs to grow against walls

Now just a few more shrubs which, though not climbers, are splendid for growing against walls. First, the pyracanthas, or firethorns, which were so over-planted at one stage that we all got heartily sick of them despite their very real charm. It is a pity, for fine examples like *Pyracantha coccinea* 'Lalandei' will go right up to the house eaves and follow an early summer show of white flowers with a truly brilliant display of orange-red berries in autumn, even in rather shaded positions. So will the rather smaller growing *P. atalantioides* with bright scarlet berries, and *P.* 'Watereri', smaller still, which is especially notable for the freedom with which it bears its red berries. Other free-fruiting varieties are 'Orange Glow' (its orange-red berries are particularly long lasting) and the American-raised 'Mohave'. This last

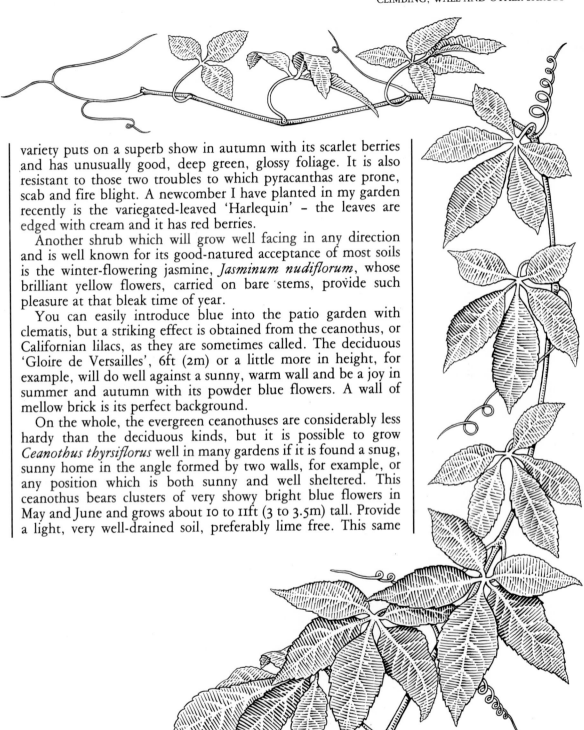

variety puts on a superb show in autumn with its scarlet berries and has unusually good, deep green, glossy foliage. It is also resistant to those two troubles to which pyracanthas are prone, scab and fire blight. A newcomer I have planted in my garden recently is the variegated-leaved 'Harlequin' – the leaves are edged with cream and it has red berries.

Another shrub which will grow well facing in any direction and is well known for its good-natured acceptance of most soils is the winter-flowering jasmine, *Jasminum nudiflorum*, whose brilliant yellow flowers, carried on bare stems, provide such pleasure at that bleak time of year.

You can easily introduce blue into the patio garden with clematis, but a striking effect is obtained from the ceanothus, or Californian lilacs, as they are sometimes called. The deciduous 'Gloire de Versailles', 6ft (2m) or a little more in height, for example, will do well against a sunny, warm wall and be a joy in summer and autumn with its powder blue flowers. A wall of mellow brick is its perfect background.

On the whole, the evergreen ceanothuses are considerably less hardy than the deciduous kinds, but it is possible to grow *Ceanothus thyrsiflorus* well in many gardens if it is found a snug, sunny home in the angle formed by two walls, for example, or any position which is both sunny and well sheltered. This ceanothus bears clusters of very showy bright blue flowers in May and June and grows about 10 to 11ft (3 to 3.5m) tall. Provide a light, very well-drained soil, preferably lime free. This same

Parthenocissus henryana

Opposite: Hedera helix *'Goldheart', understandably a very popular ivy (see p. 35).*

Ceanothus *'Gloire de Versailles' (see p. 37).*

species, *thrysiflorus*, has a very attractive variety named *repens*, a low-growing and spreading form which goes by the name of creeping blue blossom. It produces its light blue flowers in May with great prodigality and is ideal for growing against a wall facing south or west. It is especially suitable for growing under a downstairs window, for it does not grow more than 4 to 4½ft (1.25 to 1.4m) tall while having a spread of about 6ft (2m).

For growing under a ground-floor window also, or for cover anywhere low down on a wall or fence, there is the herringbone cotoneaster, *C. horizontalis*. The sprays of flat growths are a pleasing sight at any time with their herringbone pattern, but the real beauty comes in autumn when the bright red berries appear in shoals and the leaves turn to rich shades of red before being shed. You can easily keep it to a maximum height of 3ft (1m) although against a wall or other vertical surface it will double this if allowed. An excellent shrub this, too, for a north or east wall, and it will grow in any ordinary soil.

For a sunny position there is the old japonica, correctly *Chaenomeles speciosa*, and its varieties, and the splendid hybrids grouped under the name *C. superba*. In late winter and spring – the actual time of flowering depends on the position of the plant and the weather – the colourful flowers of varieties like the deep red 'Simonii', a useful, low-growing form about 4ft (1.3m) tall and more across, bright orange-scarlet 'Knap Hill Scarlet' and apple-blossom pink and white 'Moerloosei' are a joy. Consider, too, the low-growing 'Pink Lady', a spreading variety only 3ft (1m) or so tall which could be just right for a fence or to grow under a house window. Apart from a need for sunshine, they have no special cultural requirements.

Camellias also provide beautiful blooms early in the year if given wall protection – not an east wall, though, or frost-covered flowers will have their petals 'scorched' by the morning sun. These are mostly varieties of *Camellia japonica*, but they also include some *C. williamsii* hybrids of great beauty. *Camellia japonica* varieties I especially like are 'Adolphe Audusson', with crimson, semi-double blooms, the bright pink 'Elegans' and 'Alba Simplex', white. All camellias, of course, must have a lime-free soil, although if that cannot be arranged in the open garden it is always possible to grow one or two as tub specimens in lime-free compost, with excellent results. Their glossy foliage is an asset throughout the year.

Quite apart from the beauty of the *C. williamsii* hybrids, they have the advantage over the *japonica* varieties of dropping their spent blooms instead of holding on to them and looking rather untidy, unless picked over fairly frequently. The *williamsii* camellias are crosses between *C. japonica* and the more tender *C. saluenensis* and they make very handsome, tallish bushes which are a delight when bearing their flowers in late winter and spring.

The best-known variety is the delectable 'Donation', which has clear pink, semi-double flowers. Others of note include 'J. C. Williams', with pink, single flowers, and 'Francis Hanger' which has white flowers which are also single.

It is always pleasing to grow something a little out of the common run, and if you live in a warmer part of the country do consider finding a home for the pineapple-scented broom, *Cytisus battandieri,* a sizeable deciduous shrub from Morocco which is extremely attractive and is now being much more widely grown than hitherto. It is stocked by numerous leading tree and shrub nurseries.

The soft yellow flowers are borne in upright, cone-shaped clusters in June and July and, as the name suggests, have a pineapple scent. These blooms also have the perfect foil in their grey, silky textured, trifoliate leaves. But you must be prepared for it to grow to a height of 11 to 15ft (3.5 to 4.5) and to have a spread of nearly as much. It is a shrub for the angle formed by two warm walls or a sheltered south or west wall with nearly the protective qualities of the foregoing. Like all brooms, it needs a well-drained soil, preferably rather lean, and as much sunshine as can possibly be provided.

For many years one of my favourite shrubs has been *Garrya elliptica*, a tall-growing evergreen from California which has great decorative value and character. It comes into its own in the second half of winter when it clothes itself with myriad catkins of the most subtle colouring – in some lights silvery-grey, in others more greyish-green – which are borne against a background of oval to roundish, dark green, shiny leaves, greyish on their undersides. What one must be sure to do is get the male form for it is this which has the more impressive catkins, rarely less than 6in (15cm) long but in the most favourable, warm and sheltered conditions almost double that in length.

While *G. elliptica* is hardy as a free-standing shrub in all but cold gardens, it is best to plant it against a wall (for preference facing south or west); and, of course, in the patio garden, where

Chaenomeles speciosa *cultivar (see p. 38).*

space is at a premium, that is what one would wish to do. Against a wall it will reach to a height of 15ft to 20ft (4.5 to 6m). I have associated it with a rambling rose (the American-raised 'Little Compton Creeper', now, alas, no longer offered by nurseries here, at least at the time of writing) and in this way I get the pleasure of the pink flowers of the rose in early summer, its orange hips in autumn and the catkins of the garrya in winter. Perfect! Other climbing roses of the rambler type would associate with it just as well.

Quite fortuitously I planted the garrya quite near to an outside light so that on winter evenings the flick of a switch transforms this lofty shrub into a fairlyland of hanging tassels thrown into bold relief. If you are tempted to give G. *elliptica* a try take note that it must be given a well-drained soil (it need only be of average quality, and it does well on chalk or lime) and that it should be planted young, for it is tricky to transplant although otherwise trouble-free. It is sold as a pot-grown specimen. Arctic winds such as we experience in some winters can brown a proportion of the foliage but I have never known it not overcome such temporary set-backs.

Of course, if you have a good expanse of high wall with a warm and sunny aspect going begging and you live in a warmer part of the country, what better to consider growing than that other lovely Californian native, the semi-evergreen *Fremontodendron* 'California Glory', which I mentioned earlier.

This usually grows about 10 to 11ft (3 to 3.5m) tall (although it can be more) and produces an abundance of its golden-yellow, cup-shaped, waxy-textured flowers from late May until July. Again, it is helped by its foliage which is lobed and of dull green colouring and so an attractive foil for the flowers. A rather lean, well-drained soil suits it admirably and it does well on chalky soils.

If this fremontodendron has not proved to be particularly long-lived in gardens here neither has the lovely, deciduous *Abutilon vitifolium* from Chile, but that is no reason to be put off growing either shrub. *A. vitifolium* is a member of the *Malvaceae*, or mallow, family, and is a soft-wooded shrub of great elegance which really needs shelter and warmth such as it will get against a south- or west-facing wall. Given such conditions it will grow to a height of 15 to 20ft (4.5 to 6m) and produce from late May to July (at just the same time as the fremontodendron flowers) an abundance of its distinctive, hollyhock-like, mauve flowers. These also have a splendid foil in the grey, vine-like leaves. The cultivar 'Veronica Tennant' has rather bolder flowers than the species itself and is much in demand for that reason. There is also an attractive white-flowered variety, *album*. These abutilons do well on chalky soils, and indeed on all soils except those of a heavy nature.

Camellia willamsii
'Donation'

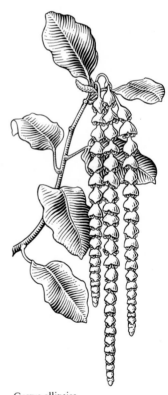

Garrya elliptica

41

Opposite: *Ivies are sympathetic companions for the pretty* Actinidia kolomikta, *the leaves of which are marked with pink and white (see p. 35).*

Its evergreen relative from Brazil, *A. megapotamicum*, is completely different and equally elegant. Growing about 6ft (2m) tall it produces (given the right conditions) a succession of colourful, Chinese-lantern-like flowers from April to autumn on a plant which forms a graceful framework of slender branches clothed with narrow, sharply-pointed leaves of rich green colouring. The pendant flowers with their bright red calyxes, yellow petals and cones of brownish stamens and stigmas are enormously eye-catching. It is a splendid shrub for a warm south- or west-facing wall or for growing in a container. In a bed, it does well in any average soil, provided it is well-drained. There is also a variety with yellow variegated leaves, *A. megapotamicum variegatum* but much as I like variegated-leaved plants generally, in this case I prefer the plain-leaved parent.

Another excellent shrub for growing against a warm, south-facing wall is the evergreen *Choisya ternata*, or Mexican orange blossom. This grows to a height of 8ft (2.5m) or so, has handsome, trifoliate, glossy-surfaced leaves and bears highly fragrant white flowers in terminal clusters in April and May. Flowering sometimes continues intermittently for several months after that. Again, it is a shrub which has no special soil needs, apart from first-class drainage.

Fremontodendron
'California Glory'
(see p. 41).

Abutilon vitifolium *(see p. 41)*

Other shrubs suitable for the patio

Before moving on to other plants I want to mention some other shrubs which would also make a very useful contribution to the patio garden. First, *Senecio* 'Sunshine', the lovely grey-foliaged evergreen shrub beloved of flower arrangers. This will grow 3 to 4ft (1 to 1.3m) tall and as much as 6ft (2m) across, but it is worth the space. What is more, it associates beautifully with a host of other plants, shrubby and perennial. Its silvery-grey leaves age to a soft olive green and are pleasing throughout the year. Sunshine and well-drained soil are all it asks for. The cheerful yellow daisy flowers in June and July can be looked upon as a useful bonus. Quite recently the botanists decided that the plants we have grown for many years in gardens under the names *Senecio greyii* and *S. laxifolius* are, in fact, invariably hybrids between the two and it is these which are now grouped together under the cultivar name 'Sunshine'.

Worth a prominent position and liking light shade is the hybrid mahonia 'Charity' – an evergreen of real value for its rank after rank of spiny leaves – each leaf consisting of up to 21 leaflets – even if one disregards the bold, deep yellow flowers borne in terminal racemes in November and December. You won't be sitting out at that time of year, but how nice to be greeted then by something of such decorative value. It grows something like 10ft (3.5m) tall and 8ft (2.5m) wide (although it can be more), and it is not difficult to please. What it will not tolerate, though, is winter wet at the roots. It can be kept more compact by pruning after flowering in spring. This can, indeed, be most beneficial as it does have a rather stiff habit. The beauty is in those wonderful leaves and flowers.

For spring flowering I would certainly commend the beautiful *Magnolia stellata*, the star magnolia as it is called. This makes a bush perhaps 8ft (2.5m) tall and as much wide, and the pure white star-shaped flowers with their many strap-like petals borne on the bare branches have a special charm. Find it a warm, sunny home where the soil is well-drained and preferably peaty. It is best without lime. Unlike most magnolias, it starts to flower at an early age.

If, on grounds of size, the easily pleased and very attractive *M. soulangiana* must be ruled out by most patio-garden owners, then there is another large magnolia which can be considered – the magnificent *M. grandiflora*, which is not all that hardy and so is invariably grown against a south- or south-west-facing wall. But it must be a high wall for it can, in time, reach a height of 26ft (8m), although it may well stick at something less. It also needs good

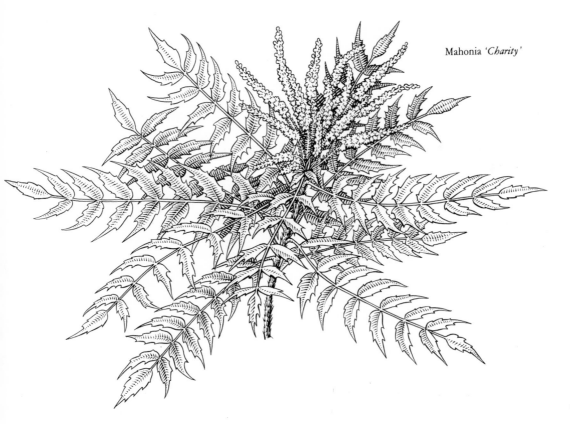

Mahonia *'Charity'*

Opposite: Pyracantha *'Orange Glow'*, *which fruits over a long period and is a favourite with many gardeners.* *(see p. 36)*

soil. What a job it is, though, when carrying its imposing creamy-white, fragrant, bowl-shaped flowers from July to September. The ovate leaves are dark green and glossy, and covered on the underside with a reddish-brown felt, as its most pronounced on young foliage. It is lime-tolerant. 'Exmouth' is a fine cultivar.

I would always try to find a home for *Paeonia lutea ludlowii* for this is a tree paeony of outstanding beauty from spring to autumn although I have to admit that it has a rather gaunt appearance in winter. It grows about 5ft (1.5m) tall and wide and is a delight when bearing the bold, deeply cut, fresh green leaves. Its peak period for effectiveness, though, is in May and June when for about three weeks these leaves form the frame for its superb rich golden-yellow, single flowers of cup-like appearance. Again, like the magnolias just referred to, this shrub needs sunshine, shelter and good soil drainage. In the patio garden even more than larger gardens it is an asset to have at least one or two different plants with very obvious "architectural" qualities (using that term in its gardening sense), for shape can be just as pleasing to the eye as beauty of flower, berry or foliage.

A shrub which associates splendidly with paving is the colourful *Hypericum* 'Hidcote', and given a well-drained soil it will flourish in sunshine or light shade. What a sight it is, too, when its rounded frame is smothered from early August until late September with the golden-yellow, saucer-like flowers – a mound of colour 4ft (1.3m) or so tall and perhaps 6ft (2m) wide.

Consider growing, too, a few potentillas, or cinquefoils as they are called, for those, mostly yellow-flowered but with some cream and white and the odd one having orange, red or pink blooms are quite low-growing – anything from 1ft to 4ft (30cm to 1.3m) tall and 3ft to 5ft (1m to 1.5m) wide, depending on cultivar – and provide colour the summer through from June to September or even October. Both the single flowers and the leaves are small and borne in profusion. Especially valuable is the cultivar 'Goldfinger', 3ft (90cm) tall, which is another of those

Magnolia soulangiana
(see p. 45).

shrubs with bright gold-yellow flowers to bring gaiety to the garden scene.

Other splendid potentiallas are 'Primrose Beauty', a lovely combination of colours with its primrose-yellow flowers and greyish-green foliage. This makes a spreading bush some 4ft (1.3m) tall and up to 6ft (2m) wide. But there are many more to choose from. 'Red Ace' is vermilion-flame, a strong colour which fades in very hot, dry weather and in very wet conditions. 'Royal Flush', with single rose-pink flowers, is highly attractive, 1ft (30cm) tall and 2ft (60cm) wide. 'Princess' has soft pink flowers and is 2½ft (75cm) tall and wide. All shrubby potentillas are extremely accommodating about soil conditions, and, although liking sunshine, they do well in light shade.

The admirable *Syringa meyeri* 'Palibin' (syn. *S. palibiniana, S. velutina*), not at all that well-known, is a natural choice for the patio garden – only 4ft (1.3m) tall and wide and with the most attractive rounded leaves, perfectly in scale, and fragrant, rosy-lilac flowers in May. Also, for the front of the border where its growth can splay over the paving, there is a delightful dwarf broom in *Cytisus kewensis*, only 1ft (30cm) tall but up to 5ft (1.5m) across, which bears sulphur-yellow flowers from late April to late May. Good soil drainage is an absolute necessity for this lime-tolerant shrub.

A dome-shaped shrub about 3ft (1m) tall which is very colourful in late May and June is *Genista hispanica*, the Spanish gorse. It smothers itself then with its bright golden-yellow pea flowers. Intensely prickly and much branched, it forms an impenetrable mass and as this network of spines and branches stays a rich green in winter it has an evergreen appearance although deciduous. What you must provide it with is a position in full sun where the soil is well drained. It will not tolerate excessive winter wet.

A dwarf cherry of great value for the patio garden is *Prunus glandulosa* 'Albiplena', another of those shrubs which although long grown in this country is not at all well-known. It grows only 3 to 4ft (1 to 1.3m) tall and wide and bears its double white flowers prolifically in late April and early May. Then in the autumn the leaves take on the most lovely tawny-red shade, sometimes suffused with lilac. It has a pink-flowered counterpart in *P. glandulosa* 'Sinensis'. A good loamy soil is appreciated by both these cherries, but whatever the composition of the soil it must be well drained – something which has to be stressed with so many shrubs. It is worth noting, too, that these cherries, like others of their kind, grow well on chalky soils.

Another prunus, which should be considered is the dwarf almond *P. tenella* 'Fire Hill', which makes a lovely show in April when the upright branches are smothered in rosy-red flowers. This is also a small shrub, 3 to 4ft (1 to 1.3m) tall and more wide.

Do not overlook either the lovely small-growing laurel, *P. laurocerasus* 'Otto Luyken', which I have described in the chapter on plants for containers (p. 120).

I shall not say much about hydrangeas, superb as these are for the patio garden, for I also deal with them in the chapter on plants to grow in containers (see p. 117), but one I must mention – the comparative newcomer *Hydrangea* 'Preziosa'. This hybrid, which has the common hydrangea, *H. macrophylla*, as one parent and *H. serrata* as the other, makes a bush at most 5ft (1.5m) tall and 4ft (1.3m) wide and usually rather less, so although showy it does not take up too much space. Its pride and joy are the round, hortensia-type (mop-headed) blooms in salmon-pink, usually borne with much freedom, and with these are combined foliage and stems tinted with purple – a delightful combination of colours. This shrub is a fine choice for any but dry soils (which all hydrangeas loathe, of course) and it is happy in sunshine or light shade.

Grow *Daphne mezereum* if you can find room, in sunshine or light shade in a rather good, moisture-retentive but well-drained soil, for the very fragrant purplish-red flowers which bedeck its bare, upright 4 to 5ft (1.3 to 1.5m) frame in February and March are a special treat. Accept, however, that this deciduous shrub can die on you for no apparent reason while still reasonably young.

Another daphne which it is well worth finding a home for is the 4 to 5ft (1.3 to 1.5m) tall *D. odora* 'Aureomarginata', an evergreen which produces in late winter and early spring richly scented small flowers in terminal heads. These flowers are near white within and purplish-red on the outside of the petals. The shiny, oval leaves are of mid-green colouring and are margined with creamy-white. Although this variety is hardier than the species itself it still needs a sheltered position, but that shouldn't be difficult to find in your patio garden. Culturally, its needs are similar to those of *D. mezereum*. There will surely be a real place in the future, too, for *D. bholua* 'Gurkha', a 7 to 8ft (2.25 to 2.5m) deciduous shrub from the Himalayas, which bears purplish-rose flowers of strong fragrance between December and February. It is upright in habit.

To grow rhododendrons and azaleas you must have a lime-free humusy soil which is retentive of moisture, but given this it can be very well worthwhile incorporating in the garden just the odd one or two of the smaller-flowering rhododendrons. I'm thinking particularly of things like the slow-growing *R. yakushimanum*, an outstanding Japanese species which grows 4ft (1.3m) tall and wide at most and has lovely bell-shaped blooms which are pink in the bud and open white. It is May-flowering.

A group of compact hybrids of small stature has been developed from this species, these being of considerable interest

Rhododendron yakushimanum

to the gardener lacking space. They have a good colour range and superb kinds include 'Morning Magic' with white flowers which are pink in the bud; 'Hydon Hunter', with pink flowers, edged with red and with orange spotting; and 'Caroline Allbrook' a lavender colour. 'Diana Pearson', a very attractive blush pink with crimson spotting was, I am delighted to say, named for my wife by Mr Arthur George, the rhododendron breeder who has had remarkable success with his 'Yak' hybrids. Other rhododen-

Rhododendron yakushiamanum *hybrids, like* 'Caroline Allbrook' *shown here, are ideal for growing on patios – of course, in lime-free soil.*

drons worth your consideration – and there are, of course, many more from which to make a choice – are the lavender-blue 'Blue Diamond', which has the most becoming small leaves, and the dark red 'Elizabeth', which makes a spreading bush not more than 4ft (1.3m) tall, or about the same as the much more compact 'Blue Diamond'. Both are April flowering.

Then there is the highly attractive 'Bow Bells' which bears bell-shaped flowers of an exquisite shade of soft pink in April and

Rhus typhina

May. It also has very attractive rounded, heart-shaped leaves, which it inherits from the *R. williamsianum* side of its parentage. It grows about 3ft (1m) tall and has a spreading habit. A hybrid which I have loved ever since I first saw it at the Chelsea Flower Show where it won an award of merit is 'Pink Pebble', a small, shapely bush with rounded leaves (from the *williamsianum* side of its parentage) and exquisite pale pink bell flowers in May which open from bright red buds.

For earlier, March, flowering a couple of small-growing rhododendron hybrids I would especially commend to attention are 'Seta' and 'Tessa Roza'. The first is an especially attractive, rather upright-growing variety up to 4ft (1.3m) tall which bears tubular bell flowers of near white colouring striped with pink; 'Tessa Roza', up to 5ft (1.5m) tall, had rose-pink flowers which are especially good for cutting for indoor decoration – if you can bring yourself to remove even a few sprigs for that purpose. Both have a common parent in *R. moupinense* which has passed on to them an ability to withstand drought conditions better than most rhododendrons. Because they flower so early in the year there is a risk of frost damage to the blooms although the plants themselves are fully hardy. For this reason it is best to avoid planting them in positions where the blooms will be exposed to early morning sunshine and damage through "scorching".

For late May colour a specimen or two of Knap Hill and Exbury hybrid deciduous azaleas could be good value, especially as the leaves often colour up well in autumn, while of the evergreen azaleas I would put in a word for the exquisite white-flowered 'Palestrina' and 'Vuyk's Rosy Red'. Again, these are May flowering, little over 4ft (1.3m) tall and 4 to 5ft (1.3 to 1.5m) across.

The stag's horn sumach, *Rhus typhina,* has a rather angular appearance and gets quite large – as much as 13 to 15ft (4 to 4.5m) tall and as much across, a low-branching tree more than a shrub, perhaps – and throws up suckers which can be a bit of a nuisance, but I still consider it very worthwhile for a sunny corner of a patio garden, at least one which is not too small. The large pinnate leaves, sometimes more than 2ft (60cm) long, are most attractive and colour beautifully in autumn – a variety of shades from red and orange to yellow and purple – and female specimens too offer another attraction in their crimson, cone-shaped fruit clusters which appear late in the year. Greenish-coloured flower panicles are borne by specimens of both sexes in July. It has no special soil needs. A cut-leaved female form named 'Laciniata' is also available and can be a source of pleasure in the garden.

A rather sprawly shrub from the Mediterranean region which is especially well-suited for patio conditions is the Jerusalem sage, *Phlomis fruticosa,* an evergreen with grey-green, sage-like leaves and pretty yellow flowers which are borne in whorls on the upper parts of the stems in early summer. About 4ft (1.3m) tall, it is a lovely sight spreading out, in its uninhibited way, over the edge of a bed on to paving. This is another of those shrubs which must be given a warm, sunny position, and it is best in rather lean soil, which must be well-drained.

Indeed, those are just the conditions to suit the rock roses I mentioned earlier (*Cistus skanbergii* [see p. 23] and a selection of hybrids of which the best is probably 'Silver Pink', up to 3ft [1m] tall and wide and very beautiful in the first half of summer when the silvery-pink flowers are borne in quantity against a background of dark green leaves). These evergreens are worth a bit of pampering. They establish best from spring planting, and love sunshine combined with shelter. Indeed, they are often known as sun roses rather than rock roses. In very severe winter weather it is a wise precaution to protect them as far as possible with dry litter.

One does not want to overdo such effects but a few really good variegated shrubs can be stunningly effective in a small garden. Two in particular I would bring to your attention: *Weigela florida variegata* and *Elaeagnus pungens* 'Maculata'. The weigela is deciduous, the elaeagnus evergreen. The first has a height and spread of 4 to 5ft (1.3 to 1.5m), the second makes a rather bigger bush. Both are happy in any reasonable, well-drained soil. The decorative value of the weigela is at its peak in early summer when the creamy-white-edged leaves make a marvellous foil for the pink, foxglove-like flowers, but the foliage alone is a decorative feature right up to leaf fall. The elaeagnus stands on the decorative value of its foliage alone, and that it does splendidly. The leaves with their rich mixture of green and gold positively glow in sunshine the year round, and they brighten the garden even in the dullest of weather.

One must always allow for the ubiquitous but invaluable forsythia to make a bush 7 to 10ft (2.3 to 3m) tall, but do find a nice corner site for it, in sunshine or shade – it will do well in either. The best known and most widely planted is the excellent *Forsythia intermedia spectabilis,* and a splendid sight it is in March and April, but even better is another variety belonging to the same *intermedia* grouping – 'Lynwood' which bears masses of large, rich yellow blooms. More upright-growing is 'Beatrix Farrand', an American-raised variety which has extra-large flowers of golden-yellow. I find it less free-flowering than the other two just mentioned.

If you are, for instance, making a feature of a birch tree (see the chapter on trees, p. 69) then you might care to give this an extra bit of sparkle by planting a few heathers around its base. Most heathers demand a lime-free soil, but an important group of winter-flowering ericas (*Erica carnea* and its numerous varieties) are among those tolerant of lime, and it is those I have in mind

Rhododendrons provide a telling backdrop to this paved area.

now to bring additional colour to the garden in the winter.

These *Erica carnea* varieties come in heights up to about 15in (38cm) so are enormously useful for providing a low carpet of colour. Two strong-growing, spreading varieties are 'Springwood White' and 'Springwood 'Pink', these flowering freely from January to March or April. Others of note are the deep red, bronze-foliaged 'Vivelli' (February-March flowering); 'Myretoun Ruby', with ruby-red flowers from February to April; the ground-

Below: Rhododendron yakushimanum *'Hydon Hunter', one of a group of hybrids of compact habit ideal for patio gardens (see p. 50).*

hugging, golden-foliaged 'Foxhollow' with pink flowers during the same period; and the vigorous 'Pink Spangles', which flowers from January to March. There are plenty of others to choose from. It is always a good thing to add plenty of peat to the soil in which heathers are to be grown, and make sure that they do not suffer from undue dryness at the roots, especially during the establishment period.

For providing low cover in less than ideal conditions I would always turn to the adaptable periwinkles or vincas, and particularly *Vinca major* 'Variegata (often known also as *V. major* 'Elegantissima'). This bears pretty purplish-blue flowers from April to June, and is attractive the year round as a foliage plant for the evergreen leaves are heavily marked with creamy-white. It grows about 1ft (30cm) tall and has a spread of about 3ft (1m).

I mentioned two hebes at the beginning of this chapter which give excellent value, 'Great Orme' and 'Autumn Glory'. The first makes a shrub some 3 to 4ft (1 to 1.3m) tall and wide, the second, one which is 2ft (60cm) tall and around 3ft (1m) wide. 'Great Orme' bears longish spikes of pink flowers from early summer to July; 'Autumn Glory' much shorter spikes of violet-blue flowers from July into autumn, so they complement each other very well indeed. Like all the hebes they do well in any well-drained soil of average quality in a sunny position.

Two low-growing, ground-covering hebes which are also very useful for patio-garden planting are 'Carl Teschner', which bears short spikes of violet-coloured flowers in mid-summer against a background of dark green leaves, and *H. pinguifolia* 'Pagei' which has a mass of glaucous-grey leaves and bears clusters of small white flowers in May. This last in particular has become very popular as a ground-coverer in recent years. Both of these plants grow about 9in to 1ft (23cm to 30cm) tall and have a spread of about 3ft (1m). *H. pinguifolia* 'Pagei' makes a lovely plant to associate with the very attractive herbaceous geranium, *G. sanguineum lancastriense,* which has pale pink flowers with red veining. This geranium flowers practically all summer.

One of the best evergreen ground-cover shrubs, not more than 1ft (30cm) tall, is the popular and eye-catching *Euonymus fortunei* 'Emerald 'n' Gold', the leaves of which are bright yellow and green and often tinged with pink. It is suitable for growing in sunshine or light shade and in any reasonable soil.

Shrubs which provide strong garden features in their own right and at the same time make splendid foils for other border plants are always to be welcomed, and *Berberis thunbergii atropurpurea* falls squarely in that category. This deciduous barberry grows about 5 to 6ft (1.5 to 2m) tall and wide and has small reddish-purple leaves which are set off by small yellow flowers in spring. Then, at the other end of the season, the leaves intensify in colour before leaf fall. This variety has a dwarf form 'Atropurpurea Nana', no more than 2ft (60cm) tall, which is a fine plant to provide special effects where space is limited, as in raised beds. Although very easy-going, like all the barberries, neither *atropurpurea* nor its dwarf form are happy in chalk soils.

Another variety of *B. thunbergii* which is admirably suited to the patio garden is 'Rose Glow', some 5ft (1.5m) tall and wide which has purple leaves mottled with silvery-pink and rose while these are at the young stage (later they become purple all over).

For a sunny position where the soil is well drained I commend also the attractive, compact form of the deciduous *Physocarpus opulifoius* named 'Dart's Gold', which grows some 2½ft to 3ft (75cm to 1m) tall and wide. From spring onwards its three- or five-lobed leaves are a rich golden-yellow, which does however take on some greenish overtones as summer advances. It bears white flowers in June, but it is the foliage which counts.

Another true dwarf form of a popular barberry is *B. stenophylla* 'Coronilla Compacta' – a frightful mouthful of a name for an attractive little 1½ft (45cm) tall shrub which bears yellow flowers in April which are coral-red in the bud stage. It's another candidate for a raised bed.

There is one other barberry to which I would give brief mention: 'Parkjuweel', a very prickly, semi-evergreen variety which is noted for its fine autumn leaf colouring. It bears yellow flowers in spring and makes a compact bush some 4ft (1.3m) tall and 2½ft (75cm) across.

For special autumnal effects don't overlook either that splendid cotoneaster, *C. conspicuus* 'Decorus', which grows some 3ft (1m) tall and more wide and smothers itself in small bright red berries during early autumn, these persisting well into winter. Then there is the low-growing *C. dammeri,* only a few inches high but with a spread of 2 to 3ft (60cm to 1m), which is an excellent ground-coverer and free in the production of its small red berries in autumn. Both can be grown in any average soil, preferably in a sunny position but in light shade if need be.

For warm, sunny positions and well-drained soils a good choice where something low-growing is required is the lavender, *Lavandula angustifolia* 'Hidcote', 2ft (60cm) tall and with spikes of violet-blue flowers in the second half of summer. If something taller is needed then a good choice would be the rosemary, *Rosmarinus officinalis* 'Fastigiatus', which is also known as 'Miss Jessop's Variety'. This grows 5 to 6ft (1.5 to 2m) tall and bears blue flowers in May and intermittently during summer.

Some of the smaller-growing forms of the Japanese maple, *Acer palmatum,* are delightful patio shrubs with their attractive shapes and foliage. Two of the most suitable are *A. palmatum* 'Dissectum' and *A. palmatum* 'Dissectum Atropurpureum' for they have deeply cut foliage, this of a fetching fresh green colour in the first case and bronze-purple in the other. In both the leaves colour well before leaf-fall, assuming red shades. These *A. palmatum* cultivars are not, however, suitable for chalky soils.

For a shady spot a splendid shrub of smallish stature is *Skimmia japonica* 'Foremanii', an evergreen with glossy leaves which grows 3ft (1m) and up to 6ft (2m) wide. It bears conspicuous red berries from autumn right through the winter but only if you plant it near a male variety of *S. japonica* 'Fragrans', for skimmia is a genus in which the sexes are divided. Both varieties bear

Skimmia japonica
'Foremanii'

Above: Euonymus fortunei
'Emerald 'n' Gold', a first-
class, low-growing evergreen
ground-cover shrub.

Opposite: Euonymus
fortunei 'Silver Queen'
associated with Hosta
sieboldiana and
Polygonatum x hybridum
(Solomon's seal) to create a
beautiful "mural corner".

white flowers in spring, those of 'Fragrans' being nicely scented, as the name suggests. *S. japonica* 'Rubella' is attractive for it bears red buds in winter which open to white flowers in April.

Another small shrub of value, but this time for a sunny position, is *Spiraea bumalda* 'Anthony Waterer', some 3ft (1m) tall and wide, with panicles of bright red flowers through most of summer set off by lance-shaped leaves of dark green, often flecked pink and cream. Any average soil suits it well. Another, no more than 2ft (60cm) high, and very free-flowering, is

Fuchsia *'Mrs Popple'*

S, japonica 'Alpina' which bears a profusion of rose-pink flowers in summer. This does well in light shade. Another I am very fond of is *S. nipponica tosaensis* (more often known as 'Snowmound') which literally does become a 4 to 5ft (1.25 to 1.50m) mound of white when it flowers in June.

Three viburnums must also be given special mention: the evergreen *V. davidii,* some 2 to 3ft (60cm to 1m) tall and as much across, *V. tinus* 'Eve Price', 6ft (2m) tall and perhaps a little more wide and *V. tinus* 'Gwenllian'. *V. davidii* has very attractive, deeply veined leaves of dark green colouring and, on female specimens (for this again is a shrub where the sexes are separated and you need to plant male and female forms to get berries), turquoise-blue berries in winter, while the compact-growing form of the popular evergreen laurustinus, *V. tinus* 'Eve Price', bears through most of the winter heads of pale pink flowers which are carmine-coloured in the bud. It is worth a prominent position. Compact-growing *V. tinus* 'Gwenllian' produces blue berries freely and is a lovely sight with these among the pink flowers. These, and indeed all, viburnums like a soil of reasonably good quality which is moisture-retentive but well drained. They should also be planted in positions open to plenty of sunshine.

I have more to say about fuchsias in the chapter on plants for containers (see p. 117) and there is no doubting the usefulness of the hardiest of these for planting permanently in sheltered borders. They include *Fuchsia magellanica* 'Versicolor' (which makes a bush of spreading habit up to 5ft [1.5m] tall) and the hardiest of the many hybrids which are available. This is a spectacular shrub with its grey-green leaves marked with creamy-white and pink and its red and violet flowers in summer (it is, however, primarily a foliage shrub), but like the other kinds referred to above it can be cut right back in severe winters. New growth breaks freely from the base in spring, however, although you should take the precaution of protecting the roots in winter with a covering of dry litter or well-weathered ashes. Winter wet is also a natural hazard, and you should make sure that the soil is free-draining by working in plenty of humus-forming material like garden compost or peat.

A few of the numerous varieties suitable for planting in this way are 'Mrs Popple', with scarlet and purple flowers; 'Margaret', crimson and violet-purple, semi-double; 'Alice Hoffman', cerise and white; 'Chillerton Beauty', white, pink and violet-mauve; and 'Tom Thumb', cerise and mauve, a popular dwarf variety. These and others will provide a mass of colour right through from mid-summer to autumn, especially in lightly shaded parts of the garden.

Don't overlook the charm of such bamboos as *Arundinaria murieliae,* the variegated *A. viridistriata* and the small 'Gauntletii'.

Only glass separates this extension to an existing house from the patio garden measuring 23ft (7m) across by 28ft (8.6m) long. To help preserve a sense of space 1ft (30cm) square tiles are used instead of larger paving slabs. The weeping birch. Betula pendula youngii, *is never likely to be a nuisance because of size.*

At the farther end of the garden 10ft (3m) square of ground is screened by runner beans and the space in between is used to grow a few vegetables and fruit on the walls. As it is so close to the house, the support for the beans is made tidy by having a sawn-timber frame with bamboo canes or cord actually

providing the support for the plants.

Two wide steps drop down beside a small pool fed by a fountain. This is sited exactly opposite a seat built into the wall on the left. It is an easily maintained garden which should give quiet satisfaction throughout the year.

The first forms a clump up to 10ft (3m) tall with arching stems which start green and later take on a yellow tinge. The 6ft (2m) *A. viridistriata* has leaves striped with yellow and purplish-green canes, while *A.* 'Gauntletii' is of only half this height and has canes which turn from a rich green to a purplish shade. These can look extremely attractive in a paved setting.

The best time of all to plant these is in April and May but October is another good planting month. Provide them with a home in a sheltered position in good soil which does not dry out.

Perhaps rather surprisingly, I am going to suggest that you also consider finding a home for that favourite of the Victorians,

Opposite: Arundinaria
viridistriata, *one of the most
striking of the variegated
bamboos (see p. 61)*

the evergreen shrub which also doubles up as a striking house
plant – *Fatsia japonica.* You will probably know it for its large,
deeply lobed, shiny leaves of darkest green, perhaps less well for
the panicles of rather handsome white flowers which appear in
late autumn. In the garden it has value as an architectural plant –
that is to say, one with beauty of form. In really cold gardens it
will have to have the protection of a warm wall, but elsewhere
any reasonably sheltered spot will suffice, and that should include
most patio gardens.

Pruning shrubs

Earlier in this chapter I outlined the pruning treatment which
clematis need for these are, as the saying goes, a rather special
case. Now I want to give a few tips on the pruning of shrubs in
general which I hope you will find useful when you come to
wield your secateurs.

I would urge above all a modicum of restraint. Do what is
necessary, but always be conscious that what you have removed
has taken a long time to develop and cannot be put back.

As with rose pruning, the way to an easy mind is to have a basic
understanding of the underlying principles, and it is these which I
shall discuss now.

With shrubs one is pruning for shapeliness, good health (by
removing dead and weak wood) and vigour. I shall at this stage
divide shrubs into two sections – the deciduous and the evergreen, the latter needing little in the way of pruning attention.

Deciduous shrubs are again sub-divided into those which
flower on wood made in the same year and those which flower on
the previous season's wood. All the earlier flowering shrubs fall
in the latter category, and these can again be split into those
which flower before growth starts in spring and those which start
to flower either coincidentally with the start of growth or rather
later in the season.

The first category, the early flowerers, like the forsythias, you
should prune as soon as flowering has finished, so that all the
growth which follows will be left to bear flowers in the following
year. If this job is done later in the year, after growth has been
made, then obviously good potential flowering wood must be
cut away – and there is no gain in that.

Those shrubs which flower at or after the start of growth in
spring are still pruned immediately after flowering finishes but it
is done in the knowledge that inevitably some potential new
flowering wood must be lost. You therefore prune with some
circumspection, only cutting away wood which you feel must go
for the overall good of the plant.

Shrubs which flower in late summer on the wood made in the
same year are easy to deal with: you can prune these at any time
during winter until growth restarts in spring.

When discussing patios the natural inclination is to think of houses or properties with a rather contemporary air, but of course many small plots accompany period terraced houses. With these, it is important that care should be taken to make the paved sitting-out area and plantings completely in character. This plot represents an area 42ft (12.6m) wide by 60ft (18m) deep and the design allows for ample sitting-out space near the building. Then there is a drop of 15in (38cm) to what could either be a small lawn or another paved area, according to taste, with or without the pool at the centre. If it were decided not to have a pool then a bowl, sundial or similar ornament set in a grouping of low-growing plants would be an admirable alternative.

Even a garden of this size can have its compost corner if this is screened from the house, as here by a carefully executed trellis screen.

With evergreens, confine the pruning to the removal of dead or weak wood and a bit of shaping up – and do this in spring when the plants have a time of strong growth ahead of them. One other thing you can do though with evergreens, if need be, is to invigorate old specimens by shortening the branches quite severely in early spring. Such treatment will encourage strong new growth to be made.

As to the execution, always use sharp secateurs or pruners and make the cuts close to a joint on the stem so that there will be no risk of die-back. Dispose of all prunings immediately to avoid the risk of decay and the spread of diseases.

4. A Small Tree for Atmosphere

Like most people I reserve a special place in my affections for trees. They do something for gardens and the landscape generally which is of inestimable value, and many of these have such character that they seem almost to have personalities of their own.

When considering trees in relation to the patio garden, though, it is necessary to curb one's enthusiasm and make quite sure that their dimensions are suitable for such a setting. There is nothing more distressing than to see some beautiful tree cut back, even mutilated, because there is insufficient room for it to develop as it should. So check first what the ultimate size of any tree you are considering is likely to be. It will vary with the conditions, of course, but it is possible to arrive at a rough mean which is a good enough guide.

What I have said about planting shrubs and their aftercare (see pp. 24 to 25) applies with equal force to trees, so I will not repeat it here. Be quite sure to provide adequate support, for if there is anything which is going to set back the re-establishment of a newly planted tree it is wind rocking, which does not give the questing roots a chance to gain a firm hold. And be sure to place the stake in position before setting the tree in the prepared hole. Doing this afterwards can easily cause severe damage to the roots.

What are the qualities to look for when choosing a tree for a patio setting? Well, it goes without saying that it must be of modest or reasonable size. Its form must be pleasing and right for the surroundings. Indeed, I think this can often be more important than the consideration of such transient pleasures as beauty of flower, berry or foliage (except in the case of evergreens). With flowering trees, and there are some delightful small ones, you must consider whether their colouring will fit in with that of other plants you expect to have in bloom at the same time. In a larger garden this is something which one need scarcely bother about, but in the confines of a small area, where everything is closely related, it is a factor to consider.

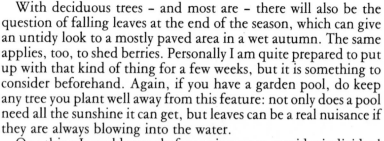

With deciduous trees – and most are – there will also be the question of falling leaves at the end of the season, which can give an untidy look to a mostly paved area in a wet autumn. The same applies, too, to shed berries. Personally I am quite prepared to put up with that kind of thing for a few weeks, but it is something to consider beforehand. Again, if you have a garden pool, do keep any tree you plant well away from this feature: not only does a pool need all the sunshine it can get, but leaves can be a real nuisance if they are always blowing into the water.

One thing I would stress before going on to consider individual trees for the patio is the action necessary if you want to remove a branch from a mature tree because it has died, is diseased or is, perhaps, just badly placed and so spoiling the symmetry of its outline.

The danger here is that when the branch is semi-severed its weight will bring it down and cause a tear in the bark which will take long to heal. You can easily stop this happening by making an undercut first. With heavy branches – anything you cannot support with your free hand – it is always wise to do the job in two stages: make the first cut about 2ft (60cm) from the trunk and finally saw it off flush with the trunk after the branch is out of the way. Then pare the edges of the wound smooth with a pruning knife and cover the whole area with a bituminous sealing agent to protect it from the weather and the entry of diseases. You can get tree wound dressings of this kind at garden stores, and they are easily painted on the wounds.

Prunus and Malus
Now for a few planting suggestions. The genus *Prunus* includes all the flowering cherries, peaches, almonds, plums and the ubiquitous and usefui laurels and offers infinite delights to gardeners of all persuasions. A splendid choice for the patio would be the pyramidal *Prunus* 'Amanogawa' which makes a slim column 15 to 20ft (4.5 to 6m) tall and smothers itself in late April and May with shell-pink blooms. Similar, but perhaps 5ft (1.5m) taller, is *P. hillieri* 'Spire', with a maximum width of about 10ft (3m), which bears soft pink flowers and provides a bonus in having good autumn colour.

For the rather more generously sized patio. I would certainly suggest the lovely flowering plum *P. blireana* as an alternative. It makes a beautifully rounded small tree, perhaps 18 to 20ft (5.5 to 6m) tall and about as wide, with double, rose-pink blooms in

Prunus '*Amanogawa*'

Opposite: Malus '*John Downie*', *an ornamental crab of excellence.*

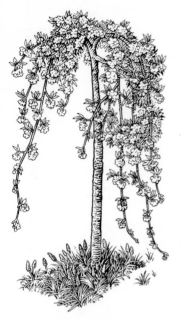

Prunus 'Kiku Shidare Sakura'

April. The coppery-bronze foliage is also an attraction from spring to autumn. One cautionary note, though: the colours of most bricks clash with the blooms, so try to avoid such a juxta-position. It is best of all with a dark background, such as in a larger garden could easily be provided by a conifer screen.

The modestly-sized winter-flowering cherry, *P. subhirtella* 'Autumnalis', is also worth considering if colour at that time of year interests you, for it produces its white, semi-double blooms intermittently right through from late autumn until March.

The Fuji cherry, *P. incisa,* is grown either as a shrub or a small tree, and in both roles it is a sheer delight, smothering itself, as winter gives way to spring, with white flowers which are pink at the bud stage. Its heavily toothed leaves usually also colour up well before leaf fall. It does not often grow much more than 15ft (4.5m). tall

A Japanese cherry to consider is the round-headed and late-flowering 'Shimidsu Sakura', another charmer, which again grows only some 15 to 18ft (4.5 to 5.5m) tall and wide. The branches droop over prettily to create a beautiful effect when it is in flower, these flowers being semi-double, pinkish in the bud stage and opening pure white. They appear in May. Even smaller in stature and a little earlier flowering (late April and early May) is the weeping 'Kiku Shidare Sakura' which bears fully double, deep pink flowers to make it the ideal weeping tree for patio-garden conditions. It can look stunning underplanted with the grape hyacinth, *Muscari armeniacum* 'Heavenly Blue', which is in flower at the same time.

Any ordinary soil suits these cherries and they like lime. They need sunshine and good drainage.

A reasonable soil, good drainage and exposure to all the sun-shine that is going is what is needed, too, by pretty ornamental crabs like *Malus* 'Golden Hornet'. This particular cultivar makes a tree of 20 to 26ft (6 to 8m) or so in height and much the same spread, and it is lovely in spring when covered in white blossom and again in autumn and winter when the long-persisting bright yellow fruits cover the branches. 'John Downie', of similar size, is another, this having pleasing yellow and red fruits.

Roughly the same size is the Japanese crab, *M. floribunda,* a spectacular sight in late April when it smothers itself with pale pink, single flowers, red at the bud stage. Yellow fruits follow in autumn. An ornamental crab of columnar habit which can also be a good choice is the variety 'Van Eseltine' which has rosy-pink, double flowers, red at the bud stage.

My favourite of them all, though, is *Malus* x *robusta* 'Yellow Siberian' which makes a small tree of great charm. It bears white flowers (sometimes flushed with pink) in April and a profusion of small yellow fruits in autumn, these being long-persisting. In flower and fruit it is a joy.

Betula pendula youngii

Elegant form and decorative bark

I am fond, too, of the weeping birch, *Betula pendula youngii*, so elegant at all times and not difficult to accommodate as it grows only some 15 to 20ft (4.5 to 6m) tall. It also relates most sympathetically to other garden features. Although taller (up to 40ft [12m]) the related Swedish birch, *B. p. dalecarlica*, whose pendulous branches carry the loveliest of finely cut leaves, does not have a great lateral spread and its natural elegance makes it worth considering for larger patios. All birches are rather greedy feeders, although they will put up with very lean fare when occasion demands. They will do best, though, in soils with plenty of body. There is much pleasure to be gained also from the yellow leaf tints which these and other birches assume in autumn. It will be up to you to decide whether their visual appeal justifies putting up with the disadvantages referred to, in a patio garden.

A choice maple to grow if you can provide a sunny, sheltered home and well-drained soil is *Acer griseum*, a species with beautiful flaking bark and good autumn colour. It does not usually grow over 20ft (6m) tall and 10ft (3m) wide. Much the same size is *A. ginnala* with most spectacular autumn colouring in deep orange and red. This you can grow as a small tree or large shrub.

Opposite: Sorbus hupehensis, *an elegant small tree which bears long-lasting fruits (see p. 72).*

Right: Sorbus *'Joseph Rock' – one of the finest of the mountain ashes.*

Quite different again are the snake-bark maples of which the small-growing *A. pensylvanicum* is an example. Its bark is beautifully striped in white and pale green and it usually makes a tree of less than 20ft (6m) in height. It can be especially delightful in winter when low-angle sunshine lights up the bark.

Very handsome in a different kind of way again is the weeping willow-leaved pear, *Pyrus salicifolia* 'Pendula'. This grows some 15 to 20ft (4.5 to 6m) tall and forms a thick mat of pendulous branches covered in silvery grey, willow-like leaves. This distinctive tree will grow in any average, well-drained soil. I saw recently a specimen of the oleaster, *Elaeagnus angustifolia,* growing near a *Pyrus salicifolia* 'Pendula' and it was suggested to me at that time that, such is the resemblance, it would make an excellent alternative to the latter, if such were needed. I'm inclined to agree. The oleaster usually grows to around 20ft (6m) tall –although it can be quite a lot more when especially well-suited –and it has silvery-grey, willow-like leaves. It is of lax habit but not fully weeping like the pyrus, however, and makes a somewhat rounded head. It is more often grown as a large shrub, rather than a small tree.

The genus Sorbus
The sorbuses – mostly belonging to the Aucuparia, or mountain ash, section of the genus – include trees of special interest. *Sorbus*

Sorbus vilmorinii

vilmorinii perhaps more than most, for it is an elegant species (from western China) with typical, pretty, fern-like foliage which colours to shades of red and purple in autumn when the fruits are also an attraction, starting off red but fading with age to pink and rosy-white. It grows to a height of some 20ft (6m) and considerably less wide. The fruits are long-lasting so it offers especially good decorative value.

Sorbus hupehensis (from the same region as *S. vilmorinii*) is likely to be a little taller than the last and this has good decorative qualities in its purplish-brown stems, its leaves comprised of many leaflets of bluish-green colouring (which turn rich red in autumn) and white, long-lasting fruits which are suffused with pink. Although it can grow to 30ft (9m) or more tall the splendid variety 'Joseph Rock' has a pyramidal habit and is excellent for its autumn colour, the leaves turning to shades of orange and yellow and the fruits starting creamy-yellow and deepening to amber-yellow as they age. For a part of the garden where little lateral space is available there is also a fastigiate form of *S. aucuparia* available, *S. a.* 'Fastigiata', which makes a column up to 20 to 26ft (6 to 8m) tall. It carries bright red fruits.

All have white flowers which are borne in May or June, but it is the decorative features already stressed which earn them their place in gardens. All are easily pleased, growing well in any reasonable soil in sunshine or light shade.

Bright foliage colour

Two trees with golden foliage which cannot be left out of the reckoning even though they can, in favourable circumstances, make quite large trees are *Robinia pseudoacacia* 'Frisia' and *Gleditsia triacanthos* 'Sunburst' – the first being raised in Holland in the mid-1930s and the second in the United States in the mid-1950s. *R. pseudoacacia* 'Frisia' will in time make a tree of about 30ft (9m) in height and about half that in width; *G. triacanthos* 'Sunburst' rather more, and with, perhaps, this last having a rather better habit for the robinia is often a little untidy in its shape.

Still, 'Frisia' is a lovely tree and it is becoming more and more widely grown as gardeners appreciate that it holds its golden-yellow colouring right through from spring to autumn, when it assumes almost apricot tints before leaf fall. And yellow, as I suggested earlier in a brief comment on colour (see p. 22) is unrivalled for giving the garden a cheerful appearance. Like all the robinias, however, 'Frisia' has rather brittle branches, easily broken in windy conditions. It is happy in any ordinary, well-drained soil but it should be given a sunny, sheltered position for preference.

The same kind of conditions suit *G. triacanthos* 'Sunburst', the fern-like, pinnate leaves of which are a bright golden-yellow in spring, gradually assuming green tones as the season advances. To a certain extent the lateral spread of this tree can be controlled by judicious pruning, but if space is a cause of concern it is best to plump for 'Frisia' which is naturally narrower.

A splendid variegated holly for providing cheerful colour is *Ilex aquifolium* 'Golden Queen' which, despite its name, is a male form and therefore non-berrying. It more than makes up for this by the excellence of its foliage, for the bold, spiny leaves are dark green in colour with pale green and grey suffusions and a broad margin of rich yellow. It grows slowly to a height of around 18 to 20ft (5.5 to 6m), with a width of about half that, but to a degree its size can be contained by careful pruning in late summer. As a design feature the year round it is most valuable. The hollies generally are, of course, extremely easy-going plants growing well in any soil of reasonable quality. They will also succeed in sunshine or shade but it is best to give them good light if this is possible.

The sexes are divided in hollies, as I've already inferred, so to get female varieties to bear berries a male variety must be planted near by. If you have room for two specimens a good one to consider would be *I. altaclarensis* 'Golden King' which, believe it or not, is a female form (how 'Golden Queen' and 'Golden King' got such inappropriate names I have not been able to discover!). This is another very striking, golden-variegated holly, this time with virtually spineless leaves boldly margined with rich yellow. It bears large red berries, and its size roughly approximates to that of 'Golden Queen'. Do not overlook also the dwarf (2ft [60cm] tall and 3 to 4ft [1 to 1.75m] in width *I. crenata* 'Golden Gem' for this non-berrying form has golden-yellow colouring which develops best in a sunny position.

Some more suggestions
The adaptability of the cotoneasters is especially marked; they will grow with gusto in any soil of average quality. It is best, however, to give them sunny positions whenever possible and that goes for the useful little *Cotoneaster* 'Hybridus Pendulus' which, when grown on a straight 6ft (2m) stem, makes a very attractive weeping specimen. It is the loveliest of sights in autumn when loaded with bright red berries. Such is the size of this weeping, evergreen tree that it can be fitted into virtually any garden – a height of about 10ft (3m) is its maximum, with a spread not exceeding this.

Willows need a soil which remains nicely moist and most of those making trees grow far too large for patio garden conditions. However, there is one which is suitable, the Kilmarnock willow, *Salix caprea* 'Kilmarnock' (formerly *S. caprea* 'Pendula') a form of our native goat willow which has an umbrella-like habit and does not usually exceed 10ft (3m) in height. It is now becoming more widely available. With its pendulous branches sweeping to the ground it makes a pleasing focal-point for a set-piece planting. Another very small weeping tree is the form of the copper beech

Above: Robinia pseudoacacia *'Frisia', now a very popular tree appreciated for its leaf coloration.*

Opposite: *A delightful association of laburnum and* Clematis montana.

named *Fagus sylvatica* 'Purpurea Pendula', excellent for chalky soils, of course, and all others with the exception of those of a very heavy nature. In this case, too, the branches sweep to the ground and though it can make a tree 18ft (5.5m) tall it is often less. Its strong purple colouring makes it an excellent tree to associate with other plants which benefit from such contrasts. For instance, containers planted for spring display with daffodils or tulips and for summer display with rich red geraniums (pelargoniums, as they should really be called).

Seen at its best there is no more beautiful small tree than *Cercis siliquastrum*, the Judas tree (the common name alludes to the belief that it was from a specimen of this tree that Judas hanged himself). At most it makes a bushy-headed tree some 26ft (8m) tall, but it must have warmth, shelter and sunshine, combined with a good, well-drained soil, to flourish. A sandy loam is ideal. It is, therefore, a tree for the more climatically congenial parts of the country, and if it is grown in the North it needs the protection of a warm wall. Its glory is the mass of rosy-purple pea flowers which appear in May before the rounded, attractive leaves arrive. Later, the 4 to 5in (10 to 13cm) long, flat seed pods appear, these later taking on reddish-purple tints. The Judas tree is not among the easiest of trees to establish, and it should always be planted as a young specimen to give it the best chance of getting off to a good start.

I've left the laburnum until now, not because it is a tree I haven't much regard for (just the reverse) but because all parts are poisonous and particularly the seed pods, thus presenting a danger if there are young children in the family. If that is not a problem you need to take account of, then the laburnum is a tree which will grow well in any well-drained soil and in sunshine or light shade. The most spectacular is *Laburnum* x *watereri* 'Vossii' with especially long racemes of flowers which, in late May and early June, makes the common name for all laburnums of golden rain seem

particularly appropriate. It makes a tree eventually up to 35ft (10.6m) tall and perhaps 25ft (7.5m) wide. But do take heed of the problem I've mentioned. Numerous garden plants are poisonous but it is the attractiveness of the fallen seed pods to toddlers which is the problem.

Conifers

Narrow-waisted conifers should not be overlooked either. In particular, ones like the ultra-narrow *Juniperus virginiana* 'Sky-rocket' which grows up to 20ft (6m) and yet has a width of little over 1ft (30cm) can be very useful for providing added interest. The dark green Irish yew, *Taxus baccata* 'Fastigiata', as well, for this only grows about 15ft (4.5m) tall and 4ft (1.30m) wide and is available in a golden form, 'Fastigiata Aureomarginata', in which the leaves are margined with yellow. With both, the girth can increase quite a bit with age, but, like all yews they are slow growing. A small juniper which is proving very useful in patio gardens is *J. squamata* 'Blue Star'. It makes, eventually, a low bush about 3ft (1m) tall and 5ft (1.5m) wide of strong silvery-blue colouring. A very small and slow-growing Lawson cypress is *Chamaecyparis lawsoniana* 'Pygmaea Argentea', which makes a globe-shaped bush of great attraction, for the bluish-green foliage

From left to right: Juniperus virginiana *'Sky-rocket'*, Juniperus squamata *'Blue Star'*, Taxus baccata *'Fastigiata'*, Chamaecyparis lawsoniana *'Pygmaea Argentea'* and Chamaecyparis lawsoniana *'Ellwoodii'*.

is tipped with creamy-white. One or two specimens of these can be very effective in a patio setting. Both junipers and yews are happy on chalky soils.

Another Lawson cypress cultivar which you might well note for your patio garden is *Chamaecyparis lawsoniana* 'Ellwoodii', which grows slowly to a height of 8 to 10ft (2.5 to 3m) and has a width of about 3ft (1m). It is attractive, too, with its feathery, grey-green foliage, and puts on growth with the kind of slowness one finds so helpful with this type of gardening. This is even more true, too, of its form 'Ellwood's Gold', which grows to around 8ft (2.5m) tall and has yellow coloration, as the name suggests, to the extent that the growths are tipped with strong yellow, especially in summer. This is seen to best advantage if the plant gets plenty of exposure to sunshine. Generally speaking, though, the Lawson cypresses do equally well in sunshine or light shade, in any reasonably moist but well-drained, soil, but remember that any conifers of yellow colouring need plenty of sunshine to bring out that colour at its best.

It is in winter that one appreciates most of all the colouring and textures of conifers. I never tire of those in my own garden for their substance complements beautifully the airy tracery of the bare branches of deciduous trees in winter. In the context of the patio garden it will almost certainly be a case of at most two trees and perhaps one conifer, but what I have just said holds true.

5. Roses - the (Almost) Indispensable Ingredient

If there is one flower which is almost indispensable for patio garden display it must surely be the rose. Whether in the form of climbers for clothing walls and fences, pillars, poles or trellis work, bush (large-flowered or cluster-flowered bush roses as, officially, hybrid tea and floridunda roses are now to be called), shrub roses for beds, or miniatures for raised beds or containers, they are a delight for a good six months of the year.

Roses are the most long-suffering of plants, but this does not mean that they will not do far better if they are given that bit of extra attention, of thoughtful care. Prepare the ground well, and make sure that the drainage is as good as it can possibly be made. Both heavy and light soils can be improved by digging in peat or garden compost, if possible a couple of months in advance of planting. This last can be done at any time from late October until the end of March, although if you have the opportunity to plant at one end or the other of this season that is what I would advise. In any case, do not plant when the frost is in the soil or when it is wet and sticky. If your plants arrive from the nursery at such an inopportune time just store them in a cool but frost-proof place or heel them in out of doors, as I suggested for shrubs in similar circumstances (see p. 25). A few days before planting, too, I would advise forking into the planting beds a dressing of bonemeal at the rate of 4oz (110g) to the square yard. This slow-acting phosphatic fertilizer will be released to the plants over a long period.

You can, of course, plant container-grown roses at any time of year.

Roses - and especially those small-growing kinds mentioned above - look particularly effective when associated with paved

areas. The stark simplicity of the paving seems to throw into high relief the colour of the blooms; as it suits the stiff appearance of the roses' growth. It is best to grow large-flowered or cluster-flowered roses in open beds where they will get a free circulation of air around them and thus be less likely to succumb to that distressing and disfiguring ailment, mildew. This fungus disease thrives in airless conditions. You then leave the beds adjoining walls and fences for climbers of one kind or another.

Climbers and ramblers

Ramblers have their place in the modern garden, things like the splendid old 'Albéric Barbier' (good for a north or east wall), whose creamy-white flowers have been enjoyed in gardens since the start of the century and 'Sanders' White' which have been around for almost as long, but it is the climbing roses of the present day like 'Pink Perpêtue', the cream, flushed rosy-pink 'Handel' (especially fine, see illustration) and the orange-scarlet 'Danse du Feu' which, with others like them, are so admirably suited for clothing pillars and poles with glorious colour to a height, on average, of 7 to 8ft (2.3 to 2.5m). Others which I would especially commend are the pink, salmon-shaded, double 'Aloha', especially to be commended for its fragrance and ability to withstand wet weather as well as its attractive foliage; the pink, semi-double, 'Bantry Bay'; the crimson 'Hamburger Phoenix', also semi-double; and the flesh pink 'New Dawn', this last an old-stager which is one parent of 'Pink Perpêtue', the other being 'Danse du Feu'. The varieties 'Hamburger Phoenix' and 'Danse du Feu' will do well against north or east walls.

For warm walls I can thoroughly recommend a very lovely old China rose, 'Mutabilis' ('Tipo Ideale') which makes a superb specimen so grown, coming into flower in June and producing the most lovely crop of single flowers which are coppery-red in the bud, open to yellow, then turn pink and red. The effect, overall, is very beautiful. After the main flowering, more blooms are produced in lesser numbers. A warm wall is, however, essential for it to do well.

Rose 'Handel'

When it won the Royal National Rose Society's Henry Edland Memorial Medal for the most fragrant new rose of its year (in 1973) the variety 'Compassion' was the first climbing rose ever to win that coveted award – and it is, at the time of writing, a record which still stands. Its double blooms are pale salmon-pink in colour with rich organge shading, and it grows to a height of 8 to 10ft (2.5 to 3m). It is a rose to keep in mind when you are next thinking of making additions to the garden. So is its primrose-yellow sport 'Highfield'.

The exquisite, miniature-flowered 'Climbing Cécile Brunner' has small pink blooms which are a lovely sight when matched with a warm-pink brick wall. This old rose, also repeat flowering, has been grown in gardens since 1894 and long may it continue to be so. It is very beautiful, and grows up to 20ft tall (6m). Another fine old climber, 'Phyllis Bide', which will reach to a height of 10ft (3m) or more, produces its pale yellow, pink-flushed blooms over most of summer. I cannot understand why it is so little grown for it is extremely attractive.

Another repeat flowerer is the *bracteata* climber 'Mermaid', but do no attempt to grow this rose unless you can provide a warm,

Rose 'Mermaid'

Rose 'Silver Jubilee'

Opposite: *'Matangi', a
striking cluster-flowered rose.*

sheltered wall facing south. The delectable, single, primrose-yellow blooms with prominent amber-yellow stamens are fully 4in (10cm) across.

The cautionary note I have struck is necessary, for this is a rose which can be damaged by severe frost. Its vigour is not in doubt, however, for here we have a rose which will grow to 26 to 30ft (8 to 9m) tall and demands a house wall to do it justice. Then you can expect to enjoy the flowers for a couple of months in mid-summer and again in autumn – but it is not, I repeat, a rose for less favoured parts of the country.

Bush roses

Almost tailor-made for patio gardens, of course, are low-growing cluster-flowered cultivars – roses like the orange-red 'Topsi' (which won the R.N.R.S. President's International Trophy – the top award – in 1972); salmon-pink 'Tip Top'; pale pink 'Gentle Touch' and yellow 'Bright Smile'; orange, golden-tinted 'Sweet Magic'; scarlet 'Wee Jock', 'Marlena', and 'Trumpeter'; 'Regensberg', pink and white, and the apricot 'Peek A Boo'. Add to these the orange-red 'Anna Ford' and you have a good idea of the choice available. Their modest height makes them especially good for patio display, and, like all cluster-flowered roses, they are free-flowering.

Other fine cluster-flowered roses for the patio are the attractive 'Anisley Dickson', pink, with reddish-salmon overtones, and winner in 1984 of the R.N.R.S. President's International Trophy; 'Korresia' with shapely, fragrant, bright yellow flowers; 'Fragrant Delight', salmon-pink and well-scented as the name implies; and that fine white 'Iceberg', introduced in 1958 and still among the best – white is always a good colour to introduce into the garden, both for its own sake and as a foil for other colours – the salmon 'City of Leeds'; golden-yellow 'Allgold' and crimson-red 'The Times'.

Others of special interest are the tallish, apricot-orange 'Southampton', with good fragrance; 'Eye Paint', with single scarlet blooms with a white eye and boss of yellow staments; 'Matangi', orange-vermilion, shaded silver at the base of the petals; and 'Margaret Merril', pale pink overlying white and sweetly scented.

It would be impossible to leave the cluster-flowered roses without saying something about two splendid cultivars, one of which was introduced in 1982 and the other a real veteran. They are 'Mountbatten', a tall cultivar with shapely buds which open to double flowers of a fetching primrose-yellow. It grows up to 5ft (1.5m) tall. The other rose is the very familiar 'Queen Elizabeth' which can top 6ft (2m) in some situations. It is still a fine and very popular rose with its lovely clear pink flowers and good foliage. One or two specimens of either of these cultivars would make a delightful feature if you sited them

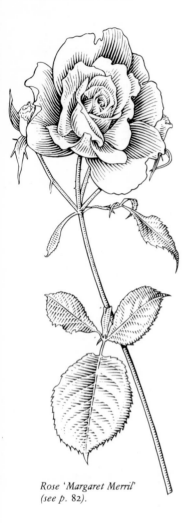

Rose 'Margaret Merril'
(see p. 82).

with care. 'Mountbatten' was voted 'Rose of the Year' in 1982 by British rose growers and breeders.

Two old polyantha roses which have much to offer are 'Nathalie Nypels' and 'The Fairy'. The first is a rose with much charm, its rose-pink, double flowers being borne on a spreading bush some 2ft (60cm) tall. 'The Fairy' has unfailing attraction for most of us with its small, double flowers being borne in great abundance from mid-summer onwards. It also is spreading and with a height of 2½ft (75cm).

The large-flowered bush rose 'Silver Jubilee', of compact habit, was the 1977 winner of the R.N.R.S. President's International Trophy already referred to in other connections. The flowers are a lovely combination of pink, apricot, peach and cream. It is also a very disease-resistant rose.

Other large-flowered bush roses of special worth are 'Alec's Red', with flowers of rich cherry-red and with what I would call a ''tidy'' habit; 'Alexander', orange-vermilion; 'Grandpa Dickson', a good yellow which fades to a paler colour and becomes pink at the edges of the petals; 'Piccadilly', scarlet and yellow; the coral-salmon 'Mischief'; dusky red 'Fragrant Cloud', salmon-pink 'Paul Shirville', and the legendary 'Peace', if you can accommodate its large frame and so enjoy its pale yellow blooms, edge with pink.

Some of the cluster-flowered and large-flowered bush roses I have just mentioned are available as standard specimens, and these can be used to good effect in the patio garden. A certain number of roses are available, too, as weeping standards, which can be extremely attractive. These include the ramblers 'Crimson Shower'; rose-pink 'Dorothy Perkins'; creamy-white 'Albéric Barbier'; and coppery-pink 'Albertine'.

Shrub roses

The modern shrub roses, like the tallest of the bush roses, can be used only with discretion in the patio garden, perhaps in ones or twos; but do consider making a set-piece planting of the creamy-white, 4ft (1.25m) tall 'Sally Holmes', or the vermilion-orange 'Fred Loads', which smothers its 6ft (2m) frame with its single blooms. And if you want a good yellow you can always turn to that excellent cultivar 'Chinatown'.

Quite my favourite shrub rose for planting near paving is the striking 'Ballerina'' a spreading bush some 3 to 4ft (1 to 1.3m) tall. It is of hydrid musk ancestry with attractive pale green foliage and carries in summer masses of pale pink, white-eyed flowers in bold clusters. The effect is striking and especially so when it sweeps its growths out over paving. 'Marjorie Fair', bred from 'Ballerina', is its deep red equivalent and a very lovely rose indeed. Other shrub roses of special worth are the rich yellow, full-petalled 'Graham Thomas'; long-flowering 'Golden Wings', with single pale yellow flowers, set off by amber stamens; and 'Robusta', scarlet. These last two are especially long floweirng. All of them grow about 4ft (1.3m) tall.

Whatever roses you choose to grow, though — and that is very much a matter of personal preference – pay particular attention to the colour blending. Some modern roses have quite strong colours and carelessness can lead to some unfortunate juxtapositions.

Miniature roses

I've left until last a group of roses which are rapidly increasing in popularity, the miniatures; none of them are over 1½ft (45cm) tall and most are under 15in (38cm) with blooms in proportion to their overall size. For raised patio beds they are ideal. The wide range of cultivars includes 'Royal Salute', a rose-pink variety which I am growing in just the kind of conditions suggested; the salmon-flowered 'Angela Rippon', 'Starina', orange-scarlet; 'Pour Toi', cream; 'Sweet Fairy', lilac-pink; 'Coralin', orange-red; and 'Perla de Alcanada', crimson. There are numerous others. What they must be given is a position where their size will seem in scale with their surroundings. Apart from narrow raised beds, they are, of course, admirable for growing in containers. But if you grow them in tubs, sinks or other containers, make sure that they have a good depth of compost to grow in and that they do not lack food or moisture. Make sure also that the soil drainage is adequate. When they are grown in pots (which is also a possibility) do not treat them as house plants apart from, perhaps, taking them indoors for the brief spell when they are at the height of their flowering. Plunge the pots to their rims in soil in the garden after they have done their stint in this way.

A guide to pruning

Pruning is a chore which always confuses the newcomer to gardening, and that is not surprising. But really it is a very straightforward job once the underlying principles are understood.

Let us take the large-flowered bush roses first. With these one is pruning for shapeliness, good health and quality – rather than quantity – of bloom. The degree of pruning given – heavy, medium or light – depends on the vigour of the variety, and that also goes for the cluster-flowered bush roses, which I shall come to in a moment. Plants which are hard pruned will make more growth than those lightly pruned, so it follows that strong-growing varieties need lighter pruning than others. In practice it will be found that most roses need only moderate pruning. Don't go mad with the secateurs.

Newly planted roses need quite different treatment in this respect to established specimens. In the March following the

Rose 'Albéric Barbier'
(see p. 80).

Opposite: The cluster-flowered rose 'Mountbatten' – worthy holder of a great name.

Left: 'The Fairy', almost indispensable for providing colour from mid-summer onwards.

planting of large-flowered bush roses, or immediately of course if you plant at the end of the planting season, cut back the shoots to within two or three 'eyes' (the gardening term for dormant buds) of the base.

Thereafter, prune in March (although see what I have to say on p. 89 about the different views on when to prune) so that the growth made in the previous year is reduced by about half, while taking account of what I said earlier about adjusting the degree of pruning to the needs of the particular variety. The aim is to produce an open-centred bush to which light and air will have free access, which is healthy – all dead or weak wood should be

Miniature rose 'Pour Toi' *(see p. 85).*

cut away at this time — and which will bear flowers of high quality. When pruning, always cut to an outward pointing bud or eye, and make the cut cleanly, say about ¼ in (0.6cm) above — in other words, leave no snags to later die back and cause further trouble. Make the cut in such a way that it slopes from just above the bud to lower down on the opposite side of the shoot. The importance of having really sharp secateurs should not need emphasising.

With newly planted cluster-flowered bush roses where the objectives are rather different — with these roses you get more colour over a longer period but not the perfection of bloom of the hybrid teas — cut back the shoots to within four or five eyes of the base, again in the March following planting.

Allowing that there are large-, medium- and small-growing cluster-flowered, bush roses, one prunes to produce a freer-growing bush than with the large-flowered type, so pruning is lighter. After the initial treatment just outlined, the annual treatment in March could consist of cutting out some of the oldest wood to within two or three eyes of the base, and then cutting back one-year-old laterals by rather more or less than half, depending on the vigour of the variety. New growths which arise from the base should be pruned very lightly indeed.

Treat standard specimens of both types in exactly the same way as their bush counterparts so far as pruning is concerned, and weeping standards like the ramblers or repeat-flowering climbers of which these are special forms, budded on to 5 or 6ft (1.5 or 2m) stems.

Newly-planted climbing and rambler roses should have their growths left at full length. Established specimens of these roses — which need quite different treatment — should be dealt with in the following manner.

Thereafter, with *wichuraiana* ramblers, which throw up new canes from the base each summer to bear the next year's crop of flowers, cut out the flowered growths to the base as soon as flowering has finished, and tie the new shoots in their place. With other ramblers, which do not make new shoots from the base annually and often develop growth higher up the sterms, confine your attentions to removing any dead shoots and unwanted wood and occasionally cutting straggly shoots back to a dormant bud low down on the stems, again when flowering has finished.

Modern repeat-flowering climbers should have their shoots just lightly tipped after planting and thereafter, in subsequent years — like the ramblers just referred to — be given practically no pruning, except for any necessary cutting back of old wood and, of course, the removal of dead and diseased wood.

Climbing sorts of large-flowered and cluster-flowered bush roses need treating with special care for they are very prone to reversion to bush form if pruning is mishandled. Again, with these, just lightly tip the shoots after planting — in March — and in subsequent years confine any pruning to the removal of dead or weak wood and the cutting of the lateral growth on mature shoots to about four buds from the main stem.

Modern shrub roses, like the shrub roses of older vintage — the old-fashioned roses as they are called — need very little pruning, either after planting or in the years to come. Just prune to remove dead or weak wood and to keep them within bounds. The same applies also to the delightful little miniature roses.

I said earlier that there are different views about when it is best to prune. Some gardeners, especially those living in climatically favoured areas, prefer mid-winter pruning which provides earlier growth and earlier flowers. They are taking a gamble with the weather, which for them may be fully justified. I think that for most of us it is best to wait until the time I have suggested, March, or possibly February, which again could be just the right time in some districts. It is all a matter of opinion, like so much else in gardening. The trouble is that our climate is fickle and early-stimulated growth can be damaged by a side-swipe from the weather.

Pruning is one aspect of making sure that you get the kind of performance from your roses you always hope to enjoy. There are others, like mulching and feeding, dead-heading, the removal of suckers and pest and disease control.

General care

With pruning out of the way and the prunings consigned to the bonfire, it will soon be time to think of applying a mulch, especially important on lightish soils which dry out quickly in warm, sunny weather. It is best to wait until the soil has had a chance to warm up though before applying such material around the plants. You can use peat, composted bark, garden compost or, if you can lay your hands on it, well rotted farmyard manure, preferably horse manure, which would, of course, provide the plants with food as well as slowing down moisture losses from the soil. To give you some idea of the kind of quantity of manure you would need, one barrowload of manure is enough to cover 10 to 12 square yards (8.36 to 10.03m²) of ground.

If you are using peat, composted bark or garden compost — you may be able to suitably camouflage a compost bin in a corner of the patio, and with efficent compost accelerators waste vegetation can soon be turned into useful material — add first a dressing of a proprietary rose fertiliser, as directed by the makers, so that the plants will get supplies of a balanced feed during the period of the year when they most need such help. Make the mulch several inches thick.

A mulch then is extremely effective in cutting down moisture losses from the soil, but do not be misled into thinking that it

absolves you from watering at all. In warm, dry spells, and indeed at intervals anyway, draw back some of the mulching material and make sure that the soil is not dry underneath. If is is, then soak the ground thoroughly for to do less is useless.

Dead-heading, a curious term which is in fact very descriptive, is the gardener's way of talking about the removal of dead flowers. With roses, this is something one should do frequently, especially in the patio garden, not only because it will encourage further flowering but also because the sight of dead rose blooms hanging forlornly on the bushes is hardly inspiring. Cut to an

'Majorie Fair', a very lovely shrub rose of rich colouring.

outward pointing bud, as I have recommended for pruning, for in its way this is what dead-heading is, and remove as short a piece of stem as possible each time.

Suckers can be an infernal nuisance, as we all know, particularly with bush roses and standards, and if you are not sure if a shoot is a sucker or not, follow it down to its point of origin. Suckers originate from the rootstock on which the particular cultivar has been budded, and where they are identified as such, either by the means I have just outlined or by their distinctive appearance — different leaf colour, shape and size, and the prickly nature of the stems — pull them out without delay. And pull is the operative word (if this is possible), for if one resorts to cutting them off there is a strong possibility that more will come in their place.

Pests and disease

I don't want to dwell too long on pests and diseases, but obviously these must be given consideration if you are going to enjoy healthy plants.

Of the pests, watch out particularly for greenfly infestations. These you can combat with an insecticide like pirimicarb, derris or malathion. Caterpillars of various kinds, for which permethrin is an effective deterrent, should also be watched for, and small numbers can of course, be dispatched in the time-honoured way — by hand picking. You can spray against leaf hoppers with permethrin or pirimiphos-methyl, and the latter insecticides will also control the leaf-rolling sawfly, if you apply it early enough in the season, before the leaves have become tightly curled to provide a protective armour and food for the developing larvae.

Gamma HCH and dimethoate are effective against those other pests, the easily recognisable cuckoo spit — the insect, the frog-hopper, makes frothy, spittle-like mounds on the plants — and thrips or thunderflies, as they are called, which make a special point of damaging the blooms, especially in the bud stage. In the latter case alternatives are malathion or pirimiphos-methyl.

Mildew, the fungus disease which is a universal problem and to which some varieties of rose are particularly prone, is, alas, only too easily identified with the white or greyish mould coating the leaves and stems as well as the flower buds. Wide fluctuations in temperature, poor soil drainage and dryness at the roots, over-lush growth brought about by incorrect feeding, and damp, stagnant air are all conditions which encourage this disease to take a hold. It is best to get your blow in first and make pre-emptive sprayings at intervals in summer with bupirimate plus triforine, propiconazole or benomyl, applied strictly in accordance with the manufacturer's instructions, as all such garden chemicals must be.

And now for that other major trouble of roses, black spot. This is one case where the gardener is a clean-air district comes off worse than the townsman who suffers the disadvantage of rather polluted air. This disease does not find sulphur-laden air at all to its liking.

Black spot is immediately recognizable by the black markings which form on the leaves. These spots spread with great rapidity and often cause premature defoliation wtih all that that means for the health of the plant. Fallen leaves affected by black spot should always be collected and burnt, for the spores remain active and can come through the winter to start the whole sorry cycle off again in spring, when the new leaves form. The answer, if you live in an area likely to be troubled by this disease, is again to take pre-emptive action by spraying with bupirimate plus triforine, propiconazole, benomyl or other recommended chemicals as directed by the manufacturers. In winter you can also spray with Bordeaux mixture to kill the over-wintering spores on the plant and in the soil.

Black spot, mildew, rust and aphids can be dealt with at the same time by applying, once every 10 to 14 days from April, the systemic fungicide/aphicide Roseclear. This contains the insecticide pirimicarb and the fungicides bupirimate and triforine. A real advantage is that the aphicide, while killing aphids quickly, leaves beneficial insects like ladybirds unharmed.

Take preventive action also against that other serious rose trouble, rose rust, which is seen as rust-coloured pustules on the undersides of the leaves from early in the season. Remove and burn all affected parts of the plant as soon as seen. The fungicides mancozeb and bupirimate plus triforine can also be used, as directed by the manufacturer.

When canker occurs – it often follows bad pruning, gaining entry through snags, etc. – cut away the diseased wood immediately and destroy it by buring. There is no chemical control. If the pruning cuts are more than ½ m (1cm) in diameter than a wound dressing should be applied as a preventative measure.

Of course there are other rose troubles of a less important nature, but the last thing I want to do is to give the impression that roses are accident-prone semi-invalids. You will know that they are not, in any case, but by the same token it is only common sense to keep a wary eye open for the troubles I have enumerated.

6. Making Good Use of Perennials

Stachys
macrantha
superba

I have been more than pleased to note in recent years a strong resurgence of interest in herbaceous perennial plants, and not so much for massed effect (although that can be stunning if you have room for an extensive border or island beds, as you certainly haven't in the patio garden) as for providing small pockets of interest and colour in all manner of different settings. The free-style use of this fascinating group of plants has given them a completely new lease of life.

It may be a small thing, too, but there is a great deal of pleasure to be gained from following their progress from the first tentative signs of growth in spring to flowering and their dying down in autumn. Some, like the hostas, paeonies and montbretias, take on lovely leaf colours in autumn – yellows, ochres, and russety-browns – which add a great deal to the enjoyment of the garden at that time. You can experience all this too on the small intimate scale of your patio garden.

The importance of foliage
If you have never given the matter a thought it might seem an extraordinary thing to say, but leaf textures and shapes and, of course, their colours, can give as much pleasure as flowers in a different way. Flowers are essential, but they are only one part of the equation in creating an integrated, satisfying garden.

A perennial I especially value (and excellent for the kind of use we are considering) is a plant called *Stachys macrantha superba* which creates a low carpet of dark green with its broadly ovate leaves, wrinkled all over their surface like the weather-beaten face of an old countryman – a delightful base from which to throw up the whorls of rosy-mauve flowers in early summer. For half the year it provides excellent ground cover. The hostas have the most alluring leaf shapes and colours, and, in a completely different way, who could not appreciate the winsome charm of the

Opposite: *Nothing could emphasise more dramatically than this tub-grown* Hosta *'Thomas Hogg' the fine decorative qualities of so many members of this genus.*

94

little epimediums with their heart-shaped leaves suspended on wire-like stems – the picture of elegance. Then there is that iris which the flower arrangers love to raid for stems – *Iris pallida variegata*, the sword-like, 2 to 3ft (60cm to 1m) leaves of which have a ground colour of soft grey and, depending on whether it is the yellow or the white form, bold longitudinal stripes of one or other of those colours. These forms are often identified in plant catalogues and elsewhere as *aureo-variegata* and *argenteo-variegata*, if not just as *variegata* with a colour description.

And so one could go on, but I think I've said enough to make the point. Do give foilage the attention it deserves. Before turning to the plants and what they can do for us in intimate patio conditions let us consider the basis of their cultivation.

Care of perennials

Most perennials need lifting and dividing about once every third or fourth year, in spring or autumn, for the clumps become overcrowded and too spreading and will almost certainly have lost vigour and quality to an unacceptable extent. It is an easy enough job to do and I will come to that in a moment, but the point I want to make now is that, once these plants are in the ground there is really nothing you can do in the way of real soil improvement for that very considerable length of time. So, get the drainage of the soil, its texture and so on right before you start. Both soils which are too light and so lack body and moisture-retentive qualities, and soil which is too heavy and perhaps is too slow to rid itself of excess moisture can be improved by digging in peat, composted bark or garden compost. Take care also to clear the ground of all perennial weeds before planting, as far as this is possible.

Still, with regard to this periodical lifting and dividing which is so beneficial for most plants, remember that there are those, like the paeonies, Japanese anemones, hellebores and oriental poppies, which do not take kindly to disturbance. They will take time to settle down and you may not get them to flower again for a couple of years, perhaps even longer.

The lifted clumps can be levered apart by placing two forks back to back through the lifted clump and forcing the handles outwards, if you cannot achieve the same end with your hands or a hand fork, as you can with smaller plants. It is the younger, outer part of the plant which is the most useful for re-planting, for the heart of the clump will often be exhausted.

Other cultural points with perennials: if they need to be staked, do this early, before wind and rain have caused any damage, and if they are of the kind which make new growths very prolifically, reduce these in number early in the season also so that better quality blooms will be obtained by concentrating the energies of the plant.

Perennials in mixed planting schemes

Another thing you can do with much success is to mix perennials with selected annuals, biennials and bulbous flowers as well as with the odd shrub or two to get the best of all possible worlds. Let us consider those perennials that I believe are of special relevance to this type of garden.

I have already mentioned hostas in passing – the plaintain lilies as they are often called – and these with their bold foliage and spikes of lily-like trumpet flowers in summer in colours from mauve to lilac and white have much to offer. They associate so well with paving and, being clump forming, make features in their own right for a good six months of the year.

Those I particularly like in *Hosta crispula*, *H. undulata* and *H. fortunei albopicta*, and I will briefly outline the attractions of each. *Hosta crispula* is perhaps my favourite, a species up to a foot (30cm) tall with handsome tapered leaves of rich green with broad white margins of indeterminate width. Its lavender-coloured flowers, on 2½ft (75cm) stems, arrive about mid-summer and last for several weeks. *H. undulata*, as its name implies, has leaves with wavy surfaces, in this case of clear green marked with a central band of creamy-white, and lilac flowers which it bears on 2 to 2½ft (60 to 75cm) stems. This makes a mat of foliage less than 1ft (30cm) tall. The third of my trio, *H. fortunei albopicta*, has broad leaves which begin life bright yellow edged with pale green and age to predominantly pale green with a darker green edging. It is very impressive and some 2ft (60cm) tall. This too has lilac flowers in mid-summer.

Hostas like light shade and a moisture-retaining soil of, for preference, a loamy texture. If the soil is lacking in substance then dig in plenty of peat before planting, something which can be done at any time from October to March, when the weather is suitable. I consider these among the best of all ground-cover plants and there are many to choose from.

Another very useful and exceedingly pretty perennial which is completely at home in association with paving is the lady's mantle, *Alchemilla mollis*, a plant with light green, rounded leaves with scalloped edges above which ride billowing sprays of delicate-looking little greenish-yellow star flowers in June and July. No wonder it is so loved by the flower arrangers – it is the epitome of grace. Only 1 to 1½ft (30 to 45cm) tall, it forms solid ground-covering clumps in sunshine or light shade and it will grow happily in most well-drained soils, preferably rather moist (which need not be a contradiction in terms).

For space-effectiveness also I would give top marks to the herbaceous geraniums or crane's bills – the true geraniums, not the pot-grown and bedding pelargoniums which, confusingly, have geranium as their common name – for these provide splendid ground cover, are adaptable, have delightful flowers,

Alchemilla mollis, *associated here, most effectively, with the small-growing cluster-flowered rose 'Golden Slippers'.*

which in some kinds are very long lasting and often very attractive foliage. Paragons of virtue, in other words.

A particularly attractive one is *Geranium psilostemon* which, in early summer, is a picture with its bushy, 2½ft (75cm) frame a mass of deeply cut leaves, above which are carried a mantle of the most lovely magenta-red, black-centred flowers. Another I consider outstanding is *G. endressii* 'A. T. Johnson' for, on clumps only 1½ft (45cm) tall, this bears masses of silvery-pink blooms over a long period in summer. Others of special note include 'Johnson's Blue', early summer flowering and with deeply cut foliage, and atractive *G. sanguineum lancastriense splendens*, a variety of the bloody crane's bill which grows some 10in (25cm)

Geranium sanguineum
lancastriense splendens

tall and flowers practically the summer through, its pretty blooms being pale pink in colour with red veining. Shorter still at 4in (10cm) is the very pretty 'Ballerina' which bears red-veined, lilac-pink flowers in the first half of summer.

You can grow most herbaceous geraniums in any well-drained soil in sun or shade, although the last-mentioned cultivar does best in sun. There are many more from which to make a choice.

Fine perennials, too, for the patio bed are the mat-forming *Polygonum affine* 'Donald Lowndes' and the better known *P. a.* 'Darjeeling Red'. Of the two the best is undoubtedly the more compact 'Donald Lowndes' which bears its pretty deep pink flower spikes on 8 to 10in (20 to 25cm) stems over a long period in

Polygonum affine 'Donald Lowndes' (see p. 99).

summer above attractive fresh green, narrow leaves which form a solid mat of growth. By autumn the flowers have deepened in colour to a russety red. 'Darjeeling Red', a little taller, starts to bear its deep rose-pink flowers a little later in the season. Both retain their leaves into winter, when they turn a pleasant warm brown colour. A moist soil is a "must", combined with good drainage. With this can go a position in sun or light shade.

For a delightful early summer show there are few plants to beat the oriental poppies (varieties of *Papaver orientale*), if they are given a sunny site and an average soil with good drainage. They come into flower in late May and continue through June, and although they take up quite a bit of room and are not an asset out of flower I would still find room myself for at least a couple of plants of, say, the orange-scarlet, black-blotched 'Marcus Perry', 'Perry's White' or the rich scarlet 'Goliath'. These are all 2½ to 3ft (75cm to 1m) tall.

A dicentra which adds distinction to any border in early summer is *Dicentra spectabilis*, the bleeding heart or Dutchman's breeches, for it bears the most lovely locket-like rose-red flowers which hang in arched stems above deeply cut foliage. It is some 2ft (60cm) tall.

A hybrid dicentra which I am sure is going to have a bright future is 'Pearl Drops', only 10in (25cm) tall and with a mass of bluish-yellow divided leaves above which are borne, from May until early autumn, a mass of white flowers. It is a real asset where space demands that every plant must earn its keep.

Another excellent perennial which makes a feature in its own right or a delightful companion for numerous other flowers is *Salvia superba*. This makes a bold clump of growth some 3ft (1m) tall and is a splendid sight in the second half of summer when bearing its spikes of purple flowers above sage-like leaves. It is a perfect companion, for instance, for the similarly sized *Achillea* 'Coronation Gold' which bears large, flat-topped golden yellow flowers at the same time. Both need lots of sunshine and a well-drained soil.

Other strong candidates for space in the patio garden are the Japanese anemones (forms of *Anemone hybrida*) providing colour from the beginning of August until the end of September. With a height of 2½ to 3ft (75cm to 1m) there are many situations where these look just right, and good varieties include the white 'Louise Uhink', pink 'Queen Charlotte' and the similarly coloured 'September Charm'. They like moist soil conditions and light shade, but are very easy going.

Perhaps one of the best of all herbaceous plants, though (certainly among the smaller ones), is *Coreopsis verticillata* for it literally smothers its bushy mound of leaves, only 1½ft (45cm) tall, with bright yellow daisy flowers from early to late summer. It's a plant for a sunny position and preferably a light soil.

What else? The bergenias — which used to be called megaseas and before that saxifrages, as they still are by some people – gardeners either love or hate. Maybe they have got leathery, rather cabbage-like leaves, as the unkind say, but what superb ground-cover plants they are, and how handsome are their bold flower trusses composed of many bell-shaped flowers. As the foliage is evergreen too, you have cover throughout the year, and the leaves of some like 'Ballawley' turn to reddish shades in winter.

'Ballawley' is in fact a particularly fine hybrid with very large leaves and rose-red flowers in April and May. The popular *B. cordifolia* has heart-shaped leaves and bears rose-coloured blooms in March and April, while the white-flowered 'Silberlicht' is another whose foliage may take on reddish tones in winter. All these grow about 1ft (30cm) tall. They will grow in almost any soil, in sun or shade.

For placing on their own, say around the base of a small tree which does not cast too much shade, and the soil is of a lightish nature, you could make a nice show with *Heuchera* 'Bressingham Hybrids'. Above a thick cover of rounded leaves in summer floats a hazy mass of tiny flowers, borne in panicles on 2½ to 3ft (75cm to 1m) stems in colours from pink to rich red. As the foliage

Salvia superba (left) and Achillea 'Coronation Gold'

Opposite: Sedum *'Autumn Joy'*, *a delight in early autumn.*

of these too is evergreen, they give good year-round ground cover. So do the little epimediums with their wiry-stemmed, heart-shaped leaves, and in spring appear delicate spikes of wispy flowers in yellow, pink or red. These love light shade and a reasonably good soil, and the ones to go for, at any rate in my opinion, are the yellow-flowered *Epimedium perralderianum*, the coppery-red *E. warleyense* and *E. macranthum* 'Rose Queen', another good red.

Tall bearded irises have a short flowering season, but how beautiful they are in late May and June. Their bold sword-like foliage can also, I believe, be turned to good use at other times if they are associated with the right plants to form a contrast. The important thing with these is to give them a position where the soil is fairly light and well drained, and to take care when planting not to set the rhizomes too deeply in the ground. Their tops should be just level with the surface of the soil and you orientate them facing south so that they get the maximum amount of sunshine which is available. You can plant them in June (immediately after flowering), in September or in March.

I mentioned earlier *Iris pallida variegata* (see p. 96) but that is a plant you grow more for its striking foliage effect than the display put on in mid-summer by its blue flowers. With the lovely winter-flowering Algerian iris, *I. unguicularis* (which many, understandably, still persist in calling by its much prettier old name of *I. stylosa*), it's a different matter, for the flowers of this 2ft (60cm) tall plant are very beautiful indeed and are borne intermittently during mild weather right through from autumn to spring.

Iris unguicularis needs a lean soil with really sharp drainage, and a sunny, sheltered position, too, not because it isn't hardy (even though it occurs in nature in Algeria and a wide spread of the eastern Mediterranean) but because the flowers can be so easily damaged by frost and rough weather. These flowers are somewhat variable in colour for there are numerous forms in commerce (few of them named) ranging from very pale lavender-blue to much deeper shades. All are delightful, although I like the deeper coloured ones best myself, and the blooms of all are a joy for cutting for room decoration. It is a plant to site against a house wall, preferably near a door you use frequently so that you enjoy its beauty to the full. I have mentioned that it should be given a lean soil. If it is richly fed it will, like annual flowers, tend to concentrate on producing foliage at the expense of flowers.

Since so many good colours have become available in the hemerocallises or day-lilies (their flowers, individually, last for only one day, although produced in succession over a long period, from June to August) they have become increasingly popular. They are so accommodating, growing well in any

Bergenia *'Ballawley'*
(see p. 101).

Iris unguicularis
(see p. 103).

ordinary, well-drained soil in sunshine or light shade, but never-theless appreciating soil with plenty of goodness in it.

Quite apart from the lily-like flowers in their yellows, creams, diverse reds, pinks, oranges and so on, the bold clumps of arched, rush-like foliage which they throw up can be used to great effect as a contrast to the colourings and forms of other near-by plants. In spring, the young foliage is a very pale green colour, which can be strikingly effective. Of the many cultivars offered, nearly all in the 2 to 3ft (60cm to 1m) height range, three of special note are the deep red 'Stafford', 'Pink Damask' and 'Hyperion', clear yellow. The recently introduced 1¾ft (55cm) tall 'Stella D'Oro' with canary-yellow flowers is ideal for patio planting.

Herbaceous paeonies take up quite a lot of room, but again I consider their foliage very decorative and if you plant something like the 3ft (1m) tall 'Bowl of Beauty' you can enjoy those large, rosy-pink, cream-centred blooms in June and July and then appreciate afterwards the matronly spread of greenery. As I said earlier, too, the leaves colour up nicely in the autumn. They like good soil and sunshine.

For edging paths remember, too, the catmint, *Nepeta faassenii* – better known, if incorrectly, as *N. mussinii* – which is only a foot (30cm) tall and so useful in producing its lavender-mauve flowers above grey-green foliage the summer through in any ordinary soil, in sun or shade. It also associates very well with roses. For a sunny, sheltered position, too, why not find a home for that lovely, very architectural spurge *Euphorbia characias* whose great heads of greenish-yellow flowers in early summer look so impos-ing above the ranks of bluish-grey leaves. This spurge is worth a prominent position on its own, preferably in a spot where you can see it from a window of the house. The similar-looking sub-shrubby *E. wulfenii* is another to consider, and this stays in flower for a longer period. Any well-drained soil of reasonable quality will suit these two.

If in shrubs one tends to look on the excellent *Senecio* 'Sun-shine' (see p. 44) as the most useful of all grey-foliaged subjects, so in herbaceous perennials I would let my thoughts turn to that excellent variety of the wormwood *Artemisia absinthium*, named 'Lambrook Silver', which was introduced by that great gardener, the late Mrs Margery Fish, who created at East Lambrook Manor, her Somerset home, such a Mecca for gardeners. The filigree of silver foliage put up by this 3ft (1m) tall plant is a constant delight, and a marvellous foil for many other plants which share its liking for a sunny position and really good soil drainage. It looks delightful, for instance, in association with the very beautiful *Aster frikartii* which produces its lavender-blue ray-flowers with gold yellow centres from July into autumn. It is of similar height to 'Lambrook Silver'.

This aster also looks stunning with *Rudbeckia fulgida* 'Goldsturm', the 2ft (60cm) variety of Black-eyed Susan, which smothers itself with its golden-yellow, black-centred ray-flowers from July to September. It is, of course, another sun-lover.

Another plant for a sunny, well-drained position which can be rewarding in patio conditions is the 2ft (60cm) tall gayfeather, *Liatris spicata*, which opens up its tufty mauvish-pink flower spikes from the top downwards. It, too, flowers from July to September and it is best in its variety 'Kobold', in which the colour is more intense – a nice plant to have near-by when you are sitting out at that time of year.

Several stonecrops or sedums are really lovely late summer and autumn flowers for sunny positions. My favourite is the hybrid 'Autumn Joy', whose large salmon-pink flower heads on 2ft (60cm) stems are impossible to ignore in any garden in September and October. As they age, the blooms deepen to shades of red and reddish-brown. This splendid plant is a cross between *S. spectabile* and *S. telephium*.

Another sedum of real quality is the *S. spectabile* variety 'Brilliant' which bears deep rose flowers on 1½ft (45cm) stems at the same time as 'Autumn Joy'. You can achieve some very good effects also by planting on the edge of a bed the cream-variegated *S. telephium variegatum*.

The same kind of warm, sunny sheltered conditions are needed by the *Agapanthus* Headbourne Hybrids, splendid plants for July-August flowering, and much hardier that the other agapanthuses, or African lilies as they are called. Even so, they are not plants for really cold gardens, and if the situation is borderline it is certainly worth protecting the crowns of the plants with a covering of dry litter or well-weathered ashes in winter. These hybrids are 2 to 4ft (60cm to 1.3m) in height, have bold, strap-shaped leaves of rich green colouring and throw up a wealth of highly decorative umbels of pale blue to violet-blue flowers on strong stems. As I've mentioned in the chapter on plants for containers, they are excellent for growing in tubs or other large, deep containers. In the garden they grow well in any ordinary, well-drained soil.

Provide just the same congenial conditions suggested for the agapanthuses for that lovely rhizomatous perennial from South Africa, *Schizostylis coccinea*, or one of its varieties like 'Major' (which has red, star-flowers like the species but of larger size) or the pale pink 'Mrs Hegarty'. Any one of these can be a lovely sight from late September to November when the delicate spikes of small flowers are borne on 2ft (60cm) stems above grass-like foliage – but they are not plants to even attempt to grow in a cold garden. You should plant the rhizomes in spring to get them off to a good start and give the roots a covering of dry litter in winter.

We have been able to enjoy for quite a few years now a range of

Paeonia *'Bowl of Beauty'*

Rudbeckia fulgida
'Goldsturm' (see p. 104).

A pink form of Schizostylis
coccinea provides welcome
colour from late September to
November (see p. 105).

106

phormiums with attractive 'architectural', evergreen foliage. Mostly, these are cultivars, bred in New Zealand, of the well-known 8 to 10ft (2.5 to 3m) tall New Zealand flax, *Phormium tenax*, which has been grown in the more climatically favoured gardens of Britain for not far short of two hundred years, but a few are derivatives of the smaller-growing *P. cookianum*, a species which has been grown here for over one hundred years

The foliage of these plants is sword-shaped and mostly two-toned, so that they have quite a lot to offer as decorative features for the patio garden, whether grown in warm, sheltered borders or in containers, for which purpose they are admirably suited (indeed, grown in that way they can be taken under cover during winter to avoid any risk of weather damage). What they must have to succeed is good soil, good drainage and exposure to plenty of sunshine

The tallest of these varieties and hybrids is around 6ft (2m) tall (*P. tenax* 'Purpureum', which has purplish leaves, as the name suggests), but the majority of them are 2 to 3ft (60cm to 1m) tall. They include 'Maori Sunrise', with pinkish, apricot and bronze-margined leaves; 'Dazzler', reddish-brown, banded with carmine-red; 'Sundowner', greyish-purple, margined with creamy-pink; and Yellow Wave', golden-yellow, edged green.

They do not take too kindly to extreme cold and they should always be given a warm, sheltered position such as can so often be provided in patio garden conditions. For the first winter at least give them protection against frost in the form of a 4in (10cm) layer of bracken, leaves or straw. Container-grown specimens, as I've already said, can be kept in a frost-proof place over-winter. I favour this method of cultivation.

There is another side also to the phormium story. If you already take an interest in phormiums generally you will know that they are as likely to be found listed in the shrub section of nurserymen's catalogues as in the perennial-plant section; like-wise in gardening books. As non-woody plants they are true perennials, but it is interesting to note that on the finer points of their taxonomy the botanists also find it difficult to make up their minds. Phormiums have recently been removed from the *Liliaceae* (or lily) family and put into the *Agavaceae* (or agave) family; but this, one gathers, may not yet be the last word on the subject. No wonder we gardeners get confused at times!

Of course, I have no more than scratched the surface of the rich array of herbaceous perennial plants on offer by nurserymen, many of them highly suitable for small set-piece plantings in patio gardens. What I have done, I hope, is to point the way to some of those most deserving of a place in a patio garden, where every inch of space is precious.

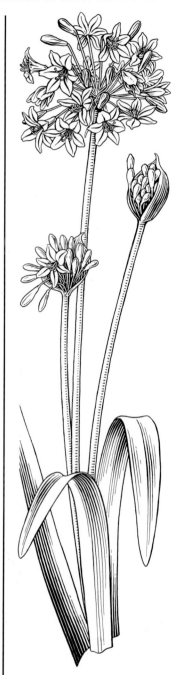

Agapanthus *Headbourne Hybrids* (see p. 105).

7. The Patio Pool

Given that you can find a nice sunny spot for it – sunshine is a necessity – a small pool can add greatly to the attractions of a patio garden. It gives the garden an air of peace and tranquillity, whether it is the still water reflecting the clouds and sky or, say, the soft babblings of a small fountain on a still summer's day. All in all, it provides beauty and interest out of all proportion to its size.

But what kind of pool? There is no reason at all why you should not have a concrete one provided you have the ability to make this really well or are prepared to go to the expense of having it made professionally so that it will be leak-proof and will not readily be breached by arctic weather. To make sure of that the concrete must be at least 5in (13cm) thick and be treated with a waterproofing preparation.

It is altogether easier though, these days, to opt for a glass-fibre pool or to use a heavy-duty plastic pool liner for which you have but to prepare a hole of the right size and shape. Certainly you have got to take care when making the preparations, for it is important when seating glass-fibre pools that the support should be even all round. If you leave loose pockets of soil around the sides the weight of the water pressing on the frame is liable to cause strain and distortion.

With the plastic pool liner the important thing is to make sure that no sharp stones are left sticking through the soil when the hole has been excavated. If you don't, then the weight of the water pressing down on sharp edges will be liable to cause tears. Lining the hole with a layer of sand before putting down the liner should ensure that this does not happen.

A pool made from either of these two materials can be effectively camouflaged with an edging of paving stones. Useful as these materials are, one does not want to be too conscious of their presence.

Planting the pool
When it comes to planting the garden pool, too, do remember the cardinal rule about design in general: keep it simple. Don't attempt to pack in too many plants. Water-lilies (nymphaeas), which everybody wants to grow, are certainly not seen to best advantage if overcrowded, nor do they grow so well.

Nymphaea *'Rose Arey'*

Let us start with water-lilies, as these are so popular. It is important to make sure that those you choose are suitable for the depth of water you can provide; and if you have a small pool – which is certainly what I would consider right for a typical patio garden – keep away from those which are too vigorous or wide-spreading.

Choose, for instance, something like the splendid 'James Brydon', a cultivar with rosy-red blooms which makes much less foliage than some others and will happily grow in anything from 7in to 2ft (18 to 60cm) of water. The yellow *Nymphaea pygmaea* 'Helvola' will grow well in as little as 6in (15cm) of water, while two for a minimum depth of 9in (23cm) are the soft pink 'Laydekeri Lilacea', which matures to rosy-red, and the rosy-crimson 'Laydekeri Purpurata'. In the same depth of water you can grow the deep red 'Froebelii' and the handsome pink 'Rose Arey'. Many others are readily available.

It is more usual nowadays to plant water-lilies in polythene containers than in prepared beds of soil on the base of the pool. It is easier this way, and the growing medium, which should consist of a rather heavy soil, is more effectively contained. If you do plant directly into a bed of soil on the base of the pool, however, this soil can be confined by a ring of stones. You can dress the soil too at planting time with a proprietary water-lily fertiliser, obtainable from garden stores.

Still, water-lilies, lovely as they are, are not the be-all and end-all of water gardening. The double marsh marigold, *Caltha palustris plena*, for instance, brings a fine splash of gold to the garden in spring. Another distinctive plant for display just a little later is the golden club, *Orontium aquaticum*. The common name is apt for the yellow flowers, individually very small, clothe the upper part of the white stems which are thrown up in spring. Then for early summer what could be better than the water iris, *Iris laevigata*, with its beautiful blue flowers on 2ft (60cm) stems; or, for late summer or early autumn display, than the pale blue-flowered *Pontederia cordata*, a plant with heart-shaped leaves. All these are suitable for shallow water, say around 3in (8cm) deep,

Iris laevigata *(see p. 109).*

but the caltha will be happy only in water 1in (3cm) deep and the orontium in water from 3 to 18in (8 to 45cm) deep.

The best planting months for aquatics are May and June with planting continuing until early August. Keep this fact in mind when you are laying your plans.

Fish and fountains

If you introduce fish like goldfish, golden orfe or shubunkins to the pool, and it is pleasant to see them darting here and there, then submerged oxygenating plants like the water violet,

Hottonia palustris, a plant which puts up to the surface stems bearing pretty lilac-coloured flowers in early summer, are a necessity to keep the water clear and sweet. Another good plant for this purpose is the water starwort, *Callitriche verna*.

A fountain can be operated by a submersible or external pump, electrically powered. Underwater lighting kits, complete with low-voltage transformers, add a new dimension of interest to a water feature, and have a special attraction in a patio garden where you will want to sit out on summer evenings. A very pleasing prospect.

III

8. Plants in Containers

There is no need to stress the value of plants grown in tubs, window-boxes and containers of other kinds in the context of the patio garden, and the smaller patio area the greater part they have to play. Large containers, too, can be used for permanent plantings of climbers and shrubs, if they are treated as I suggest later (see p. 122).

Choice of compost

This kind of gardening is immensely enjoyable and rewarding, but like everything else it imposes its own set of rules and disciplines. It is necessary to appreciate right from the start that if you are going to confine plants in such close quarters it is essential to provide them with good fare. Old worn-out soil from the garden just is not good enough.

So what should it be? The choice is quite wide: the John Innes potting composts (Nos. 1, 2 and 3), proprietary soilless mixtures and composts which you can make up yourself.

Let us look at each in turn. I make much use of the soilless, peat-based composts but to fill a large container with one of these costs quite a lot of money, as indeed it does if the John Innes composts are used. Of these two types the John Innes are a better choice for shrubs and larger plants generally of a permanent nature as they provide more support for the plants in windy weather and do not need the regular feeding which is essential with soilless composts, after the initial food content of the compost has been used up. It is important to appreciate that with soilless composts a complete fertiliser including trace elements must be used as directed by the manufacturer.

If you use John Innes composts, however, pay proper attention to the grade you use for these vary in their fertiliser content. So, it should be No. 1 grade for plants which are of a transient nature; No. 2 for what might be termed semi-permanent plants, and No. 3 for long-term occupants of containers, bearing in mind that very small plants should not be introduced to the No. 3 grade until they have grown larger.

As John Innes composts contain ground chalk they should not be used for lime-hating plants like rhododendrons, azaleas and camellias. The same applies to the loamless composts, of course, and in both types of compost (soil-based and soilless) there are lime-free versions – termed ericaceous mixtures – available. Alternatively, use a mixture consisting of lime-free loam to which liberal quantities of peat and sand have been added.

I mentioned home-made mixtures. It is possible to buy proprietary compost-making kits which allow you to make up your own soilless, peat-based composts to a given formula, or rather any one of numerous formulas for a wide range of purposes. For those prepared to go to the trouble involved in making up such mixtures there are definite cost advantages. Quite different again is a method of compost-making for permanent container plants like shrubs, and indeed, for shorter-term plants like bulbous flowers and summer bedders, which I have found completely satisfactory over the past two to three years. This is to mix equal quantities of composted bark (available from garden centres and stores) with good garden loam. Naturally, I feed the plants with liquid fertiliser, as necessary.

Points to remember
Drainage must be good for any container-grown plant so the container must have an adequate number of holes in its base for drainage, with a layer of porous material between this and the growing compost. With the dominance of plastic pots and containers nowadays over their clay equivalents crocks are hard to come by but pebbles and small stones are good substitutes. Cover these in turn with rough-textured material from the compost heap or elsewhee to stop the compost filtering through.

Make sure, too, that the container's base is raised off the ground so that excess moisture can drain away freely. With window-boxes, of course, it is the wall fittings or brackets which must be strong enough to do their job properly. A box laden with soil and plants can be surprisingly heavy and can be a menace if not properly secured.

Which brings me to another point. One of the plus factors with containers is their mobility, but if you think you are going to do a lot of scene shifting with the seasons you may be in for a disappointment. If a window-box or large pot can be heavy that is nothing to a typical garden tub or concrete plant container with all its impedimenta. It is usually more than a single-handed job, which means that in practice you leave them alone as much as possible.

With container plants – and even more with hanging baskets – you must be constantly aware of their need for water. On a hot summer day, with the sun beating down, the compost can dry out in next to no time. So try to get a neighbour or a friend to give them a drink in such weather even if you have to be away yourself.

Tulipa kaufmanniana

Opposite: Superbly grown pot plants like these tuberous begonias, pelargoniums, fuchsias and so on can only be seen to best advantage if positioned with sensitivity to provide interest at different levels.

Bulbs

A wide range of plants can be used for window-box display and for growing in other containers to give vibrant colour for many months of the year – from bulbous flowers early on to annuals like the showy marigolds, antirrhinums, nasturtiums and the like later in the season.

Bulbs can make a heart-warming show in spring for a quite modest expenditure weighed against the pleasure they give. For example, such strong-growing trumpet daffodil varieties as 'Golden Harvest' and 'King Alfred' will put up an impressive show from plantings made in September or October, setting the bulbs 4in (10cm) deep. The beautiful water-lily tulips, too, the varieties and hybrids of *Tulipa kaufmanniana*, are ideal for container gardening, providing brilliant colour in March and April; some of the hybrids also have the most exquisitely marked foliage as a result of crossing *T. kaufmanniana* with *T. greigii*. These hybrids are anything from 4in to 10in (10 to 25cm) tall.

Other tulips you could grow would be the lovely varieties and hybrids of *T. fosteriana*, at least the shorter ones (they range in height from 9in to 18in (23 to 45cm), and certain of the *T. greigii* kinds like the scarlet, black and bronze 'Red Riding Hood' and the richly coloured 'Cape Cod' (bronze-yellow and black with bold red stripes on the outside of the petals), which do not make so much height as the others. Find them a nice sunny position and plant the bulbs 4in (10cm) deep and 6in (15cm) apart an any time between September and November.

You can do the same also with the Double Earlies, which are very attractive. For all, it is essential that the compost should be well drained.

What else? Well, of course, hyacinths are delightful for flowering in late March and early April, and these you plant in September or October, 4in (10cm) deep; also snowdrops, which you plant at the same time and at the same depth. Either *Galanthus nivalis*, the common snowdrop, or *G. elwesii* will put up a splendid show early in the year.

The Siberian squill, *Scilla sibirica*, muscari (grape hyacinths) in variety, dwarf irises like the beautiful little *Iris reticulata* which flowers in February and March, and a whole range of dwarf narcissi and crocuses can be pressed into service to provide a display. These last all need planting about 3in (8cm) deep in September or October.

Just a mention, too, of the regal lily, *Lilium regale*, more fully described on p. 132, which makes a splendid tub plant for providing colour in July. Its trumpet flowers are white, flushed yellow in the throat and rose-purple on the outside of the petals. It needs a sunny position.

For all of these you could use one of the compost mixtures I have suggested for general use (p. 112), but if the bulbs are

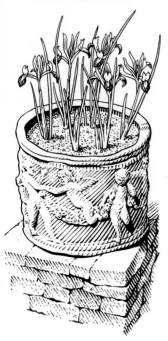

Iris reticulata *(see p. 114)*.

replacing plants which have been giving a summer display do not bother to bring in fresh compost. The same mixture will be quite adequate, provided it is of an open texture so that the drainage is beyond reproach. If necessary, take the old compost out and mix in with it some peat and sharp sand.

Watch the watering as well and make sure that at no time is the compost allowed to become dry.

Bedding plants

There is nothing like the joy of seeing spring flowers, especially on those days – and we do get them – when the weather is warm enough to sit among them and take in their beauty in a contemplative way. All the same, it is the summer bedding plants, either raised oneself if the facilities are available or bought in as young plants, which are the really significant plants for use in containers on the patio, as they are for small beds, if the design allows for such display. A whole host of lovely things can be used to good effect, from impatiens (busy lizzies) and petunias to calendulas and tagetes (marigolds) to nasturtiums, ageratums and smaller-growing antirrhinums to celosias (cockscombs), salvias, dwarf varieties of *Begonia semperflorens, Phlox drummondii* varieties, China asters (callistephuses) and other plants raised from seed.

If you buy boxes of these make quite sure that the roots of the plants are thoroughly moistened before planting, for if you don't you will find that is extremely difficult to get the dry root balls to take up moisture later. What usually happens is that the plant remains dry while the new compost gets over-moist and in extreme cases becomes sour – a very unsatisfactory state of affairs.

Shrubs and sub-shrubs

Clematis are marvellous patio plants whether grown in beds or in containers. The early, large-flowered hybrids (which I discussed on p. 28) are wonderfully convenient, easy and successful climbers to grow in tubs or other large containers made of wood or stone. Likewise the cultivars of *Clematis alpina* and *C. macropetala* (see p. 28). These last two types also look extremely attractive grown in old strawberry pots. The *C. montana* cultivars are really a little too vigorous for container cultivation, and that is true also of the mid-season flowering hybrids like 'Marie Boisselot', the 'Jackmanii' types and the later flowering species. The role of these highly decorative kinds lies elsewhere, as indicated earlier (p. 29).

The zonal and ivy-leaved pelargoniums (or geraniums) are, of course, indispensible container plants, like the hortensia cultivars of the common hydrangea, *H. macrophylla*, and the fuchsias which are available in such variety.

It is well known, of course, that the colour of the flowers of

A hortensia hydrangea.

hortensia hydrangeas is directly related to the chemical composition of the soil. You don't get blue shades on alkaline, or limy, soils but shades of pink and red. In such circumstances you can, of course, apply a proprietary blueing agent if you so desire. One of my favourite varieties is the splendid 'Génerale Vicomtesse de Vibraye', for it is notably generous in producing its blooms – either a lovely clear blue or rose-pink, depending on the soil you grow it in. Other excellent varieties include the deep rose-pink or deep blue 'Hamburg', the deep pink or purplish-blue 'Maréchal Foch', and the superb 'Madame E. Mouillière', white. You could also make a very nice show with the hybrid 'Preziosa' grown in this way. It is described on p. 49.

These hydrangeas can be grown in sunshine or light shade, like fuchsias. Of the latter there are also many varieties from which to make a choice, among them excellent ones like the dwarf cerise and mauve 'Tom Thumb', the white, pink and violet-mauve 'Chillerton Beauty' and 'Mrs Popple', a very good performer with scarlet and purple flowers.

At the end of the season you can store your container-grown hydrangeas and fuchsias in any cool, frost-proof place like the

Opposite: *Fuchsias and pelargoniums provide a riot of late-season colour.*

Left: Hedera helix *'Buttercup' – one of the most effective of all the ivies.*

Azalea (see p. 120).

garage, until the warmer weather returns. Pelargoniums need overwintering in good light and frost-proof conditions.

Of course, if you have little space to grow plants in beds, and that is quite often the case in the small patio garden, you can grow all manner of things successfully in containers, provided they are large enough. Shrubs like the evergreen azaleas and Japanese maples (cultivars of *Acer palmatum*), the cheery yellow-flowered winter jasmine (*Jasminium nudiflorum*) and *Forsythia intermedia spectabilis* or the excellent 'Lynwood' are a natural choice, not to mention ornamental vines like the Virginia creeper (*Parthenocissus quinquefolia*); ivies like the variegated Persian type, *Hedera colchica* 'Dentata Variegata', and the splendid *H. helix* 'Buttercup'; the beautiful camellias, lovely in leaf alone even when they are not

Viburnum davidii

Pinus mugo pumilio

carrying their exotic-looking flowers, roses and clematises. There are numerous others, like the bold-leaved *Fatsia japonica* (see p. 62), the bay laurel, *Laurus nobilis* (so long as its site does not subject it to severe cold), and the very handsome-foliaged, small-growing variety of the common laurel, *Prunus laurocerasus* 'Otto Luyken'. This has small, narrow leaves which are dark green and shiny and it makes a wide-spreading shrub about 3 to 4ft (1 to 1.3m) tall. It bears spikes of white flowers in May.

I must put in a word, too, for the charming little variegated evergreen *Euonymus fortunei* 'Silver Queen', which, free-standing in a tub or a bed, will remain small and spreading – not more than 2ft (60cm) tall – but which up against a wall will climb to a height of about 10ft (3m). The small leaves are margined with creamy-white and it is an attraction at all seasons. Then there is that recently introduced foliage plant, the evergreen *Euonymus fortunei* 'Emerald 'n' Gold', about 1ft (30cm) high, which clothes itself in bright yellow and green leaves slightly tinged with pink (in the garden it is an excellent ground cover).

Also excellent for container growing are *Berberis stenophylla* 'Corallina Compacta', *Elaeagnus pungens* 'Maculata', *Viburnum davidii* and *Daphne odora* 'Aureomarginata', all of which I have discussed in the chapter on shrubs (see pp. 23 to 64 and index).

Of the above, though, do note that the evergreen azaleas and camellias demand a lime-free soil. Make a special note too, of the following azaleas, for they are especially attractive: 'Hinodegiri', bright crimson, 'Vuyk's Scarlet', the pure white 'Palestrina' and the salmon-pink 'Blaauw's Pink', all of which make modestly sized shrubs and flower in May. A sheltered, very lightly shaded position suits them best of all but they will grow well in sun if need be.

Dwarf conifers

Don't overlook either the value of dwarf and slow-growing conifers as tub specimens, for the foliage can provide year-round interest with its colour and texture. A conifer which is often grown in this way is *Chamaecyparis lawsoniana* 'Ellwoodii', columnar in habit and grey-green foliaged, but a rather better choice might be the form known as *C. lawsoniana* 'Ellwood's Gold' (see p. 78), in that the yellow tips to the growths give it a more lively appearance. For this coloration to be good, though, it needs to be placed in a sunny position.

Another *lawsoniana* variety to consider is the small, globular *C. lawsoniana* 'Minima Glauca', little over 2ft (60cm) tall, which has sea-green foliage and is very slow to put on growth, which is no disadvantage in a container plant.

I'm very fond of the dwarf form of the mountain pine, *Pinus mugo pumilio*, another conifer which can be used very satisfactorily for this purpose with its mass of dark green, tufty, spreading growths. It has a lot of character and is unlikely to be more than 3ft (1m) tall grown in this way. The ultra-slow growing *Juniperus communis* 'Compressa' is, of course, the one used so often in sink gardens, and very attractive it is making its conical mat of growth and eventually reaching, after years, a height of perhaps 2ft (60cm). Another juniper to consider is the distinctive *J. media* 'Blaauw', which makes a quite sizeable specimen with upward-thrusting branches which arch over at the top. Its foliage colour is greyish-green. There are, of course, numerous others which can be grown in this way.

What has given me great pleasure over the past two years is a collection of dwarf and slow-growing conifers which I am growing in clay pots of various sizes, some of small size. There are over 40 of them all together, all of different kinds, and it is amazing how much interest these provide at every season. Moreover, they take up very little room, a point of importance if such a collection is made in a corner of a patio garden – something I would recommend.

Juniperus media *'Blaauw'*

Mine include the three just referred to, namely *Pinus mugo pumilio*, *Chamaecyparis lawsoniana* 'Minima Glauca' and *Juniperus communis* 'Compressa', and other attractive plants like the prostrate-growing *Microcachrys tetragona* which bears showy little red cones from autumn onwards throughout the winter; *Chamaecyparis lawsoniana* 'Pygmaea Argentea', the foliage tips of which are creamy-white; *Picea abies* 'Gregoryana', which makes a rounded bush, eventually of 1 to 1½ft (30 to 45cm) in height, with light green foliage in spring which contrasts with the darker, older foliage; the very small growing *Thuja occidentalis* 'Hetz Midget' and the very dwarf *Cedrus libani* 'Nana'. All are very distinctive and fascinating to observe over a period of time.

I grow all of these conifers in John Innes No. 2 potting compost, replacing a little of the surface compost in the spring with fresh compost of like kind – and taking care, of course, not to disturb the roots in the process. The plants are also given a light dressing of bone-meal in spring. No other feeding is necessary or desirable.

Be very careful to water the plants correctly. Conifers grown in pots will almost certainly need daily watering in summer (so make arrangements for this when you are going on holiday) except in dull, rainy weather, but between October and spring only water when this is really necessary. To let conifers dry right out is likely to lead to disaster, for plants allowed to suffer in this way rarely recover.

Specialist nurseries offer the conifers I have referred to, and many others as well.

Note that the interesting new range of phormiums (ornamented flaxes) which I have discussed in the chapter on perennials (see p. 107) are highly suited for container cultivation. Their clearly

Above: *A dwarf broom and pine,* Bellis perennis *(daisy) and violas make a charming container planting.*

Opposite: *This hanging basket and vase planting gives the scene an almost Mediterranean air.*

defined 'architectural' forms and colourings could add much to the attractions of a paved area (see illustration on p. 18). The *Agapanthus* Headbourne Hybrids, described on p. 105, are also excellent plants for growing in tubs or other large, deep containers.

There is advice on growing strawberries in containers on p.168.

Care of plants in containers

Whatever permanent plants you grow in containers, though, you must take the trouble to see that they are provided with the optimum growing conditions. This means really efficient drainage, the right kind of compost, sunshine or shade as the case may be. Attend to their watering needs, too, with particular assiduity for containers can dry out remarkably quickly in hot, sunny weather, a point already noted in relation to pot-grown conifers.

Make it a matter of routine, too, to give such permanent plants a top-dressing of new compost each spring, again just as suggested for conifers in pots. Remove with great care the top few inches of old soil – or as much as you can without disturbing the roots of the plants – and replace this with new compost which you firm in place with your fingers. This always gives the plants a

Sometimes a new house or a conversion of an old house opens on to a garden area enclosed by walls on at least two sides. The area represented here is about 60ft (18m) across by 40ft (12m) deep, and the design exploits the intimate atmosphere already partly provided by the end of an adjoining property and the wall which abuts on to it. Slight changes of level provide

additional interest and it should be noted that such a feature, with raised beds, can have practical advantages as well if the soil is heavy and the drainage none too good.

The panel of grass on the left increases the usable sitting-out space in summer and its greenness can be very welcome in winter, when muted tones predominate.

Note, also, how the two small trees give the garden a sense of balance with the shrubs, the tall conifer and the climbers on the far wall breaking up what would otherwise be a hard line which, inevitably, would jar on the senses. With relative ease a site like this can be transformed into a patio garden of considerable charm.

new lease of life. It is usually necessary to feed container-grown shrubs in the growing season as well for they cannot fend for themselves in a similar way to those grown in the open ground. There are numerous proprietary liquid feeds available.

Hanging baskets

Another type of container display which can give added charm to the patio garden in summer is to have flower-filled hanging baskets dotted around, perhaps hung on brackets near a door into the house or attached to some other wall or fence. They can indeed be great fun and immensely colourful if you use plants like ivy-leaved pelargoniums (geraniums), blue-flowered trailing lobelia and verbena, petunias and nasturtiums. Here again, too, fuchsias come into their own and tuberous and fibrous-rooted begonias.

Once again, though, I would advise taking more than usual care in the preparation of the baskets and watch especially the subsequent watering. On a very hot summer's day the baskets need, ideally, several soakings, but for busy people away from home all day I realise that that may be a counsel of perfection. What I do say is that you should make a thorough job of watering, the best way being by immersing the basket in a container for perhaps 10 minutes or so but otherwise doing this in the ordinary way with a watering can. As with other container-grown plants, also give the plants a liquid feed at regular intervals in summer. Once a fortnight is not too often for the plants really are in very confined conditions.

Preparing a hanging basket is simple enough. First line the basket with well-moistened sphagnum moss or plastic sheeting, then add compost and firm it well with the fingers. Plant the trailing plants around the sides first (if plastic sheeting is used, making slits in this for planting) and then put in the rest of the plants so that you end up by filling the last bare space in the centre of the basket. Water thoroughly with a watering can (not by immersion until the compost has had a chance to settle down) and all is then ready to hang the basket in position.

If you try your hand at the kind of container gardening I have been suggesting, I shall be very surprised if you do not find it immensely rewarding. Try experimenting with all kinds of plants – for that is half the fun of gardening – and gradually find out what is most suitable for your patio.

Baskets of flowers can add much interest to a patio garden.

9. Colourful Bulbs

Opposite: *Snowdrops (galanthus) in all their wide diversity are a great joy early in the year.*

In the last chapter, I mentioned some bulbous plants which are excellent for growing in containers. Of course, all can be grown with equal or greater effect in beds if the space can be found.

Early flowering bulbs

Two snowdrops of quite outstanding beauty and quality which I would recommend for a special position are a form of the common snowdrop, *Galanthus nivalis*, named 'S. Arnott', which comes into flower in February, and the so-called giant snowdrop, *G. elwesii*, which opens its large, globular blooms rather later in the same month. For a terrace bed I can think of few more welcome pleasures at that time of year, if that is not being too disloyal to the pretty little *Crocus tomasinianus* which produces its mauvy-blue flowers from quite early in February in some gardens, although usually a few weeks later than that in my garden. There are various forms of this last, including one called 'Whitewell Purple' with violet-purple blooms.

Crocus tomasinianus naturalises itself freely and looks superb, for instance, around the base of a tall conifer. Plant the corms of these, as of other crocuses, like the colourful varieties of *C. chrysanthus* – also February flowering – in which are found shades from purple to blue and yellow, cream and white, in September or at latest October. Set them 3in (8cm) deep and much the same apart, in well-drained soil in a sunny position on the patio. For February-March flowering, too, there is the easily pleased winter aconite, *Eranthis hyemalis*, with its well-known yellow flowers. These again are followed by scillas like *Scilla sibirica*. Plant both 2in (5cm) deep in September or October.

Bulbs for spring

What would spring be like without the daffodils in their multitudinous forms? A much duller season, without a doubt. A whole host of the larger kinds from the trumpet varieties to the large- and small-cupped kinds and the doubles can be put to good use in the patio garden, growing around shrubs and roses and in other situations where their early colour will be appreciated. They like good soil but will put up with very mediocre concoctions if need be. On poorer soils it is well worth lacing the

Crocus tomasinianus

Narcissus *'February Gold'*

Narcissus cyclamineus

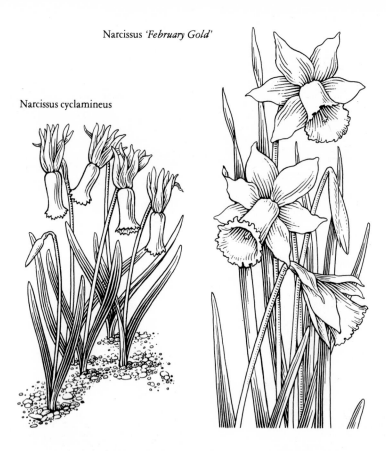

planting area with bone-meal at the rate of 4oz (113g) to the square yard when the soil is being prepared. Plant the bulbs in August or as soon thereafter as practicable, setting them 4 to 6in (10 to 15cm) deep, the greater depth on light soils.

But it is the exquisite little dwarf narcissi which really capture one's heart, and these are ideal for patio garden conditions. Particularly lovely is the February-March flowering *Narcissus cyclamineus* and its offspring. Many very attractive garden hybrids have been obtained by crossing this species with trumpet varieties. The species itself has reflexed perianth segments resembling those of a cyclamen – hence the name – and the narrow trumpet combines with these to make a flower of great charm. To be grown well, though, it needs rather a moist soil which contains plenty of humus. The hybrids I've just referred to include varieties like 'February Gold', 'March Sunshine', 'Peeping Tom', 'Dove Wings', 'Jenny' and 'Charity May'. All are excellent and they are nearly all 10 to 12in (25 to 30cm) tall, with 'Peeping Tom' being one of those which has a height of up to 15in (38cm).

Then there is the beautiful hoop petticoat daffodil, *N. bulbocodium*, with is distinctive, flared, trumpet-shaped yellow blooms which appear in February and March as well.

For April flowering there are the crosses between *N. triandrus* and *N. jonquilla* with names like 'April Tears', 'Hawera' and 'Rippling Waters'. The first two are about 9in (23cm) tall and very pretty with, in the case of 'April Tears', up to five deep yellow flowers to a stem, rather less in the case of the lemon-yellow 'Hawera'. 'Rippling Waters' has three pure white, cup-shaped blooms to a stem. The bulbs of all these small narcissi should also be planted in August or as soon thereafter as possible, but only 2 to 3in (6 to 8cm) deep, the greater depth being in light soil.

Of course, one of the most popular small bulbous plants is the muscari (or grape hyacinth) in its various species and forms. Nothing could be more accommodating, either, for it will grow happily in sunshine or light shade in almost any reasonable soil. Grown with daffodils, as in the raised beds which so often form a part of a paved patio area, they can be a delight in April – and none more so than the well-known *Muscari armeniacum* 'Heavenly Blue', some 6in (15cm) tall and with flowers of a vivid blue. An interesting, rather earlier flowering species is *M. tuberginianum* 8in (20cm) tall which got its name of Oxford and Cambridge grape hyacinth from its way of bearing dark blue flowers at the top of the spike, pale blue ones lower down. It is often in flower before March is out. Plant the bulbs 3in (8cm) deep between late August and early November, but preferably as early as possible.

More, too, about the scillas which I mentioned earlier in passing. These also are easy-going little plants, but they will always do best where there is plenty of moisture in the soil combined with free drainage. Sunshine or light shade suits them equally well. One of the best for brightening March days is the 6in (15cm) *Scilla sibirica atrocoerulea*, or 'Spring Beauty' as it is often called. For ordinary garden conditions it is the best one to grow.

Of course, the other very popular group of bulbous plants is the tulips, to which I have already made reference in respect of the species and their varieties and hybrids (see p. 114). How pleasant also to find a home for some of the colourful bedding kinds, allowing that these should be lifted and the bulbs stored in a cool, dry place after the foliage has died down in summer until planting time comes round once more. The planting time for these tulips is in October and November and you set the bulbs between 4 and 5in (10 to 13cm) deep, the lighter the soil the deeper the planting. What they need, too, is an especially well-drained soil, in sun or light shade.

Before looking at some of the bedding kinds, though, I must sing the praises of some of the species and their hybrids for special parts of the garden, and it should be noted that these do not need lifting every season, like the bedding kinds. For example, the *T. kaufmanniana* varieties and hybrids, which I have recommended

Scilla sibirica
atrocoerulea

Tulipa kaufmanniana
*'Gluck', one of the numerous
hybrids of this species, which
can be associated most
beautifully with bedding plants
like polyanthus.*

Lilium candidum

for container growing, look quite magnificent in a bed set in paving, and these together with the *T. fosteriana* hybrids and the *T. greigii* hybrids – these last flower from late April – are splendid for a raised bed. Even a few make a striking display. Note, however, that tulips of this type need planting in a sunny position and the bulbs need planting some 4in (10cm) deep.

To go back to the bedding tulips, take special note of the single early and double early kinds which are around 1ft (30cm) tall and make a striking display in the second half of April, and of the spectacular Darwin hybrids which flower from late April and are unsurpassed for a formal display in a small bed set in paving. These have single blooms on 2ft (60cm) stems. Just a few May-flowering lily-flowered tulips are also a joy for these have a grace which demands attention.

Hyacinths can be planted in beds and make a colourful display in spring and these you should plant 4in (10cm) deep between September and November. They like a good soil and excellent drainage and you should lift the bulbs in summer when the foliage has withered and store – after removing the remains of the foliage – in a cool, airy place until planting time arrives again.

If part of your patio is lightly shaded and the soil there is nicely moisture-retentive then you might think of growing one of my favourite bulbs, the so-called summer snowflake, *Leucojum aestivum*, which, despite its common name, flowers in April and May. It is a very elegant plant with its white, bell-shaped flowers with green markings on the tips of the petals, these being borne in nodding umbels on stems some 2ft (60cm) tall. In some ways this plant looks like an outsize snowdrop. The strong foliage is strap-shaped and makes the perfect foil for the flowers. But get the form 'Gravetye Variety', which is even better than the species. Plant the bulbs in September or October 4in (10cm) deep. This plant increases freely and should be left alone until the quality of the blooms starts dropping off. Then lift, divide and replant the bulbs after flowering has finished and the foliage has died back.

Lilies

I am going to mention only a couple of lilies although there are rich pickings here for anybody keen on this beautiful genus. First, the very popular regal lily, *Lilium regale*, which makes a superb tub plant and a first-class border plant as well for it grows well in practically all soils – it does not mind lime – provided they are well drained. The white trumpet flowers, carried in bold heads on 4 to 6ft (1.3 to 2m) stems in July, have yellow throat markings and rosy-purple suffusions on the outside of the petals. What it does need is plenty of sunshine, and you should plant the bulbs in autumn as soon as these can be obtained from the supplier for no lily bulb improves by being out of the ground for long.

The regal lily is stem rooting so the bulbs should be set 8 to 10in (20 to 25cm) deep in the soil and, like all lilies, be bedded in sharp sand at the base of the planting hole to avoid the possibility of rotting in wet weather.

The other lily is *L. candidum*, the Madonna lily, with a history which goes back into the mists of time. Indeed, its glorious white, broad-petalled blooms set off by golden-yellow anthers have been enjoyed in Britain for centuries, and this species from the eastern Mediterranean was reproduced on pottery by Cretan craftsmen before 1500 B.C. Ten or more flower heads are borne on each 4 to 5ft (1.3 to 1.5m) stem in June and July, sometimes as many as 20 flowers, but that is still well below the maximum you can get in the inflorescence of *L. regale*.

This also is a lily which does not mind lime in the soil, and the conditions it needs are similar to those liked by *L. regale*, a well-drained soil, of reasonable quality, warmth and sunshine, but its planting regime is different – indeed it is different from that of almost every other lily. It needs to be planted in July or August, just as soon as the bulbs can be obtained. Also untypically they need to be planted only 1in (2.5cm) deep. This lily is subject to attack by botrytis, in hot, airless weather and as soon as this is noticed the plants should be sprayed with Bordeaux mixture. Have no hesitation though in lifting and burning any really badly attacked plants.

Sternbergia and nerine

Another sun-loving bulbous plant is *Sternbergia lutea*, which produces in September and October attractive crocus-like flowers above strap-shaped leaves. A well-drained bed at the foot of a warm wall is ideal for this plant and it appreciates good soil. The sheltered conditions found in the typical patio garden are the kind of home it likes. Leave the bulbs undisturbed until the quality of the flowers starts to drop off and then lift and divide in July or August, the time when you buy the plant bulbs when starting off. Plant the bulbs 4in (10cm) deep.

Sternbergia lutea is not all that well known, and it does need a warm spot, so you may have been wondering why I haven't mentioned the autumn crocus, *Colchicum autumnale*, and its forms which put on a show at the same time of year. I'm fond of them in fact, but one cannot overlook the obtrusiveness of the large leaves from early spring to mid-summer in the confines of a small garden. Still, there are the very gay autumn crocuses proper, the varieties of *Crocus speciosus*, with their very good colour range. These are suitable for sunny positions.

I am going to leave the bulbs with a mention of a barely hardy plant of great beauty, *Nerine bowdenii*, which needs very similar conditions to the sternbergia just referred to, and a good loamy soil with excellent drainage. If you can find a sheltered spot for it

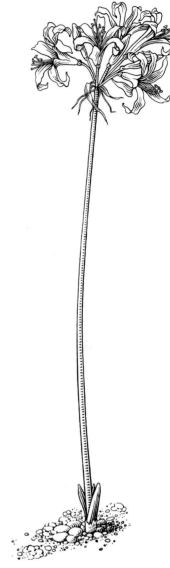

Nerine bowdenii

at the foot of a sheltered, south-facing wall that would be ideal. The flowers are borne in umbels of six or more on 2ft (60cm) stems, each flower consisting of narrow, reflexed segments in pale pink colouring with a darker line down the centre. The strap-like leaves do not usually arrive until after the flowers, which are there to be enjoyed from late September until

The regal lily, Lilium regale, *rightly popular with its beautiful flowers which are borne in July (see p.132).*

November. An especially fine form is 'Fenwick's Variety' with flowers of a richer pink. Dry litter protection – bracken, if you can get it, or straw for example – must be given in winter and you leave the plants undisturbed until the need for division is self-evident. This should be done in July or August, setting the bulbs 4in (10cm) deep.

10. Making a Trough Garden

What is it about plants which makes them of such compelling interest? Primarily, I suppose, their perfect proportions, for what exquisite beauty there is in the flowers, say, of a cushion-type saxifrage, the thrift, *Armeria caespitosa*, or a dwarf phlox. All arouse one's protective interest, although they are more than capable of looking after themselves given anything like the right conditions.

And there is no question that, as a patio gardener, you are on an equal footing with anyone else in what you can achieve. You don't need much space for this kind of gardening. A trough

The interest provided by a trough garden can be immense.

garden or two also look very handsome in the setting of a patio garden. If planted with skill and care these will look attractive as well when nothing is in flower, but it is, of course, for the succession of colour they can provide that one gives them garden space.

Real stone sinks are now hard to lay one's hands on but manufactured substitutes are easy to obtain and old stone kitchen sinks with glazed surfaces are still occasionally available and quite acceptable if the surface is "doctored", faced with hypertufa. What you should avoid doing at all costs is to grow alpine and rock plants in plastic containers, for these heat up far too much in hot weather and get excessively cold in frosty conditions.

With this kind of container gardening again you must also make sure that the drainage is really good, and this means having at least one hole in the base if the trough is small, and more if it is larger. The internal depth of the trough must also be at least 6in (15cm) and nearer a foot for preference. Each drainage hole should be covered with a piece of perforated zinc to stop insects creeping into the trough, before covering this again with a layer of small crocks (pieces of broken pot), weathered ashes or small stones. Then cover this with a layer of fibrous roughage before adding the compost in which the plants will grow.

Preparing the container

But what compost should be used? I have tried several mixtures over the years, some better than others, but I am going to pass on, with his permission, two recipes which my good friend Mr Royton E. Heath, an outstandingly successful alpine plant specialist of amateur status, has found the best through long experience. For sun-loving alpine and rock garden plants he uses a mixture of equal parts loam, leaf-mould and sharp sand; for shade lovers, a mixture of equal parts loam, leaf-mould, peat and sharp sand. Finish off with a sprinkling of lime-free stone chippings in the ordinary way, to help keep the roots of the plant cool and conserve moisture in warm weather.

If you are growing lime-loving plants, too, it is a good idea to add a top-dressing of limestone chippings. Rock plants in general detest winter wet and you can ensure even better drainage of whatever compost you use if you mix in a smattering of broken crocks of very small size – if you happen to have any broken clay pots lying around.

Again, although these plants do not need feeding in the accepted sense, just a sprinkling of bone-meal added to the compost will not come amiss for this will provide extra phosphate over a long period. One has to remember that with this kind of planting an awful lot of roots are competing for a very limited amount of space.

A few small rocks can be added for effect, and there are some

Gentiana verna *'Angulosa'*
(right).

Dianthus *'La Bourbrille'*
(far right, see p. 140*)*.

small plants which will grow all the better for the quicker root drainage proximity to these will ensure – cushion plants like the very pretty little white encrusted saxifrage, *Saxifraga cochlearis* 'Minor', a treat for the eye in May, and some of the late spring flowering androsaces. In April the flowers of the cushion-forming drabas arrive – lovely things like *Draba bryoides imbricata* with yellow blooms on the slenderest of stems.

Raise your sink, or sinks, off the ground to ensure that excess water can get away freely. This also serves the very useful purpose of bringing the plants nearer to normal eye level.

Usually you will want to find a sheltered home for the sink in a sunny part of the patio, but you could of course deliberately choose a site with less favourable light conditions. I would suggest leaving that to the more specialised gardener, though, and concentrate on those plants which do like sunshine. That is the vast majority.

What plants to grow

What to grow is, of course, the next thing you will want to know. A wealth of rock plants and small bulbous plants are admirably suited for this kind of cultivation, and I will make a few suggestions which I hope will prove helpful for troughs in sunny positions.

To begin with there is the thrift, *Armeria caespitosa*, a charming little plant when its cushion growths are covered in May with almost stemless pink blooms. Also, for flowering at the same time, the pretty mat-forming *Phlox douglasii* 'Snow Queen' which, as its name implies, has pure white flowers; and *Erodium reichardii* 'Roseum' (formerly *E. chamaedryoides* 'Roseum'), a very attractive sight when carrying its deep pink flowers just above an inch-high (2.5cm) spread of fresh green small leaves. This is also the time when that lovely gentian, *Gentiana verna* 'Angulosa',

Opposite: Narcissus bulbocodium, *the pretty hoop-petticoat daffodil, for February-March flowering (see p. 143).*

A representation of a tiny backyard only 15ft (4.5m) across. There are times when it is necessary to hide something from view, even in a garden of this size, such as, perhaps, a back entrance door, and an alternative to a trellis screen could be a panel of precast concrete screen blocks similar to those shown here. The containers forms an integral part of the design.

flowers, bearing rich blue star-shaped blooms with great aplomb. I recommend, too, the rhizomatous *Oxalis adenophylla* which bears pinkish-mauve flowers on 2 to 3in (5 to 8cm) stems in May and June against grey-coloured foliage.

In summer comes the aromatic little thyme, *Thymus doerfleri*, with deep pink flowers on 1in (2.5cm) stems; the little bellflower, *Campanula arvatica* with violet blooms, and that excellent dianthus, *D.* 'La Bourbrille' with clear pink flowers, prettily displayed against a mat of grey foliage. And, of course, there are

This garden is 52ft (16m) long and 60ft (18m) wide, and the traditional or period house imposes restrictions on the layout. The small, symmetrical house, indeed, calls for a symmetrical response from the designer. In this design there is very little bed space and what there is is raised so that, should the soil be poor, deep excavation and the making of beds would be avoided. The centre panel would, however, need at least 6 to 9in (15 to 23cm) of good soil to support a small lawn. Containers or sinks are placed against the side walls or fences and a single ornament makes a focal point on the lawn.

numerous other dianthus which could be planted as well. Just a mention, too, of the violet- and orange-flowered *Linaria alpina* whose effectiveness is enhanced by its bluish-grey foliage, and the lavender, mat-forming *Globularia cordifolia*, only 2in (5cm) tall. The easily-grown and very attractive houseleeks or sempervivums are also delightful trough-garden plants; *Sempervivum arachnoideum* and *S. tectorum* and their cultivars are especially recommended.

Miniature roses are other possibilities; these could include

orange-red 'Starina'; lavender-coloured 'Lavender Jewel'; shell-pink 'Dresden Doll', with 'mossed' buds; 'Baby Masquerade', red and yellow; 'Golden Angel', yellow; and 'Pour Toi', cream. See p. 85 for more on miniature roses.

There are many bulbous plants which are ideal for this kind of display – from grape hyacinths (muscari), dwarf crocuses and dwarf narcissi like the exquisite *Narcissus cyclamineus, N. bulbocodium* and *N. triandrus albus* to dwarf irises such as *I. reticulata* and *I. histrioides*, the last bearing its rich blue flowers as early as January. Small tulip species like the yellow- and white-flowered *Tulipa tarda*, which makes its display in April, can also be grown in this way.

A dwarf conifer gives character to a trough garden and by far the most popular for this purpose is the very small growing *Juniperus communis* 'Compressa' with glaucous green foliage. This takes many years to reach a height of 2ft (60cm). A lovely little "bun" conifer is *Chamaecyparis obtusa caespitosa* with rich green foliage, while another is the small and very attractive little conifer *Thuja occidentalis* 'Hetz Midget', globular in shape, dark green in colour and very slow growing.

The Lilliputian world of the trough garden can be a joy. But now a few other cultural details which may help you in your trough gardening. Pot-grown alpine plants can be put in at almost any time during reasonable weather, but spring is an especially good time with the growing season ahead. As with containers of other kinds, be very conscious that they will dry out rapidly in hot, sunny weather and pay attention to their watering needs accordingly. It is a great help to have a layer of stone chipping on the compost's surface to lessen such moisture losses.

There are quite a lot of rock plants which object to winter damp, including the dianthus and the draba I have mentioned; overhead shelter can be provided using a pane of glass attached to a wire frame.

Tulipa tarda

Opposite: Linaria alpina *with violet and orange flowers, grows here with* Asperula suberosa *(see p. 141).*

11. Plants in Paving

Growing rock plants in a sun-bathed paved area has its attractions for the patio gardener. It is as well, though, to go into things quite carefully early on, for the visual effect can be marred if the ratio between plants and paving is not conducive to a basic harmony. Try to imagine what the overall feature will look like when the plants are mature, and endeavour to create a pattern of textures and colours.

A lot of plants do well in these conditions with their roots delving down into cool soil. I particularly like to see the thrift, *Armeria maritima,* grown thus, and a campanula like *G. garganica* with its blue, star-like flowers, provides a lovely show in summer; also the Corsican mint, *Mentha requienii,* with its tiny aromatic leaves, smelling of peppermint, and lilac-mauve flowers in summer.

Gaily coloured rock roses (helianthemums), which make evergreen clumps up to 9in (23cm) high in colours from orange, shades of red, pink and yellow throughout the summer months, are difficult to fault for a sunny site. Numerous dianthuses and aubrietas can also be effectively exploited as well as cultivars of *Saxifraga paniculata* (syn. *S. aizoon*); the cobweb houseleek, *Sempervivum arachnoideum,* and such attractive varieties of the thyme, *Thymus serpyllum,* as 'Pink Chintz'. For summer colour there is also the pretty *Viola cornuta,* with lavender-coloured blooms, and its white cultivar, 'Alba'. Other useful paving plants are the acaenas, and especially *Acaena microphylla,* which has greenish bronze leaves and crimson burrs (seed heads) from mid-summer onwards.

A prostrate juniper like *Juniperus communis* 'Hornibrookii' can also look attractive spreading over paving, for its stems, heavy with little greyish-green leaves, are at a most a foot high, and it has a spread of up to 5ft (1.5m). Perhaps twice as tall and with much the same kind of spread as the last-mentioned in time, is the well-known and excellent *Juniperus sabina tamariscifolia,* with rich green foliage. It is an asset to any garden but much will depend on how much room you have to spare for this kind of thing.

The junipers I have mentioned grow well in most soils, including chalk, and they appreciate plenty of sunshine. So, too, does the colourful *Thuja occidentalis* 'Rheingold' of conical shape,

which has foliage of a warm yellow which turns to bronzy-gold in winter. After a long time this may grow as much as 10ft (3m) tall, though it is more likely to be rather less than half that height.

A delightful very slow-growing small spruce, too, for which a planting pocket might be found in a paved area is *Picea abies nidiformis,* which ultimately makes a densely branched, flat-topped bush some 3ft (1m) tall and 5ft (1.5m) wide with dark green colouring. If your garden lies in what is called a frost pocket, though (i.e. cold air drains into it from higher levels), this would not be a good choice as the new growth can be damaged when severe frost occur in early spring. It has the rather delightful common name of bird's nest spruce.

I think that we shall see much more use made of dwarf and slow-growing conifers in paved areas in the years ahead, with, of course, planting pockets of appropriate size being left for them. I remember being very impressed by a paved patio garden which I saw in Switzerland a year or so ago where, apart from climbing and wall shrubs planted against the white house walls, the only plants consisted of dwarf and slow-growing conifers set most attractively among the paving in the way I have just suggested. Most in evidence were forms of the mountain pine of central and south-east Europe, *Pinus mugo,* and very handsome they looked, too. One of the best of these forms, freely available here, is 'Mops' which makes a bun-shaped bush of greyish-green of around 1½ft (45cm) and 2ft (60cm) wide in time. This cultivar is, of course, a great favourite with rock gardening enthusiasts.

I found this small Swiss garden fascinating to see but what I am not sure about is how long it would remain really satisfying if one had to live with it over a period of years – perhaps in its concentration on one type of plant it is just too much of a good

When planting paved areas, the aim should be to create a pattern of pleasing textures and colours.

145

The pretty little herbaceous Geranium cinereum *'Ballerina' which flowers in the first half of summer.*

thing. Its real interest lies in the stimulus it gives to devote, say, part of a paved area to this kind of display. Dwarf conifers certainly have impact, especially if you can emulate the kind of picture I have tried to draw. And the maintenance needed, of course, is minimal, which, if you are either extremely busy or not too active, could be a consideration.

Do not overlook either the use of prostrate shrubs such as *Cotoneaster dammeri* with its bright red berries or the 3ft (1m) tall *C. conspicuus* 'Decorus', also extremely free-berrying. Both of these are described on p. 57. The smaller growing potentillas I have discussed on pp. 46 and 48 would also be admirable for the purpose in question, and the charming little herbaceous geranium, 'Ballerina'.

But whatever plants you use for planting in a paved area, remember my earlier advice to keep the ratio between plants and paving in balance.

12. Annuals for a Quick Display

There are numerous annuals, many of them half-hardy – those you can't plant out until the danger of frost has passed – which you can put to good use as container-grown plants for summer display. And if you have no greenhouse for raising the half-hardies yourself, you can always buy young plants by the box in late May and early June. However, I would suggest that you take a look at some of the really small and neat lean-to greenhouses available nowadays for they are certainly of a size suitable for a patio setting. Bedding plants can now be quite costly to buy and raising your own is also great fun. You can make sowings of half-hardy annuals in a warm greenhouse from late February to April providing a germinating temperature of about 15°C (59°F) –earlier sowing is not usually necessary – or in a cold greenhouse or frame in late March and April. The resulting plants must not be planted out in the garden until late May or early June, after hardening-off.

Of course, you can easily provide for some delightful splashes of summer colour around the patio by sowing seeds of hardy annuals between late March and early May in whatever pockets of spare ground you happen to have available, provided they are open to a fair bit of sunshine.

Summer bedding

Again, you can buy in young plants of half-hardy annuals as I have just suggested (or raise them yourself) and enjoy a fine display, for little trouble, if you make border plantings of things like the brightly coloured impatiens (busy lizzies) – strains such as 'Super Elfin' and 'Accent' – which do well in light shade, French and African marigolds, petunias, cultivars of *Phlox drummondii,* lobelias, antirrhinums and asters of various kinds, salvias, nemesias, ursinias and zinnias.

Another half-hardy plant which is extremely attractive and used for summer bedding is the fibrous-rooted begonia (the *semperflorens* type) which is available in wide variety and in heights from 6in to 1ft (15 to 30cm) depending on the strain.

Phlox drummondii

These plants are extremely free-flowering and are in bloom from July until October. My favourite strain is 'Organdy', some 6in (15cm) tall, always very eye-catching and with colours from red and pink in various shades to white. It is very resistant to wet weather. The leaf colouring can be either green or bronze. Of special interest are 'Danica Scarlet' and 'Danica Rose', rosy-red, 14in (35cm) tall hybrids which have larger flowers than the general run of these plants, attractive bronze foliage and good weather resistance. All the fibrous begonias of this type give a fine display of colour, with flowers ranging from orangy-red to scarlet, salmon and pink to white.

Then, of course, there are the annual pinks (dianthus), lovely flowers for a sunny, well-drained position, especially the 6in (15cm) tall Magic Charms strain which includes colours like crimson, pink, salmon and white as well as bicolours; multi-coloured dahlias like the well-known Coltness Hybrids and strains like Dandy and Redskin with flowers of numerous colours; and the brilliantly coloured (orange, red and yellow) *Tagetes signata pumila* cultivars which are so excellent for edging beds.

Growing from seed

I must make particular mention of the intermediate-sized strain of sweet pea named Jet Set. The significance of it is that the modestly sized plants, only 3ft (1m) tall, bear a wealth of blooms whose size and length and sturdiness of stem match up to that of the traditional tall Spencer-type cultivars. The colours include scarlet, crimson, cerise, salmon, mauve, blue and cream. You can grow these Jet Sets from a spring sowing made where the plants are to flower. With that kind of stature one can think of many uses for them in the patio garden, and of course, like all sweet peas, they are in a class of their own as cut flowers, both for their beauty of form and colour and their fragrance.

These Jet Sets are an improved strain of the Knee-Hi sweet peas which have become popular in recent years, and need only the support of short sticks or netting to keep them in trim. Of much the same stature is the Little Elf strain and shorter by far are the Patio and Dwarf Bijiou strains for these are little over 1ft (30cm) tall. A quite different sweet pea is 'Snoopea' 2ft (60cm) tall and without the usual tendrils, and the improved form of this, 'Supersnoop', with larger flowers in a wide range of colours. This makes a good border plant with its fine range of colour and pleasant fragrance.

Sweet peas like the sun, of course, and need a deeply dug soil with plenty of humus-forming material in it so that they do not lack moisture at the roots.

If you can provide a sunny spot where the soil is poor there is nothing like the nasturtiums – hardy annuals you sow in April or May. Climbing or trailing, the typical tall, 6 to 8ft (2 to 2.5m)

Dahlia *Coltness Hybrids*

nasturium with its single blooms, in shades of red, orange and yellow, is a considerable asset from July to September, and so are the double-flowered semi-tall and dwarf kinds which have heights of 15in (38cm) and 6 to 9in (15 to 23cm) respectively, and are very useful for bedding. Particularly good are the semi-tall Gleam hybrids and the Jewel Mixed dwarfs, which carry their very colourful flowers well above the foliage. 'Empress of India' with crimson flowers and dark foliage can look especially gay if it is given the contrast of a white background. The typical back spur of the flower is missing from the dwarf 'Whirlybird', a free-flowering mixture in which the flowers of various colours face upwards on top of the stems and above the foliage to create a very colourful show. Give nasturtiums (tropaeolum is, of course, their botanical name) too good a soil and the flowers will be drowned by the foliage, so lushly will they grow – the poorer the better in this case.

One of my favourite hardy annuals is *Layia elegans,* called tidy tips, which bears showy daisy flowers for most of the summer. It is really a very pretty plant, its blooms having a centre of deep yellow surrounded by golden-yellow ray-florets, which are tipped with white. With a height of about 1½ft (45cm) it is useful in the patio garden and the blooms last well when cut for the house. Another favourite of mine is *Limnanthes douglasii,* a lovely sprawling plant from north-west America which produces a

Jet Set sweet pea

mass of white flowers with yellow centres to earn itself the rather amusing name of poached egg-flower. It is especially good for planting beside a low flight of steps which it can ''invade'', and it is very good value as it flowers from early in summer to August. You can sow the seeds where the plants are to flower in September or in March, with the September planting, of course, giving earlier flowering.

   You can sow seeds of the Californian poppy, eschscholzia, and
godetia (also, as it happens, a Californian native) in September if
you wish, but March or April is the more usual sowing time.
September sowing brings earlier flower but it means taking a
chance that there will not be abnormally bad weather conditions
in winter.
   Two goods strains of eschscholzia, both about 1ft (30cm) tall,

are Harlequin and Ballerina. The colour range is good and the flowers are either double or semi-double. By far the best known and most popular godetia is 'Sybil Sherwood', a truly delightful cultivar with salmon-pink, white-edged blooms which are borne in abundance. This also is about 1ft (30cm) tall and so admirable for narrow patio borders. Alternatively, you could decide that the slightly taller Azalea-flowered strain with an excellent range of colours would be preferable. The blooms do resemble those of azaleas, so the name has relevance.

Two hardy annuals of unusual distinction are *Lavatera* 'Silver Cup' and *L.* 'Mont Blanc'. Both are some 2ft (60cm) tall and literally smother their bushy frames with the highly attractive, trumpet-shaped single blooms. Those of 'Silver Cup' are rose-pink with silvery shading; those of 'Mont Blanc' pure white. Their cultivation is of the easiest, the seeds being sown where the plants are to flower at any time in spring. In importance I would rate them with the three rudbeckias whose descriptions follow.

Resistance to bad weather
Some of the finest and most exciting new flowers from seed to be introduced for years are the rudbeckias 'Marmalade', 'Rustic Dwarfs' and 'Goldilocks' which, from a sowing made in a heated greenhouse in February or March will provide plants for setting out after all danger of frost has passed in late May or early June to provide colour from July into autumn. Alternatively, seeds can be sown between April to June to give plants for setting out in autumn or in the following spring. Both 'Marmalade' and 'Rustic Dwarfs' make plants about 1½ft (45cm) tall which smother themselves with the most striking ray flowers – in the first case rich golden-yellow and in the second case in shades of mahogany-red, bronze, golden and yellow. The flowers of 'Marmalade' are up to 5in (13cm) across, those of 'Rustic Dwarfs' if anything slightly more. 'Goldilocks' is taller (about 2ft or 60cm) and has semi-double golden-yellow flowers which are very showy. They make excellent cut flowers for the house. One other thing of

Rudbeckia *'Rustic Dwarfs'*

importance: they stand up remarkably well to bad weather – an important factor in our climate!

If you are using petunias for bedding or for growing in containers (and what better!) take note than the Resisto strain, of which there is a dwarf section, has especially weather-resistant blooms. To see them against other petunias in a wet spell shows this up clearly. These, like other petunias, you can sow up till the end of March in a heated greenhouse to provide plants, duly hardened off, for planting out in a sunny part of the garden in late May or early June.

I have been impressed also by the performance of the handsome cultivar of the perennial *Coreopsis grandiflora* named 'Sunray'. Masses of double, golden-yellow blooms are borne on a plant 18in (45cm) tall. By sowing seed under glass early in the year (February or March) and setting the plants out in May, flowering will take place from July onwards. This is another plant which performs well in wet weather and the blooms are excellent for cutting.

A 4ft (1.3m) sunflower (helianthus), too, like 'Autumn Sunshine', with flowers in shades of yellow and red, can create a good impression, if well placed. And, at the other end of the scale, a sweet william like 'Wee Willy', only 6in (15cm) tall, can be just right for edging a small plant bed. It is a biennial, but you grow it as a hardy annual or as half-hardy annual if you wish.

There is something especially satisfying about growing plants like this from seed. One thing we can all appreciate is the quick results which annuals give. It is possible to experiment with different plants and plant combinations to one's heart content.

Other plants of distinction
Another superb plant which won a Fleuroselect bronze medal in 1978 and which has made its presence felt increasingly since then is *Salvia farinacea* 'Victoria', really a perennial but grown as a half-hardy annual. From a base of arched rich green leaves arise bold spikes of purplish-blue flowers to a height of about 2ft (60cm). Its makes an ideal companion for many other plants, and not only annuals.

Another group of half-hardy annuals which has come much to the fore in recent years is the nicotianas or tobacco plants, notable for their fragrance (especially in the evenings) and in quite a few modern hybrids and strains opening up their flowers in the daytime and not in the evening only, as is the nicotiana's natural inclination. These have heights of between 1ft (30cm) or even a little less and 3ft (1m), as in the case of the highly scented 'Evening Fragrance' mixture in which are found shades of purple, mauve, red, pink and white. 'Lime Green' is a firm favourite, especially with the flower arrangers, for it has pale yellowish-

green flowers which associate beautifully with the flowers of many other plants, being borne on 2ft (60cm) stems.

The 2½ft (75cm) tall Sensation mixture also has an excellent colour range and makes a telling feature in the right situation. Much smaller at 1ft (30cm) is the Nicki mixture, also with a good colour range and the kind of stature which makes it very useful in the confines of a patio garden. The same can be said of the Domino mixture which is of much the same height. Sensation, Nicki and Domino mixtures all open their flowers in the daytime.

I would rate the pretty, extremely free-flowering nemesias among the finest of half-hardy annuals for patio gardening (or for use in any garden for that matter). The funnel-shaped blooms come in numerous attractive colours and in the delightful Carnival mixture are borne on stems no more than 7 to 8in (18 to 20cm) high. The colours of this strain range from orange and red to pink, pale yellow and white. I personally prefer the compact kinds to the rather taller ones with a height of 1ft (30cm) or thereabouts, but all are marvellous plants for bedding purposes.

Above: *For providing colour from mid-summer onwards, few seed-raised plants can beat the petunias, in containers or beds.*

Opposite: Rudbeckia *'Marmalade', one of the most significant and colourful plants in the seedsmen's lists.*

13. Something for the Table

It can be great fun to use a little space in even a small garden to grow a few fruits and vegetables, especially the latter, and I want to just briefly discuss the possibilities in this direction, using any spare bit of ground or containers you may have.

Vegetables and salad crops
Vegetables first, for growing these is an interest of so many people these days. Very popular indeed is growing tomatoes outdoors, even though you have got to have the weather on your side to achieve the best results. It is a gamble well worth taking, and you will naturally set aside a really warm, sheltered spot in which to grow the plants, either a bed or a container, where they will get all the sunshine which is going.

If you do not have the facilities to raise your own plants from seed you will buy hardened off plants at the end of May or in early June for immediate planting, not before the latter date in colder parts of the country. Prepare the ground well in advance of this and dig in either some well-decayed farmyard manure (if you can get it) or garden compost and make sure that the soil is well drained.

Set the plants 1½ft (45cm) apart in the row and don't plant too deeply. Have something like ½in (1cm) of soil over the ball of roots. Stake at the time of planting and take out the side shoots so that the plant is kept to a single stem. Then, when the third or fourth flower truss has formed pinch out the tip of the leading shoot. Start to feed regularly with a proprietary tomato feed when the first fruits begin to develop, and make sure that they get enough water. All the fruit must be gathered before the frost occurs, and any which are still green ripened in boxes in a warm room.

Bush varieties like ''The Amateur'' and F_1 hybrids like 'Alfresco', 'Red Alert' and 'Totem' (compact and especially good for patio cultivation) do not need pinching out, of course. A quite recent introduction of special interest to the patio gardener is the cultivar 'Minibel' which bears quantities of quite small fruits of good quality on a plant 1ft (30cm) tall. It performs well as a pot-grown plant and is excellent, of course, for cultivating in growing bags, as is 'Totem', in particular.

Other varieties for outdoors include 'Outdoor Girl' and 'Sweet 100' which bears masses of small, sweetly flavoured fruits.

Very convenient for the patio gardener are the proprietary growing bags which I alluded to above. These are filled with specially formulated soil-less compost in which crops like tomatoes, runner beans, marrows, herbs and flowers can be grown with ease. They can increase your growing area very appreciably.

If you want to try your hand at growing some runner beans make a sowing in mid-May in a rather rich soil which is well supplied with moisture. Sow the seed 2in (5cm) deep and 9in (23cm) apart in a single row or a double row 1ft (30cm) apart. In preparation for this it is advisable to dig the ground over deeply at least a couple of months beforehand and add some well-decayed manure at that time if it can be obtained, or garden compost. If you are not supporting your runner beans on trellis work or setting against a wall or fence, stake the plants very early on with long poles, and make quite sure that the plants are getting plenty of moisture at the roots during the flowering period and when the pods are developing. A peat mulch applied in early summer will be very helpful in conserving soil moisture. Two excellent varieties are 'Scarlet Emperor' and 'Streamline'. Pick the pods as soon as they become ready, and you should get a good three months of supply from your plants from July onwards.

But don't be over-hasty about getting in the seeds for this is a frost-sensitive vegetable. It is excellent, too, for container growing if you cannot manage to find a bit of spare ground.

If you have a warm, sunny corner spare where the soil is of really good quality what better crop to grow, too, than small bush Courgette marrows, which you cut for use when about 6in (15cm) long. This way you catch this vegetable at its most succulent and it encourages better cropping. Sow the seeds at the end of May or in early June where the plants are to be grown in rich soil laced with well-rotted manure or garden compost if you have no facility for raising plants under glass. This is another crop which needs much moisture and the watering must be watched, particularly in dry weather. It pays to hand fertilise the female flowers with the male flowers to ensure a good crop. (The female flowers have an unformed marrow behind them, which shows as a swollen area.)

How rewarding it can be, too, to give a little ground to lettuces, sowing little and often to provide a succession over many months. (With cloche protection and a greenhouse in which to raise plants it is possible to have lettuces the year round, but I'm not thinking on those ambitious lines.) To get the quick growth which is needed you should grow lettuces in good soil

The bush marrow 'Golden Zucchini'.

with excellent moisture-retaining properties while still being well-drained. The plants must never be allowed to suffer from lack of moisture. Grow them also in a position open to plenty of sunshine.

Good butterhead cultivars of the cabbage type include 'Tom Thumb' (for March-April sowing), a very useful small-headed kind; 'Salad Bowl' (for sowing from April to July) and the excellent 'Avondefiance' for sowing from June to early August.

An extremely useful cos lettuce is 'Little Gem' (it is a compact-growing cultivar which is part cos and part cabbage lettuce in appearance) and this is suitable for sowing outdoors from March to mid-summer. Another good cos variety is 'Lobjoit's Green Cos'. Sow seeds ½in (1cm) deep in rows set 12in (30cm) apart and thin out the resulting seedling to 9 to 12in (23 to 30cm) apart in the rows.

Again, you could consider growing radishes and onions for

salad use. Both give an excellent return for the small amount of ground they take up.

Little and often is definitely the rule with radish sowings (as with lettuces) for this is a crop which needs to be grown well and quickly for use as required. To achieve this you need to make the sowings in soil of good quality and with good moisture-retentive qualities (or you must watch the need for water with special care).

Make successional sowings of radishes outdoors as often as once a fortnight (or at a little longer interval than that, depending on your need) from March until August. (Earlier sowings than that can be made, of course, with glass protection, and there are winter-hardy varieties for sowing in July and August, but we won't go into that here). For the sowings I've suggested, consider growing such varieties as the well-known 'French Breakfast', 'Cherry Belle', 'Scarlet Globe' or 'Long White Icicle'.

Sow the seeds in drills ¼ in (0.5cm) deep and with 5 to 6in (13 to 15cm) between the rows. Sow thinly. Never let the plants be checked in growth through lack of water at the roots. Water as necessary. Very light shade is needed for summer crops of radish but sunny positions for the early crops.

'White Lisbon' is the variety of onion to grow for salad purposes, and you can make successional sowings from March to June in drills set 9in to 1ft (23 to 30cm) apart. Sow thinly and pull the resulting onions as they reach the required size and are needed. You can also make a sowing in July or August of 'White Lisbon – Winter Hardy' to provide onions for pulling in spring.

Lastly, a little bit of fun: growing first-early potatoes in a tub or other large container, in John Innes No. 3 potting compost or some other really good growing mixture of your own concoction. Plant the tubers (after sprouting them in a frost-proof, well-ventilated place open to good light) in late March or early April. If you want to do the equivalent of mounding up the potatoes later, then only just over half-fill the container with compost and add more as top growth develops. Otherwise, start off with more compost and keep the light away from the tubers by letting the plants grow through a covering of black polythene.

Any first-early variety can be grown in this way, and, as always nowadays, with most seed potatoes being obtained locally, it is a question of making a choice from thoses on offer. Naturally, you will want to plant a first-early variety for the novelty has gone out of the operation once there are plenty of new potatoes around. Earliness is the thing.

Herbs

Now a few words about herbs, which are useful in the kitchen and can be grown in odd corners of the garden. Parsley is something it is always useful to have around and it is usual to make two sowings a year, where the plants are to mature: the first in March or April, the second in late June or July. The seeds take five or even more weeks to germinate so don't expect results too quickly. The soil should be kept moist at this time. Sow in drills ¼ in (o.5cm) deep and thin the resulting seedlings to 6in (15cm) apart. At the end of the season you could cover some of the plants from the second sowing with a cloche. The best-known cultivar is 'Moss Curled'.

The common thyme, *Thymus vulgaris*, makes a bush a foot high and likes a sunny position and a well-drained, preferably limy soil. Sow seeds in March and thin the resulting seedlings to 12in (30cm) apart. You can also raise plants of pot marjoram, *Origanum onites*, from a sowing made in May, but it is better to buy young plants and put these in in spring, 1ft (30cm) apart. This herb likes a moist, well-drained soil.

Mint is useful but it does spread, especially when given the conditions it likes – sunshine, and a rather rich, moist soil – and for that reason some gardeners like to grow it in a container, just to keep it within bounds. Buy plants for spring or autumn planting.

Top fruit

Now to fruit. As I remarked earlier you could consider growing the Morello cherry as a fan-trained specimen against a north-facing wall if you have such available. All it really needs to do well is good drainage and a soil well-supplied with lime. An espalier trained apple or pear could be grown against a wall facing south or south-west if you have 10 to 15ft (3 to 4.5cm) of clear space and the soil is loamy and well-drained and there is reasonable shelter from winds. You could also grow cordon apples or pears against a wall or fence of similar aspect.

As I remarked earlier there is no reason why you shouldn't have a "family tree", with three varieties of dessert apples or three varieties of pears grafted on to the one bush, all carefully chosen to have matching flowering periods and readily cross-pollinating one another. It must be understood, however, that such bushes will have a height of 12 to 15ft (3.8 to 4.5m) eventually. It is interesting to note, for instance, that two excellent new apple varieties are among the varieties obtainable in this way – 'Merton Knave', a nicely flavoured dessert variety which matures from late August to mid-September, and 'Spartan', a variety of especially good eating quality which can be eaten straight from the tree or to be kept until Christmas (its season is October to December). You can have a bush on which the varieties 'Merton Knave', 'Egremont Russett' and 'Golden Delicious' have been worked, or, alternatively, 'James Grieve', 'Spartan' and 'Cox's Orange Pippin'. There are numerous other combinations of apples available in addition to the two mentioned, mostly dessert cultivars but one selection all cookers and another two dessert

and one cooker. I have used as examples combination offered by Highfield Nurseries, Whitminster, Gloucester. They are also offering on one bush the pears 'Williams' Bon Chrétien', 'Conference' and 'Doyenné du Comice'. Between them, these

'Cox's Orange Pippin', the
aristocrat of dessert apples
which is in season from October
to early January. It is only
suitable, however, for growing
in good conditions (in other than
cold gardens) and is prone to
attack by canker and mildew.
'Sunset', with something
of Cox's quality and
flavour without the draw-
backs, is an attractive
alternative. It is in season
from October to mid-December'.

apples and pears provide a succession of fruit over the period
August to March. Other fruit specialists offer other combinations,
and family trees are available also through selected garden
centres.

New developments

Before the sweet cherry 'Stella' arrived on the scene in the early 1970s – bred at a research station in British Columbia – there was no self-fertile sweet cherry. 'Stella' is still, at the time of writing, the only self-fertile cultivar of its type. Morever, it is now married to the semi-vigorous rootstock Colt and, for the first time, it is possible to think of growing a sweet cherry, within reasonable space, in a small garden and with no need to provide another compatible pollinating cultivar.

Even with 'Stella' on Colt, however, you will have a bush or half-standard tree with an eventual height of around 20ft (6cm), and the answer in the patio garden is to grow this cultivar as a fan-trained specimen. All that is needed then is a tall wall with room for the cherry to have a lateral spread of 15ft (4.5m). 'Stella' is vigorous with an upright habit and throws laterals in a manner very suitable for training.

'Stella' is certainly worth finding space for, for, in the summer of 1982, it won the accolade of a first class certificate from the Royal Horticultural Society – a high award given sparingly at the best of times and hardly ever to a fruit. Its large, dark red fruits, which have good flavour, ripen in late July and it is a heavy cropper. Another point in its favour is that it has good resistance to bacterial canker, which is a serious trouble of cherries. It is something to think about, if you have the space available against a south- or west-facing wall. But remember that sweet cherries need a good, well-drained soil to grow in, and plenty of moisture in the soil, especially when the fruits are developing. The latest development is a more compact narrower form of 'Stella', named 'Compact Stella', from the same Canadian source which Highfield are the first to offer. This has obvious possibilties for patio cultivation.

An extremely dwarfing apple rootstock, M27, has been developed at the Institute of Horticultural Research, East Malling, Maidstone, Kent, of which more in a moment, and a dwarfing rootstock for plums named Pixy, of special interest to all gardeners with an enthusiasm for fruit growing but space problems of one kind or another.

Highfield Nurseries (referred to on p. 162 in connection with family trees of apples and pears) developed a few years ago a novel form of training for the self-fertile dessert plum 'Victoria' worked onto Pixy rootstock – "festooning", as they call it. It has real practical advantages in increasing fruitfulness, and is of special interest to patio gardeners, who want every plant given space to realise its full potential. The system works equally well with apples grown on certain dwarfing rootstocks, but more of that in a moment.

It is a good method to adopt whether you are growing the fruits just mentioned in a bed or in large containers.

But first the plum 'Victoria' grown on Pixy rootstock, which

This garden at the corner of a road is about 60ft (18m) square, and the entrance through the wrought iron gate is screened from the drawing room window by a narrow yew hedge. This also serves as a backcloth for the sculpture on the edge of the small pool. If so desired, the pool could be a plant bed, but water adds greatly to the attractions of small patio gardens of this type. The curved, raised bed adjoining the water feature would make an admirable home for alpine and rock plants. The small conifer helps the yew hedge to screen the sitting-out area from the gate. Note how the tree interrupts the line of the wall and so counters effectively the sense of enclosure which this induces.

makes trees up to two-thirds the size of those on the much-used St. Julien A rootstock. (Another different but very interesting development is that this rootstock has made it possible to grow plums as cordons, with 'Victoria' again highly suitable for the purpose).

Essentially, festooning consists of taking a two-year-old tree with a framework of three or four branches and bending these branches down and securing them to the stem. The objective is to divert the tree's energies into the formation and development of fruit buds rather than have it make excessive branch growth ('Victoria' is strong growing). Indeed, the system often induces such prolific fruiting that thinning of the fruitlets is necessary to get fruits of acceptable size (with small fruits the stone comprises most of the volume).

Under the Highfield system the laterals on the main branches are reduced in length by almost half a year or so later, this pruning being done in late summer with the cuts being made back to a bud in each case. New branches which have developed since the original training can, if so desired, be similarly "festooned".

They also recommend festooning some branches on older trees if these are making excessive growth to the detriment of fruit production. Try it, if you have a tree which is not performing as it should do, and so achieve a better balance between growth and fruiting.

Highfield have shown, too, that it is possible to stimulate increased fruit production by festooning apple varieties worked onto the very dwarfing M27 rootstock – not suitable for weak-growing varieties – and the dwarfing M9 rootstock. I would emphasies, however, that apples grown on M27 and M9 must be grown in really good soil, and in John Innes No 3 potting compost if they are grown in containers (this also applies to plum 'Victoria' grown in this way). The apples should be fed also in the growing season with a fertiliser with a high potash content. Such bushes need the support of stakes throughout their lives. Those grown in containers will also need to have the top inch or so of compost replaced each spring with fresh compost of the same type after the first year.

The space-saving benefits these rootstocks confer are real. The M27 rootstock provides a bush at maturity of around 5ft (1.5m) in height and similar spread, while M9 gives a bush some 8 to 9ft (2.4 to 2.7m) tall and wide. Fruiting starts early, too, normally in the third year from planting and often in two years in the case of bushes on M27, and the fruits are often better coloured than those on rootstocks making larger bushes or trees.

Don't overlook the necessity of ensuring efficient cross-pollination with apples, for, while many are self-fertile, all will give better crops with cross-pollination, and some are self-sterile and will bear no fruit at all without this facility. So, whatever variety you choose to grow should have a compatible variety near

The rear of a country cottage modernised by the addition of a patio in simple rectangular slabs and a brick-edged cobbled area containing an abstract sculpture. Three shallow, easily negotiated steps lead down to the small lawn in the foreground. The sitting-out area is kept free of draughts by the wall leading from the corner of the house, this containing a door to another part of the garden.

The tree on the patio is a Malus or flowering crab, but it could be, just as suitably, a variety of Sorbus aucuparia (mountain ash), a labumum or a flowering cherry. The steps are heavily planted with a selection of rock plants and good ground-cover plants such as Vinca (periwinkle) and Ajuga (bugle). A way up and down the steps is provided by the single slab on each step.

variety you choose to grow should have a compatible variety near by which shares its flowering period, early, mid-season or late, and will allow cross-pollination – the transfer of pollen and subsequent fertilisation. There is no problem about what to plant with what for the catalogues of fruit specialists give advice on the compatibility of the varieties they offer, whether it is apples, pears, cherries or plums in which you are interested.

Soft fruit

The new high yielding autumn fruiting raspberry. 'Autumn Bliss', is a good choice for growing in large containers, cropping being much heavier than that of other autumn fruiting varieties over a period from mid-August to the end of September. Grow in John Innes No. 3 potting compost.

Of the summer-fruiting raspberries for planting in a bed, a good choice would be the early cultivar 'Glen Moy' for July cropping and 'Leo' for August cropping. Raspberries do well in sunshine or light shade in a soil which should be fertile and moisture-retentive but well drained.

Most people like strawberries, and the best way to grow these is in the ground, but if this is not possible they can be grown very satisfactorily in 9in (23cm) pots on the patio, when they will give a good yield (or in barrels or other containers). Use John Innes No. 3 potting compost for this purpose. The whole range of strawberry varieties can be grown in this way. Two cultivars of particular interest for this purpose are the Dutch-raised summer-fruiting 'Tamella' and the perpetual (or remontant) variety 'Ostara'. 'Tamella' is a high-yielding cultivar which can be used for dessert, freezing, jam-making or bottling—'Ostara' (also Dutch-raised), like others of its kind, fruits early (in June) and again later in the season (August to October). To keep up the yield it is best only to leave strawberries in containers for the one year. Plant container-grown strawberries in August or early September even though planting can go on into autumn, just as with those grown in the open ground. It is best to get the job done as soon as possible. Remember also that strawberries should be grown in a sunny position.

With pot-grown plants, pot them in August, and with the arrival of winter turn the pots on their sides to avoid the compost becoming too wet. In early February turn the pots right side up and when growth begins start to water, increasing the amounts given as the plants develop. You can grow strawberries in this way without any glass protection at all.

Tiered pots are available for strawberry growing called Tower-pots, these being made of polypropylene and locking together to make a column of 4 pots with 12 planting stations. Modern versions of the traditional strawberry barrel are also available.

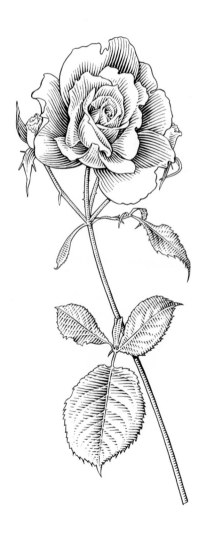

Afterword

A cynic once said that gardening books tell you everything except the answer to the problem which is plaguing you at the moment. There is a grain of truth in this, alas, for with a subject so broad and with so many fascinating facets and byways the author's problem is what to leave out rather than what to put in, even when the subject matter is as specific as it is in this case.

What I have attempted to do more than anything else is to give you ideas, to set you thinking by bringing to your notice a host of good garden plants. Some, at least, should match your tastes and the kind of garden you have been hoping to create. For a garden is a very personal possession; it provides opportunities for self-expression and personal fulfilment which are difficult to describe in words. It is a mirror of yourself.

Gardening is the most rewarding of pastimes, whether you have the smallest of plots or something more ambitious, and a patio garden, with its intimate atmosphere, can be a haven of delight. If you haven't had it already, I hope you will soon have confirmation of that through your own experiences.

Index

(Page numbers in italics indicate illustrations)